SERIOUS CRYPTOGRAPHY

SERIOUS CRYPTOGRAPHY

A Practical Introduction to Modern Encryption

by Jean-Philippe Aumasson

no starch press

San Francisco

Printed in USA

First printing

21 20 19 18 17   1 2 3 4 5 6 7 8 9

ISBN-10: 1-59327-826-8
ISBN-13: 978-1-59327-826-7

Publisher: William Pollock
Production Editor: Laurel Chun
Cover Illustration: Jonny Thomas
Interior Design: Octopod Studios
Developmental Editors: William Pollock, Jan Cash, and Annie Choi
Technical Reviewers: Erik Tews and Samuel Neves
Copyeditor: Barton D. Reed
Compositor: Meg Sneeringer
Proofreader: James Fraleigh

For information on distribution, translations, or bulk sales, please contact No Starch Press, Inc. directly:
No Starch Press, Inc.
245 8th Street, San Francisco, CA 94103
phone: 1.415.863.9900; sales@nostarch.com
www.nostarch.com

Library of Congress Control Number: 2017940486

BRIEF CONTENTS

CONTENTS IN DETAIL

2
RANDOMNESS
21

3
CRYPTOGRAPHIC SECURITY
39

4
BLOCK CIPHERS
53

FOREWORD

If you've read a book or two on computer security, you may have encountered a common perspective on the field of cryptography. "Cryptography," they say, "is the strongest link in the chain." Strong praise indeed, but it's also somewhat dismissive. If cryptography is in fact the strongest part of your system, why invest time improving it when there are so many other areas of the system that will benefit more from your attention?

If there's one thing that I hope you take away from this book, it's that this view of cryptography is idealized; it's largely a myth. Cryptography *in theory* is strong, but cryptography in practice is as prone to failure as any other aspect of a security system. This is particularly true when cryptographic implementations are developed by non-experts without sufficient care or experience, as is the case with many cryptographic systems deployed today. And it gets worse: when cryptographic implementations fail, they often do so in uniquely spectacular ways.

But why should you care, and why this book?

When I began working in the field of applied cryptography nearly two decades ago, the information available to software developers was often piecemeal and outdated. Cryptographers developed algorithms and protocols, and cryptographic engineers implemented them to create opaque, poorly documented cryptographic libraries designed mainly for other experts. There was—and there has been—a huge divide between those who know and understand cryptographic algorithms and those who use them (or ignore them at their peril). There are a few decent textbooks on the market, but even fewer have provided useful tools for the practitioner.

The results have not been pretty. I'm talking about compromises with labels like "CVE" and "Severity: High," and in a few alarming cases, attacks on slide decks marked "TOP SECRET." You may be familiar with some of the more famous examples if only because they've affected systems that you rely on. Many of these problems occur because cryptography is subtle and mathematically elegant, and because cryptographic experts have failed to share their knowledge with the engineers who actually write the software.

Thankfully, this has begun to change and this book is a symptom of that change.

Serious Cryptography was written by one of the foremost experts in applied cryptography, but it's not targeted at other experts. Nor, for that matter, is it intended as a superficial overview of the field. On the contrary, it contains a thorough and up-to-date discussion of cryptographic engineering, designed to help practitioners who plan to work in this field do better. In these pages, you'll learn not only how cryptographic algorithms work, but how to use them in real systems.

The book begins with an exploration of many of the key cryptographic primitives, including basic algorithms like block ciphers, public encryption schemes, hash functions, and random number generators. Each chapter provides working examples of how the algorithms work and what you should or should *not* do. Final chapters cover advanced subjects such as TLS, as well as the future of cryptography—what to do after quantum computers arrive to complicate our lives.

While no single book can solve all our problems, a bit of knowledge can go a long way. This book contains plenty of knowledge. Perhaps enough to make real, deployed cryptography live up to the high expectations that so many have of it.

Happy reading.

Matthew D. Green
Professor
Information Security Institute
Johns Hopkins University

PREFACE

I wrote this book to be the one I wish I had when I started learning crypto. In 2005, I was studying for my masters degree near Paris, and I eagerly registered for the crypto class in the upcoming semester. Unfortunately, the class was canceled because too few students had registered. "Crypto is too hard," the students argued, and instead, they enrolled en masse in the computer graphics and database classes.

I've heard "crypto is hard" more than a dozen times since then. But is crypto really *that* hard? To play an instrument, master a programming language, or put the applications of any fascinating field into practice, you need to learn some concepts and symbols, but doing so doesn't take a PhD. I think the same applies to becoming a competent cryptographer. I also believe that crypto is perceived as hard because cryptographers haven't done a good job of teaching it.

Another reason why I felt the need for this book is that crypto is no longer just about crypto—it has expanded into a multidisciplinary field. To do anything useful and relevant in crypto, you'll need some understanding of the concepts *around* crypto: how networks and computers work, what users and systems need, and how attackers can abuse algorithms and their implementations. In other words, you need a connection to reality.

This Book's Approach

The initial title of this book was *Crypto for Real* to stress the practice-oriented, real-world, no-nonsense approach I aimed to follow. I didn't want to make cryptography approachable by dumbing it down, but instead tie it to real applications. I provide source code examples and describe real bugs and horror stories.

Along with a clear connection to reality, other cornerstones of this book are its simplicity and modernity. I focus on simplicity in form more than in substance: I present many non-trivial concepts, but without the dull mathematical formalism. Instead, I attempt to impart an understanding of cryptography's core ideas, which are more important than remembering a bunch of equations. To ensure the book's modernity, I cover the latest developments and applications of cryptography, such as TLS 1.3 and post-quantum cryptography. I don't discuss the details of obsolete or insecure algorithms such as DES or MD5. An exception to this is RC4, but it's only included to explain how weak it is and to show how a stream cipher of its kind works.

Serious Cryptography isn't a guide for crypto software, nor is it a compendium of technical specifications—stuff that you'll easily find online. Instead, the foremost goal of this book is to get you excited about crypto and to teach you its fundamental concepts along the way.

Who This Book Is For

While writing, I often imagined the reader as a developer who'd been exposed to crypto but still felt clueless and frustrated after attempting to read abstruse textbooks and research papers. Developers often need—and want—a better grasp of crypto to avoid unfortunate design choices, and I hope this book will help.

But if you aren't a developer, don't worry! The book doesn't require any coding skills, and is accessible to anyone who understands the basics of computer science and college-level math (notions of probabilities, modular arithmetic, and so on).

This book can nonetheless be intimidating, and despite its relative accessibility, it requires some effort to get the most out of it. I like the mountaineering analogy: the author paves the way, providing you with ropes and ice axes to facilitate your work, but you make the ascent yourself. Learning the concepts in this book will take an effort, but there will be a reward at the end.

How This Book Is Organized

The book has fourteen chapters, loosely split into four parts. The chapters are mostly independent from one another, except for Chapter 9, which lays the foundations for the three subsequent chapters. I also recommend reading the first three chapters before anything else.

Fundamentals

- **Chapter 1: Encryption** introduces the notion of secure encryption, from weak pen-and-paper ciphers to strong, randomized encryption.
- **Chapter 2: Randomness** describes how a pseudorandom generator works, what it takes for one to be secure, and how to use one securely.
- **Chapter 3: Cryptographic Security** discusses theoretical and practical notions of security, and compares provable security with probable security.

Symmetric Crypto

- **Chapter 4: Block Ciphers** deals with ciphers that process messages block per block, focusing on the most famous one, the Advanced Encryption Standard (AES).
- **Chapter 5: Stream Ciphers** presents ciphers that produce a stream of random-looking bits that are XORed with messages to be encrypted.
- **Chapter 6: Hash Functions** is about the only algorithms that don't work with a secret key, which turn out to be the most ubiquitous crypto building blocks.
- **Chapter 7: Keyed Hashing** explains what happens if you combine a hash function with a secret key, and how this serves to authenticate messages.
- **Chapter 8: Authenticated Encryption** shows how some algorithms can both encrypt and authenticate a message with examples, such as the standard AES-GCM.

Asymmetric Crypto

- **Chapter 9: Hard Problems** lays out the fundamental concepts behind public-key encryption, using notions from computational complexity.
- **Chapter 10: RSA** leverages the factoring problem in order to build secure encryption and signature schemes with a simple arithmetic operation.
- **Chapter 11: Diffie–Hellman** extends asymmetric cryptography to the notion of key agreement, wherein two parties establish a secret value using only non-secret values.
- **Chapter 12: Elliptic Curves** provides a gentle introduction to elliptic curve cryptography, which is the fastest kind of asymmetric cryptography.

Applications

- **Chapter 13: TLS** focuses on Transport Layer Security (TLS), arguably the most important protocol in network security.
- **Chapter 14: Quantum and Post-Quantum** concludes with a note of science fiction by covering the concepts of quantum computing and a new kind of cryptography.

Acknowledgments

I'd like to thank Jan, Annie, and the rest of the No Starch staff who contributed to this book, especially Bill for believing in this project from the get-go, for his patience digesting difficult topics, and for turning my clumsy drafts into readable pages. I am also thankful to Laurel for making the book look so nice and for handling my many correction requests.

On the technical side, the book would contain many more errors and inaccuracies without the help of the following people: Jon Callas, Bill Cox, Niels Ferguson, Philipp Jovanovic, Samuel Neves, David Reid, Phillip Rogaway, Erik Tews, as well as all readers of the early access version who reported errors. Finally, thanks to Matt Green for writing the foreword.

I'd also like to thank my employer, Kudelski Security, for allowing me time to work on this book. Finally, I offer my deepest thanks to Alexandra and Melina for their support and patience.

Lausanne, 05/17/2017 (three prime numbers)

ABBREVIATIONS

AE	authenticated encryption	CPA	chosen-plaintext attackers
AEAD	authentication encryption with associated data	CRT	Chinese remainder theorem
		CTR	counter mode
AES	Advanced Encryption Standard	CVP	closest vector problem
AES-NI	AES native instructions	DDH	decisional Diffie–Hellman
AKA	authenticated key agreement	DES	Data Encryption Standard
API	application program interface	DH	Diffie–Hellman
ARX	add-rotate-XOR	DLP	discrete logarithm problem
ASIC	application-specific integrated circuit	DRBG	deterministic random bit generator
CA	certificate authority	ECB	electronic codebook
CAESAR	Competition for Authenticated Encryption: Security, Applicability, and Robustness	ECC	elliptic curve cryptography
		ECDH	elliptic curve Diffie–Hellman
		ECDLP	elliptic-curve discrete logarithm problem
CBC	cipher block chaining		
CCA	chosen-ciphertext attackers	ECDSA	elliptic-curve digital signature algorithm
CDH	computational Diffie–Hellman		
CMAC	cipher-based MAC	FDH	Full Domain Hash
COA	ciphertext-only attackers	FHE	fully homomorphic encryption

FIPS	Federal Information Processing Standards	NP	nondeterministic polynomial-time
FPE	format-preserving encryption	OAEP	Optimal Asymmetric Encryption Padding
FPGA	field-programmable gate array	OCB	offset codebook
FSR	feedback shift register	P	polynomial time
GCD	greatest common divisor	PLD	programmable logic device
GCM	Galois Counter Mode	PRF	pseudorandom function
GNFS	general number field sieve	PRNG	pseudorandom number generator
HKDF	HMAC-based key derivation function	PRP	pseudorandom permutation
HMAC	hash-based message authentication code	PSK	pre-shared key
		PSS	Probabilistic Signature Scheme
HTTPS	HTTP Secure	QR	quarter-round
IND	indistinguishablity	QRNG	quantum random number generator
IP	Internet Protocol		
IV	initial value	RFC	request for comments
KDF	key derivation function	RNG	random number generator
KPA	known-plaintext attackers	RSA	Rivest–Shamir–Adleman
LFSR	linear feedback shift register	SHA	Secure Hash Algorithm
LSB	least significant bit	SIS	short integer solution
LWE	learning with errors	SIV	synthetic IV
MAC	messsage authentication code	SPN	substitution–permutation network
MD	message digest	SSH	Secure Shell
MitM	meet-in-the-middle	SSL	Secure Socket Layer
MQ	multivariate quadratics	TE	tweakable encryption
MQV	Menezes–Qu–Vanstone	TLS	Transport Layer Security
MSB	most significant bit	TMTO	time-memory trade-off
MT	Mersenne Twister	UDP	User Datagram Protocol
NFSR	nonlinear feedback shift register	UH	universal hash
NIST	National Institute of Standards and Technology	WEP	Wireless Encrypted Protocol
		WOTS	Winternitz one-time signature
NM	non-malleability	XOR	exclusive OR

1

ENCRYPTION

Encryption is the principal application of cryptography; it makes data incomprehensible in order to ensure its *confidentiality*. Encryption uses an algorithm called a *cipher* and a secret value called the *key*; if you don't know the secret key, you can't decrypt, nor can you learn any bit of information on the encrypted message—and neither can any attacker.

This chapter will focus on symmetric encryption, which is the simplest kind of encryption. In *symmetric encryption*, the key used to decrypt is the same as the key used to encrypt (unlike *asymmetric encryption*, or *public-key encryption*, in which the key used to decrypt is different from the key used to encrypt). You'll start by learning about the weakest forms of symmetric encryption, classical ciphers that are secure against only the most illiterate attacker, and then move on to the strongest forms that are secure forever.

The Basics

When we're encrypting a message, *plaintext* refers to the unencrypted message and *ciphertext* to the encrypted message. A cipher is therefore composed of two functions: *encryption* turns a plaintext into a ciphertext, and *decryption* turns a ciphertext back into a plaintext. But we'll often say "cipher" when we actually mean "encryption." For example, Figure 1-1 shows a cipher, **E**, represented as a box taking as input a plaintext, *P*, and a key, *K*, and producing a ciphertext, *C*, as output. I'll write this relation as $C = \mathbf{E}(K, P)$. Similarly, when the cipher is in decryption mode, I'll write $\mathbf{D}(K, C)$.

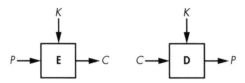

Figure 1-1: Basic encryption and decryption

NOTE   *For some ciphers, the ciphertext is the same size as the plaintext; for some others, the ciphertext is slightly longer. However, ciphertexts can never be shorter than plaintexts.*

Classical Ciphers

Classical ciphers are ciphers that predate computers and therefore work on letters rather than on bits. They are much simpler than a modern cipher like DES—for example, in ancient Rome or during WWI, you couldn't use a computer chip's power to scramble a message, so you had to do everything with only pen and paper. There are many classical ciphers, but the most famous are the Caesar cipher and Vigenère cipher.

The Caesar Cipher

The Caesar cipher is so named because the Roman historian Suetonius reported that Julius Caesar used it. It encrypts a message by shifting each of the letters down three positions in the alphabet, wrapping back around to A if the shift reaches Z. For example, ZOO encrypts to CRR, FDHVDU decrypts to CAESAR, and so on, as shown in Figure 1-2. There's nothing special about the value 3; it's just easier to compute in one's head than 11 or 23.

The Caesar cipher is super easy to break: to decrypt a given ciphertext, simply shift the letters three positions back to retrieve the plaintext. That said, the Caesar cipher may have been strong enough during the time of Crassus and Cicero. Because no secret key is involved (it's always 3), users of Caesar's cipher only had to assume that attackers were illiterate or too uneducated to figure it out—an assumption that's much less realistic today. (In fact, in 2006, the Italian police arrested a mafia boss after decrypting messages written on small scraps of paper that were encrypted using a variant of the Caesar cipher: ABC was encrypted to 456 instead of DEF, for example.)

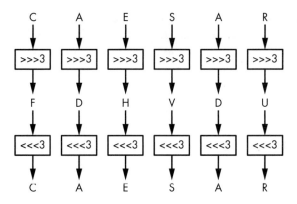

Figure 1-2: The Caesar cipher

Could the Caesar cipher be made more secure? You can, for example, imagine a version that uses a secret shift value instead of always using 3, but that wouldn't help much because an attacker could easily try all 25 possible shift values until the decrypted message makes sense.

The Vigenère Cipher

It took about 1500 years to see a meaningful improvement of the Caesar cipher in the form of the Vigenère cipher, created in the 16th century by an Italian named Giovan Battista Bellaso. The name "Vigenère" comes from the Frenchman Blaise de Vigenère, who invented a different cipher in the 16th century, but due to historical misattribution, Vigenère's name stuck. Nevertheless, the Vigenère cipher became popular and was later used during the American Civil War by Confederate forces and during WWI by the Swiss Army, among others.

The Vigenère cipher is similar to the Caesar cipher, except that letters aren't shifted by three places but rather by values defined by a *key*, a collection of letters that represent numbers based on their position in the alphabet. For example, if the key is DUH, letters in the plaintext are shifted using the values 3, 20, 7 because *D* is three letters after *A*, *U* is 20 letters after *A*, and *H* is seven letters after *A*. The 3, 20, 7 pattern repeats until you've encrypted the entire plaintext. For example, the word CRYPTO would encrypt to FLFSNV using DUH as the key: *C* is shifted three positions to *F*, *R* is shifted 20 positions to *L*, and so on. Figure 1-3 illustrates this principle when encrypting the sentence THEY DRINK THE TEA.

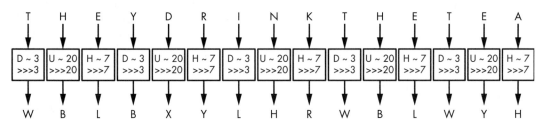

Figure 1-3: The Vigenère cipher

The Vigenère cipher is clearly more secure than the Caesar cipher, yet it's still fairly easy to break. The first step to breaking it is to figure out the key's length. For example, take the example in Figure 1-3, wherein THEY DRINK THE TEA encrypts to WBLBXYLHRWBLWYH with the key DUH. (Spaces are usually removed to hide word boundaries.) Notice that in the ciphertext WBLBXYLHRWBLWYH, the group of three letters WBL appears twice in the ciphertext at nine-letter intervals. This suggests that the same three-letter word was encrypted using the same shift values, producing WBL each time. A cryptanalyst can then deduce that the key's length is either nine or a value divisible by nine (that is, three). Furthermore, they may guess that this repeated three-letter word is THE and therefore determine DUH as a possible encryption key.

The second step to breaking the Vigenère cipher is to determine the actual key using a method called *frequency analysis*, which exploits the uneven distribution of letters in languages. For example, in English, *E* is the most common letter, so if you find that *X* is the most common letter in a ciphertext, then the most likely plaintext value at this position is *E*.

Despite its relative weakness, the Vigenère cipher may have been good enough to securely encrypt messages when it was used. First, because the attack just outlined needs messages of at least a few sentences, it wouldn't work if the cipher was used to encrypt only short messages. Second, most messages needed to be secret only for short periods of time, so it didn't matter if ciphertexts were eventually decrypted by the enemy. (The 19th-century cryptographer Auguste Kerckhoffs estimated that most encrypted wartime messages required confidentiality for only three to four hours.)

How Ciphers Work

Based on simplistic ciphers like the Caesar and Vigenère ciphers, we can try to abstract out the workings of a cipher, first by identifying its two main components: a permutation and a mode of operation. A *permutation* is a function that transforms an item (in cryptography, a letter or a group of bits) such that each item has a unique inverse (for example, the Caesar cipher's three-letter shift). A *mode of operation* is an algorithm that uses a permutation to process messages of arbitrary size. The mode of the Caesar cipher is trivial: it just repeats the same permutation for each letter, but as you've seen, the Vigenère cipher has a more complex mode, where letters at different positions undergo different permutations.

In the following sections, I discuss in more detail what these are and how they relate to a cipher's security. I use each component to show why classical ciphers are doomed to be insecure, unlike modern ciphers that run on high-speed computers.

The Permutation

Most classical ciphers work by replacing each letter with another letter—in other words, by performing a *substitution*. In the Caesar and Vigenère ciphers, the substitution is a shift in the alphabet, though the alphabet or set of symbols can vary: instead of the English alphabet, it could be the Arabic alphabet; instead of letters, it could be words, numbers, or ideograms, for example. The representation or encoding of information is a separate matter that is mostly irrelevant to security. (We're just considering Latin letters because that's what classical ciphers use.)

A cipher's substitution can't be just any substitution. It should be a permutation, which is a rearrangement of the letters *A* to *Z*, such that each letter has a unique inverse. For example, a substitution that transforms the letters *A*, *B*, *C*, and *D*, respectively to *C*, *A*, *D*, and *B* is a permutation, because each letter maps onto another single letter. But a substitution that transforms *A*, *B*, *C*, *D* to *D*, *A*, *A*, *C* is not a permutation, because both B and C map onto A. With a permutation, each letter has exactly one inverse.

Still, not every permutation is secure. In order to be secure, a cipher's permutation should satisfy three criteria:

- **The permutation should be determined by the key**, so as to keep the permutation secret as long as the key is secret. In the Vigenère cipher, if you don't know the key, you don't know which of the 26 permutations was used; hence, you can't easily decrypt.

- **Different keys should result in different permutations**. Otherwise, it becomes easier to decrypt without the key: if different keys result in identical permutations, that means there are fewer distinct keys than distinct permutations, and therefore fewer possibilities to try when decrypting without the key. In the Vigenère cipher, each letter from the key determines a substitution; there are 26 distinct letters, and as many distinct permutations.

- **The permutation should look random**, loosely speaking. There should be no pattern in the ciphertext after performing a permutation, because patterns make a permutation predictable for an attacker, and therefore less secure. For example, the Vigenère cipher's substitution is pretty predictable: if you determine that *A* encrypts to *F*, you could conclude that the shift value is 5 and you would also know that *B* encrypts to *G*, that *C* encrypts to *H*, and so on. However, with a randomly chosen permutation, knowing that *A* encrypts to *F* would only tell you that *B* does *not* encrypt to *F*.

We'll call a permutation that satisfies these criteria a *secure permutation*. But as you'll see next, a secure permutation is necessary but not sufficient on its own for building a secure cipher. A cipher will also need a mode of operation to support messages of any length.

The Mode of Operation

Say we have a secure permutation that transforms *A* to *X*, *B* to *M*, and *N* to *L*, for example. The word BANANA therefore encrypts to MXLXLX, where each occurrence of *A* is replaced by an *X*. Using the same permutation for all the letters in the plaintext thus reveals any duplicate letters in the plaintext. By analyzing these duplicates, you might not learn the entire message, but you'll learn *something* about the message. In the BANANA example, you don't need the key to guess that the plaintext has the same letter at the three *X* positions and another same letter at the two *L* positions. So if you know, for example, that the message is a fruit's name, you could determine that it's BANANA rather than CHERRY, LYCHEE, or another six-letter fruit.

The mode of operation (or just *mode*) of a cipher mitigates the exposure of duplicate letters in the plaintext by using different permutations for duplicate letters. The mode of the Vigenère cipher partially addresses this: if the key is *N* letters long, then *N* different permutations will be used for every *N* consecutive letters. However, this can still result in patterns in the ciphertext because every *N*th letter of the message uses the same permutation. That's why frequency analysis works to break the Vigenère cipher, as you saw earlier.

Frequency analysis can be defeated if the Vigenère cipher only encrypts plaintexts that are of the same length as the key. But even then, there's another problem: reusing the same key several times exposes similarities between plaintexts. For example, with the key KYN, the words TIE and PIE encrypt to DGR and ZGR, respectively. Both end with the same two letters (*GR*), revealing that both plaintexts share their last two letters as well. Finding these patterns shouldn't be possible with a secure cipher.

To build a secure cipher, you must combine a secure permutation with a secure mode. Ideally, this combination prevents attackers from learning anything about a message other than its length.

Why Classical Ciphers Are Insecure

Classical ciphers are doomed to be insecure because they're limited to operations you can do in your head or on a piece of paper. They lack the computational power of a computer and are easily broken by simple computer programs. Let's see the fundamental reason why that simplicity makes them insecure in today's world.

Remember that a cipher's permutation should look random in order to be secure. Of course, the best way to look random is to *be* random—that is, to select every permutation randomly from the set of all permutations. And there are many permutations to choose from. In the case of the 26-letter English alphabet, there are approximately 2^{88} permutations:

$$26! = 403291461126605635584000000 \approx 2^{88}$$

Here, the exclamation point (!) is the factorial symbol, defined as follows:

$$n! = n \times (n-1) \times (n-2) \times \ldots \times 3 \times 2$$

(To see why we end up with this number, count the permutations as lists of reordered letters: there are 26 choices for the first possible letter, then 25 possibilities for the second, 24 for the third, and so on.) This number is huge: it's of the same order of magnitude as the number of atoms in the human body. But classical ciphers can only use a small fraction of those permutations—namely, those that need only simple operations (such as shifts) and that have a short description (like a short algorithm or a small look-up table). The problem is that a secure permutation can't accommodate both of these limitations.

You can get secure permutations using simple operations by picking a random permutation, representing it as a table of 25 letters (enough to represent a permutation of 26 letters, with the 26th one missing), and applying it by looking up letters in this table. But then you wouldn't have a short description. For example, it would take 250 letters to describe 10 different permutations, rather than just the 10 letters used in the Vigenère cipher.

You can also produce secure permutations with a short description. Instead of just shifting the alphabet, you could use more complex operations such as addition, multiplication, and so on. That's how modern ciphers work: given a key of typically 128 or 256 bits, they perform hundreds of bit operations to encrypt a single letter. This process is fast on a computer that can do billions of bit operations per second, but it would take hours to do by hand, and would still be vulnerable to frequency analysis.

Perfect Encryption: The One-Time Pad

Essentially, a classical cipher can't be secure unless it comes with a huge key, but encrypting with a huge key is impractical. However, the one-time pad is such a cipher, and it is the most secure cipher. In fact, it guarantees *perfect secrecy*: even if an attacker has unlimited computing power, it's impossible to learn anything about the plaintext except for its length.

In the next sections, I'll show you how a one-time pad works and then offer a sketch of its security proof.

Encrypting with the One-Time Pad

The one-time pad takes a plaintext, P, and a random key, K, that's the same length as P and produces a ciphertext C, defined as

$$C = P \oplus K$$

where C, P, and K are bit strings of the same length and where $\oplus$ is the bitwise exclusive OR operation (XOR), defined as $0 \oplus 0 = 0$, $0 \oplus 1 = 1$, $1 \oplus 0 = 1$, $1 \oplus 1 = 0$.

NOTE *I'm presenting the one-time pad in its usual form, as working on bits, but it can be adapted to other symbols. With letters, for example, you would end up with a variant of the Caesar cipher with a shift index picked at random for each letter.*

The one-time pad's decryption is identical to encryption; it's just an XOR: $P = C \oplus K$. Indeed, we can verify $C \oplus K = P \oplus K \oplus K = P$ because XORing K with itself gives the all-zero string $000 \ldots 000$. That's it—even simpler than the Caesar cipher.

For example, if $P = 01101101$ and $K = 10110100$, then we can calculate the following:

$$C = P \oplus K = 01101101 \oplus 10110100 = 11011001$$

Decryption retrieves P by computing the following:

$$P = C \oplus K = 11011001 \oplus 10110100 = 01101101$$

The important thing is that a one-time pad can only be used *one time*: each key K should be used only once. If the same K is used to encrypt P_1 and P_2 to C_1 and C_2, then an eavesdropper can compute the following:

$$C_1 \oplus C_2 = \left(P_1 \oplus K \right) \oplus \left(P_2 \oplus K \right) = P_1 \oplus P_2 \oplus K \oplus K = P_1 \oplus P_2$$

An eavesdropper would thus learn the XOR difference of P_1 and P_2, information that should be kept secret. Moreover, if either plaintext message is known, then the other message can be recovered.

Of course, the one-time pad is utterly inconvenient to use because it requires a key as long as the plaintext and a new random key for each new message or group of data. To encrypt a one-terabyte hard drive, you'd need another one-terabyte drive to store the key! Nonetheless, the one-time pad has been used throughout history. For example, it was used by the British Special Operations Executive during WWII, by KGB spies, by the NSA, and is still used today in specific contexts. (I've heard of Swiss bankers who couldn't agree on a cipher trusted by both parties and ended up using one-time pads, but I don't recommend doing this.)

Why Is the One-Time Pad Secure?

Although the one-time pad is not practical, it's important to understand what makes it secure. In the 1940s, American mathematician Claude Shannon proved that the one-time pad's key must be at least as long as the message to achieve perfect secrecy. The proof's idea is fairly simple. You assume that the attacker has unlimited power, and thus can try all the keys. The goal is to encrypt such that the attacker can't rule out any possible plaintext given some ciphertext.

The intuition behind the one-time pad's perfect secrecy goes as follows: if K is random, the resulting C looks as random as K to an attacker because the XOR of a random string with any fixed string yields a random string. To see this, consider the probability of getting 0 as the first bit of a random string (namely, a probability of $1/2$). What's the probability that a random bit XORed with the second bit is 0? Right, $1/2$ again. The same argument can be iterated over bit strings of any length. The ciphertext C thus looks random to an attacker that doesn't know K, so it's literally impossible to learn anything about P given C, even for an attacker with unlimited time and power. In other words, knowing the ciphertext gives no information whatsoever about the plaintext except its length—pretty much the definition of a secure cipher.

For example, if a ciphertext is 128 bits long (meaning the plaintext is 128 bits as well), there are 2^{128} possible ciphertexts; therefore, there should be 2^{128} possible plaintexts from the attacker's point of view. But if there are fewer than 2^{128} possible keys, the attacker can rule out some plaintexts. If the key is only 64 bits, for example, the attacker can determine the 2^{64} possible plaintexts and rule out the overwhelming majority of 128-bit strings. The attacker wouldn't learn what the plaintext is, but they would learn what the plaintext is not, which makes the encryption's secrecy imperfect.

As you can see, you must have a key as long as the plaintext to achieve perfect security, but this quickly becomes impractical for real-world use. Next, I'll discuss the approaches taken in modern-day encryption to achieve the best security that's both possible and practical.

PROBABILITY IN CRYPTOGRAPHY

A *probability* is a number that expresses the likelihood, or chance, of some event happening. It's expressed as a number between 0 and 1, where 0 means "never" and 1 means "always." The higher the probability, the greater the chance. You'll find many explanations of probability, usually in terms of white balls and red balls in a bag and the probability of picking a ball of either color.

Cryptography often uses probabilities to measure an attack's chances of success, by 1) counting the number of successful events (for example, the event "find the one correct secret key") and 2) counting the total number of possible events (for example, the total number of keys is 2^n if we deal with *n*-bit keys). In this example, the probability that a randomly chosen key is the correct one is $1/2^n$, or the count of successful events (1 secret key) and the count of possible events (2^n possible keys). The number $1/2^n$ is negligibly small for common key lengths such as 128 and 256.

The probability of an event *not happening* is $1 - p$, if the event's probability is p. The probability of getting a wrong key in our previous example is therefore $1 - 1/2^n$, a number very close to 1, meaning almost certainty.

Encryption Security

You've seen that classical ciphers aren't secure and that a perfectly secure cipher like the one-time pad is impractical. We'll thus have to give a little in terms of security if we want secure *and* usable ciphers. But what does "secure" really mean, besides the obvious and informal "eavesdroppers can't decrypt secure messages"?

Intuitively, a cipher is secure if, even given a large number of plaintext–ciphertext pairs, *nothing can be learned* about the cipher's behavior when applied to other plaintexts or ciphertexts. This opens up new questions:

- How does an attacker come by these pairs? How large is a "large number"? This is all defined by *attack models*, assumptions about what the attacker can and cannot do.

- What could be "learned" and what "cipher's behavior" are we talking about? This is defined by *security goals*, descriptions of what is considered a successful attack.

Attack models and security goals must go together; you can't claim that a system is secure without explaining against whom or from what it's safe. A *security notion* is thus the combination of some security goal with some attack model. We'll say that a cipher *achieves* a certain security notion if any attacker working in a given model can't achieve the security goal.

Attack Models

An attack model is a set of assumptions about how attackers might interact with a cipher and what they can and can't do. The goals of an attack model are as follows:

- To set requirements for cryptographers who design ciphers, so that they know what attackers and what kinds of attacks to protect against.

- To give guidelines to users, about whether a cipher will be safe to use in their environment.

- To provide clues for cryptanalysts who attempt to break ciphers, so they know whether a given attack is valid. An attack is only valid if it's doable in the model considered.

Attack models don't need to match reality exactly; they're an approximation. As the statistician George E. P. Box put it, "all models are wrong; the practical question is how wrong do they have to be to not be useful." To be useful in cryptography, attack models should at least encompass what attackers can actually do to attack a cipher. It's okay and a good thing if a model overestimates attackers' capabilities, because it helps anticipate future attack techniques—only the paranoid cryptographers survive. A bad model underestimates attackers and provides false confidence in a cipher by making it seem secure in theory when it's not secure in reality.

Kerckhoffs's Principle

One assumption made in all models is the so-called *Kerckhoffs's principle*, which states that the security of a cipher should rely only on the secrecy of the key and not on the secrecy of the cipher. This may sound obvious today, when ciphers and protocols are publicly specified and used by everyone. But historically, Dutch linguist Auguste Kerckhoffs was referring to military encryption machines specifically designed for a given army or division.

Quoting from his 1883 essay "La Cryptographie Militaire," where he listed six requirements of a military encryption system: "The system must not require secrecy and can be stolen by the enemy without causing trouble."

Black-Box Models

Let's now consider some useful attack models expressed in terms of what the attacker can observe and what queries they can make to the cipher. A *query* for our purposes is the operation that sends an input value to some function and gets the output in return, without exposing the details of that function.

An *encryption query*, for example, takes a plaintext and returns a corresponding ciphertext, without revealing the secret key.

We call these models *black-box models*, because the attacker only sees what goes in and out of the cipher. For example, some smart card chips securely protect a cipher's internals as well as its keys, yet you're allowed to connect to the chip and ask it to decrypt any ciphertext. The attacker would then receive the corresponding plaintext, which may help them determine the key. That's a real example where *decryption queries* are possible.

There are several different black-box attack models. Here, I list them in order from weakest to strongest, describing attackers' capabilities for each model:

- *Ciphertext-only attackers (COA)* observe ciphertexts but don't know the associated plaintexts, and don't know how the plaintexts were selected. Attackers in the COA model are passive and can't perform encryption or decryption queries.

- *Known-plaintext attackers (KPA)* observe ciphertexts and do know the associated plaintexts. Attackers in the KPA model thus get a list of plaintext–ciphertext pairs, where plaintexts are assumed to be randomly selected. Again, KPA is a passive attacker model.

- *Chosen-plaintext attackers (CPA)* can perform encryption queries for plaintexts of their choice and observe the resulting ciphertexts. This model captures situations where attackers can choose all or part of the plaintexts that are encrypted and then get to see the ciphertexts. Unlike COA or KPA, which are passive models, CPA are *active* attackers, because they influence the encryption processes rather than passively eavesdropping.

- *Chosen-ciphertext attackers (CCA)* can both encrypt and decrypt; that is, they get to perform encryption queries and decryption queries. The CCA model may sound ludicrous at first—if you can decrypt, what else do you need?—but like the CPA model, it aims to represent situations where attackers can have some influence on the ciphertext and later get access to the plaintext. Moreover, decrypting something is not always enough to break a system. For example, some video-protection devices allow attackers to perform encryption queries and decryption queries using the device's chip, but in that context attackers are interested in the key in order to redistribute it; in this case, being able to decrypt "for free" isn't sufficient to break the system.

In the preceding models, ciphertexts that are observed as well as queried don't come for free. Each ciphertext comes from the computation of the encryption function. This means that generating 2^N plaintext–ciphertext pairs through encryption queries takes about as much computation as trying 2^N keys, for example. The cost of queries should be taken into account when you're computing the cost of an attack.

Gray-Box Models

In a *gray-box model*, the attacker has access to a cipher's *implementation*. This makes gray-box models more realistic than black-box models for applications such as smart cards, embedded systems, and virtualized systems, to which attackers often have physical access and can thus tamper with the algorithms' internals. By the same token, gray-box models are more difficult to define than black-box ones because they depend on physical, analog properties rather than just on an algorithm's input and outputs, and crypto theory will often fail to abstract the complexity of the real world.

Side-channel attacks are a family of attacks within gray-box models. A side channel is a source of information that depends on the implementation of the cipher, be it in software or hardware. Side-channel attackers observe or measure analog characteristics of a cipher's implementation but don't alter its integrity; they are *noninvasive*. For pure software implementations, typical side channels are the execution time and the behavior of the system that surrounds the cipher, such as error messages, return values, branches, and so on. In the case of implementations on smart cards, for example, typical side-channel attackers measure power consumption, electromagnetic emanations, or acoustic noise.

Invasive attacks are a family of attacks on cipher implementations that are more powerful than side-channel attacks, and more expensive because they require sophisticated equipment. You can run basic side-channel attacks with a standard PC and an off-the-shelf oscilloscope, but invasive attacks require tools such as a high-resolution microscopes and a chemical lab. Invasive attacks thus consist of a whole set of techniques and procedures, from using nitric acid to remove a chip's packaging to microscopic imagery acquisition, partial reverse engineering, and possible modification of the chip's behavior with something like laser fault injection.

Security Goals

I've informally defined the goal of security as "nothing can be learned about the cipher's behavior." To turn this idea into a rigorous mathematical definition, cryptographers define two main security goals that correspond to different ideas of what it means to learn something about a cipher's behavior:

Indistinguishability (IND)   Ciphertexts should be indistinguishable from random strings. This is usually illustrated with this hypothetical game: if an attacker picks two plaintexts and then receives a ciphertext of one of the two (chosen at random), they shouldn't be able to tell which plaintext was encrypted, even by performing encryption queries with the two plaintexts (and decryption queries, if the model is CCA rather than CPA).

Non-malleability (NM)   Given a ciphertext $C_1 = \mathbf{E}(K, P_1)$, it should be impossible to create another ciphertext, C_2, whose corresponding plaintext, P_2, is related to P_1 in a meaningful way (for example, to create a P_2 that is equal to $P_1 \oplus 1$ or to $P_1 \oplus X$ for some known value X). Surprisingly, the one-time pad is malleable: given a ciphertext $C_1 = P_1 \oplus K$, you can define $C_2 = C_1 \oplus 1$, which is a valid ciphertext of $P_2 = P_1 \oplus 1$ under the same key K. Oops, so much for our perfect cipher.

Next, I'll discuss these security goals in the context of different attack models.

Security Notions

Security goals are only useful when combined with an attack model. The convention is to write a security notion as *GOAL-MODEL*. For example, IND-CPA denotes indistinguishability against chosen-plaintext attackers, NM-CCA denotes nonmalleability against chosen-ciphertext attackers, and so on. Let's start with the security goals for an attacker.

Semantic Security and Randomized Encryption: IND-CPA

The most important security notion is IND-CPA, also called *semantic security*. It captures the intuition that ciphertexts shouldn't leak any information about plaintexts as long as the key is secret. To achieve IND-CPA security, encryption must return different ciphertexts if called twice on the same plaintext; otherwise, an attacker could identify duplicate plaintexts from their ciphertexts, contradicting the definition that ciphertexts shouldn't reveal any information.

One way to achieve IND-CPA security is to use *randomized encryption*. As the name suggests, it randomizes the encryption process and returns different ciphertexts when the same plaintext is encrypted twice. Encryption can then be expressed as $C = \mathbf{E}(K, R, P)$, where R is fresh random bits. Decryption remains deterministic, however, because given $\mathbf{E}(K, R, P)$, you should always get P, regardless of the value of R.

What if encryption isn't randomized? In the IND game introduced in "Security Goals" on page 12, the attacker picks two plaintexts, P_1 and P_2, and receives a ciphertext of one of the two, but doesn't know which plaintext the ciphertext corresponds to. That is, they get $C_i = \mathbf{E}(K, P_i)$ and have to guess whether i is 1 or 2. In the CPA model, the attacker can perform encryption queries to determine both $C_1 = \mathbf{E}(K, P_1)$ and $C_2 = \mathbf{E}(K, P_2)$. If encryption isn't randomized, it suffices to see if C_i is equal to C_1 or to C_2 in order to determine which plaintext was encrypted and thereby win the IND game. Therefore, randomization is key to the IND-CPA notion.

NOTE *With randomized encryption, ciphertexts must be slightly longer than plaintexts in order to allow for more than one possible ciphertext per plaintext. For example, if there are 2^{64} possible ciphertexts per plaintext, ciphertexts must be at least 64 bits longer than plaintexts.*

Achieving Semantically Secure Encryption

One of the simplest constructions of a semantically secure cipher uses a *deterministic random bit generator (DRBG)*, an algorithm that returns random-looking bits given some secret value:

$$\mathbf{E}\big(K, R, P\big) = \big(\mathbf{DRBG}\big(K \parallel R\big) \oplus P, R\big)$$

Here, R is a string randomly chosen for each new encryption and given to a DRBG along with the key ($K \parallel R$ denotes the string consisting of K followed by R). This approach is reminiscent of the one-time pad: instead of picking a random key of the same length as the message, we leverage a random bit generator to get a random-looking string.

The proof that this cipher is IND-CPA secure is simple, if we assume that the DRBG produces random bits. The proof works ad absurdum: if you can distinguish ciphertexts from random strings, which means that you can distinguish $\mathbf{DRBG}(K \parallel R) \oplus P$ from random, then this means that you can distinguish $\mathbf{DRBG}(K \parallel R)$ from random. Remember that the CPA model lets you get ciphertexts for chosen values of P, so you can XOR P to $\mathbf{DRBG}(K, R) \oplus P$ and get $\mathbf{DRBG}(K, R)$. But now we have a contradiction, because we started by assuming that $\mathbf{DRBG}(K, R)$ can't be distinguished from random, producing random strings. So we conclude that ciphertexts can't be distinguished from random strings, and therefore that the cipher is secure.

NOTE *As an exercise, try to determine what other security notions are satisfied by the above cipher $E(K, R, P) = (DRBG(K \parallel R) \oplus P, R)$. Is it NM-CPA? IND-CCA? You'll find the answers in the next section.*

Comparing Security Notions

You've learned that attack models such as CPA and CCA are combined with security goals such as NM and IND to build the security notions NM-CPA, NM-CCA, IND-CPA, and IND-CCA. How are these notions related? Can we prove that satisfying notion X implies satisfying notion Y?

Some relations are obvious: IND-CCA implies IND-CPA, and NM-CCA implies NM-CPA, because anything a CPA attacker can do, a CCA attacker can do as well. That is, if you can't break a cipher by performing chosen-ciphertext and chosen-plaintext queries, you can't break it by performing chosen-plaintext queries only.

A less obvious relation is that IND-CPA does not imply NM-CPA. To understand this, observe that the previous IND-CPA construction

($\mathbf{DRBG}(K, R) \oplus P, R$) is not NM-CPA: given a ciphertext (X, R), you can create the ciphertext $(X \oplus 1, R)$, which is a valid ciphertext of $P \oplus 1$, thus contradicting the notion of non-malleability.

But the opposite relation does hold: NM-CPA implies IND-CPA. The intuition is that IND-CPA encryption is like putting items in a bag: you don't get to see them, but you can rearrange their positions in the bag by shaking it up and down. NM-CPA is more like a safe: once inside, you can't interact with what you put in there. But this analogy doesn't work for IND-CCA and NM-CCA, which are equivalent notions that each imply the presence of the other. I'll spare you the proof, which is pretty technical.

TWO TYPES OF ENCRYPTION APPLICATIONS

There are two main types of encryption applications. *In-transit encryption* protects data sent from one machine to another: data is encrypted before being sent and decrypted after being received, as in encrypted connections to e-commerce websites. *At-rest encryption* protects data stored on an information system. Data is encrypted before being written to memory and decrypted before being read. Examples include disk encryption systems on laptops as well as virtual machine encryption for cloud virtual instances. The security notions we've seen apply to both types of applications, but the right notion to consider may depend on the application.

Asymmetric Encryption

So far we've considered only symmetric encryption, where two parties share a key. In *asymmetric encryption*, there are two keys: one to encrypt and another to decrypt. The encryption key is called a *public key* and is generally considered publicly available to anyone who wants to send you encrypted messages. The decryption key, however, must remain secret and is called a *private key*.

The public key can be computed from the private key, but obviously the private key can't be computed from the public key. In other words, it's easy to compute in one direction, but not in the other—and that's the point of *public-key cryptography*, whose functions are easy to compute in one direction but practically impossible to invert.

The attack models and security goals for asymmetric encryption are about the same as for symmetric encryption, except that because the encryption key is public, any attacker can make encryption queries by using the public key to encrypt. The default model for asymmetric encryption is therefore the chosen-plaintext attacker (CPA).

Symmetric and asymmetric encryption are the two main types of encryption, and they are usually combined to build secure communication systems. They're also used to form the basis of more sophisticated schemes, as you'll see next.

When Ciphers Do More Than Encryption

Basic encryption turns plaintexts into ciphertexts and ciphertexts into plaintexts, with no requirements other than security. However, some applications often need more than that, be it extra security features or extra functionalities. That's why cryptographers created variants of symmetric and asymmetric encryption. Some are well-understood, efficient, and widely deployed, while others are experimental, hardly used, and offer poor performance.

Authenticated Encryption

Authenticated encryption (AE) is a type of symmetric encryption that returns an *authentication tag* in addition to a ciphertext. Figure 1-4 shows authenticated encryption sets $\mathbf{AE}(K, P) = (C, T)$, where the authentication tag T is a short string that's impossible to guess without the key. Decryption takes K, C, and T and returns the plaintext P only if it verifies that T is a valid tag for that plaintext–ciphertext pair; otherwise, it aborts and returns some error.

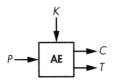

Figure 1-4: Authenticated encryption

The tag ensures the *integrity* of the message and serves as evidence that the ciphertext received is identical to the one sent in the first place by a legitimate party that knows the key K. When K is shared with only one other party, the tag also guarantees that the message was sent by that party; that is, it implicitly *authenticates* the expected sender as the actual creator of the message.

NOTE *I use "creator" rather than "sender" here because an eavesdropper can record some (C, T) pairs sent by party A to party B and then send them again to B, pretending to be A. This is called a replay attack, and it can be prevented, for example, by including a counter number in the message. When a message is decrypted, its counter i is increased by one: i + 1. In this way, one could check the counter to see if a message has been sent twice, indicating that an attacker is attempting a replay attack by resending the message. This also enables the detection of lost messages.*

Authenticated encryption with associated data (AEAD) is an extension of authenticated encryption that takes some cleartext and unencrypted data and uses it to generate the authentication tag $\mathbf{AEAD}(K, P, A) = (C, T)$. A typical application of AEAD is used to protect protocols' datagrams with a cleartext header and an encrypted payload. In such cases, at least some header data has to remain in the clear; for example, destination addresses need to be clear in order to route network packets.

For more on authenticated encryption, jump to Chapter 8.

Format-Preserving Encryption

A basic cipher takes bits and returns bits; it doesn't care whether bits represents text, an image, or a PDF document. The ciphertext may in turn be encoded as raw bytes, hexadecimal characters, base64, and other formats. But what if you need the ciphertext to have the same format as the plaintext, as is sometimes required by database systems that can only record data in a prescribed format?

Format-preserving encryption (FPE) solves this problem. It can create ciphertexts that have the same format as the plaintext. For example, FPE can encrypt IP addresses to IP addresses (as shown in Figure 1-5), ZIP codes to ZIP codes, credit card numbers to credit card numbers with a valid checksum, and so on.

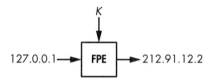

Figure 1-5: Format-preserving encryption
for IP addresses

Fully Homomorphic Encryption

Fully homomorphic encryption (FHE) is the holy grail to cryptographers: it enables its users to replace a ciphertext, $C = \mathbf{E}(K, P)$, with another ciphertext, $C' = \mathbf{E}(K, \mathbf{F}(P))$, for $\mathbf{F}(P)$ can be any function of P, and without ever decrypting the initial ciphertext C. For example, P can be a text document, and $\mathbf{F}$ can be the modification of part of the text. You can imagine a cloud application that stores your encrypted data, but where the cloud provider doesn't know what the data is or the type of changes made when you change that data. Sounds amazing, doesn't it?

But there's a flip side: this type of encryption is slow—so slow that even the most basic operation would take an unacceptably long time. The first FHE scheme was created in 2009, and since then more efficient variants appeared, but it remains unclear whether FHE will ever be fast enough to be useful.

Searchable Encryption

Searchable encryption enables searching over an encrypted database without leaking the searched terms by encrypting the search query itself. Like fully homomorphic encryption, searchable encryption could enhance the privacy of many cloud-based applications by hiding your searches from your cloud provider. Some commercial solutions claim to offer searchable encryption, though they're mostly based on standard cryptography with a few tricks to enable partial searchability. As of this writing, however, searchable encryption remains experimental within the research community.

Tweakable Encryption

Tweakable encryption (TE) is similar to basic encryption, except for an additional parameter called the tweak, which aims to simulate different versions of a cipher (see Figure 1-6). The tweak might be a unique per-customer value to ensure that a customer's cipher can't be cloned by other parties using the same product, but the main application of TE is *disk encryption*. However, TE is not bound to a single application and is a lower-level type of encryption used to build other schemes, such as authentication encryption modes.

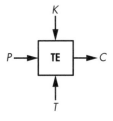

Figure 1-6: Tweakable encryption

In disk encryption, TE encrypts the content of storage devices such as hard drives or solid-state drives. (Randomized encryption can't be used because it increases the size of the data, which is unacceptable for files on storage media.) To make encryption unpredictable, TE uses a tweak value that depends on the position of the data encrypted, which is usually a sector number or a block index.

How Things Can Go Wrong

Encryption algorithms or implementations thereof can fail to protect confidentiality in many ways. This can be due to a failure to match the security requirements (such as "be IND-CPA secure") or to set requirements matching reality (if you target only IND-CPA security when attackers can actually perform chosen-ciphertext queries). Alas, many engineers don't even think about cryptographic security requirements and just want to be "secure" without understanding what that actually means. That's usually a recipe for disaster. Let's look at two examples.

Weak Cipher

Our first example concerns ciphers that can be attacked using cryptanalysis techniques, as occurred with the 2G mobile communication standard. Encryption in 2G mobile phones used a cipher called A5/1 that turned out to be weaker than expected, enabling the interception of calls by anyone with the right skills and tools. Telecommunication operators had to find workarounds to prevent the attack.

NOTE *The 2G standard also defined A5/2, a cipher for areas other than the EU and US. A5/2 was purposefully weaker to prevent the use of strong encryption everywhere.*

That said, attacking A5/1 isn't trivial, and it took more than 10 years for researchers to come up with an effective cryptanalysis method. Furthermore, the attack is a *time-memory trade-off (TMTO)*, a type of method that first runs computations for days or weeks in order to build large look-up tables, which are subsequently used for the actual attack. For A5/1, the precomputed tables are more than 1TB. Later standards for mobile encryption, such as 3G and LTE, specify stronger ciphers, but that doesn't mean that their encryption won't be compromised; rather, it simply means that the encryption won't be compromised by breaking the symmetric cipher that's part of the system.

Wrong Model

The next example concerns an invalid attack model that overlooked some side channels.

Many communication protocols that use encryption ensure that they use ciphers considered secure in the CPA or CCA model. However, some attacks don't require encryption queries, as in the CPA model, nor do they require decryption queries, as in the CCA model. They simply need *validity queries* to tell whether a ciphertext is valid, and these queries are usually sent to the system responsible for decrypting ciphertexts. *Padding oracle attacks* are an example of such attacks, wherein an attacker learns whether a ciphertext conforms to the required format.

Specifically, in the case of padding oracle attacks, a ciphertext is valid only if its plaintext has the proper *padding*, a sequence of bytes appended to the plaintext to simplify encryption. Decryption fails if the padding is incorrect, and attackers can often detect decryption failures and attempt to exploit them. For example, the presence of the Java exception `javax.crypto`
`.BadPaddingException` would indicate that an incorrect padding was observed.

In 2010, researchers found padding oracle attacks in several web application servers. The validity queries consisted of sending a ciphertext to some system and observing whether it threw an error. Thanks to these queries, they could decrypt otherwise secure ciphertexts without knowing the key.

Cryptographers often overlook attacks like padding oracle attacks because they usually depend on an application's behavior and on how users can interact with the application. But if you don't anticipate such attacks and fail to include them in your model when designing and deploying cryptography, you may have some nasty surprises.

Further Reading

We discuss encryption and its various forms in more detail throughout this book, especially how modern, secure ciphers work. Still, we can't cover everything, and many fascinating topics won't be discussed. For example, to learn the theoretical foundations of encryption and gain a deeper understanding of the notion of indistinguishability (IND), you should read the 1982 paper that introduced the idea of semantic security, "Probabilistic Encryption and How to Play Mental Poker Keeping Secret All Partial Information" by Goldwasser and Micali. If you're interested in physical attacks and cryptographic hardware, the proceedings of the CHES conference are the main reference.

There are also many more types of encryption than those presented in this chapter, including attribute-based encryption, broadcast encryption, functional encryption, identity-based encryption, message-locked encryption, and proxy re-encryption, to cite but a few. For the latest research on those topics, you should check *https://eprint.iacr.org/*, an electronic archive of cryptography research papers.

2

RANDOMNESS

Randomness is found everywhere in cryptography: in the generation of secret keys, in encryption schemes, and even in the attacks on cryptosystems. Without randomness, cryptography would be impossible because all operations would become predictable, and therefore insecure.

This chapter introduces you to the concept of randomness in the context of cryptography and its applications. We discuss pseudorandom number generators and how operating systems can produce reliable randomness, and we conclude with real examples showing how flawed randomness can impact security.

Random or Non-Random?

You've probably already heard the phrase "random bits," but strictly speaking there is no such thing as a series of random bits. What is random is actually the algorithm or process that produces a series of random bits; therefore, when we say "random bits," we actually mean randomly generated bits.

What do random bits look like? For example, to most people, the 8-bit string 11010110 is more random than 00000000, although both have the same chance of being generated (namely, 1/256). The value 11010110 looks more random than 00000000 because it has the signs typical of a randomly generated value. That is, 11010110 has no obvious pattern.

When we see the string 11010110, our brain registers that it has about as many zeros (three) as it does ones (five), just like 55 other 8-bit strings (11111000, 11110100, 11110010, and so on), but only one 8-bit string has eight zeros. Because the pattern three-zeros-and-five-ones is more likely to occur than the pattern eight-zeros, we identify 11010110 as random and 00000000 as non-random, and if a program produces the bits 11010110, you may think that it's random, even if it's not. Conversely, if a randomized program produces 00000000, you'll probably doubt that it's random.

This example illustrates two types of errors people often make when identifying randomness:

Mistaking non-randomness for randomness Thinking that an object was randomly generated simply because it *looks* random.

Mistaking randomness for non-randomness Thinking that patterns appearing by chance are there for a reason other than chance.

The distinction between random-looking and actually random is crucial. Indeed, in crypto, non-randomness is often synonymous with insecurity.

Randomness as a Probability Distribution

Any randomized process is characterized by a *probability distribution*, which gives all there is to know about the randomness of the process. A probability distribution, or simply distribution, lists the outcomes of a randomized process where each outcome is assigned a *probability*.

A probability measures the likelihood of an event occurring. It's expressed as a real number between 0 and 1 where a probability 0 means impossible and a probability of 1 means certain. For example, when tossing a two-sided coin, each side has a probability of landing face up of 1/2, and we usually assume that landing on the edge of the coin has probability zero.

A probability distribution must include all possible outcomes, such that the sum of all probabilities is 1. Specifically, if there are N possible events, there are N probabilities $p_1, p_2, \ldots, p_N$ with $p_1 + p_2 + \ldots + p_N = 1$. In the case of the coin toss, the distribution is 1/2 for heads and 1/2 for tails. The sum of both probabilities is equal to $1/2 + 1/2 = 1$, because the coin will fall on one of its two faces.

A *uniform distribution* occurs when all probabilities in the distribution are equal, meaning that all outcomes are equally likely to occur. If there are N events, then each event has probability $1/N$. For example, if a 128-bit key is picked uniformly at random—that is, according to a uniform distribution—then each of the 2^{128} possible keys should have a probability of $1/2^{128}$.

In contrast, when a distribution is *non-uniform*, probabilities aren't all equal. A coin toss with a non-uniform distribution is said to be biased, and may yield heads with probability $1/4$ and tails with probability $3/4$, for example.

Entropy: A Measure of Uncertainty

Entropy is the measure of uncertainty, or disorder in a system. You might think of entropy as the amount of surprise found in the result of a randomized process: the higher the entropy, the less the certainty found in the result.

We can compute the entropy of a probability distribution. If your distribution consists of probabilities $p_1, p_2, \ldots, p_N$, then its entropy is the negative sum of all probabilities multiplied by their logarithm, as shown in this expression:

$$-p_1 \times \log(p_1) - p_2 \times \log(p_2) - \ldots p_N \times \log(p_N)$$

Here the function *log* is the *binary logarithm*, or logarithm in base two. Unlike the natural logarithm, the binary logarithm expresses the information in bits and yields integer values when probabilities are powers of two. For example, $\log(1/2) = -1$, $\log(1/4) = -2$, and more generally $\log(1/2^n) = -n$. (That's why we actually take the *negative sum*, in order to end up with a positive number.) Random 128-bit keys produced using a uniform distribution therefore have the following entropy:

$$2^{128} \times \left(-2^{-128} \times \log\left(2^{-128}\right)\right) = -\log\left(2^{-128}\right) = 128 \text{ bits}$$

If you replace 128 by any integer n you will find that the entropy of a uniformly distributed n-bit string will be n bits.

Entropy is maximized when the distribution is uniform because a uniform distribution maximizes uncertainty: no outcome is more likely than the others. Therefore, n-bit values can't have more than n bits of entropy.

By the same token, when the distribution is not uniform, entropy is lower. Consider the coin toss example. The entropy of a fair toss is the following:

$$-(1/2) \times \log(1/2) - (1/2) \times \log(1/2) = 1/2 + 1/2 = 1 \text{ bit}$$

What if one side of the coin has a higher probability of landing face up than the other? Say heads has a probability of $1/4$ and tails $3/4$ (remember that the sum of all probabilities should be 1).

The entropy of such a biased toss is this:

$$-(3/4) \times \log(3/4) - (1/4) \times \log(1/4) \approx -(3/4) \times (-0.415) - (1/4) \times (-2) \approx 0.81 \text{ bit}$$

The fact that 0.81 is less than the 1-bit entropy of a fair toss tells us that the more biased the coin, the less uniform the distribution and the lower the entropy. Taking this example further, if heads has a probability of 1/10, the entropy is 0.469; if the probability drops to 1/100, the entropy drops to 0.081.

NOTE *Entropy can also be viewed as a measure of information. For example, the result of a fair coin toss gives you exactly one bit of information—heads or tails—and you're unable to predict the result of the toss in advance. In the case of the unfair coin toss, you know in advance that tails is more probable, so you can usually predict the outcome of the toss. The result of the coin toss gives you the information needed to predict the result with certainty.*

Random Number Generators (RNGs) and Pseudorandom Number Generators (PRNGs)

Cryptosystems need randomness to be secure and therefore need a component from which to get their randomness. The job of this component is to return random bits when requested to do so. How is this randomness generation done? You'll need two things:

- A source of uncertainty, or *source of entropy*, provided by random number generators (RNGs).
- A cryptographic algorithm to produce high-quality random bits from the source of entropy. This is found in pseudorandom number generators (PRNGs).

Using RNGs and PRNGs is the key to making cryptography practical and secure. Let's briefly look at how RNGs work before exploring PRNGs in depth.

Randomness comes from the environment, which is analog, chaotic, uncertain, and hence unpredictable. Randomness can't be generated by computer-based algorithms alone. In cryptography, randomness usually comes from *random number generators (RNGs)*, which are software or hardware components that leverage entropy in the analog world to produce unpredictable bits in a digital system. For example, an RNG might directly sample bits from measurements of temperature, acoustic noise, air turbulence, or electrical static. Unfortunately, such analog entropy sources aren't always available, and their entropy is often difficult to estimate.

RNGs can also harvest the entropy in a running operating system by drawing from attached sensors, I/O devices, network or disk activity, system logs, running processes, and user activities such as key presses and mouse movement. Such system- and human-generated activities can be a good source of entropy, but they can be fragile and manipulated by an attacker. Also, they're slow to yield random bits.

Quantum random number generators (QRNGs) are a type of RNG that relies on the randomness arising from quantum mechanical phenomena such as radioactive decay, vacuum fluctuations, and observing photons' polarization. These can provide *real* randomness, rather than just apparent randomness. However, in practice, QRNGs may be biased and don't produce bits quickly; like the previously cited entropy sources, they need an additional component to produce reliably at high speed.

Pseudorandom number generators (PRNGs) address the challenge we face in generating randomness by reliably producing many artificial random bits from a few true random bits. For example, an RNG that translates mouse movements to random bits would stop working if you stop moving the mouse, whereas a PRNG always returns pseudorandom bits when requested to do so.

PRNGs rely on RNGs but behave differently: RNGs produce true random bits relatively slowly from analog sources, in a nondeterministic way, and with no guarantee of high entropy. In contrast, PRNGs produce random-looking bits quickly from digital sources, in a deterministic way, and with maximum entropy. Essentially, PRNGs transform a few unreliable random bits into a long stream of reliable pseudorandom bits suitable for crypto applications, as shown in Figure 2-1.

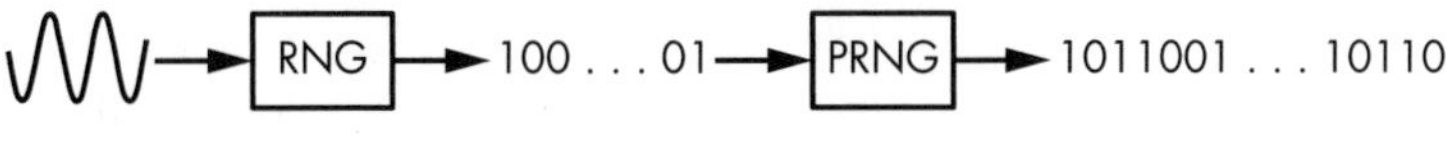

Figure 2-1: RNGs produce few unreliable bits from analog sources, whereas PRNGs expand those bits to a long stream of reliable bits.

How PRNGs Work

A PRNG receives random bits from an RNG at regular intervals and uses them to update the contents of a large memory buffer, called the *entropy pool*. The entropy pool is the PRNG's source of entropy, just like the physical environment is to an RNG. When the PRNG updates the entropy pool, it mixes the pool's bits together to help remove any statistical bias.

In order to generate pseudorandom bits, the PRNG runs a deterministic random bit generator (DRBG) algorithm that expands some bits from the entropy pool into a much longer sequence. As its name suggests, a DRBG is deterministic, not randomized: given one input you will always get the same output. The PRNG ensures that its DRBG never receives the same input twice, in order to generate unique pseudorandom sequences.

In the course of its work, the PRNG performs three operations, as follows:

init()   Initializes the entropy pool and the internal state of the PRNG

refresh(R)   Updates the entropy pool using some data, *R*, usually sourced from an RNG

next(N)   Returns *N* pseudorandom bits and updates the entropy pool

The *init* operation resets the PRNG to a fresh state, reinitializes the entropy pool to some default value, and initializes any variables or memory buffers used by the PRNG to carry out the *refresh* and *next* operations.

The *refresh* operation is often called *reseeding*, and its argument *R* is called a *seed*. When no RNG is available, seeds may be unique values hard-coded in a system. The *refresh* operation is typically called by the operating system, whereas *next* is typically called or requested by applications. The *next* operation runs the DRBG and modifies the entropy pool to ensure that the next call will yield different pseudorandom bits.

Security Concerns

Let's talk briefly about the way that PRNGs address some high-level security concerns. Specifically, PRNGs should guarantee *backtracking resistance* and *prediction resistance*. Backtracking resistance (also called *forward secrecy*) means that previously generated bits are impossible to recover, whereas prediction resistance (*backward secrecy*) means that future bits should be impossible to predict.

In order to achieve backtracking resistance, the PRNG should ensure that the transformations performed when updating the state through the *refresh* and *next* operations are irreversible so that if an attacker compromises the system and obtains the entropy pool's value, they can't determine the previous values of the pool or the previously generated bits. To achieve prediction resistance, the PRNG should call *refresh* regularly with *R* values that are unknown to an attacker and that are difficult to guess, thus preventing an attacker from determining future values of the entropy pool, even if the whole pool is compromised. (Even if the list of *R* values used were known, you'd need to know the order in which *refresh* and *next* calls were made in order to reconstruct the pool.)

The PRNG Fortuna

Fortuna is a PRNG construction used in Windows originally designed in 2003 by Niels Ferguson and Bruce Schneier. Fortuna superseded *Yarrow*, a 1998 design by Kelsey and Schneier now used in the macOS and iOS operating systems. I won't provide the Fortuna specification here or show you how to implement it, but I will try to explain how it works. You'll find a complete description of Fortuna in Chapter 9 of *Cryptography Engineering* by Ferguson, Schneier, and Kohno (Wiley, 2010).

Fortuna's internal memory includes the following:

- Thirty-two entropy pools, $P_1, P_2, \ldots, P_{32}$, such that P_i is used every 2^i reseeds.

- A key, *K*, and a counter, *C* (both 16 bytes). These form the internal state of Fortuna's DRBG.

In simplest terms, Fortuna works like this:

- *init*() sets K and C to zero and empties the 32 entropy pools P_i, where $i = 1 \ldots 32$.
- *refresh*(R) appends the data, R, to one of the entropy pools. The system chooses the RNGs used to produce R values, and it should call *refresh* regularly.
- *next*(N) updates K using data from one or more entropy pools, where the choice of the entropy pools depends mainly on how many updates of K have already been done. The N bits requested are then produced by encrypting C using K as a key. If encrypting C is not enough, Fortuna encrypts $C + 1$, then $C + 2$, and so on, to get enough bits.

Although Fortuna's operations look fairly simple, implementing them correctly is hard. For one thing, you need to get all the details of the algorithm right—namely, how entropy pools are chosen, the type of cipher to be used in *next*, how to behave when no entropy is received, and so on. Although the specs define most of the details, they don't include a comprehensive test suite to check that an implementation is correct, which makes it difficult to ensure that your implementation of Fortuna will behave as expected.

Even if Fortuna is correctly implemented, security failures may occur for reasons other than the use of an incorrect algorithm. For example, Fortuna might not notice if the RNGs fail to produce enough random bits, and as a result Fortuna will produce lower-quality pseudorandom bits, or it may stop delivering pseudorandom bits altogether.

Another risk inherent in Fortuna implementations lies in the possibility of exposing associated *seed files* to attackers. The data in Fortuna seed files is used to feed entropy to Fortuna through *refresh* calls when an RNG is not immediately available, such as immediately after a system reboot and before the system's RNGs have recorded any unpredictable events. However, if an identical seed file is used twice, then Fortuna will produce the same bit sequence twice. Seed files should therefore be erased after being used to ensure that they aren't reused.

Finally, if two Fortuna instances are in the same state because they are sharing a seed file (meaning they are sharing the same data in the entropy pools, including the same C and K), then the *next* operation will return the same bits in both instances.

Cryptographic vs. Non-Cryptographic PRNGs

There are both cryptographic and non-cryptographic PRNGs. Non-crypto PRNGs are designed to produce uniform distributions for applications such as scientific simulations or video games. However, you should never use non-crypto PRNGs in crypto applications, because they're insecure—they're only concerned with the quality of the bits' probability distribution and not with their predictability. Crypto PRNGs, on the other hand, are unpredictable, because they're also concerned with the strength of the underlying *operations* used to deliver well-distributed bits.

Unfortunately, most PRNGs exposed by programming languages, such as libc's rand and drand48, PHP's rand and mt_rand, Python's random module, Ruby's Random class, and so on, are non-cryptographic. Defaulting to a non-crypto PRNG is a recipe for disaster because it often ends up being used in crypto applications, so be sure to use only crypto PRNGs in crypto applications.

A Popular Non-Crypto PRNG: Mersenne Twister

The *Mersenne Twister* (MT) algorithm is a non-cryptographic PRNG used (at the time of this writing) in PHP, Python, R, Ruby, and many other systems. MT will generate uniformly distributed random bits without statistical bias, but it's predictable: given a few bits produced by MT, it's easy enough to tell which bits will follow.

Let's look under the hood to see what makes the Mersenne Twister insecure. The MT algorithm is much simpler than that of crypto PRNGs: its internal state is an array, S, consisting of 624 32-bit words. This array is initially set to $S_1, S_2, \ldots, S_{624}$ and evolves to $S_2, \ldots, S_{625}$, then $S_3, \ldots, S_{626}$, and so on, according to this equation:

$$S_{k+624} = S_{k+397} \oplus \mathbf{A}\big(\big(S_k \wedge 0x80000000\big) \vee \big(S_{k+1} \wedge 0x7fffffff\big)\big)$$

Here, $\oplus$ denotes the bitwise XOR (^ in the C programming language), $\wedge$ denotes the bitwise AND (& in C), $\vee$ denotes the bitwise OR (| in C), and $\mathbf{A}$ is a function that transforms some 32-bit word, x, to $(x \gg 1)$, if x's most significant bit is 0, or to $(x \gg 1) \oplus 0x9908b0df$ otherwise.

Notice in this equation that bits of S interact with each other only through XORs. The operators $\wedge$ and $\vee$ never combine two bits of S together, but just bits of S with bits from the constants 0x80000000 and 0x7fffffff. This way, any bit from S_{625} can be expressed as an XOR of bits from S_{398}, S_1, and S_2, and any bit from any future state can be expressed as an XOR combination of bits from the initial state $S_1, \ldots, S_{624}$. (When you express, say, $S_{228+624} = S_{852}$ as a function of S_{625}, S_{228}, and S_{229}, you can in turn replace S_{625} by its expression in terms of S_{398}, S_1, and S_2.)

Because there are exactly $624 \times 32 = 19,968$ bits in the initial state (or 624 32-bit words), any output bit can be expressed as an equation with at most 19,969 terms (19,968 bits plus one constant bit). That's just about 2.5 kilobytes of data. The converse is also true: bits from the initial state can be expressed as an XOR of output bits.

Linearity Insecurity

We call an XOR combination of bits a *linear combination*. For example, if X, Y, and Z are bits, then the expression $X \oplus Y \oplus Z$ is a linear combination, whereas $(X \wedge Y) \oplus Z$ is not because there's an AND ($\wedge$). If you flip a bit of X in $X \oplus Y \oplus Z$, then the result changes as well, regardless of the value of the Y and Z. In contrast, if you flip a bit of X in $(X \wedge Y) \oplus Z$, the result changes only if Y's bit at the same position is 1. The upshot is that linear combinations are predictable, because you don't need to know the value of the bits in order to predict how a change in their value will affect the result.

For comparison, if the MT algorithm were cryptographically strong, its equations would be *nonlinear* and would involve not only single bits but also AND-combinations (*products*) of bits, such as $S_1 S_{15} S_{182}$ or $S_{17} S_{256} S_{257} S_{354} S_{498} S_{601}$. Although linear combinations of those bits include at most 624 variables, nonlinear combinations allow for up to 2^{624} variables. It would be impossible to solve, let alone write down the whole of these equations. (Note that 2^{305}, a much smaller number, is the estimated information capacity of the observable universe.)

The key here is that linear transformations lead to short equations (comparable in size to the number of variables), which are easy to solve, whereas nonlinear transformations give rise to equations of exponential size, which are practically unsolvable. The game of cryptographers is thus to design PRNG algorithms that emulate such complex nonlinear transformations using only a small number of simple operations.

NOTE *Linearity is just one of many security criteria. Although necessary, nonlinearity alone does not make a PRNG cryptographically secure.*

The Uselessness of Statistical Tests

Statistical test suites like TestU01, Diehard, or the National Institute of Standards and Technology (NIST) test suite are one way to test the quality of pseudorandom bits. These tests take a sample of pseudorandom bits produced by a PRNG (say, one megabyte worth), compute some statistics on the distribution of certain patterns in the bits, and compare the results with the typical results obtained for a perfect, uniform distribution. For example, some tests count the number of 1 bits versus the number of 0 bits, or the distribution of 8-bit patterns. But statistical tests are largely irrelevant to cryptographic security, and it's possible to design a cryptographically weak PRNG that will fool any statistical test.

When you run statistical tests on randomly generated data, you will usually see a bunch of statistical indicators as a result. These are typically *p*-values, a common statistical indicator. These results aren't always easy to interpret, because they're rarely as simple as passed or failed. If your first results seem abnormal, don't worry: they may be the result of some accidental deviation, or you may be testing too few samples. To ensure that the results you see are normal, compare them with those obtained for some reliable sample of identical size; for example, one generated with the OpenSSL toolkit using the following command:

```
$ openssl rand <number of bytes> -out <output file>
```

Real-World PRNGs

Let's turn our attention to how to implement PRNGs in the real world. You'll find crypto PRNGs in the operating systems (OSs) of most platforms, from desktops and laptops to embedded systems such as routers and set-top boxes, as well as virtual machines, mobile phones, and so on. Most of these PRNGs are software based, but some are pure hardware. Those PRNGs are used by applications running on the OS, and sometimes other PRNGs running on top of cryptographic libraries or applications.

Next we'll look at the most widely deployed PRNGs: the one for Linux, Android, and many other Unix-based systems; the one in Windows; and the one in recent Intel microprocessors, which is hardware based.

Generating Random Bits in Unix-Based Systems

The device file */dev/urandom* is the userland interface to the crypto PRNG of common *nix systems, and it's what you will typically use to generate reliable random bits. Because it's a device file, requesting random bits from */dev/urandom* is done by reading it as a file. For example, the following command uses */dev/urandom* to write 10MB of random bits to a file:

```
$ dd if=/dev/urandom of=<output file> bs=1M count=10
```

The Wrong Way to Use /dev/urandom

You could write a naive and insecure C program like the one shown in Listing 2-1 to read random bits, and hope for the best, but that would be a bad idea.

```
int random_bytes_insecure(void *buf, size_t len)
{
    int fd = open("/dev/urandom", O_RDONLY);
    read(fd, buf, len);
    close(fd);
    return 0;
}
```

Listing 2-1: Insecure use of /dev/urandom

This code is insecure; it doesn't even check the return values of open() and read(), which means your expected random buffer could end up filled with zeroes, or left unchanged.

A Safer Way to Use /dev/urandom

Listing 2-2, copied from LibreSSL, shows a safer way to use */dev/urandom*.

```
int random_bytes_safer(void *buf, size_t len)
{
    struct stat st;
    size_t i;
    int fd, cnt, flags;
    int save_errno = errno;

start:
    flags = O_RDONLY;
```

```
#ifdef O_NOFOLLOW
    flags |= O_NOFOLLOW;
#endif
#ifdef O_CLOEXEC
    flags |= O_CLOEXEC;
#endif
    fd = ❶open("/dev/urandom", flags, 0);
    if (fd == -1) {
        if (errno == EINTR)
            goto start;
        goto nodevrandom;
    }
#ifndef O_CLOEXEC
    fcntl(fd, F_SETFD, fcntl(fd, F_GETFD) | FD_CLOEXEC);
#endif

    /* Lightly verify that the device node looks sane */
    if (fstat(fd, &st) == -1 || !S_ISCHR(st.st_mode)) {
        close(fd);
        goto nodevrandom;
    }
    if (ioctl(fd, RNDGETENTCNT, &cnt) == -1) {
        close(fd);
        goto nodevrandom;
    }
    for (i = 0; i < len; ) {
        size_t wanted = len - i;
        ssize_t ret = ❷read(fd, (char *)buf + i, wanted);

        if (ret == -1) {
            if (errno == EAGAIN || errno == EINTR)
                continue;
            close(fd);
            goto nodevrandom;
        }
        i += ret;
    }
    close(fd);
    if (gotdata(buf, len) == 0) {
        errno = save_errno;
        return 0;                    /* satisfied */
    }
nodevrandom:
    errno = EIO;
    return -1;
}
```

Listing 2-2: Safe use of /dev/urandom

Unlike Listing 2-1, Listing 2-2 makes several sanity checks. Compare, for example, the call to open() at ❶ and the call to read() at ❷ with those in Listing 2-1: you'll notice that the safer code checks the return values of those functions, and upon failure closes the file descriptor and returns –1.

Differences Between /dev/urandom and /dev/random on Linux

Different Unix versions use different PRNGs. The Linux PRNG, defined in *drivers/char/random.c* in the Linux kernel, mainly uses the hash function SHA-1 to turn raw entropy bits into reliable pseudorandom bits. The PRNG harvests entropy from various sources (including the keyboard, mouse, disk, and interrupt timings) and has a primary entropy pool of 512 bytes, as well as a non-blocking pool for */dev/urandom* and a blocking pool for */dev/random*.

What's the difference between */dev/urandom* and */dev/random*? The short story is that */dev/random* attempts to estimate the amount of entropy and refuses to return bits if the level of entropy is too low. Although this may sound like a good idea, it's not. For one thing, entropy estimators are notoriously unreliable and can be fooled by attackers (which is one reason why Fortuna ditched Yarrow's entropy estimation). Furthermore, */dev/random* runs out of estimated entropy pretty quickly, which can produce a denial-of-service condition, slowing applications that are forced to wait for more entropy. The upshot is that in practice, */dev/random* is no better than */dev/urandom* and creates more problems than it solves.

Estimating the Entropy of /dev/random

You can observe how */dev/random*'s entropy estimate evolves by reading its current value in bits in */proc/sys/kernel/random/entropy_avail* on Linux. For example, the shell script shown in Listing 2-3 first minimizes the entropy estimate by reading 4KB from */dev/random*, waits until it reaches an estimate of 128 bits, reads 64 bits from */dev/random*, and then shows the new estimate. When running the script, notice how user activity accelerates entropy recovery (bytes read are printed to stdout encoded in base64).

```
#!/bin/sh
ESTIMATE=/proc/sys/kernel/random/entropy_avail
timeout 3s dd if=/dev/random bs=4k count=1 2> /dev/null | base64
ent=`cat $ESTIMATE`
while [ $ent -lt 128 ]
do
    sleep 3
    ent=`cat $ESTIMATE`
    echo $ent
done
dd if=/dev/random bs=8 count=1 2> /dev/null | base64
cat $ESTIMATE
```

Listing 2-3: A script showing the evolution of /dev/urandom's entropy estimate

A sample run of Listing 2-3 gave the output shown in Listing 2-4. (Guess when I started randomly moving the mouse and hitting the keyboard to gather entropy.)

```
xFNX/f2R87/zrrNJ6Ibr5R1L913tl+F4GNzKb6OBC+qQnHQcyA==
2
18
19
```

```
27
28
72
124
193
jq8XWCt8
129
```

Listing 2-4: A sample execution of the entropy estimate evolution script in Listing 2-3

As you can see in Listing 2-4, we have 193 − 64 = 129 bits of entropy left in the pool, as per */dev/random*'s estimator. Does it make sense to consider a PRNG as having *N* less entropy bits just because *N* bits were just read from the PRNG? (Spoiler: it does not.)

NOTE *Like /dev/random, Linux's getrandom() system call blocks if it hasn't gathered enough initial entropy. However, unlike /dev/random, it won't attempt to estimate the entropy in the system and will never block after its initialization stage. And that's fine. (You can force getrandom() to use /dev/random and to block by tweaking its flags, but I don't see why you'd want to do that.)*

The CryptGenRandom() Function in Windows

In Windows, the legacy userland interface to the system's PRNG is the CryptGenRandom() function from the Cryptography application programming interface (API). The CryptGenRandom() function has been replaced in recent Windows versions with the BcryptGenRandom() function in the Cryptography API: Next Generation (CNG) API. The Windows PRNG takes entropy from the kernel mode driver *cng.sys* (formerly *ksecdd.sys*), whose entropy collector is loosely based on Fortuna. As is usually the case in Windows, the process is complicated.

Listing 2-5 shows a typical C++ invocation of CryptGenRandom() with the required checks.

```cpp
int random_bytes(unsigned char *out, size_t outlen)
{
    static HCRYPTPROV handle = 0; /* only freed when the program ends */
    if(!handle) {
        if(!CryptAcquireContext(&handle, 0, 0, PROV_RSA_FULL,
                        CRYPT_VERIFYCONTEXT | CRYPT_SILENT)) {
            return -1;
        }
    }
    while(outlen > 0) {
        const DWORD len = outlen > 1048576UL ? 1048576UL : outlen;
        if(!CryptGenRandom(handle, len, out)) {
            return -2;
        }
        out    += len;
        outlen -= len;
    }
}
```

```
        return 0;
}
```

Listing 2-5: Using the Windows `CryptGenRandom()` PRNG interface

Notice in Listing 2-5 that prior to calling the actual PRNG, you need
to declare a *cryptographic service provider* (`HCRYPTPROV`) and then acquire a
cryptographic context with `CryptAcquireContext()`, which increases the chances
of things going wrong. For instance, the final version of the TrueCrypt
encryption software was found to call `CryptAcquireContext()` in a way that
could silently fail, leading to suboptimal randomness without notifying the
user. Fortunately, the newer `BCryptGenRandom()` interface for Windows is much
simpler and doesn't require the code to explicitly open a handle (or at least
makes it much easier to use without a handle).

A Hardware-Based PRNG: RDRAND in Intel Microprocessors

We've discussed only software PRNGs so far, so let's have a look at a hardware one. The *Intel Digital Random Number Generator* is a hardware PRNG
introduced in 2012 in Intel's Ivy Bridge microarchitecture, and it's based
on NIST's SP 800-90 guidelines with the Advanced Encryption Standard
(AES) in CTR_DRBG mode. Intel's PRNG is accessed through the `RDRAND`
assembly instruction, which offers an interface independent of the operating system and is in principle faster than software PRNGs.

Whereas software PRNGs try to collect entropy from unpredictable
sources, `RDRAND` has a single entropy source that provides a serial stream
of entropy data as zeroes and ones. In hardware engineering terms, this
entropy source is a dual differential jamb latch with feedback; essentially, a
small hardware circuit that jumps between two states (0 or 1) depending on
thermal noise fluctuations, at a frequency of 800 MHz. This kind of thing is
usually pretty reliable.

The `RDRAND` assembly instruction takes as an argument a register of 16,
32, or 64 bits and then writes a random value. When invoked, `RDRAND` sets the
carry flag to 1 if the data set in the destination register is a valid random
value, and to 0 otherwise, which means you should be sure to check the `CF`
flag if you write assembly code directly. Note that the C intrinsics available
in common compilers don't check the `CF` flag but do return its value.

NOTE   *Intel's PRNG framework provides an assembly instruction other than `RDRAND`: the
RDSEED assembly instruction returns random bits directly from the entropy source,
after some conditioning or cryptographic processing. It's intended to be able to seed
other PRNGs.*

Intel's PRNG is only partially documented, but it's built on known standards, and has been audited by the well-regarded company Cryptography
Research (see their report titled "Analysis of Intel's Ivy Bridge Digital
Random Number Generator"). Nonetheless, there have been some concerns about its security, especially following Snowden's revelations about

cryptographic backdoors, and PRNGs are indeed the perfect target for sabotage. If you're concerned but still wish to use RDRAND or RDSEED, just mix them with other entropy sources. Doing so will prevent effective exploitation of a hypothetical backdoor in Intel's hardware or in the associated microcode in all but the most far-fetched scenarios.

How Things Can Go Wrong

To conclude, I'll present a few examples of randomness failures. There are countless examples to choose from, but I've chosen four that are simple enough to understand and illustrate different problems.

Poor Entropy Sources

In 1996, the SSL implementation of the Netscape browser was computing 128-bit PRNG seeds according to the pseudocode shown in Listing 2-6, copied from Goldberg and Wagner's page at *http://www.cs.berkeley.edu/~daw/papers/ddj-netscape.html*.

```
global variable seed;

RNG_CreateContext()
    (seconds, microseconds) = time of day; /* Time elapsed since 1970 */
    pid = process ID;  ppid = parent process ID;
    a = mklcpr(microseconds);
 ❶  b = mklcpr(pid + seconds + (ppid << 12));
    seed = MD5(a, b); /* Derivation of a 128-bit value using the hash MD5 */

mklcpr(x) /* not cryptographically significant; shown for completeness */
    return ((0xDEECE66D * x + 0x2BBB62DC) >> 1);

MD5() /* a very good standard mixing function, source omitted */
```

Listing 2-6: Pseudocode of the Netscape browser's generation of 128-bit PRNG seeds

The problem here is that the PIDs and microseconds are guessable values. Assuming that you can guess the value of seconds, microseconds has only 10^6 possible values and thus an entropy of $\log(10^6)$, or about 20 bits. The process ID (PID) and parent process ID (PPID) are 15-bit values, so you'd expect $15 + 15 = 30$ additional entropy bits. But if you look at how b is computed at ❶, you'll see that the overlap of three bits yields an entropy of only about $15 + 12 = 27$ bits, for a total entropy of only 47 bits, whereas a 128-bit seed should have 128 bits of entropy.

Insufficient Entropy at Boot Time

In 2012, researchers scanned the whole internet and harvested public keys from TLS certificates and SSH hosts. They found that a handful of systems had identical public keys, and in some cases very similar keys (namely, RSA keys with shared prime factors): in short, two numbers, $n = pq$ and $n' = p'q'$, with $p = p'$, whereas normally all ps and qs should be different in distinct modulus values.

After further investigation, it turned out that many devices generated their public key early, at first boot, before having collected enough entropy, despite using an otherwise decent PRNG (typically */dev/urandom*). PRNGs in different systems ended up producing identical random bits due to a same base entropy source (for example, a hardcoded seed).

At a high level, the presence of identical keys is due to key-generation schemes like the following, in pseudocode:

```
prng.seed(seed)
p = prng.generate_random_prime()
q = prng.generate_random_prime()
n = p*q
```

If two systems run this code given an identical seed, they'll produce the same p, the same q, and therefore the same n.

The presence of shared primes in different keys is due to key-generation schemes where additional entropy is injected during the process, as shown here:

```
prng.seed(seed)
p = prng.generate_random_prime()
prng.add_entropy()
q = prng.generate_random_prime()
n = p*q
```

If two systems run this code with the same seed, they'll produce the same p, but the injection of entropy through `prng.add_entropy()` will ensure distinct qs.

The problem with shared prime factors is that given $n = pq$ and $n' = pq'$, it's trivial to recover the shared p by computing the *greatest common divisor* (GCD) of n and n'. For the details, see the paper "Mining Your Ps and Qs" by Heninger, Durumeric, Wustrow, and Halderman, available at *https://factorable.net/*.

Non-cryptographic PRNG

Earlier we discussed the difference between crypto and non-crypto PRNGs and why the latter should never be used for crypto applications. Alas, many systems overlook that detail, so I thought I should give you at least one such example.

The popular MediaWiki application runs on Wikipedia and many other wikis. It uses randomness to generate things like security tokens and temporary passwords, which of course should be unpredictable. Unfortunately, a now obsolete version of MediaWiki used a non-crypto PRNG, the Mersenne Twister, to generate these tokens and passwords. Here's a snippet from the vulnerable MediaWiki source code. Look for the function called to get a random bit, and be sure to read the comments.

```
/**
 * Generate a hex-y looking random token for various uses.
 * Could be made more cryptographically sure if someone cares.
 * @return string
 */
function generateToken( $salt = '' ) {
    $token = dechex(mt_rand()).dechex(mt_rand());
    return md5( $token . $salt );
}
```

Did you notice mt_rand() in the preceding code? Here, mt stands for Mersenne Twister, the non-crypto PRNG discussed earlier. In 2012, researchers showed how to exploit the predictability of Mersenne Twister to predict future tokens and temporary passwords, given a couple of security tokens. MediaWiki was patched in order to use a crypto PRNG.

Sampling Bug with Strong Randomness

The next bug shows how even a strong crypto PRNG with sufficient entropy can produce a biased distribution. The chat program Cryptocat was designed to offer secure communication. It used a function that attempted to create a uniformly distributed string of decimal digits—namely, numbers in the range 0 through 9. However, just taking random bytes modulo 10 doesn't yield a uniform distribution, because when taking all numbers between 0 and 255 and reducing them modulo 10, you don't get an equal number of values in 0 to 9.

Cryptocat did the following to address that problem and obtain a uniform distribution:

```
Cryptocat.random = function() {
    var x, o = '';
    while (o.length < 16) {
        x = state.getBytes(1);
        if (x[0] <= 250) {
            o += x[0] % 10;
        }
    }
    return parseFloat('0.' + o)
}
```

And that was almost perfect. By taking only the numbers up to a multiple of 10 and discarding others, you'd expect a uniform distribution of the digits 0 through 9. Unfortunately, there was an off-by-one error in the if condition. I'll leave the details to you as an exercise. You should find that the values generated had an entropy of 45 instead of approximately 53 bits (hint: <= should have been < instead).

Further Reading

I've just scratched the surface of randomness in cryptography in this chapter. There is much more to learn about the theory of randomness, including topics such as different entropy notions, randomness extractors, and even the power of randomization and derandomization in complexity theory. To learn more about PRNGs and their security, read the classic 1998 paper "Cryptanalytic Attacks on Pseudorandom Number Generators" by Kelsey, Schneier, Wagner, and Hall. Then look at the implementation of PRNGs in your favorite applications and try to find their weaknesses. (Search online for "random generator bug" to find plenty of examples.)

We're not done with randomness, though. We'll encounter it again and again throughout this book, and you'll discover the many ways it helps to construct secure systems.

3

CRYPTOGRAPHIC SECURITY

Cryptographic definitions of security are not the same as those that apply to general computer security. The main difference between software security and cryptographic security is that the latter can be *quantified*. Unlike in the software world, where applications are usually seen as either secure or insecure, in the cryptographic world it's often possible to calculate the amount of effort required to break a cryptographic algorithm. Also, whereas software security focuses on preventing attackers from abusing a program's code, the goal of cryptographic security is to make well-defined problems impossible to solve.

Cryptographic problems involve mathematical notions, but not complex math—or at least not in this book. This chapter walks you through some of these security notions and how they're applied to solve real-world problems. In the following sections, I discuss how to quantify crypto security in ways that are both theoretically sound and practically relevant. I discuss the notions of informational versus computational security, bit security versus full attack cost, provable versus heuristic security, and symmetric versus asymmetric key generation. I conclude the chapter with actual examples of failures in seemingly strong cryptography.

Defining the Impossible

In Chapter 1, I described a cipher's security relative to an attacker's capabilities and goals, and deemed a cipher secure if it was impossible to reach these goals given an attacker's known capabilities. But what does *impossible* mean in this context?

Two notions define the concept of impossible in cryptography: informational security and computational security. Roughly speaking, *informational security* is about theoretical impossibility whereas *computational security* is about practical impossibility. Informational security doesn't quantify security because it views a cipher as either secure or insecure, with no middle ground; it's therefore useless in practice, although it plays an important role in theoretical cryptography. Computational security is the more relevant and practical measure of the strength of a cipher.

Security in Theory: Informational Security

Informational security is based not on how hard it is to break a cipher, but whether it's conceivable to break it at all. A cipher is informationally secure only if, even given unlimited computation time and memory, it cannot be broken. Even if a successful attack on a cipher would take trillions of years, such a cipher is informationally *insecure*.

For example, the one-time pad introduced in Chapter 1 is informationally secure. Recall that the one-time pad encrypts a plaintext, P, to a ciphertext, $C = P \oplus K$, where K is a random bit string that is unique to each plaintext. The cipher is informationally secure because given a ciphertext and unlimited time to try all possible keys, K, and compute the corresponding plaintext, P, you would still be unable to identify the right K because there are as many possible Ps as there are Ks.

Security in Practice: Computational Security

Unlike informational security, computational security views a cipher as secure if it cannot be broken within a *reasonable* amount of time, and with reasonable resources such as memory, hardware, budget, energy, and so on. Computational security is a way to quantify the security of a cipher or any crypto algorithm.

For example, consider a cipher, **E**, for which you know a plaintext–ciphertext pair (P, C) but not the 128-bit key, K, that served to compute $C = \mathbf{E}(K, P)$. This cipher is not informationally secure because you could break it after trying the 2^{128} possible 128-bit Ks until you find the one that satisfies $\mathbf{E}(K, P) = C$. But in practice, even testing 100 billion keys per second, it would take more than 100,000,000,000,000,000,000 years. In other words, reasonably speaking, this cipher is computationally secure because it's practically impossible to break.

Computational security is sometimes expressed in terms of two values:

- t, which is a limit on the number of operations that an attacker will carry out
- ε (called "epsilon"), which is a limit on the probability of success of an attack

We then say that a cryptographic scheme is (t, ε)-secure if an attacker performing at most t operations—whatever those operations are—has a probability of success that is no higher than ε, where ε is at least 0 and at most 1. Computational security gives a limit on how hard it is to break a cryptographic algorithm.

Here it's important to know that t and ε are just limits: if a cipher is (t, ε)-secure, then no attacker performing fewer than t operations will succeed (with probability ε). But that doesn't imply that an attacker doing exactly t operations will succeed, and it doesn't tell you how many operations are needed, which may be much larger than t. We say that t is a *lower bound* on the computation effort needed, because you'd need at least t operations to compromise security.

We sometimes know precisely how much effort it takes to break a cipher; in such cases we say that a *(t, ε)-security* gives us a *tight bound* when an attack exists that breaks the cipher with probability ε and exactly t operations.

For example, consider a symmetric cipher with a 128-bit key. Ideally, this cipher should be $(t, t/2^{128})$-secure for any value of t between 1 and 2^{128}. The best attack should be *brute force* (trying all keys until you find the correct one). Any better attack would have to exploit some imperfection in the cipher, so we strive to create ciphers where brute force is the best possible attack.

Given the statement $(t, t/2^{128})$-secure, let's examine the probability of success of three possible attacks:

- In the first case, $t = 1$, an attacker tries one key and succeeds with a probability of $\varepsilon = 1/2^{128}$.
- In the second case, $t = 2^{128}$, an attacker tries all 2^{128} keys and one succeeds. Thus, the probability $\varepsilon = 1$ (if the attacker tries all keys, obviously the right one must be one of them).
- In the third case, an attacker tries only $t = 2^{64}$ keys, and succeeds with a probability of $\varepsilon = 2^{64}/2^{128} = 2^{-64}$. When an attacker only tries a fraction of all keys, the success probability is proportional to the number of keys tried.

We can conclude that a cipher with a key of n bits is at best $(t, t/2^n)$-secure, for any t between 1 and 2^n, because no matter how strong the cipher, a brute-force attack against it will always succeed. The key thus needs be long enough to blunt brute-force attacks in practice.

In this example, we are counting the number of evaluations of the cipher, not the absolute time or number of processor clock cycles. Computational security is technology agnostic, which is good: a cipher that is (t, ε)-secure today will be (t, ε)-secure tomorrow, but what's considered secure in practice today might not be considered secure tomorrow.

Quantifying Security

When an attack is found, the first thing you want to know is how efficient it is in theory, and how practical it is, if at all. Likewise, given a cipher that's allegedly secure, you want to know what amount of work it can withstand. To address those questions, I'll explain how cryptographic security can be measured in bits (the theoretical view) and what factors affect the actual cost of an attack.

Measuring Security in Bits

When speaking of computational security, we say that a cipher is *t-secure* when a successful attack needs at least t operations. We thus avoid the unintuitive $(t, ε)$ notation by assuming a success probability of $ε$ close to 1, or what we care about in practice. We then express security in bits, where "n-bit security" means that about 2^n operations are needed to compromise some particular security notion.

If you know approximately how many operations it takes to break a cipher, you can determine its security level in bits by taking the binary logarithm of the number of operations: if it takes 1000000 operations, the security level is $\log_2(1000000)$, or about 20 bits (that is, 1000000 is approximately equal to 2^{20}). Recall that an n-bit key will give at most n-bit security because a brute-force attack with all 2^n possible keys will always succeed. But the key size doesn't always match the security level—it just gives an *upper bound*, or the highest possible security level.

A security level may be smaller than the key size for one of two reasons:

- An attack broke the cipher in fewer operations than expected—for example, using a method that recovers the key by trying not all 2^n keys, but only a subset of those.
- The cipher's security level intentionally differs from its key size, as with most public key algorithms. For example, the RSA algorithm with a 2048-bit secret key provides less than 100-bit security.

Bit security proves useful when comparing ciphers' security levels but doesn't provide enough information on the actual cost of an attack. It is sometimes too simple an abstraction because it just assumes that an n-bit-secure cipher takes 2^n operations to break, whatever these operations are. Two ciphers with the same bit security level can therefore have vastly different real-world security levels when you factor in the actual cost of an attack to a real attacker.

Say we have two ciphers, each with a 128-bit key and 128-bit security. Each must be evaluated 2^{128} times in order to be broken, except that the second cipher is 100 times slower than the first. Evaluating the second cipher 2^{128} times thus takes the same time as $100 \times 2^{128} \approx 2^{134.64}$ evaluations of the first. If we count in terms of the first, fast cipher, then breaking the slower one takes $2^{134.64}$ operations. If we count in terms of the second, slow cipher, it only takes 2^{128} operations. Should we then say that the second cipher is stronger than the first? In principle, yes, but we rarely see such a hundred-fold performance difference between commonly used ciphers.

The inconsistent definition of an operation raises more difficulties when comparing the efficiency of attacks. Some attacks claim to reduce a cipher's security because they perform 2^{120} evaluations of some operation rather than 2^{128} evaluations of the cipher, but the speed of each type of attack is left out of the analysis. The 2^{120}-operation attack won't always be faster than a 2^{128} brute-force attack.

Nevertheless, bit security remains a useful notion as long as the operation is reasonably defined—meaning about as fast as an evaluation of the cipher. After all, in real life, all it takes to determine whether a security level is sufficient is an order of magnitude.

Full Attack Cost

Bit security expresses the cost of the fastest attack against a cipher by estimating the order of magnitude of the number of operations it needs to succeed. But other factors affect the cost of an attack, and these must be taken into account when estimating the actual security level. I'll explain the four main ones: parallelism, memory, precomputation, and the number of targets.

Parallelism

The first factor to consider is computational parallelism. For example, consider two attacks of 2^{56} operations each. The difference between the two is that the second attack can be parallelized but not the first: the first attack performs 2^{56} *sequentially dependent* operations, such as $x_{i+1} = f_i(x_i)$ for some x_0 and some functions f_i (with i from 1 to 2^{56}), whereas the second performs 2^{56} *independent* operations, such as $x_i = f_i(x)$ for some x and i from 1 to 2^{56}, which can be executed in parallel. Parallel processing can be orders of magnitude faster than sequential processing. For example, if you had $2^{16} = 65536$ processors available, you could divide the workload of the parallel attacks into 2^{16} independent tasks, each performing $2^{56} / 2^{16} = 2^{40}$ operations. The first attack, however, cannot benefit from having multiple cores available because each operation relies on the previous operation's result. Therefore, the parallel attack will complete 65536 times faster than the sequential one, even though they perform the same number of operations.

NOTE *Algorithms that become N times faster to attack when N cores are available are called* embarrassingly parallel, *and we say that their execution times scale linearly with respect to the number of computing cores.*

Memory

The second factor when determining the cost of an attack is memory. Cryptanalytic attacks should be evaluated with respect to their use of time and space: how many operations do they perform over time, how much memory or space do they consume, how do they use the space they consume, and what's the speed of the available memory? Unfortunately, bit security is concerned only with the time it takes to perform an attack.

Concerning the way space is used, it's important to consider how many memory lookups are required as part of an attack, the speed of memory accesses (which may differ between reads and writes), the size of the data accessed, the access pattern (contiguous or random memory addresses), and how data is structured in memory. For example, on one of today's general-purpose CPUs, reading from a register takes one cycle, whereas reading from the CPU's cache memory takes around 20 cycles (for the L3 cache), and reading from DRAM usually takes at least 100 cycles. A factor of 100 can make the difference between one day and three months.

Precomputation

Precomputation operations are those that need to be performed only once and can be reused over subsequent executions of the attack. Precomputation is sometimes called the *offline stage* of an attack.

For example, consider the time-memory trade-off attack. When performing this kind of attack, the attacker performs one huge computation that produces large lookup tables that are then stored and reused to perform the actual attack. For example, one attack on 2G mobile encryption took two months to build two terabytes' worth of tables, which were then used to break the encryption in 2G and recover a secret session key in only a few seconds.

Number of Targets

Finally, we come to the number of targets of the attack. The greater the number of targets, the greater the attack surface, and the more attackers can learn about the keys they're after.

For example, consider a brute-force key search: if you target a single n-bit key, it will take 2^n attempts to find the correct key with certainty. But if you target multiple n-bit keys—say, a number M—and if for a single P you have M distinct ciphertexts, where $C = \mathbf{E}(K, P)$ for each of the M keys (K) that you're after, it will again take 2^n attempts to find each key. But if you're only interested in *at least one* of the M keys and not in every one, it would take on average $2^n / M$ attempts to succeed. For example, to break one 128-bit key of $2^{16} = 65536$ target keys, it will take on average $2^{128 - 16} = 2^{112}$ evaluations of the cipher. That is, the cost (and speed) of the attack decreases as the number of targets increases.

Choosing and Evaluating Security Levels

Choosing a security level often involves selecting between 128-bit and 256-bit security because most standard crypto algorithms and implementations are available in one of these two security levels. Below 128 bits you'll find schemes with 64- or 80-bit security, but these are generally not secure enough for real-world use.

At a high level, 128-bit security means that you'd need to carry out approximately 2^{128} operations to break that crypto system. To give you a sense of what this number means, consider the fact that the universe is approximately 2^{88} nanoseconds old (there's a billion nanoseconds in a second). Since testing a key with today's technology takes no less than a nanosecond, you'd need several times the age of the universe for an attack to succeed (2^{40} times to be precise) if it takes exactly one nanosecond to test a key.

But can't parallelism and multiple targets dramatically reduce the time it takes to complete a successful attack? Not exactly. Say you're interested in breaking any of a million targets, and that you have a million parallel cores available. That brings the search time down from 2^{128} to $(2^{128} / 2^{20}) / 2^{20} = 2^{88}$, which is equivalent to only one universe lifetime.

Another thing to consider when evaluating security levels is the evolution of technology. Moore's law posits that computing efficiency doubles roughly every two years. We can think of this as a loss of one bit of security every two years: if today a $1000 budget allows you to break, say, a 40-bit key in one hour, then Moore's law says that two years later, you could break a 41-bit key in one hour for the same $1000 budget (I'm simplifying). We can extrapolate from this to say that, according to Moore's law, we'll have 40 fewer bits of security in 80 years compared to today. In other words, in 80 years doing 2^{128} operations may cost as much as doing 2^{88} operations today. Accounting for parallelism and multiple targets, as discussed earlier, we're down to 2^{48} nanoseconds of computation, or about three days. But this extrapolation is highly inaccurate, because Moore's law won't and can't scale that much. Still, you get the idea: what looks infeasible today may be realistic in a century.

There will be times when a security level lower than 128 bits is justified. For example, when you need security for only a short time period and when the costs of implementing a higher security level will negatively impact the cost or usability of a system. A real-world example is that of pay TV systems, wherein encryption keys are either 48 or 64 bits. This sounds ridiculously low, but that's a sufficient security level because the key is refreshed every 5 or 10 seconds.

Nevertheless, to ensure long-term security, you should choose 256-bit security or a bit less. Even in a worst-case scenario—the existence of quantum computers, see Chapter 14—a 256-bit secure scheme is unlikely to be broken in the foreseeable future. More than 256 bits of security is practically unnecessary, except as a marketing device.

As NIST cryptographer John Kelsey once put it, "The difference between 80 bits and 128 bits of key search is like the difference between a mission to Mars and a mission to Alpha Centauri. As far as I can see, there is no meaningful difference between 192-bit and 256-bit keys in terms of practical brute-force attacks; impossible is impossible."

Achieving Security

Once you've chosen a security level, it's important to guarantee that your cryptographic schemes will stick to it. In other words, you want *confidence*, not just hope and uncertainty, that things will work as planned, all the time.

When building confidence in the security of a crypto algorithm, you can rely on mathematical proofs, an approach called *provable security*, or on evidence of failed attempts to break the algorithm, which I'll call *heuristic security* (though it's sometimes called *probable* security). These two approaches are complementary and neither is better than the other, as you'll see.

Provable Security

Provable security is about proving that breaking your crypto scheme is at least as hard as solving another problem known to be hard. Such a *security proof* guarantees that the crypto remains safe as long as the hard problem remains hard. This type of proof is called a *reduction*, and it comes from the field of complexity theory. We say that breaking some cipher is reducible to problem X if any method to solve problem X also yields a method to break the cipher.

Security proofs come in two flavors, depending on the type of presumably hard problem used: proofs relative to a mathematical problem and proofs relative to a cryptographic problem.

Proofs Relative to a Mathematical Problem

Many security proofs (such as those for public-key crypto) show that breaking a crypto scheme is at least as hard as solving some hard mathematical problem. We're talking of problems for which a solution is known to exist, and is easy to verify once it's known, but is computationally hard to find.

> **NOTE** *There's no real proof that seemingly hard math problems are actually hard. In fact, proving this for a specific class of problems is one of the greatest challenges in the field of complexity theory, and as I write this there is a $1,000,000 bounty for anyone who can solve it, awarded by the Clay Mathematics Institute. This is discussed in more detail in Chapter 9.*

For example, consider the challenge of solving the *factoring problem*, which is the best-known math problem in crypto: given a number that you know is the product of two prime numbers ($n = pq$), find the said primes. For example, if $n = 15$, the answer is 3 and 5. That's easy for a small number, but it becomes exponentially harder as the size of the number grows. For example, if a number, n, is 3000 bits long (about 900 decimal digits) or more, factoring is believed to be practically infeasible.

RSA is the most famous crypto scheme to rely on the factoring problem: RSA encrypts a plaintext, P, seen as a large number, by computing $C = P^e \bmod n$, where the number e and $n = pq$ are the public key. Decryption recovers a plaintext from a ciphertext by computing $P = C^d \bmod n$, where d is the private key associated to e and n. If we can factor n, then we can break

RSA (by recovering the private key from the public key), and if we can obtain the private key, then we can factor n; in other words, recovering an RSA private key and factoring n are equivalently hard problems. That's the kind of reduction we're looking for in provable security. However, there is no guarantee that recovering an RSA plaintext is as hard as factoring n, since the knowledge of a plaintext doesn't reveal the private key.

Proofs Relative to Another Crypto Problem

Instead of comparing a crypto scheme to a math problem, you can compare it to another crypto scheme and prove that you can only break the second if you can break the first. Security proofs for symmetric ciphers usually follow this approach.

For example, if all you have is a single permutation algorithm, then you can build symmetric ciphers, random bit generators, and other crypto objects such as hash functions by combining calls to the permutations with various types of inputs (as you'll see in Chapter 6). Proofs then show that the newly created schemes are secure if the permutation is secure. In other words, we know for sure that the newly created algorithm is *not weaker* than the original one. Such proofs usually work by crafting an attack on the smaller component given an attack on the larger one—that is, by showing a reduction.

When you're proving that a crypto algorithm is no weaker than another, the main benefit is that of a reduced attack surface: instead of analyzing both the core algorithm and the combination, you can simply look at the new cipher's core algorithm. Specifically, if you write a cipher that uses a newly developed permutation and a new combination, you may prove that the combination doesn't weaken security compared to the core algorithm. Therefore, to break the combination, you need to break the new permutation.

Caveats

Cryptography researchers rely heavily on security proofs, whether with respect to math problem schemes or to other crypto schemes. But the existence of a security proof does not guarantee that a cryptographic scheme is perfect, nor is it an excuse for neglecting the more practical aspects of implementation. After all, as cryptographer Lars Knudsen once said, "If it's provably secure, it's probably not," meaning that a security proof shouldn't be taken as an absolute guarantee of security. Worse, there are multiple reasons why a "provably secure" scheme may lead to a security failure.

One issue is with the phrase "proof of security" itself. In mathematics, a proof is the demonstration of an *absolute truth*, but in crypto, a proof is only the demonstration of a *relative truth*. For example, a proof that your cipher is as hard to break as it is to compute discrete logarithms—finding the number x given g and $g^x \bmod n$—guarantees that if your cipher fails, a whole lot of other ciphers will fail as well, and nobody will blame you if the worst happens.

Another caveat is that security proofs are usually proven with respect to a single notion of security. For example, you might prove that recovering the private key of a cipher is as hard as the factoring problem. But if you can recover plaintexts from ciphertext without the key, you'll bypass the proof, and recovering the key hardly matters.

Then again, proofs are not always correct, and it may be easier to break an algorithm than originally thought.

Unfortunately, few researchers carefully check security proofs, which commonly span dozens of pages, thus complicating quality control. That said, demonstrating that a proof is incorrect doesn't necessarily imply that the proof's goal is completely wrong; if the result is correct, the proof may be salvaged by correcting its errors.

Another important consideration is that hard math problems sometimes turn out to be easier to solve than expected. For example, certain weak parameters make breaking RSA easy. Or the math problem may be hard in certain cases, but not on average, as often happens when the reference problem is new and not well understood. That's what happened when the 1978 knapsack encryption scheme by Merkle and Hellman was later totally broken using lattice reduction techniques.

Finally, although the proof of an algorithm's security may be fine, the implementation of the algorithm can be weak. For example, attackers may exploit side-channel information such as power consumption or execution time to learn about an algorithm's internal operations in order to break it, thus bypassing the proof. Or implementers may misuse the crypto scheme: if the algorithm is too complicated with too many knobs to configure, chances are higher that the user or developer will get a configuration wrong, which may render the algorithm completely insecure.

Heuristic Security

Provable security is a great tool to gain confidence in a crypto scheme, but it doesn't apply to all kinds of algorithms. In fact, most symmetric ciphers don't have a security proof. For example, every day we rely on the Advanced Encryption Standard (AES) to securely communicate using our mobile phones, laptops, and desktop computers, but AES is not provably secure; there's no proof that it's as hard to break as some well-known problem. AES can't be related to a math problem or to another algorithm because it is the hard problem itself.

In cases where provable security doesn't apply, the only reason to trust a cipher is because many skilled people tried to break it and failed. This is sometimes called *heuristic security.*

When can we be sure that a cipher is secure then? We can never be sure, but we can be pretty confident that an algorithm won't be broken when hundreds of experienced cryptanalysts have each spent hundreds of hours trying to break it and published their findings—usually by attempting attacks on *simplified versions* of a cipher (often versions with fewer operations, or fewer *rounds*, which are short series of operations that ciphers iterate in order to mix bits together).

When analyzing a new cipher, cryptanalysts first try to break one round, then two, three, or as many as they can. The *security margin* is then the difference between the total number of rounds and the number of rounds that were successfully attacked. When after years of study a cipher's security margin is still high, we become confident that it's (probably) secure.

Generating Keys

If you plan to encrypt something, you'll have to generate keys, whether they are temporary "session keys" (like the ones generated when browsing an HTTPS site) or long-term public keys. Recall from Chapter 2 that secret keys are the crux of cryptographic security and should be randomly generated so that they are unpredictable and secret.

For example, when you browse an HTTPS website, your browser receives the site's public key and uses it to establish a symmetric key that's only valid for the current session, and that site's public key and its associated private key may be valid for years. Therefore, it'd better be hard to find for an attacker. But generating a secret key isn't always as simple as dumping enough pseudorandom bits. Cryptographic keys may be generated in one of three ways:

- *Randomly*, using a pseudorandom number generator (PRNG) and, when needed, a key-generation algorithm
- From a *password*, using a key derivation function (KDF), which transforms the user-supplied password into a key
- Through a *key agreement protocol*, which is a series of message exchanges between two or more parties that ends with the establishment of a shared key

For now, I'll explain the simplest method: randomized generation.

Generating Symmetric Keys

Symmetric keys are secret keys shared by two parties, and they are the simplest to generate. They are usually the same length as the security level they provide: a 128-bit key provides 128-bit security, and any of the 2^{128} possible keys is a valid one that can do the job as well as any other key.

To generate a symmetric key of n bits using a cryptographic PRNG, you simply ask it for n pseudorandom bits and use those bits as the key. That's it. You can, for example, use the OpenSSL toolkit to generate a random symmetric key by dumping pseudorandom bytes, as in the following command (obviously, your result will differ from mine):

```
$ openssl rand 16 -hex
65a4400ea649d282b855bd2e246812c6
```

Generating Asymmetric Keys

Unlike symmetric keys, asymmetric keys are usually longer than the security level they provide. But that's not the main problem. Asymmetric keys are trickier to generate than symmetric ones because you can't just dump n bits from your PRNG and get away with the result. Asymmetric keys aren't just raw bit sequences; instead, they represent a specific type of object, such as a large number with specific properties (in RSA, a product of two primes). A random bit string value (and thus a random number) is unlikely to have the specific properties needed, and therefore won't be a valid key.

To generate an asymmetric key, you send pseudorandom bits as a seed to a *key-generation algorithm*. This key-generation algorithm takes as input a seed value that's at least as long as the intended security level and then constructs from it a private key and its respective public key, ensuring that both satisfy all the necessary criteria. For example, a naive key-generation algorithm for RSA would generate a number, $n = pq$, by using an algorithm to generate two random primes of about the same length. That algorithm would pick random numbers until one happens to be prime—so you'd also need an algorithm to test whether a number is prime.

To save yourself the burden of manually implementing the key-generation algorithm, you can use OpenSSL to generate a 4096-bit RSA private key, like this:

```
$ openssl genrsa 4096
Generating RSA private key, 4096 bit long modulus
.....................................................................
...........................++
...............................................++
e is 65537 (0x10001)
-----BEGIN RSA PRIVATE KEY-----
MIIJKQIBAAKCAgEA3Qgm6OjMy61YVstaGawk22A9LyMXhiQUU4N8F5QZXEef2Pjq
vTtAIA1hzpK2AJsv16INpNkYcTjNmechAJOxHraftO6cp2pZFP85dvknsMfUoe8u
btKXZiYvJwpSOfQQ4tzlDtH45Gj8sMHcwFxTO3HSIxoXVOowfJTLMzZbSE3TDlN+
JdW8d9Xd5UVB+o9gUCI8tSfnOjF2dHlLNiOhlfT4wORf+G35USIyUJZtOQODh8M+
--snip--
zO/dbYtqRkMT8Ubb/OQ1IWOq8eOWnFetzkwPzAIjwZGXTOkWJu3RYj1OXbTYDr2c
xBRVC/ujoDL6O3NaqPxkWY5HJVmkyKIE5pCO4RFNyaQ8+o4APyobabPMylQq5Vo5
N5L2c4mhy1/OH8fvKBRDuvCk2oZinjdoKUo8ZA5DOa4pdvIQfR+b4/4Jjsx4
-----END RSA PRIVATE KEY-----
```

Notice that the key comes in a specific format—namely, base64-encoded data between the BEGIN RSA PRIVATE KEY and END RSA PRIVATE KEY markers. That's a standard encoding format supported by most systems, which then convert this representation to raw bytes of data. The dot sequences at the beginning are a kind of progress bar, and e is 65537 (0x10001) indicates the parameter to use when encrypting (remember that RSA encrypts by computing $C = P^e$ mod n).

Protecting Keys

Once you have a secret key, you need to keep it secret, yet available when you need it. There are three ways to address this problem.

Key wrapping (encrypting the key using a second key)
The problem with this approach is that the second key must be available when you need to decrypt the protected key. In practice, this

second key is often generated from a password supplied by the user when he needs to use the protected key. That's how private keys for the Secure Shell (SSH) protocol are usually protected.

On-the-fly generation from a password
Here, no encrypted file needs to be stored because the key comes straight out from the password. Modern systems like miniLock use this method. Although this method is more direct than key wrapping, it's less widespread, in part because it's more vulnerable to weak passwords. Say, for example, that an attacker captured some encrypted message: if key wrapping was used, the attacker first needs to get the protected key file, which is usually stored locally on the user's file system and therefore not easy to access. But if on-the-fly generation was used, the attacker can directly search for the correct password by attempting to decrypt the encrypted message with candidate passwords. And if the password is weak, the key is compromised.

Storing the key on a hardware token (smart card or USB dongle)
In this approach, the key is stored in secure memory and remains safe even if the computer is compromised. This is the safest approach to key storage, but also the costliest and least convenient because it requires you to carry the hardware token with you and run the risk of losing it. Smart cards and USB dongles usually require you to enter a password to unlock the key from the secure memory.

NOTE *Whatever method you use, make sure not to mistake the private key for the public one when exchanging keys, and don't accidentally publish the private key through email or source code. (I've actually found private keys on GitHub.)*

To test key wrapping, run the OpenSSL command shown here with the argument -aes128 to tell OpenSSL to encrypt the key with the cipher AES-128 (AES with a 128-bit key):

```
$ openssl genrsa -aes128 4096
Generating RSA private key, 4096 bit long modulus
..........++
.................................................................
...........................................++
e is 65537 (0x10001)
Enter pass phrase:
```

The passphrase requested will be used to encrypt the newly created key.

How Things Can Go Wrong

Cryptographic security can go wrong in many ways. The biggest risk is when we have a false sense of security thanks to security proofs or to well-studied protocols, as illustrated by the following two examples.

Incorrect Security Proof

Even proofs of security by renowned researchers may be wrong. One of the most striking examples of a proof gone terribly wrong is that of *Optimal Asymmetric Encryption Padding (OAEP)*, a method of secure encryption that used RSA and was implemented in many applications. Yet, an incorrect proof of OAEP's security against chosen-ciphertext attackers was accepted as valid for seven years, until a researcher found the flaw in 2001. Not only was the proof wrong, the result was wrong as well. A new proof later showed that OAEP is only almost secure against chosen-ciphertext attackers. We now have to trust the new proof and hope that it's flawless. (For further details, see the 2001 paper "OAEP Reconsidered" by Victor Shoup.)

Short Keys for Legacy Support

In 2015, researchers found that some HTTPS sites and SSH servers supported public-key cryptography with shorter keys than expected: namely, 512 bits instead of at least 2048 bits. Remember, with public-key schemes, the security level isn't equal to the key size, and in the case of HTTPS, keys of 512 bits offer a security level of approximately 60 bits. These keys could be broken after only about two weeks of computation using a cluster of 72 processors. Many websites were affected, including the FBI's. Although the software was ultimately fixed (thanks to patches for OpenSSL and for other software), the problem was quite an unpleasant surprise.

Further Reading

To learn more about provable security for symmetric ciphers, read the sponge functions documentation (*http://sponge.noekeon.org/*). Sponge functions introduced the permutation-based approach in symmetric crypto, which describes how to construct a bunch of different cryptographic functions using only one permutation.

Some must-reads on the real cost of attacks include Bernstein's 2005 paper "Understanding Brute Force" and Wiener's 2004 paper "The Full Cost of Cryptanalytic Attacks," both available online for free.

To determine the security level for a given key size, visit *http://www.keylength.com/*. This site also offers an explanation on how private keys are protected in common cryptographic utilities, such as SSH, OpenSSL, GnuPG, and so on.

Finally, as an exercise, pick an application (such as a secure messaging application) and identify its crypto schemes, key length, and respective security levels. You'll often find surprising inconsistencies, such as a first scheme providing a 256-bit security level but a second scheme providing only 100-bit security. The security of the whole system is often only as strong as that of its weakest component.

4

BLOCK CIPHERS

During the Cold War, the US and Soviets developed their own ciphers. The US government created the Data Encryption Standard (DES), which was adopted as a federal standard from 1979 to 2005, while the KGB developed GOST 28147-89, an algorithm kept secret until 1990 and still used today. In 2000, the US-based National Institute of Standards and Technology (NIST) selected the successor to DES, called the *Advanced Encryption Standard (AES)*, an algorithm developed in Belgium and now found in most electronic devices. AES, DES, and GOST 28147-89 have something in common: they're all *block ciphers*, a type of cipher that combines a core algorithm working on blocks of data with a mode of operation, or a technique to process sequences of data blocks.

This chapter reviews the core algorithms that underlie block ciphers, discusses their modes of operation, and explains how they all work together. It also discusses how AES works and concludes with coverage of a classic attack tool from the 1970s, the meet-in-the-middle attack, and a favorite attack technique of the 2000s—padding oracles.

What Is a Block Cipher?

A block cipher consists of an encryption algorithm and a decryption algorithm:

- The *encryption algorithm* (**E**) takes a key, K, and a plaintext block, P, and produces a ciphertext block, C. We write an encryption operation as $C = \mathbf{E}(K, P)$.

- The *decryption algorithm* (**D**) is the inverse of the encryption algorithm and decrypts a message to the original plaintext, P. This operation is written as $P = \mathbf{D}(K, C)$.

Since they're the inverse of each other, the encryption and decryption algorithms usually involve similar operations.

Security Goals

If you've followed earlier discussions about encryption, randomness, and indistinguishability, the definition of a secure block cipher will come as no surprise. Again, we'll define security as random-lookingness, so to speak.

In order for a block cipher to be secure, it should be a *pseudorandom permutation (PRP)*, meaning that as long as the key is secret, an attacker shouldn't be able to compute an output of the block cipher from any input. That is, as long as K is secret and random from an attacker's perspective, they should have no clue about what $\mathbf{E}(K, P)$ looks like, for any given P.

More generally, attackers should be unable to discover any *pattern* in the input/output values of a block cipher. In other words, it should be impossible to tell a block cipher from a truly random permutation, given black-box access to the encryption and decryption functions for some fixed and unknown key. By the same token, they should be unable to recover a secure block cipher's secret key; otherwise, they would be able to use that key to tell the block cipher from a random permutation. Of course that also implies that attackers can't predict the plaintext that corresponds to a given ciphertext produced by the block cipher.

Block Size

Two values characterize a block cipher: the block size and the key size. Security depends on both values. Most block ciphers have either 64-bit or 128-bit blocks—DES's blocks have 64 (2^6) bits, and AES's blocks have 128 (2^7) bits. In computing, lengths that are powers of two simplify data processing, storage, and addressing. But why 2^6 and 2^7 and not 2^4 or 2^{16} bits?

For one thing, it's important that blocks are not too large in order to minimize both the length of ciphertext and the memory footprint. With regard to the length of the ciphertext, block ciphers process blocks, not bits. This means that in order to encrypt a 16-bit message when blocks are 128 bits, you'll first need to convert the message into a 128-bit block, and only then will the block cipher process it and return a 128-bit ciphertext. The wider the blocks, the longer this overhead. As for the *memory footprint*, in order to process a 128-bit block, you need at least 128 bits of memory. This is small enough to fit in the registers of most CPUs or to be implemented using dedicated hardware circuits. Blocks of 64, 128, or even 512 bits are short enough to allow for efficient implementations in most cases. But larger blocks (for example, several kilobytes long) can have a noticeable impact on the cost and performance of implementations.

When ciphertexts' length or memory footprint is critical, you may have to use 64-bit blocks, because these will produce shorter ciphertexts and consume less memory. Otherwise, 128-bit or larger blocks are better, mainly because 128-bit blocks can be processed more efficiently than 64-bit ones on modern CPUs and are also more secure. In particular, CPUs can leverage special CPU instructions in order to efficiently process one or more 128-bit blocks in parallel—for example, the Advanced Vector Extensions (AVX) family of instructions in Intel CPUs.

The Codebook Attack

While blocks shouldn't be too large, they also shouldn't be too small; otherwise, they may be susceptible to *codebook attacks*, which are attacks against block ciphers that are only efficient when smaller blocks are used. The codebook attack works like this with 16-bit blocks:

1. Get the 65536 (2^{16}) ciphertexts corresponding to each 16-bit plaintext block.
2. Build a lookup table—the *codebook*—mapping each ciphertext block to its corresponding plaintext block.
3. To decrypt an unknown ciphertext block, look up its corresponding plaintext block in the table.

When 16-bit blocks are used, the lookup table needs only $2^{16} \times 16 = 2^{20}$ bits of memory, or 128 kilobytes. With 32-bit blocks, memory needs grow to 16 gigabytes, which is still manageable. But with 64-bit blocks, you'd have to store 2^{70} bits (a zetabit, or 128 exabytes), so forget about it. Codebook attacks won't be an issue for larger blocks.

How to Construct Block Ciphers

There are hundreds of block ciphers but only a handful of techniques to construct one. First, a block cipher used in practice isn't a gigantic algorithm but a repetition of *rounds*, a short sequence of operations that is weak on its own but strong in number. Second, there are two main techniques to construct a round: substitution–permutation networks (as in AES) and Feistel schemes (as in DES). In this section, we look at how these work, after viewing an attack that works when all rounds are identical to each other.

A Block Cipher's Rounds

Computing a block cipher boils down to computing a sequence of *rounds*. In a block cipher, a round is a basic transformation that is simple to specify and to implement, and which is iterated several times to form the block cipher's algorithm. This construction, consisting of a small component repeated many times, is simpler to implement and to analyze than a construction that would consist of a single huge algorithm.

For example, a block cipher with three rounds encrypts a plaintext by computing $C = \mathbf{R}_3(\mathbf{R}_2(\mathbf{R}_1(P)))$, where the rounds are $\mathbf{R}_1$, $\mathbf{R}_2$, and $\mathbf{R}_3$ and P is a plaintext. Each round should also have an inverse in order to make it possible for a recipient to compute back to plaintext. Specifically, $P = \mathbf{iR}_1(\mathbf{iR}_2(\mathbf{iR}_3(C)))$, where $\mathbf{iR}_1$ is the inverse of $\mathbf{R}_1$, and so on.

The round functions—$\mathbf{R}_1$, $\mathbf{R}_2$, and so on—are usually identical algorithms, but they are parameterized by a value called the *round key*. Two round functions with two distinct round keys will behave differently, and therefore will produce distinct outputs if fed with the same input.

Round keys are keys derived from the main key, K, using an algorithm called a *key schedule*. For example, $\mathbf{R}_1$ takes the round key K_1, $\mathbf{R}_2$ takes the round key K_2, and so on.

Round keys should always be different from each other in every round. For that matter, not all round keys should be equal to the key K. Otherwise, all the rounds would be identical and the block cipher would be less secure, as described next.

The Slide Attack and Round Keys

In a block cipher, no round should be identical to another round in order to avoid a *slide attack*. Slide attacks look for two plaintext/ciphertext pairs (P_1, C_1) and (P_2, C_2), where $P_2 = \mathbf{R}(P_1)$ if $\mathbf{R}$ is the cipher's round (see Figure 4-1). When rounds are identical, the relation between the two plaintexts, $P_2 = \mathbf{R}(P_1)$, implies the relation $C_2 = \mathbf{R}(C_1)$ between their respective ciphertexts. Figure 4-1 shows three rounds, but the relation $C_2 = \mathbf{R}(C_1)$ will hold no matter the number of rounds, be it 3, 10, or 100. The problem is that knowing the input and output of a single round often helps recover the key. (For details, read the 1999 paper by Biryukov and Wagner called "Advanced Slide Attacks," available at *https://www.iacr.org/archive/eurocrypt2000/1807/18070595-new.pdf*)

The use of different round keys as parameters ensures that the rounds will behave differently and thus foil slide attacks.

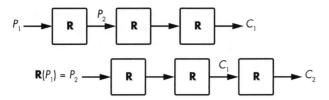

Figure 4-1: The principle of the slide attack, against block ciphers with identical rounds

NOTE *One potential byproduct and benefit of using round keys is protection against side-channel attacks, or attacks that exploit information leaked from the implementation of a cipher (for example, electromagnetic emanations). If the transformation from the main key, K, to a round key, K_i, is not invertible, then if an attacker finds K_i, they can't use that key to find K. Unfortunately, few block ciphers have a one-way key schedule. The key schedule of AES allows attackers to compute K from any round key, K_i, for example.*

Substitution–Permutation Networks

If you've read textbooks about cryptography, you'll undoubtedly have read about *confusion* and *diffusion*. Confusion means that the input (plaintext and encryption key) undergoes complex transformations, and diffusion means that these transformations depend equally on all bits of the input. At a high level, confusion is about depth whereas diffusion is about breadth. In the design of a block cipher, confusion and diffusion take the form of substitution and permutation operations, which are combined within substitution–permutation networks (SPNs).

Substitution often appears in the form of *S-boxes*, or *substitution boxes*, which are small lookup tables that transform chunks of 4 or 8 bits. For example, the first of the eight S-boxes of the block cipher Serpent is composed of the 16 elements (3 8 f 1 a 6 5 b e d 4 2 7 0 9 c), where each element represents a 4-bit nibble. This particular S-box maps the 4-bit nibble 0000 to 3 (0011), the 4-bit nibble 0101 (5 in decimal) to 6 (0110), and so on.

NOTE *S-boxes must be carefully chosen to be cryptographically strong: they should be as nonlinear as possible (inputs and outputs should be related with complex equations) and have no statistical bias (meaning, for example, that flipping an input bit should potentially affect any of the output bits).*

The permutation in a substitution–permutation network can be as simple as changing the order of the bits, which is easy to implement but doesn't mix up the bits very much. Instead of a reordering of the bits, some ciphers use basic linear algebra and matrix multiplications to mix up the bits: they perform a series of multiplication operations with fixed values (the matrix's coefficients) and then add the results. Such linear algebra operations can quickly create dependencies between all the bits within a cipher and thus ensure strong diffusion. For example, the block cipher FOX transforms a 4-byte vector (a, b, c, d) to (a', b', c', d'), defined as follows:

$$a' = a + b + c + (2 \times d)$$
$$b' = a + (253 \times b) + (2 \times c) + d$$
$$c' = (253 \times a) + (2 \times b) + c + d$$
$$d' = (2 \times a) + b + (253 \times c) + d$$

In the above equations, the numbers 2 and 253 are interpreted as binary polynomials rather than integers; hence, additions and multiplications are defined a bit differently than what we're used to. For example, instead of having $2 + 2 = 4$, we have $2 + 2 = 0$. Regardless, the point is that each byte in the initial state affects all 4 bytes in the final state.

Feistel Schemes

In the 1970s, IBM engineer Horst Feistel designed a block cipher called Lucifer that works as follows:

1. Split the 64-bit block into two 32-bit halves, L and R.

2. Set L to $L \oplus \mathbf{F}(R)$, where $\mathbf{F}$ is a substitution–permutation round.

3. Swap the values of L and R.

4. Go to step 2 and repeat 15 times.

5. Merge L and R into the 64-bit output block.

This construction became known as a *Feistel scheme*, as shown in Figure 4-2. The left side is the scheme as just described; the right side is a functionally equivalent representation where, instead of swapping L and R, rounds alternate the operations $L = L \oplus \mathbf{F}(R)$ and $R = R \oplus \mathbf{F}(L)$.

I've omitted the keys from Figure 4-2 to simplify the diagrams, but note that the first $\mathbf{F}$ takes a first round key, K_1, and the second $\mathbf{F}$ takes another round key, K_2. In DES, the $\mathbf{F}$ functions take a 48-bit round key, which is derived from the 56-bit key, K.

In a Feistel scheme, the $\mathbf{F}$ function can be either a pseudorandom permutation (PRP) or a pseudorandom function (PRF). A PRP yields distinct outputs for any two distinct inputs, whereas a PRF will have values X and Y for which $\mathbf{F}(X) = \mathbf{F}(Y)$. But in a Feistel scheme, that difference doesn't matter as long as $\mathbf{F}$ is cryptographically strong.

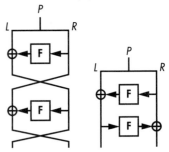

Figure 4-2: The Feistel scheme block cipher construction in two equivalent forms

How many rounds should there be in a Feistel scheme? Well, DES performs 16 rounds, whereas GOST 28147-89 performs 32 rounds. If the **F** function is as strong as possible, four rounds are in theory sufficient, but real ciphers use more rounds to defend against potential weaknesses in **F**.

The Advanced Encryption Standard (AES)

AES is the most-used cipher in the universe. Prior to the adoption of AES, the standard cipher in use was DES, with its ridiculous 56-bit security, as well as the upgraded version of DES known as Triple DES, or 3DES.

Although 3DES provides a higher level of security (112-bit security), it's inefficient because the key needs to be 168 bits long in order to get 112-bit security, and it's slow in software (DES was created to be fast in integrated circuits, not on mainstream CPUs). AES fixes both issues.

NIST standardized AES in 2000 as a replacement for DES, at which point it became the world's de facto encryption standard. Most commercial encryption products today support AES, and the NSA has approved it for protecting top-secret information. (Some countries do prefer to use their own cipher, largely because they don't want to use a US standard, but AES is actually more Belgian than it is American.)

NOTE *AES used to be called Rijndael (a portmanteau for its inventors' names, Rijmen and Daemen, pronounced like "rain-dull") when it was one of the 15 candidates in the AES competition, the process held by NIST from 1997 to 2000 to specify "an unclassified, publicly disclosed encryption algorithm capable of protecting sensitive government information well into the next century," as stated in the 1997 announcement of the competition in the Federal Register. The AES competition was kind of a "Got Talent" competition for cryptographers, where anyone could participate by submitting a cipher or breaking other contestants' ciphers.*

AES Internals

AES processes blocks of 128 bits using a secret key of 128, 192, or 256 bits, with the 128-bit key being the most common because it makes encryption slightly faster and because the difference between 128- and 256-bit security is meaningless for most applications.

Whereas some ciphers work with individual bits or 64-bit words, AES manipulates *bytes.* It views a 16-byte plaintext as a two-dimensional array of bytes ($s = s_0, s_1, \ldots, s_{15}$), as shown in Figure 4-3. (The letter *s* is used because this array is called the *internal state,* or just *state.*) AES transforms the bytes, columns, and rows of this array to produce a final value that is the ciphertext.

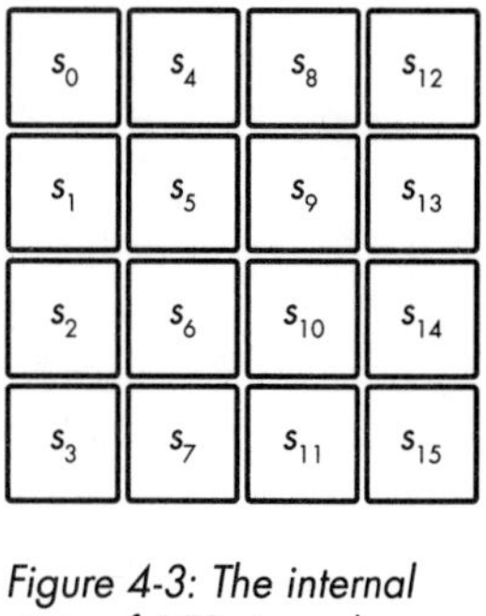

Figure 4-3: The internal state of AES viewed as a 4 × 4 array of 16 bytes

In order to transform its state, AES uses an SPN structure like the one shown in Figure 4-4, with 10 rounds for 128-bit keys, 12 for 192-bit keys, and 14 for 256-bit keys.

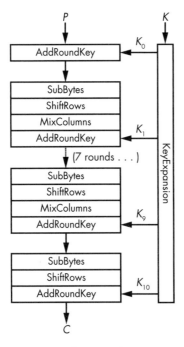

Figure 4-4: The internal operations of AES

Figure 4-4 shows the four building blocks of an AES round (note that all but the last round are a sequence of SubBytes, ShiftRows, MixColumns, and AddRoundKey):

AddRoundKey   XORs a round key to the internal state.

SubBytes   Replaces each byte (s_0, s_1, . . . , s_{15}) with another byte according to an S-box. In this example, the S-box is a lookup table of 256 elements.

ShiftRows   Shifts the ith row of i positions, for i ranging from 0 to 3 (see Figure 4-5).

MixColumns   Applies the same linear transformation to each of the four columns of the state (that is, each group of cells with the same shade of gray, as shown on the left side of Figure 4-5).

Remember that in an SPN, the S stands for substitution and the P for permutation. Here, the substitution layer is SubBytes and the permutation layer is the combination of ShiftRows and MixColumns.

The key schedule function *KeyExpansion*, shown in Figure 4-4, is the AES key schedule algorithm. This expansion creates 11 round keys (K_0, K_1, . . . , K_{10}) of 16 bytes each from the 16-byte key, using the same S-box as SubBytes and a combination of XORs. One important property of

KeyExpansion is that given any round key, K_i, an attacker can determine all other round keys as well as the main key, K, by reversing the algorithm. The ability to get the key from any round key is usually seen as an imperfect defense against side-channel attacks, where an attacker may easily recover a round key.

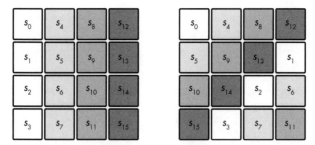

Figure 4-5: ShiftRows rotates bytes within each row of the internal state.

Without these operations, AES would be totally insecure. Each operation contributes to AES's security in a specific way:

- Without KeyExpansion, all rounds would use the same key, K, and AES would be vulnerable to slide attacks.

- Without AddRoundKey, encryption wouldn't depend on the key; hence, anyone could decrypt any ciphertext without the key.

- SubBytes brings nonlinear operations, which add cryptographic strength. Without it, AES would just be a large system of linear equations that is solvable using high-school algebra.

- Without ShiftRows, changes in a given column would never affect the other columns, meaning you could break AES by building four 2^{32}-element codebooks for each column. (Remember that in a secure block cipher, flipping a bit in the input should affect all the output bits.)

- Without MixColumns, changes in a byte would not affect any other bytes of the state. A chosen-plaintext attacker could then decrypt any ciphertext after storing 16 lookup tables of 256 bytes each that hold the encrypted values of each possible value of a byte.

Notice in Figure 4-4 that the last round of AES doesn't include the MixColumns operation. That operation is omitted in order to save useless computation: because MixColumns is linear (meaning, predictable), you could cancel its effect in the very last round by combining bits in a way that doesn't depend on their value or the key. SubBytes, however, can't be inverted without the state's value being known prior to AddRoundKey.

To decrypt a ciphertext, AES unwinds each operation by taking its inverse function: the inverse lookup table of SubBytes reverses the SubBytes transformation, ShiftRow shifts in the opposite direction,

MixColumns's inverse is applied (as in the matrix inverse of the matrix encoding its operation), and AddRoundKey's XOR is unchanged because the inverse of an XOR is another XOR.

AES in Action

To try encrypting and decrypting with AES, you can use Python's cryptography library, as in Listing 4-1.

```
#!/usr/bin/env python

from cryptography.hazmat.primitives.ciphers import Cipher, algorithms, modes
from cryptography.hazmat.backends import default_backend
from binascii import hexlify as hexa
from os import urandom

# pick a random 16-byte key using Python's crypto PRNG
k = urandom(16)
print "k = %s" % hexa(k)
# create an instance of AES-128 to encrypt a single block
cipher = Cipher(algorithms.AES(k), modes.ECB(), backend = default_backend())
aes_encrypt = cipher.encryptor()

# set plaintext block p to the all-zero string
p = '\x00'*16
# encrypt plaintext p to ciphertext c
c = aes_encrypt.update(p) + aes_encrypt.finalize()
print "enc(%s) = %s" % (hexa(p), hexa(c))
# decrypt ciphertext c to plaintext p
aes_decrypt = cipher.decryptor()
p = aes_decrypt.update(c) + aes_decrypt.finalize()
print "dec(%s) = %s" % (hexa(c), hexa(p))
```

Listing 4-1: Trying AES with Python's cryptography library

Running this script produces something like the following output:

```
$ ./aes_block.py
k = 2c6202f9a582668aa96d511862d8a279
enc(00000000000000000000000000000000) = 12b620bb5eddcde9a07523e59292a6d7
dec(12b620bb5eddcde9a07523e59292a6d7) = 00000000000000000000000000000000
```

You'll get different results because the key is randomized at every new execution.

Implementing AES

Real AES software works differently than the algorithm shown in Figure 4-4. You won't find production-level AES code calling a SubBytes() function, then a ShiftRows() function, and then a MixColumns() function because that would be inefficient. Instead, fast AES software uses special techniques called table-based implementations and native instructions.

Table-Based Implementations

Table-based implementations of AES replace the sequence SubBytes-ShiftRows-MixColumns with a combination of XORs and lookups in tables hardcoded into the program and loaded in memory at execution time. This is possible because MixColumns is equivalent to XORing four 32-bit values, where each depends on a single byte from the state and on SubBytes. Thus, you can build four tables with 256 entries each, one for each byte value, and implement the sequence SubBytes-MixColumns by looking up four 32-bit values and XORing them together.

For example, the table-based C implementation in the OpenSSL toolkit looks like Listing 4-2.

```
/* round 1: */
t0 = Te0[s0 >> 24] ^ Te1[(s1 >> 16) & 0xff] ^ Te2[(s2 >> 8) & 0xff] ^ Te3[s3 & 0xff] ^ rk[ 4];
t1 = Te0[s1 >> 24] ^ Te1[(s2 >> 16) & 0xff] ^ Te2[(s3 >> 8) & 0xff] ^ Te3[s0 & 0xff] ^ rk[ 5];
t2 = Te0[s2 >> 24] ^ Te1[(s3 >> 16) & 0xff] ^ Te2[(s0 >> 8) & 0xff] ^ Te3[s1 & 0xff] ^ rk[ 6];
t3 = Te0[s3 >> 24] ^ Te1[(s0 >> 16) & 0xff] ^ Te2[(s1 >> 8) & 0xff] ^ Te3[s2 & 0xff] ^ rk[ 7];
/* round 2: */
s0 = Te0[t0 >> 24] ^ Te1[(t1 >> 16) & 0xff] ^ Te2[(t2 >> 8) & 0xff] ^ Te3[t3 & 0xff] ^ rk[ 8];
s1 = Te0[t1 >> 24] ^ Te1[(t2 >> 16) & 0xff] ^ Te2[(t3 >> 8) & 0xff] ^ Te3[t0 & 0xff] ^ rk[ 9];
s2 = Te0[t2 >> 24] ^ Te1[(t3 >> 16) & 0xff] ^ Te2[(t0 >> 8) & 0xff] ^ Te3[t1 & 0xff] ^ rk[10];
s3 = Te0[t3 >> 24] ^ Te1[(t0 >> 16) & 0xff] ^ Te2[(t1 >> 8) & 0xff] ^ Te3[t2 & 0xff] ^ rk[11];
--snip--
```

Listing 4-2: The table-based C implementation of AES in OpenSSL

A basic table-based implementation of AES encryption needs four kilobytes' worth of tables because each table stores 256 32-bit values, which occupy $256 \times 32 = 8192$ bits, or one kilobyte. Decryption requires another four tables, and thus four more kilobytes. But there are tricks to reduce the storage from four kilobytes to one, or even fewer.

Alas, table-based implementations are vulnerable to *cache-timing attacks*, which exploit timing variations when a program reads or writes elements in cache memory. Depending on the relative position in cache memory of the elements accessed, access time varies. Timings thus leak information about which element was accessed, which in turn leaks information on the secrets involved.

Cache-timing attacks are difficult to avoid. One obvious solution would be to ditch lookup tables altogether by writing a program whose execution time doesn't depend on its inputs, but that's almost impossible to do and still retain the same speed, so chip manufacturers have opted for a radical solution: instead of relying on potentially vulnerable software, they rely on *hardware*.

Native Instructions

AES native instructions (AES-NI) solve the problem of cache-timing attacks on AES software implementations. To understand how AES-NI works, you need to think about the way software runs on hardware: to run a program, a microprocessor translates binary code into a series of instructions executed by integrated circuit components. For example, a MUL assembly instruction between two 32-bit values will activate the transistors implementing a 32-bit multiplier in the microprocessor. To implement a crypto algorithm, we usually just express a combination of such basic operations—additions, multiplications, XORs, and so on—and the microprocessor activates its adders, multipliers, and XOR circuits in the prescribed order.

AES native instructions take this to a whole new level by providing developers with dedicated assembly instructions that compute AES. Instead of coding an AES round as a sequence of assembly instructions, when using AES-NI, you just call the instruction AESENC and the chip will compute the round for you. Native instructions allow you to just tell the processor to run an AES round instead of requiring you to program rounds as a combination of basic operations.

A typical assembly implementation of AES using native instructions looks like Listing 4-3.

```
PXOR        %xmm5,  %xmm0
AESENC      %xmm6,  %xmm0
AESENC      %xmm7,  %xmm0
AESENC      %xmm8,  %xmm0
AESENC      %xmm9,  %xmm0
AESENC      %xmm10, %xmm0
AESENC      %xmm11, %xmm0
AESENC      %xmm12, %xmm0
AESENC      %xmm13, %xmm0
AESENC      %xmm14, %xmm0
AESENCLAST  %xmm15, %xmm0
```

Listing 4-3: AES native instructions

This code encrypts the 128-bit plaintext initially in the register xmm0, assuming that registers xmm5 to xmm15 hold the precomputed round keys, with each instruction writing its result into xmm0. The initial PXOR instruction XORs the first round key prior to computing the first round, and the final AESENCLAST instruction performs the last round slightly different from the others (MixColumns is omitted).

NOTE *AES is about ten times faster on platforms that implement native instructions, which as I write this, are virtually all laptop, desktop, and server microprocessors, as well as most mobile phones and tablets. In fact, on the latest Intel microarchitecture the* AESENC *instruction has a latency of four cycles with a reciprocal throughput of one cycle, meaning that a call to* AESENC *takes four cycles to complete and that a new call can be made every cycle. To encrypt a series of blocks consecutively it thus takes 4 × 10 = 40 cycles to complete the 10 rounds or 40 / 16 = 2.5 cycles per byte. At 2 GHz (2×10^9 cycles per second), that gives a throughput of about 736 megabytes per second. If the blocks to encrypt or decrypt are independent of each other, as certain modes of operation allow, then four blocks can be processed in parallel to take full advantage of the* AESENC *circuit in order to reach a latency of 10 cycles per block instead of 40, or about 3 gigabytes per second.*

Is AES Secure?

AES is as secure as a block cipher can be, and it will never be broken. Fundamentally, AES is secure because all output bits depend on all input bits in some complex, pseudorandom way. To achieve this, the designers of AES carefully chose each component for a particular reason—MixColumns for its maximal diffusion properties and SubBytes for its optimal non-linearity—and they have shown that this composition protects AES against whole classes of cryptanalytic attacks.

But there's no proof that AES is immune to all possible attacks. For one thing, we don't know what all possible attacks are, and we don't always know how to prove that a cipher is secure against a given attack. The only way to really gain confidence in the security of AES is to crowdsource attacks: have many skilled people attempt to break AES and, hopefully, fail to do so.

After more than 15 years and hundreds of research publications, the theoretical security of AES has only been scratched. In 2011 cryptanalysts found a way to recover an AES-128 key by performing about 2^{126} operations instead of 2^{128}, a speed-up of a factor four. But this "attack" requires an insane amount of plaintext–ciphertext pairs—about 2^{88} bits worth. In other words, it's a nice finding but not one you need to worry about.

The upshot is that you should care about a million things when implementing and deploying crypto, but AES security is not one of those. The biggest threat to block ciphers isn't in their core algorithms but in their modes of operation. When an incorrect mode is chosen, or when the right one is misused, even a strong cipher like AES won't save you.

Modes of Operation

In Chapter 1, I explained how encryption schemes combine a permutation with a mode of operation to handle messages of any length. In this section, I'll cover the main modes of operations used by block ciphers, their security and function properties, and how (not) to use them. I'll begin with the dumbest one: electronic codebook.

The Electronic Codebook (ECB) Mode

The simplest of the block cipher encryption modes is electronic codebook (ECB), which is barely a mode of operation at all. ECB takes plaintext blocks $P_1, P_2, \ldots, P_N$ and processes each independently by computing $C_1 = \mathbf{E}(K, P_1)$, $C_2 = \mathbf{E}(K, P_2)$, and so on, as shown in Figure 4-6. It's a simple operation but also an insecure one. I repeat: ECB is insecure and you should not use it!

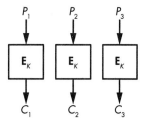

Figure 4-6: The ECB mode

Marsh Ray, a cryptographer at Microsoft, once said, "Everybody knows ECB mode is bad because we can see the penguin." He was referring to a famous illustration of ECB's insecurity that uses an image of Linux's mascot, Tux, as shown in Figure 4-7. You can see the original image of Tux on the left, and the image encrypted in ECB mode using AES (though the underlying cipher doesn't matter) on the right. It's easy to see the penguin's shape in the encrypted version because all the blocks of one shade of gray in the original image are encrypted to the same new shade of gray in the new image; in other words, ECB encryption just gives you the same image but with different colors.

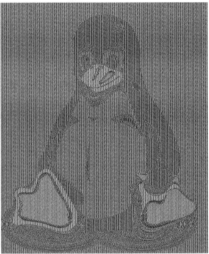

Figure 4-7: The original image (left) and the ECB-encrypted image (right)

The Python program in Listing 4-4 also shows ECB's insecurity. It picks a pseudorandom key and encrypts a 32-byte message p containing two blocks of null bytes. Notice that encryption yields two identical blocks and that repeating encryption with the same key and the same plaintext yields the same two blocks again.

```python
#!/usr/bin/env python

from cryptography.hazmat.primitives.ciphers import Cipher, algorithms, modes
from cryptography.hazmat.backends import default_backend
from binascii import hexlify as hexa
from os import urandom

BLOCKLEN = 16
def blocks(data):
    split = [hexa(data[i:i+BLOCKLEN]) for i in range(0, len(data), BLOCKLEN)]
    return ' '.join(split)

k = urandom(16)
print "k = %s" % hexa(k)

# create an instance of AES-128 to encrypt and decrypt
cipher = Cipher(algorithms.AES(k), modes.ECB(), backend=default_backend())
aes_encrypt = cipher.encryptor()
```

```
# set plaintext block p to the all-zero string
p = '\x00'*BLOCKLEN*2

# encrypt plaintext p to ciphertext c
c = aes_encrypt.update(p) + aes_encrypt.finalize()
print "enc(%s) = %s" % (blocks(p), blocks(c))
```

Listing 4-4: Using AES in ECB mode in Python

Running this script gives ciphertext blocks like this, for example:

```
$ ./aes_ecb.py
k = 50a0ebeff8001250e87d31d72a86e46d
enc(00000000000000000000000000000000 00000000000000000000000000000000) =
5eb4b7af094ef7aca472bbd3cd72f1ed 5eb4b7af094ef7aca472bbd3cd72f1ed
```

As you can see, when the ECB mode is used, identical ciphertext blocks reveal identical plaintext blocks to an attacker, whether those are blocks within a single ciphertext or across different ciphertexts. This shows that block ciphers in ECB mode aren't semantically secure.

Another problem with ECB is that it only takes complete blocks of data, so if blocks were 16 bytes, as in AES, you could only encrypt chunks of 16 bytes, 32 bytes, 48 bytes, or any other multiple of 16 bytes. There are a few ways to deal with this, as you'll see with the next mode, CBC. (I won't tell you how these tricks work with ECB because you shouldn't be using ECB in the first place.)

The Cipher Block Chaining (CBC) Mode

Cipher block chaining (CBC) is like ECB but with a small twist that makes a big difference: instead of encrypting the ith block, P_i, as $C_i = \mathbf{E}(K, P_i)$, CBC sets $C_i = \mathbf{E}(K, P_i \oplus C_{i-1})$, where C_{i-1} is the previous ciphertext block—thereby *chaining* the blocks C_{i-1} and C_i. When encrypting the first block, P_1, there is no previous ciphertext block to use, so CBC takes a random initial value (IV), as shown in Figure 4-8.

The CBC mode makes each ciphertext block dependent on all the previous blocks, and ensures that identical plaintext blocks won't be identical ciphertext blocks. The random initial value guarantees that two identical plaintexts will encrypt to distinct ciphertexts when calling the cipher twice with two distinct initial values.

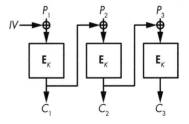

Figure 4-8: The CBC mode

Listing 4-5 illustrates these two benefits. This program takes an all-zero, 32-byte message (like the one in Listing 4-4), encrypts it twice with CBC, and shows the two ciphertexts. The line iv = urandom(16), shown in bold, picks a new random IV for each new encryption.

```
#!/usr/bin/env python

from cryptography.hazmat.primitives.ciphers import Cipher, algorithms, modes
from cryptography.hazmat.backends import default_backend
from binascii import hexlify as hexa
from os import urandom

BLOCKLEN = 16
# the blocks() function splits a data string into space-separated blocks
def blocks(data):
    split = [hexa(data[i:i+BLOCKLEN]) for i in range(0, len(data), BLOCKLEN)]
    return ' '.join(split)
k = urandom(16)
print "k = %s" % hexa(k)
# pick a random IV
iv = urandom(16)
print "iv = %s" % hexa(iv)
# pick an instance of AES in CBC mode
aes = Cipher(algorithms.AES(k), modes.CBC(iv), backend=default_backend()).encryptor()

p = '\x00'*BLOCKLEN*2
c = aes.update(p) + aes.finalize()
print "enc(%s) = %s" % (blocks(p), blocks(c))
# now with a different IV and the same key
iv = urandom(16)
print "iv = %s" % hexa(iv)
aes = Cipher(algorithms.AES(k), modes.CBC(iv), backend=default_backend()).encryptor()
c = aes.update(p) + aes.finalize()
print "enc(%s) = %s" % (blocks(p), blocks(c))
```

Listing 4-5: Using AES in CBC mode

The two plaintexts are the same (two all-zero blocks), but the encrypted blocks should be distinct, as in this example execution:

```
$ ./aes_cbc.py
k = 9cf0d31ad2df24f3cbbefc1e6933c872
iv = 0a75c4283b4539c094fc262aff0d17af
enc(00000000000000000000000000000000 00000000000000000000000000000000) =
370404dcab6e9ecbc3d24ca5573d2920 3b9e5d70e597db225609541f6ae9804a
iv = a6016a6698c3996be13e8739d9e793e2
enc(00000000000000000000000000000000 00000000000000000000000000000000) =
655e1bb3e74ee8cf9ec1540afd8b2204 b59db5ac28de43b25612dfd6f031087a
```

Alas, CBC is often used with a constant IV instead of a random one, which exposes identical plaintexts and plaintexts that start with identical blocks. For example, say the two-block plaintext $P_1 \parallel P_2$ is encrypted in CBC mode to the two-block ciphertext $C_1 \parallel C_2$. If $P_1 \parallel P_2'$ is encrypted with the same IV, where P_2' is some block distinct from P_2, then the ciphertext will look like $C_1 \parallel C_2'$, with C_2' different from C_2 but with the same first block C_1. Thus, an attacker can guess that the first block is the same for both plaintexts, even though they only see the ciphertexts.

NOTE *In CBC mode, decryption needs to know the IV used to encrypt, so the IV is sent along with the ciphertext, in the clear.*

With CBC, decryption can be much faster than encryption due to parallelism. While encryption of a new block, P_i, needs to wait for the previous block, C_{i-1}, decryption of a block computes $P_i = \mathbf{D}(K, C_i) \oplus C_{i-1}$, where there's no need for the previous plaintext block, P_{i-1}. This means that all blocks can be decrypted in parallel simultaneously, as long as you also know the previous ciphertext block, which you usually do.

How to Encrypt Any Message in CBC Mode

Let's circle back to the block termination issue and look at how to process a plaintext whose length is not a multiple of the block length. For example, how would we encrypt an 18-byte plaintext with AES-CBC when blocks are 16 bytes? What do we do with the two bytes left? We'll look at two widely used techniques to deal with this problem. The first one, padding, makes the ciphertext a bit longer than the plaintext, while the second one, *ciphertext stealing*, produces a ciphertext of the same length as the plaintext.

Padding a Message

Padding is a technique that allows you to encrypt a message of any length, even one smaller than a single block. Padding for block ciphers is specified in the PKCS#7 standard and in RFC 5652, and is used almost everywhere CBC is used, such as in some HTTPS connections.

Padding is used to expand a message to fill a complete block by adding extra bytes to the plaintext. Here are the rules for padding 16-byte blocks:

- If there's one byte left—for example, if the plaintext is 1 byte, 17 bytes, or 33 bytes long—pad the message with 15 bytes 0f (15 in decimal).
- If there are two bytes left, pad the message with 14 bytes 0e (14 in decimal).
- If there are three bytes left, pad the message with 13 bytes 0d (13 in decimal).

If there are 15 plaintext bytes and a single byte missing to fill a block, padding adds a single 01 byte. If the plaintext is already a multiple of 16, the block length, add 16 bytes 10 (16 in decimal). You get the idea. The trick generalizes to any block length up to 255 bytes (for larger blocks, a byte is too small to encode values greater than 255).

Decryption of a padded message works like this:

1. Decrypt all the blocks as with unpadded CBC.
2. Make sure that the last bytes of the last block conform to the padding rule: that they finish with at least one 01 byte, at least two 02 bytes, or at least three 03 bytes, and so on. If the padding isn't valid—for example, if the last bytes are 01 02 03—the message is rejected. Otherwise, decryption strips the padding bytes and returns the plaintext bytes left.

One downside of padding is that it makes ciphertext longer by at least one byte and at most a block.

Ciphertext Stealing

Ciphertext stealing is another trick used to encrypt a message whose length isn't a multiple of the block size. Ciphertext stealing is more complex and less popular than padding, but it offers at least three benefits:

-   Plaintexts can be of any *bit* length, not just bytes. You can, for example, encrypt a message of 131 bits.
-   Ciphertexts are exactly the same length as plaintexts.
-   Ciphertext stealing is not vulnerable to padding oracle attacks, powerful attacks that sometimes work against CBC with padding (as we'll see in "Padding Oracle Attacks" on page 74).

In CBC mode, ciphertext stealing extends the last incomplete plaintext block with bits from the previous ciphertext block, and then encrypts the resulting block. The last, incomplete ciphertext block is made up of the first blocks from the previous ciphertext block; that is, the bits that have not been appended to the last plaintext block.

In Figure 4-9, we have three blocks, where the last block, P_3, is incomplete (represented by a zero). P_3 is XORed with the last bits from the previous ciphertext block, and the encrypted result is returned as C_2. The last ciphertext block, C_3, then consists of the first bits from the previous ciphertext block. Decryption is simply the inverse of this operation.

There aren't any major problems with ciphertext stealing, but it's inelegant and hard to get right, especially when NIST's standard specifies three different ways to implement it (see Special Publication 800-38A).

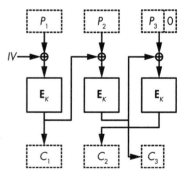

Figure 4-9: Ciphertext stealing for CBC-mode encryption

The Counter (CTR) Mode

To avoid the troubles and retain the benefits of ciphertext stealing, you should use counter mode (CTR). CTR is hardly a block cipher mode: it turns a block cipher into a stream cipher that just takes bits in and spits bits out and doesn't embarrass itself with the notion of blocks. (I'll discuss stream ciphers in detail in Chapter 5.)

In CTR mode (see Figure 4-10), the block cipher algorithm won't transform plaintext data. Instead, it will encrypt blocks composed of a *counter* and a *nonce*. A counter is an integer that is incremented for each block. No two blocks should use the same counter within a message, but different messages can use the same sequence of counter values $(1, 2, 3, \ldots)$. A nonce is a number used only once. It is the same for all blocks in a single message, but no two messages should use the same nonce.

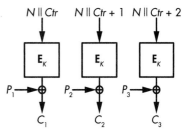

Figure 4-10: The CTR mode

As shown in Figure 4-10, in CTR mode, encryption XORs the plaintext and the stream taken from "encrypting" the nonce, N, and counter, Ctr. Decryption is the same, so you only need the encryption algorithm for both encryption and decryption. The Python script in Listing 4-6 gives you a hands-on example.

```python
#!/usr/bin/env python

from Crypto.Cipher import AES
from Crypto.Util import Counter
from binascii import hexlify as hexa
from os import urandom
from struct import unpack

k = urandom(16)
print "k = %s" % hexa(k)

# pick a starting value for the counter
nonce = unpack('<Q', urandom(8))[0]
# instantiate a counter function
ctr = Counter.new(128, initial_value=nonce)

# pick an instance of AES in CTR mode, using ctr as counter
aes = AES.new(k, AES.MODE_CTR, counter=ctr)

# no need for an entire block with CTR
p = '\x00\x01\x02\x03'

# encrypt p
c = aes.encrypt(p)
print "enc(%s) = %s" % (hexa(p), hexa(c))
```

```
# decrypt using the encrypt function
ctr = Counter.new(128, initial_value=nonce)
aes = AES.new(k, AES.MODE_CTR, counter=ctr)
p = aes.encrypt(c)
print "enc(%s) = %s" % (hexa(c), hexa(p))
```

Listing 4-6: Using AES in CTR mode

The example execution encrypts a 4-byte plaintext and gets a 4-byte ciphertext. It then decrypts that ciphertext using the encryption function:

```
$ ./aes_ctr.py
k = 130a1aa77fa58335272156421cb2a3ea
enc(00010203) = b23d284e
enc(b23d284e) = 00010203
```

As with the initial value in CBC, CTR's nonce is supplied by the encryp-ter and sent with the ciphertext in the clear. But unlike CBC's initial value, CTR's nonce doesn't need to be random, it simply needs to be unique. A nonce should be unique for the same reason that a one-time pad shouldn't be reused: when calling the pseudorandom stream, S, if you encrypt P_1 to $C_1 = P_1 \oplus S$ and P_2 to $C_2 = P_2 \oplus S$ using the same nonce, then $C_1 \oplus C_2$ reveals $P_1 \oplus P_2$.

A random nonce will do the trick only if it's long enough; for example, if the nonce is n bits, chances are that after $2^{n/2}$ encryptions and as many nonces you'll run into duplicates. Sixty-four bits are therefore insufficient for a random nonce, since you can expect a repetition after approximately 2^{32} nonces, which is an unacceptably low number.

The counter is guaranteed unique if it's incremented for every new plaintext, and if it's long enough; for example, a 64-bit counter.

One particular benefit to CTR is that it can be faster than in any other mode. Not only is it parallelizable, but you can also start encrypting even before knowing the message by picking a nonce and computing the stream that you'll later XOR with the plaintext.

How Things Can Go Wrong

There are two must-know attacks on block ciphers: meet-in-the-middle attacks, a technique discovered in the 1970s but still used in many crypt-analytic attacks (not to be confused with man-in-the-middle attacks), and padding oracle attacks, a class of attacks discovered in 2002 by academic cryptographers, then mostly ignored, and finally rediscovered a decade later along with several vulnerable applications.

Meet-in-the-Middle Attacks

The 3DES block cipher is an upgraded version of the 1970s standard DES that takes a key of $56 \times 3 = 168$ bits (an improvement on DES's 56-bit key). But the security level of 3DES is 112 bits instead of 168 bits, because of the *meet-in-the-middle (MitM)* attack.

As you can see in Figure 4-11, 3DES encrypts a block using the DES encryption and decryption functions: first encryption with a key, K_1, then decryption with a key, K_2, and finally encryption with another key, K_3. If $K_1 = K_2$, the first two calls cancel themselves out and 3DES boils down to a single DES with key K_3. 3DES does encrypt-decrypt-encrypt rather than encrypting thrice to allow systems to emulate DES when necessary using the new 3DES interface.

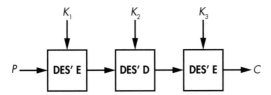

Figure 4-11: The 3DES block cipher construction

Why use triple DES and not just double DES, that is, $\mathbf{E}(K_1, \mathbf{E}(K_2, P))$? It turns out that the MitM attack makes double DES only as secure as single DES. Figure 4-12 shows the MitM attack in action.

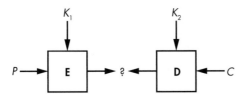

Figure 4-12: The meet-in-the-middle attack

The meet-in-the-middle attack works as follows to attack double DES:

1. Say you have P and $C = \mathbf{E}(K_2, \mathbf{E}(K_1, P))$ with two unknown 56-bit keys, K_1 and K_2. (DES takes 56-bit keys, so double DES takes 112 key bits in total.) You build a key–value table with 2^{56} entries of $\mathbf{E}(K_1, P)$, where $\mathbf{E}$ is the DES encryption function and K_1 is the value stored.

2. For all 2^{56} values of K_2, compute $\mathbf{D}(K_2, C)$ and check whether the resulting value appears in the table as an index (thus as a middle value, represented by a question mark in Figure 4-12).

3. If a middle value is found as an index of the table, you fetch the corresponding K_1 from the table and verify that the (K_1, K_2) found is the right one by using other pairs of P and C. Encrypt P using K_1 and K_2 and then check that the ciphertext obtained is the given C.

This method recovers K_1 and K_2 by performing about 2^{57} instead of 2^{112} operations: step 1 encrypts 2^{56} blocks and then step 2 decrypts at most 2^{56} blocks, for $2^{56} + 2^{56} = 2^{57}$ operations in total. You also need to store 2^{56} elements of 15 bytes each, or about 128 petabytes. That's a lot, but there's a trick that allows you to run the same attack with only negligible memory (as you'll see in Chapter 6).

As you can see, you can apply the MitM attack to 3DES in almost the same way you would to double DES, except that the third stage will go through all 2^{112} values of K_2 and K_3. The whole attack thus succeeds after performing about 2^{112} operations, meaning that 3DES gets only 112-bit security despite having 168 bits of key material.

Padding Oracle Attacks

Let's conclude this chapter with one of the simplest and yet most devastating attacks of the 2000s: the padding oracle attack. Remember that padding fills the plaintext with extra bytes in order to fill a block. A plaintext of 111 bytes, for example, is a sequence of six 16-byte blocks followed by 15 bytes. To form a complete block, padding adds a 01 byte. For a 110-byte plaintext, padding adds two 02 bytes, and so on.

A *padding oracle* is a system that behaves differently depending on whether the padding in a CBC-encrypted ciphertext is valid. You can see it as a black box or an API that returns either a *success* or an *error* value. A padding oracle can be found in a service on a remote host sending error messages when it receives malformed ciphertexts. Given a padding oracle, padding oracle attacks record which inputs have a valid padding and which don't, and exploit this information to decrypt chosen ciphertext values.

Say you want to decrypt ciphertext block C_2. I'll call X the value you're looking for, namely $\mathbf{D}(K, C_2)$, and P_2 the block obtained after decrypting in CBC mode (see Figure 4-13). If you pick a random block C_1 and send the two-block ciphertext $C_1 \parallel C_2$ to the oracle, decryption will only succeed if $C_1 \oplus P_2 = X$ ends with valid padding—a single 01 byte, two 02 bytes, or three 03 bytes, and so on.

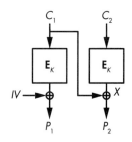

Based on this observation, padding oracle attacks on CBC encryption can decrypt a block C_2 like this (bytes are denoted in array notation: $C_1[0]$ is C_1's first byte, $C_1[1]$ its second byte, and so on up to $C_1[15]$, C_1's last byte):

Figure 4-13: Padding oracle attacks recover X by choosing C_1 and checking the validity of padding.

1. Pick a random block C_1 and vary its last byte until the padding oracle accepts the ciphertext as valid. Usually, in a valid ciphertext, $C_1[15] \oplus X[15] = 01$, so you'll find $X[15]$ after trying around 128 values of $C_1[15]$.

2. Find the value $X[14]$ by setting $C_1[15]$ to $X[15] \oplus 02$ and searching for the $C_1[14]$ that gives correct padding. When the oracle accepts the ciphertext as valid, it means you have found $C_1[14]$ such that $C_1[14] \oplus X[14] = 02$.

3. Repeat steps 1 and 2 for all 16 bytes.

The attack needs on average 128 queries to the oracle for each of the 16 bytes, which is about 2000 queries in total. (Note that each query must use the same initial value.)

NOTE *In practice, implementing a padding oracle attack is a bit more complicated than what I've described, because you have to deal with wrong guesses at step 1. A ciphertext may have valid padding not because P_2 ends with a single 01 but because it ends with two 02 bytes or three 03 bytes. But that's easily managed by testing the validity of ciphertexts where more bytes are modified.*

Further Reading

There's a lot to say about block ciphers, be it in how algorithms work or in how they can be attacked. For instance, Feistel networks and SPNs aren't the only ways to build a block cipher. The block ciphers IDEA and FOX use the Lai–Massey construction, and Threefish uses ARX networks, a combination of addition, word rotations, and XORs.

There are also many more modes than just ECB, CBC, and CTR. Some modes are folklore techniques that nobody uses, like CFB and OFB, while others are for specific applications, like XTS for tweakable encryption or GCM for authenticated encryption.

I've discussed Rijndael, the AES winner, but there were 14 other algorithms in the race: CAST-256, CRYPTON, DEAL, DFC, E2, FROG, HPC, LOKI97, Magenta, MARS, RC6, SAFER+, Serpent, and Twofish. I recommend that you look them up to see how they work, how they were designed, how they have been attacked, and how fast they are. It's also worth checking out the NSA's designs (Skipjack, and more recently, SIMON and SPECK) and more recent "lightweight" block ciphers such as KATAN, PRESENT, or PRINCE.

5

STREAM CIPHERS

Symmetric ciphers can be either block ciphers or stream ciphers. Recall from Chapter 4 that block ciphers mix chunks of plaintext bits together with key bits to produce chunks of ciphertext of the same size, usually 64 or 128 bits. Stream ciphers, on the other hand, don't mix plaintext and key bits; instead, they generate pseudorandom bits from the key and encrypt the plaintext by XORing it with the pseudorandom bits, in the same fashion as the one-time pad explained in Chapter 1.

Stream ciphers are sometimes shunned because historically they've been more fragile than block ciphers and are more often broken—both the experimental ones designed by amateurs and the ciphers deployed in systems used by millions, including mobile phones, Wi-Fi, and public transport smart cards. But that's all history. Fortunately, although it has taken

20 years, we now know how to design secure stream ciphers, and we trust them to protect things like Bluetooth connections, mobile 4G communications, TLS connections, and more.

This chapter first presents how stream ciphers work and discusses the two main classes of stream ciphers: stateful and counter-based ciphers. We'll then study hardware- and software-oriented stream ciphers and look at some insecure ciphers (such as A5/1 in GSM mobile communications and RC4 in TLS) and some secure, state-of-the-art ones (such as Grain-128a for hardware and Salsa20 for software).

How Stream Ciphers Work

Stream ciphers are more akin to deterministic random bit generators (DRBGs) than they are to full-fledged pseudorandom number generators (PRNGs) because, like DRBGs, stream ciphers are deterministic. Stream ciphers' determinism allows you to decrypt by regenerating the pseudorandom bits used to encrypt. With a PRNG, you could encrypt but never decrypt—which is secure, but useless.

What sets stream ciphers apart from DRBGs is that DRBGs take a single input value whereas stream ciphers take two values: a key and a nonce. The key should be secret and is usually 128 or 256 bits. The nonce doesn't have to be secret, but it should be unique for each key and is usually between 64 and 128 bits.

Stream ciphers produce a pseudorandom stream of bits called the *keystream*. The keystream is XORed to a plaintext to encrypt it and then XORed again to the ciphertext to decrypt it. Figure 5-1 shows the basic stream cipher encryption operation, where **SC** is the stream cipher algorithm, *KS* the keystream, *P* the plaintext, and *C* the ciphertext.

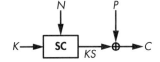

Figure 5-1: How stream ciphers encrypt, taking a secret key, K, and a public nonce, N

A stream cipher computes $KS = \textbf{SC}(K, N)$, encrypts as $C = P \oplus KS$, and decrypts as $P = C \oplus KS$. The encryption and decryption functions are the same because both do the same thing—namely, XOR bits with the keystream. That's why, for example, certain cryptographic libraries provide a single encrypt function that's used for both encryption and decryption.

Stream ciphers allow you to encrypt a message with key K_1 and nonce N_1 and then encrypt another message with key K_1 and nonce N_2 that is different from N_1, or with key K_2, which is different from K_1 and nonce N_1. However, you should never again encrypt with K_1 and N_1, because you would then use twice the same keystream KS. You would then have a first ciphertext $C_1 = P_1 \oplus KS$, a second ciphertext $C_2 = P_2 \oplus KS$, and if you know P_1, then you could determine $P_2 = C_1 \oplus C_2 \oplus P_1$.

NOTE *The name* nonce *is actually short for* number used only once. *In the context of stream ciphers, it's sometimes called the* IV, *for* initial value.

Stateful and Counter-Based Stream Ciphers

From a high-level perspective, there are two types of stream ciphers: stateful and counter based. *Stateful stream ciphers* have a secret internal state that evolves throughout keystream generation. The cipher initializes the state from the key and the nonce and then calls an update function to update the state value and produce one or more keystream bits from the state, as shown in Figure 5-2. For example, the famous RC4 is a stateful cipher.

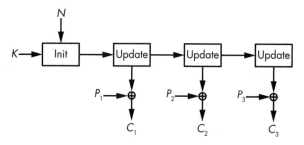

Figure 5-2: The stateful stream cipher

Counter-based stream ciphers produce chunks of keystream from a key, a nonce, and a counter value, as shown in Figure 5-3. Unlike stateful stream ciphers, such as Salsa20, no secret state is memorized during keystream generation.

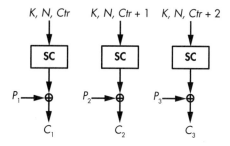

Figure 5-3: The counter-based stream cipher

These two approaches define the high-level architecture of the stream cipher, regardless of how the core algorithms work. The internals of the stream cipher also fall into two categories, depending on the target platform of the cipher: hardware oriented and software oriented.

Hardware-Oriented Stream Ciphers

When cryptographers talk about hardware, they mean application-specific integrated circuits (ASICs), programmable logic devices (PLDs), and field-programmable gate arrays (FPGAs). A cipher's hardware implementation is an electronic circuit that implements the cryptographic algorithm at the bit level and that can't be used for anything else; in other words, the circuit is *dedicated hardware*. On the other hand, software implementations of cryptographic algorithms simply tell a microprocessor what instructions to execute in order to run the algorithm. These instructions operate on bytes or words and then call pieces of electronic circuit that implement general-purpose operations such as addition and multiplication. Software deals with bytes or words of 32 or 64 bits, whereas hardware deals with bits. The first stream ciphers worked with bits in order to save complex word-wise operations and thus be more efficient in hardware, their target platform at the time.

The main reason why stream ciphers were commonly used for hardware implementations is that they were cheaper than block ciphers. Stream ciphers needed less memory and fewer logical gates than block ciphers, and therefore occupied a smaller area on an integrated circuit, which reduced fabrication costs. For example, counting in gate-equivalents, the standard area metric for integrated circuits, you could find stream ciphers taking less than 1000 gate-equivalents; by contrast, typical software-oriented block ciphers needed at least 10000 gate-equivalents, making crypto an order of magnitude more expensive than with stream ciphers.

Today, however, block ciphers are no longer more expensive than stream ciphers—first, because there are now hardware-friendly block ciphers about as small as stream ciphers, and second, because the cost of hardware has plunged. Yet stream ciphers are often associated with hardware because they used to be the best option.

In the next section, I'll explain the basic mechanism behind hardware stream ciphers, called *feedback shift registers (FSRs)*. Almost all hardware stream ciphers rely on FSRs in some way, whether that's the A5/1 cipher used in 2G mobile phones or the more recent cipher Grain-128a.

NOTE *The first standard block cipher, the Data Encryption Standard (DES), was optimized for hardware rather than for software. When the US government standardized DES in the 1970s, most target applications were hardware implementations. It's therefore no surprise that the S-boxes in DES are small and fast to compute when implemented as a logical circuit in hardware but inefficient in software. Unlike DES, the current Advanced Encryption Standard (AES) deals with bytes and is therefore more efficient in software than DES.*

Feedback Shift Registers

Countless stream ciphers have used FSRs because they're simple and well understood. An FSR is simply an array of bits equipped with an update *feedback function*, which I'll denote as **f**. The FSR's state is stored in the array, or register, and each *update* of the FSR uses the feedback function to change the state's value and to produce one output bit.

In practice, an FSR works like this: if R_0 is the initial value of the FSR, the next state, R_1, is defined as R_0 left-shifted by 1 bit, where the bit leaving the register is returned as output, and where the empty position is filled with $\mathbf{f}(R_0)$.

The same rule is repeated to compute the subsequent state values R_2, R_3, and so on. That is, given R_t, the FSR's state at time t, the next state, R_{t+1}, is the following:

$$R_{t+1} = (R_t \ll 1) \mid \mathbf{f}(R_t)$$

In this equation, | is the logical OR operator and $\ll$ is the shift operator, as used in the C language. For example, given the 8-bit string 00001111, we have this:

$$00001111 \ll 1 = 00011110$$
$$00011110 \ll 1 = 00111100$$
$$00111100 \ll 1 = 01111000$$

The bit shift moves the bits to the left, losing the leftmost bit in order to retain the state's bit length, and zeroing the rightmost bit. The update operation of an FSR is identical, except that instead of being set to 0, the rightmost bit is set to $\mathbf{f}(R_t)$.

Consider, for example, a 4-bit FSR whose feedback function $\mathbf{f}$ XORs all 4 bits together. Initialize the state to the following:

$$1 \ 1 \ 0 \ 0$$

Now shift the bits to the left, where 1 is output and the rightmost bit is set to the following:

$$\mathbf{f}(1100) = 1 \oplus 1 \oplus 0 \oplus 0 = 0$$

Now the state becomes this:

$$1 \ 0 \ 0 \ 0$$

The next update outputs 1, left-shifts the state, and sets the rightmost bit to the following:

$$\mathbf{f}(1000) = 1 \oplus 0 \oplus 0 \oplus 0 = 1$$

Now the state is this:

$$0 \ 0 \ 0 \ 1$$

The next three updates return three 0 bits and give the following state values:

$$0 \ 0 \ 1 \ 1$$
$$0 \ 1 \ 1 \ 0$$
$$1 \ 1 \ 0 \ 0$$

We thus return to our initial state of 1100 after five iterations, and we can see that updating the state five times from any of the values observed throughout this cycle will return us to this initial value. We say that 5 is the *period* of the FSR given any one of the values 1100, 1000, 0001, 0011, or 0110. Because the period of this FSR is 5, clocking the register 10 times will yield twice the same 5-bit sequence. Likewise, if you clock the register 20 times, starting from 1100, the output bits will be 11000110001100011000, or four times the same 5-bit sequence of 11000. Intuitively, such repeating patterns should be avoided, and a longer period is better for security.

NOTE   *If you plan to use an FSR in a stream cipher, avoid using one with short periods, which make the output more predictable. Some types of FSRs make it easy to figure out their period, but it's almost impossible to do so with others.*

Figure 5-4 shows the structure of this cycle, along with the other cycles of that FSR, with each cycle shown as a circle whose dots represent a state of the register.

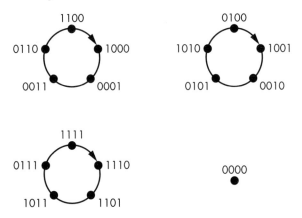

Figure 5-4: Cycles of the FSR whose feedback function XORs the 4 bits together

Indeed, this particular FSR has two other period-5 cycles—namely, {0100, 1001, 0010, 0101, 1010} and {1111, 1110, 1101, 1011, 0111}. Note that any given state can belong to only one cycle of states. Here, we have three cycles of five states each, covering 15 of all the $2^4 = 16$ possible values of our 4-bit register. The 16th possible value is 0000, which, as Figure 5-4 shows, is a period-1 cycle because the FSR will transform 0000 to 0000.

You've seen that an FSR is essentially a register of bits, where each update of the register outputs a bit (the leftmost bit of the register) and where a function computes the new rightmost bit of the register. (All other bits are left-shifted.) The period of an FSR, from some initial state, is the number of updates needed until the FSR enters the same state again. If it takes N updates to do so, the FSR will produce the same N bits again and again.

Linear Feedback Shift Registers

Linear feedback shift registers (LFSRs) are FSRs with a *linear* feedback function—namely, a function that's the XOR of some bits of the state, such as the example of a 4-bit FSR in the previous section and its feedback function returning the XOR of the register's 4 bits. Recall that in cryptography, linearity is synonymous with predictability and suggestive of a simple underlying mathematical structure. And, as you might expect, thanks to this linearity, LFSRs can be analyzed using notions like linear complexity, finite fields, and primitive polynomials—but I'll skip the math details and just give you the essential facts.

The choice of which bits are XORed together is crucial for the period of the LFSR and thus for its cryptographic value. The good news is that we know how to select the position of the bits in order to guarantee a maximal period, of $2^n - 1$. Specifically, we take the indices of the bits, from 1 for the rightmost to n for the leftmost, and write the polynomial expression $1 + X + X^2 + \ldots + X^n$, where the term X^i is only included if the ith bit is one of the bits XORed in the feedback function. The period is maximal *if and only if* that polynomial is *primitive*. To be primitive, the polynomial must have the following qualities:

- The polynomial must be irreducible, meaning that it can't be factorized; that is, written as a product of smaller polynomials. For example, $X + X^3$ is not irreducible because it's equal to $(1 + X)(X + X^2)$:

$$(1 + X)(X + X^2) = X + X^2 + X^2 + X^3 = X + X^3$$

- The polynomial must satisfy certain other mathematical properties that cannot be easily explained without nontrivial mathematical notions but are easy to test.

NOTE *The maximal period of an n-bit LFSR is $2^n - 1$, not 2^n, because the all-zero state always loops on itself infinitely. Because the XOR of any number of zeros is zero, new bits entering the state from the feedback functions will always be zero; hence, the all-zero state is doomed to stay all zeros.*

For example, Figure 5-5 shows a 4-bit LFSR with the feedback polynomial $1 + X + X^3 + X^4$ in which the bits at positions 1, 3, and 4 are XORed together to compute the new bit set to L_1. However, this polynomial isn't primitive because it can be factorized into $(1 + X^3)(1 + X)$.

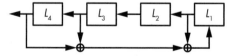

Figure 5-5: An LFSR with the feedback polynomial
$1 + X + X^3 + X^4$

Indeed, the period of the LFSR shown in Figure 5-5 isn't maximal. To prove that, start from the state 0001.

$$0\ 0\ 0\ 1$$

Now left-shift by 1 bit and set the new bit to $0 + 0 + 1 = 1$:

$$0\ 0\ 1\ 1$$

Repeating the operation four times gives the following state values:

$$0\ 1\ 1\ 1$$
$$1\ 1\ 0\ 0$$
$$1\ 0\ 0\ 0$$
$$0\ 0\ 0\ 1$$

And as you can see, the state after five updates is the same as the initial one, demonstrating that we're in a period-5 cycle and proving that the LFSR's period isn't the maximal value of 15.

Now, by way of contrast, consider the LFSR shown in Figure 5-6.

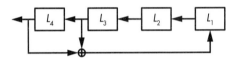

Figure 5-6: An LFSR with the feedback polynomial
$1 + X^3 + X^4$, a primitive polynomial, ensuring
a maximal period

This feedback polynomial is a primitive polynomial described by $1 + X^3 + X^4$, and you can verify that its period is indeed maximal (namely 15). Specifically, from an initial value, the state evolves as follows:

0 0 0 1	0 0 1 1	0 1 0 1	1 1 1 0
0 0 1 0	0 1 1 0	1 0 1 1	1 1 0 0
0 1 0 0	1 1 0 1	0 1 1 1	1 0 0 0
1 0 0 1	1 0 1 0	1 1 1 1	0 0 0 1

The state spans all possible values except 0000 with no repetition until it eventually loops. This demonstrates that the period is maximal and proves that the feedback polynomial is primitive.

Alas, using an LFSR as a stream cipher is insecure. If n is the LFSR's bit length, an attacker needs only n output bits to recover the LFSR's initial state, allowing them to determine all previous bits and predict all future bits. This attack is possible because the Berlekamp–Massey algorithm can be used to solve the equations defined by the LFSR's mathematical structure to find not only the LFSR's initial state but also its feedback polynomial. In fact, you don't even need to know the exact length of the LFSR to succeed; you can repeat the Berlekamp–Massey algorithm for all possible values of n until you hit the right one.

The upshot is that LFSRs are cryptographically weak because they're linear. Output bits and initial state bits are related by simple and short equations that can be easily solved with high-school linear algebra techniques.

To strengthen LFSRs, let's thus add a pinch of nonlinearity.

Filtered LFSRs

To mitigate the insecurity of LFSRs, you can hide their linearity by passing their output bits through a nonlinear function before returning them to produce what is called a *filtered LFSR* (see Figure 5-7).

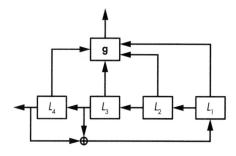

The **g** function in Figure 5-7 must be a *nonlinear* function—one that both XORs bits together and combines them with logical AND or OR operations. For example,

Figure 5-7: A filtered LFSR

$L_1L_2 + L_3L_4$ is a nonlinear function (I've omitted the multiply sign, so L_1L_2 means $L_1 \times L_2$, or L_1 & L_2 using C syntax).

> **NOTE** *You can write feedback functions either directly in terms of an FSR's bits, like $L_1L_2 + L_3L_4$, or using the equivalent polynomial notation $1 + XX^2 + X^3X^4$. The direct notation is easier to grasp, but the polynomial notation better serves the mathematical analysis of an FSR's properties. We'll now stick to the direct notation unless we care about the mathematical properties.*

Filtered LFSRs are stronger than plain LFSRs because their nonlinear function thwarts straightforward attacks. Still, more complex attacks such as the following will break the system:

- *Algebraic attacks* will solve the nonlinear equation systems deduced from the output bits, where unknowns in the equations are bits from the LFSR state.

- *Cube attacks* will compute derivatives of the nonlinear equations in order to reduce the degree of the system down to one and then solve it efficiently like a linear system.

- *Fast correlation attacks* will exploit filtering functions that, despite their nonlinearity, tend to behave like linear functions.

The lesson here, as we've seen in previous examples, is that Band-Aids don't fix bullet holes. Patching a broken algorithm with a slightly stronger layer won't make the whole thing secure. The problem has to be fixed at the core.

Nonlinear FSRs

Nonlinear FSRs (NFSRs) are like LFSRs but with a nonlinear feedback function instead of a linear one. That is, instead of just bitwise XORs, the feedback function can include bitwise AND and OR operations—a feature with both pros and cons.

One benefit of the addition of nonlinear feedback functions is that they make NFSRs cryptographically stronger than LFSRs because the output bits depend on the initial secret state in a complex fashion, according to equations of exponential size. The LFSRs' linear function keeps the relations simple, with at most n terms ($N_1, N_2, \ldots, N_n$, if the N_is are the NFSR's state bits). For example, a 4-bit NFSR with an initial secret state (N_1, N_2, N_3, N_4) and a feedback function ($N_1 + N_2 + N_1 N_2 + N_3 N_4$) will produce a first output bit equal to the following:

$$N_1 + N_2 + N_1 N_2 + N_3 N_4$$

The second iteration replaces the N_1 value with that new bit. Expressing the second output bit in terms of the initial state, we get the following equation:

$$\left(N_1 N_2 + N_3 N_4 + N_1 + N_2 \right) + N_1 + \left(N_1 N_2 + N_3 N_4 + N_1 + N_2 \right) N_1 + N_2 N_3$$
$$= N_1 N_3 N_4 + N_1 N_2 + N_2 N_3 + N_3 N_4 + N_1 + N_2$$

This new equation has algebraic degree 3 (the highest number of bits multiplied together, here in $N_1 N_3 N_4$) rather than degree 2 of the feedback function, and it has six terms instead of four. As a result, iterating the nonlinear function quickly yields unmanageable equations because the size of the output grows exponentially. Although you'll never compute those equations when running the NFSR, an attacker would have to solve them in order to break the system.

One downside to NFSRs is that there's no efficient way to determine an NFSR's period, or simply to know whether its period is maximal. For an NFSR of n bits, you'd need to run close to 2^n trials to verify that its period is maximal. This calculation is impossible for large NFSRs of 80 bits or more.

Fortunately, there's a trick to using an NFSR without worrying about short periods: you can combine LFSRs and NFSRs to get both a guaranteed maximal period and the cryptographic strength—and that's exactly how Grain-128a works.

Grain-128a

Remember the AES competition discussed in Chapter 4, in the context of the AES block cipher? The stream cipher Grain is the offspring of a similar project called the eSTREAM competition. This competition closed in 2008 with a shortlist of recommended stream ciphers, which included four hardware-oriented ciphers and four software-oriented ones. Grain is one of these hardware ciphers, and Grain-128a is an upgraded version from the original authors of Grain. Figure 5-8 shows the action mechanism of Grain-128a.

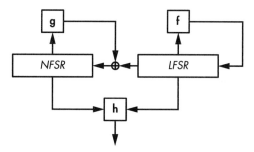

Figure 5-8: The mechanism of Grain-128a, with a 128-bit NFSR and a 128-bit LFSR

As you can see in Figure 5-8, Grain-128a is about as simple as a stream cipher can be, combining a 128-bit LFSR, a 128-bit NFSR, and a filter function, **h**. The LFSR has a maximal period of $2^{128} - 1$, which ensures that the period of the whole system is at least $2^{128} - 1$ to protect against potential short cycles in the NFSR. At the same time, the NFSR and the nonlinear filter function **h** add cryptographic strength.

Grain-128a takes a 128-bit key and a 96-bit nonce. It copies the 128 key bits into the NFSR's 128 bits and copies the 96 nonce bits into the first 96 LFSR bits, filling the 32 bits left with ones and a single zero bit at the end. The initialization phase updates the whole system 256 times before returning the first keystream bit. During initialization, the bit returned by the **h** function is thus not output as a keystream, but instead goes into the LFSR to ensure that its subsequent state depends on both the key and the nonce.

Grain-128a's LFSR feedback function is

$$\mathbf{f}(L) = L_{32} + L_{47} + L_{58} + L_{90} + L_{121} + L_{128}$$

where $L_1, L_2, \ldots, L_{128}$ are the bits of the LFSR. This feedback function takes only 6 bits from the 128-bit LFSR, but that's enough to get a primitive polynomial that guarantees a maximal period. The small number of bits minimizes the cost of a hardware implementation.

Here is the feedback polynomial of Grain-128a's NFSR ($N_1, \ldots, N_{128}$):

$$\mathbf{g}(N) = N_{32} + N_{37} + N_{72} + N_{102} + N_{128} + N_{44}N_{60} + N_{61}N_{125} + N_{63}N_{67} + N_{69}N_{101}$$
$$+ N_{80}N_{88} + N_{110}N_{111} + N_{115}N_{117} + N_{46}N_{50}N_{58} + N_{103}N_{104}N_{106} + N_{33}N_{35}N_{36}N_{40}$$

This function was carefully chosen to maximize its cryptographic strength while minimizing its implementation cost. It has an algebraic degree of 4 because its term with the most variables has four variables (namely, $N_{33}N_{35}N_{36}N_{40}$). Moreover, **g** can't be approximated by a linear function because it is highly nonlinear. Also, in addition to **g**, Grain-128a XORs the bit coming out from the LFSRs to feed the result back as the NFSR's new, rightmost bit.

The filter function **h** is another nonlinear function; it takes 9 bits from the NFSR and 7 bits from the LFSR and combines them in a way that ensures good cryptographic properties.

As I write this, there is no known attack on Grain-128a, and I'm confident that it will remain secure. Grain-128a is used in some low-end embedded systems that need a compact and fast stream cipher—typically industrial proprietary systems—which is why Grain-128a is little known in the open-source software community.

A5/1

A5/1 is a stream cipher that was used to encrypt voice communications in the 2G mobile standard. The A5/1 standard was created in 1987 but only published in the late 1990s after it was reverse engineered. Attacks appeared in the early 2000s, and A5/1 was eventually broken in a way that allows actual (rather than theoretical) decryption of encrypted communications. Let's see why and how.

A5/1's Mechanism

A5/1 relies on three LFSRs and uses a trick that looks clever at first glance but actually fails to be secure (see Figure 5-9).

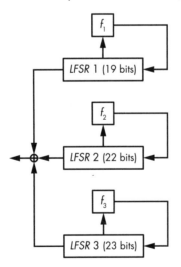

Figure 5-9: The A5/1 cipher

As you can see in Figure 5-9, A5/1 uses LFSRs of 19, 22, and 23 bits, with the polynomials for each as follows:

$$1 + X^{14} + X^{17} + X^{18} + X^{19}$$
$$1 + X^{21} + X^{22}$$
$$1 + X^8 + X^{21} + X^{22} + X^{23}$$

How could this be seen as secure with only LFSRs and no NFSR? The trick lies in A5/1's update mechanism. Instead of updating all three LFSRs at each clock cycle, the designers of A5/1 added a clocking rule that does the following:

1. Checks the value of the ninth bit of LFSR 1, the 11th bit of LFSR 2, and the 11th bit of LFSR 3, called the *clocking bits*. Of those three bits, either all have the same value (1 or 0) or exactly two have the same value.

2. Clocks the registers whose clocking bits are equal to the majority value, 0 or 1. Either two or three LFSRs are clocked at each update.

Without this simple rule, A5/1 would provide no security whatsoever, and bypassing this rule is enough to break the cipher. However, that is easier said than done, as you'll see.

NOTE *In A5/1's irregular clocking rule, each register is clocked with a probability of 3/4 at any update. Namely, the probability that at least one other register has the same bit value is $1 - (1/2)^2$, where $(1/2)^2$ is the chance that both of the other two registers have a different bit value.*

2G communications use A5/1 with a key of 64 bits and a 22-bit nonce, which is changed for every new data frame. Attacks on A5/1 recover the 64-bit initial state of the system (the 19 + 22 + 23 LFSR initial value), thus in turn revealing the nonce (if it was not already known) and the key, by unwinding the initialization mechanism. The attacks are referred to as *known-plaintext attacks (KPAs)* because part of the encrypted data is known, which allows attackers to determine the corresponding keystream parts by XORing the ciphertext with the known plaintext chunks.

There are two main types of attacks on A5/1:

Subtle attacks   Exploit the internal linearity of A5/1 and its simple irregular clocking system

Brutal attacks   Only exploit the short key of A5/1 and the invertibility of the frame number injection

Let's see how these attacks work.

Subtle Attacks

In a subtle attack called a *guess-and-determine* attack, an attacker guesses certain secret values of the state in order to determine others. In cryptanalysis, "guessing" means brute-forcing: for each possible value of LFSRs 1 and 2, and all possible values of LFSR 3's clocking bit during the first 11 clocks, the attack reconstructs LFSR 3's bits by solving equations that depend on the bits guessed. When the guess is correct, the attacker gets the right value for LFSR 3.

The attack's pseudocode looks like this:

```
For all 2¹⁹ values of LFSR 1's initial state
    For all 2²² values of LFSR 2's initial state
        For all 2¹¹ values of LFSR 3's clocking bit during the first 11 clocks
            Reconstruct LFSR 3's initial state
            Test whether guess is correct; if yes, return; else continue
```

How efficient is this attack compared to the 2^{64}-trial brute-force search discussed in Chapter 3? This attack makes at most $2^{19} \times 2^{22} \times 2^{11} = 2^{52}$ operations in the worst case, when the algorithm only succeeds at the very last test. That's 2^{12} (or about 4000) times faster than in the brute-force search, assuming that the last two operations in the above pseudocode require about as much computation as testing a 64-bit key in a brute-force search. But is this assumption correct?

Recall our discussion of the full attack cost in Chapter 3. When evaluating the cost of an attack, we need to consider not only the amount of computation required to perform the attack but also parallelism and memory consumption. Neither are issues here: as with any brute-force attack, the guess-and-determine attack is embarrassingly parallel (or N times faster when run on N cores) and doesn't need more memory than just running the cipher itself.

Our 2^{52} attack cost estimate is inaccurate for another reason. In fact, each of the 2^{52} operations (testing a key candidate) takes about four times as many clock cycles as does testing a key in a brute-force attack. The upshot is that the real cost of this particular attack is closer to $4 \times 2^{52} = 2^{54}$ operations, when compared to a brute-force attack.

The guess-and-determine attack on A5/1 can decrypt encrypted mobile communications, but it takes a couple of hours to recover the key when run on a cluster of dedicated hardware devices. In other words, it's nowhere near real-time decryption. For that, we have another type of attack.

Brutal Attacks

The time-memory trade-off (TMTO) attack is the brutal attack on A5/1. This attack doesn't care about A5/1's internals; it cares only that its state is 64 bits long. The TMTO attack sees A5/1 as a black box that takes in a 64-bit value (the state) and spits out a 64-bit value (the first 64 keystream bits).

The idea behind the attack is to reduce the cost of a brute-force search in exchange for using lots of memory. The simplest type of TMTO is the codebook attack. In a codebook attack, you precompute a table of 2^{64} elements containing a combination of key and value pairs (*key:value*), and store the output value for each of the 2^{64} possible keys. To use this precomputed table for the attack, you simply collect the output of an A5/1 instance and then look up in the table which key corresponds to that output. The attack itself is fast—taking only the amount of time necessary to look up a value in memory—but the creation of the table takes 2^{64} computations of A5/1. Worse, codebook attacks require an insane amount of memory: $2^{64} \times (64 + 64)$ bits, which is 2^{68} bytes or 256 exabytes. That's dozens of data centers, so we can forget about it.

TMTO attacks reduce the memory required by a codebook attack at the price of increased computation during the online phase of the attack; the smaller the table, the more computations required to crack a key. Regardless, it will still cost about 2^{64} operations to prepare the table, but that needs to be done only once.

In 2010, researchers took about two months to generate two terabytes' worth of tables, using graphics processing units (GPUs) and running 100000 instances of A5/1 in parallel. With the help of such large tables, calls encrypted with A5/1 could be decrypted almost in real time. Telecommunication operators have implemented workarounds to mitigate the attack, but a real solution came with the later 3G and 4G mobile telephony standards, which ditched A5/1 altogether.

Software-Oriented Stream Ciphers

Software stream ciphers work with bytes or 32- or 64-bit words instead of individual bits, which proves to be more efficient on modern CPUs where instructions can perform arithmetic operations on a word in the same amount of time as on a bit. Software stream ciphers are therefore better suited than hardware ciphers for servers or browsers running on personal computers, where powerful general-purpose processors run the cipher as native software.

Today, there is considerable interest in software stream ciphers for a few reasons. First, because many devices embed powerful CPUs and hardware has become cheaper, there's less of a need for small bit-oriented ciphers. For example, the two stream ciphers in the mobile communications standard 4G (the European SNOW3G and the Chinese ZUC) work with 32-bit words and not bits, unlike the older A5/1.

Second, stream ciphers have gained popularity in software at the expense of block ciphers, notably following the fiasco of the padding oracle attack against block ciphers in CBC mode. In addition, stream ciphers are easier to specify and to implement than block ciphers: instead of mixing message and key bits together, stream ciphers just ingest key bits as a secret. In fact, one of the most popular stream ciphers is actually a block cipher in disguise: AES in counter mode (CTR).

One software stream cipher design, used by SNOW3G and ZUC, copies hardware ciphers and their FSRs, replacing bits with bytes or words. But these aren't the most interesting designs for a cryptographer. As of this writing, the two designs of most interest are RC4 and Salsa20, which are used in numerous systems, despite the fact that one is completely broken.

RC4

Designed in 1987 by Ron Rivest of RSA Security, then reverse engineered and leaked in 1994, RC4 has long been the most widely used stream cipher. RC4 has been used in countless applications, most famously in the first Wi-Fi encryption standard Wireless Equivalent Privacy (WEP) and in the Transport Layer Security (TLS) protocol used to establish HTTPS connections. Unfortunately, RC4 isn't secure enough for most applications, including WEP and TLS. To understand why, let's see how RC4 works.

How RC4 Works

RC4 is among the simplest ciphers ever created. It doesn't perform any crypto-like operations, and it has no XORs, no multiplications, no S-boxes . . . nada. It simply swaps bytes. RC4's internal state is an array, S, of 256 bytes, first set to $S[0] = 0$, $S[1] = 1$, $S[2] = 2$, . . . , $S[255] = 255$, and then initialized from an n-byte K using its *key scheduling algorithm (KSA)*, which works as shown in the Python code in Listing 5-1.

```
j = 0
# set S to the array S[0] = 0, S[1] = 1, . . . , S[255] = 255
S = range(256)
# iterate over i from 0 to 255
for i in range(256):
    # compute the sum of v
    j = (j + S[i] + K[i % n]) % 256
    # swap S[i] and S[j]
    S[i], S[j] = S[j], S[i]
```

Listing 5-1: The key scheduling algorithm of RC4

Once this algorithm completes, array S still contains all the byte values from 0 to 255, but now in a random-looking order. For example, with the all-zero 128-bit key, the state S (from $S[0]$ to $S[255]$) becomes this:

$$0, 35, 3, 43, 9, 11, 65, 229, (\ldots), 233, 169, 117, 184, \ 31, 39$$

However, if I flip the first key bit and run the KSA again, I get a totally different, apparently random state:

$$32, 116, 131, 134, 138, 143, 149, (\ldots), 152, 235, 111, \ 48, 80, 12$$

Given the initial state S, RC4 generates a keystream, KS, of the same length as the plaintext, P, in order to compute a ciphertext: $C = P \oplus KS$. The bytes of the keystream KS are computed from S according to the Python code in Listing 5-2, if P is m bytes long.

```
i = 0
j = 0
```

```
for b in range(m):
    i = (i + 1) % 256
    j = (j + S[i]) % 256
    S[i], S[j] = S[j], S[i]
    KS[b] = S[(S[i] + S[j]) % 256]
```

Listing 5-2: The keystream generation of RC4, where S is the state initialized in Listing 5-1

In Listing 5-2, each iteration of the for loop modifies up to 2 bytes of RC4's internal state S: the $S[i]$ and $S[j]$ whose values are swapped. That is, if $i = 0$ and $j = 4$, and if $S[0] = 56$ and $S[4] = 78$, then the swap operation sets $S[0]$ to 78 and $S[4]$ to 56. If j equals i, then $S[i]$ isn't modified.

This looks too simple to be secure, yet it took 20 years for cryptanalysts to find exploitable flaws. Before the flaws were revealed, we only knew RC4's weaknesses in specific implementations, as in the first Wi-Fi encryption standard, WEP.

RC4 in WEP

WEP, the first generation Wi-Fi security protocol, is now completely broken due to weaknesses in the protocol's design and in RC4.

In its WEP implementation, RC4 encrypts payload data of 802.11 frames, the datagrams (or packets) that transport data over the wireless network. All payloads delivered in the same session use the same secret key of 40 or 104 bits but have what is a supposedly unique 3-byte nonce encoded in the frame header (the part of the frame that encodes metadata and comes before the actual payload). See the problem?

The problem is that RC4 doesn't support a nonce, at least not in its official specification, and a stream cipher can't be used without a nonce. The WEP designers addressed this limitation with a workaround: they included a 24-bit nonce in the wireless frame's header and prepended it to the WEP key to be used as RC4's secret key. That is, if the nonce is the bytes $N[0]$, $N[1]$, $N[2]$ and the WEP key is $K[0]$, $K[1]$, $K[2]$, $K[3]$, $K[4]$, the actual RC4 key is $N[0]$, $N[1]$, $N[2]$, $K[0]$, $K[1]$, $K[2]$, $K[3]$, $K[4]$. The net effect is to have 40-bit secret keys yield 64-bit effective keys, and 104-bit keys yield 128-bit effective keys. The result? The advertised 128-bit WEP protocol actually offers only 104-bit security, at best.

But here are the real problems with WEP's nonce trick:

- **The nonces are too small at only 24 bits**. This means that if a nonce is chosen randomly for each new message, you'll have to wait about $2^{24/2} = 2^{12}$ packets, or a few megabytes' worth of traffic, until you can find two packets encrypted with the same nonce, and thus the same keystream. Even if the nonce is a counter running from 0 to $2^{24} - 1$, it will take a few gigabytes' worth of data until a rollover, when the repeated nonce can allow the attacker to decrypt packets. But there's a bigger problem.

- **Combining the nonce and key in this fashion helps recover the key.**
  WEP's three non-secret nonce bytes let an attacker determine the value
  of S after three iterations of the key scheduling algorithm. Because of
  this, cryptanalysts found that the first keystream byte strongly depends
  on the first secret key byte—the fourth byte ingested by the KSA—and
  that this bias can be exploited to recover the secret key.

Exploiting those weaknesses requires access to both ciphertexts
and the keystream; that is, known or chosen plaintexts. But that's easy
enough: known plaintexts occur when the Wi-Fi frames encapsulate data
with a known header, and chosen plaintexts occur when the attacker
injects known plaintext encrypted with the target key. The upshot is that
the attacks work in practice, not just on paper.

Following the appearance of the first attacks on WEP in 2001, researchers found faster attacks that required fewer ciphertexts. Today, you can even
find tools such as aircrack-ng that implement the entire attack, from network sniffing to cryptanalysis.

WEP's insecurity is due to both weaknesses in RC4, which takes a single
one-use key instead of a key and nonce (as in any decent stream cipher),
and weaknesses in the WEP design itself.

Now let's look at the second biggest failure of RC4.

RC4 in TLS

TLS is the single most important security protocol used on the internet.
It is best known for underlying HTTPS connections, but it's also used to
protect some virtual private network (VPN) connections, as well as email
servers, mobile applications, and many others. And sadly, TLS has long
supported RC4.

Unlike WEP, the TLS implementation doesn't make the same blatant
mistake of tweaking the RC4 specs in order to use a public nonce. Instead,
TLS just feeds RC4 a unique 128-bit session key, which means it's a bit less
broken than WEP.

The weakness in TLS is due only to RC4 and its inexcusable flaws: statistical biases, or non-randomness, which we know is a total deal breaker for a
stream cipher. For example, the second keystream byte produced by RC4 is
zero, with a probability of $1/128$, whereas it should be $1/256$ ideally. (Recall
that a byte can take 256 values from 0 to 255; hence, a truly random byte
is zero with a chance of $1/256$.) Crazier still is the fact that most experts
continued to trust RC4 as late as 2013, even though its statistical biases have
been known since 2001.

RC4's known statistical biases should have been enough to ditch the
cipher altogether, even if we didn't know how to exploit the biases to compromise actual applications. In TLS, RC4's flaws weren't publicly exploited
until 2011, but the NSA allegedly managed to exploit RC4's weaknesses to
compromise TLS's RC4 connections well before then.

As it turned out, not only was RC4's second keystream byte biased, but all of the first 256 bytes were biased as well. In 2011, researchers found that the probability that one of those bytes comes to zero equals $1/256 + c/256^2$, for some constant, c, taking values between 0.24 and 1.34. It's not just for the byte zero but for other byte values as well. The amazing thing about RC4 is that it fails where even many noncryptographic PRNGs succeed—namely, at producing uniformly distributed pseudorandom bytes (that is, where each of the 256 bytes has a chance of $1/256$ of showing up).

Even the weakest attack model can be used to exploit RC4's flawed TLS implementation: basically, you collect ciphertexts and look for the plaintext, not the key. But there's a caveat: you'll need many ciphertexts, encrypting *the same plaintext* several times using different secret keys. This attack model is sometimes called the *broadcast model*, because it's akin to broadcasting the same message to multiple recipients.

For example, say you want to decrypt the plaintext byte P_1 given many ciphertext bytes obtained by intercepting the different ciphertexts of the same message. The first four ciphertext bytes will therefore look like this:

$$C_1^2 = P_1 \oplus KS_1^2$$
$$C_1^3 = P_1 \oplus KS_1^3$$
$$C_1^4 = P_1 \oplus KS_1^4$$

Because of RC4's bias, keystream bytes KS_1^i are more likely to be zero than any other byte value. Therefore, C_1^i bytes are more likely to be equal to P_1 than to any other value. In order to determine P_1 given the C_1^i bytes, you simply count the number of occurrences of each byte value and return the most frequent one as P_1. However, because the statistical bias is very small, you'll need millions of values to get it right with any certainty.

The attack generalizes to recover more than one plaintext byte and to exploit more than one biased value (zero here). The algorithm just becomes a bit more complicated. However, this attack is hard to put into practice because it needs to collect many ciphertexts encrypting the same plaintext but using different keys. For example, the attack can't break all TLS-protected connections that use RC4 because you need to trick the server into encrypting the same plaintext to many different recipients, or many times to the same recipient with different keys.

Salsa20

Salsa20 is a simple, software-oriented cipher optimized for modern CPUs that has been implemented in numerous protocols and libraries, along with its variant, ChaCha. Its designer, respected cryptographer Daniel J. Bernstein, submitted Salsa20 to the eSTREAM competition in 2005 and won a place in eSTREAM's software portfolio. Salsa20's simplicity and speed have made it popular among developers.

Salsa20 is a counter-based stream cipher—it generates its keystream by repeatedly processing a counter incremented for each block. As you can see in Figure 5-10, the *Salsa20 core* algorithm transforms a 512-bit block using a key (*K*), a nonce (*N*), and a counter value (*Ctr*). Salsa20 then adds the result to the original value of the block to produce a *keystream block*. (If the algorithm were to return the core's permutation directly as an output, Salsa20 would be totally insecure, because it could be inverted. The final addition of the initial secret state *K* || *N* || *Ctr* makes the transform key-to-keystream-block non-invertible.)

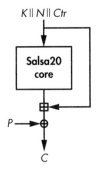

Figure 5-10: Salsa20's encryption scheme for a 512-bit plaintext block

The Quarter-Round Function

Salsa20's core permutation uses a function called *quarter-round* (**QR**) to transform four 32-bit words (*a*, *b*, *c*, and *d*), as shown here:

$$b = b \oplus \left[(a + d) <<< 7 \right]$$
$$c = c \oplus \left[(b + a) <<< 9 \right]$$
$$d = d \oplus \left[(c + b) <<< 13 \right]$$
$$a = a \oplus \left[(d + c) <<< 18 \right]$$

These four lines are computed from top to bottom, meaning that the new value of *b* depends on *a* and *d*, the new value of *c* depends on *a* and on the new value of *b* (and thus *d* as well), and so on.

The operation <<< is wordwise left-rotation by the specified number of bits, which can be any value between 1 and 31 (for 32-bit words). For example, <<< 8 rotates a word's bits of eight positions toward the left, as shown in these examples:

$$0x01234567 <<< 8 = 0x23456701$$
$$0x01234567 <<< 16 = 0x45670123$$
$$0x01234567 <<< 22 = 0x59c048d1$$

Transforming Salsa20's 512-bit State

Salsa20's core permutation transforms a 512-bit internal state viewed as a 4 × 4 array of 32-bit words. Figure 5-11 shows the initial state, using a key of eight words (256 bits), a nonce of two words (64 bits), a counter of two words (64 bits), and four fixed constant words (128 bits) that are identical for each encryption/decryption and all blocks.

To transform the initial 512-bit state, Salsa20 first applies the **QR** transform to all four columns independently (known as the *column-round*) and then to all four rows independently (the *row-round*), as shown in Figure 5-12. The sequence column-round/row-round is called a *double-round*. Salsa20 repeats 10 double-rounds, for 20 rounds in total, thus the *20* in *Salsa20*.

c_0	k_0	k_1	k_2
k_3	c_1	v_0	v_1
t_0	t_1	c_2	k_4
k_5	k_6	k_7	c_3

Figure 5-11: The initialization of Salsa20's state

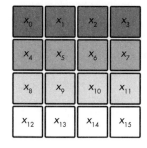
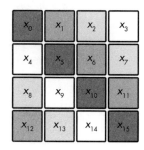

Figure 5-12: Columns and rows transformed by Salsa20's quarter-round (QR) function

The **column-round** transforms the four columns like so:

$$\mathbf{QR}\left(x_0, x_4, x_8, x_{12}\right)$$
$$\mathbf{QR}\left(x_1, x_5, x_9, x_{13}\right)$$
$$\mathbf{QR}\left(x_2, x_6, x_{10}, x_{14}\right)$$
$$\mathbf{QR}\left(x_3, x_7, x_{11}, x_{15}\right)$$

The **row-round** transforms the rows by doing the following:

$$\mathbf{QR}\left(x_0, x_1, x_2, x_3\right)$$
$$\mathbf{QR}\left(x_5, x_6, x_7, x_4\right)$$
$$\mathbf{QR}\left(x_{10}, x_{11}, x_8, x_9\right)$$
$$\mathbf{QR}\left(x_{15}, x_{12}, x_{13}, x_{14}\right)$$

Notice that in a column-round, each **QR** takes x_i arguments ordered from the top to the bottom line, whereas a row-round's **QR** takes as a first argument the words on the diagonal (as shown in the array on the right in Figure 5-12) rather than words from the first column.

Evaluating Salsa20

Listing 5-3 shows Salsa20's initial states for the first and second blocks when initialized with an all-zero key (00 bytes) and an all-one nonce (ff bytes). These two states differ in only one bit, in the counter, as shown in bold: specifically, 0 for the first block and 1 for the second.

```
61707865 00000000 00000000 00000000      61707865 00000000 00000000 00000000
00000000 3320646e ffffffff ffffffff      00000000 3320646e ffffffff ffffffff
00000000 00000000 79622d32 00000000      00000001 00000000 79622d32 00000000
00000000 00000000 00000000 6b206574      00000000 00000000 00000000 6b206574
```

Listing 5-3: Salsa20's initial states for the first two blocks with an all-zero key and an all-one nonce

Yet, despite only a one-bit difference, the respective internal states after 10 double-rounds are totally different from each other, as Listing 5-4 shows.

```
e98680bc f730ba7a 38663ce0 5f376d93      1ba4d492 c14270c3 9fb05306 ff808c64
85683b75 a56ca873 26501592 64144b6d      b49a4100 f5d8fbbd 614234a0 e20663d1
6dcb46fd 58178f93 8cf54cfe cfdc27d7      12e1e116 6a61bc8f 86f01bcb 2efead4a
68bbe09e 17b403a1 38aa1f27 54323fe0      77775a13 d17b99d5 eb773f5b 2c3a5e7d
```

Listing 5-4: The states from Listing 5-3 after 10 Salsa20 double-rounds

But remember, even though word values in the keystream block may look random, we've seen that it's far from a guarantee of security. RC4's output looks random, but it has blatant biases. Fortunately, Salsa20 is much more secure than RC4 and doesn't have statistical biases.

Differential Cryptanalysis

To demonstrate why Salsa20 is more secure than RC4, let's have a look at the basics of *differential cryptanalysis*, the study of the differences between states rather than their actual values. For example, the two initial states in Figure 5-13 differ by one bit in the counter, or by the word x_8 in the Salsa20 state array. The bitwise difference between these two states is thus shown in this array:

```
00000000 00000000 00000000 00000000
00000000 00000000 00000000 00000000
00000001 00000000 00000000 00000000
00000000 00000000 00000000 00000000
```

The difference between the two states is actually the XOR of these states. The 1 bit shown in bold corresponds to a 1-bit difference between the two states. In the XOR of the two states, any nonzero bits indicate differences.

To see how fast changes propagate in the initial state as a result of Salsa20's core algorithm, let's look at the difference between two states throughout the rounds iteration. After one round, the difference propagates across the first column to two of the three other words in that column:

```
80040003 00000000 00000000 00000000
00000000 00000000 00000000 00000000
00000001 00000000 00000000 00000000
00002000 00000000 00000000 00000000
```

After two rounds, differences further propagate across the rows that already include a difference, which is all but the second row. At this point the differences between the states are rather sparse; not many bits have changed within a word as shown here:

```
9ed7eb7f 060002c0 18028b0c 57ca83c0
00000000 00000000 00000000 00000000
00000001 0000e000 801c0006 00000000
00002000 00400000 04000008 0060f300
```

After three rounds, the differences between the states become more dense, though the many zero nibbles indicate that many bit positions are still not affected by the initial difference:

```
3ab3c25d 9f40a5c9 10070e30 07bd03c0
db1ee2ce 43ee9401 21a702c3 48fd800c
403c1e72 00034003 4dc843be 700b8857
5625b75b 09c00e00 06000348 23f712d4
```

After four rounds, differences look random to a human observer, and they are also almost random statistically as well, as shown here:

```
d93bed6d a267bf47 760c2f9f 4a41d54b
0e03d792 7340e010 119e6a00 e90186af
7fa9617e b6aca0d7 4f6e9a4a 564b34fd
98be796d 64908d32 4897f7ca a684a2df
```

So after only four rounds, a single difference propagates to most of the bits in the 512-bit state. In cryptography, this is called *full diffusion*.

We've seen that differences propagate quickly throughout Salsa20 rounds. But not only do differences propagate across all states, they also do so according to complex equations that make future differences hard to predict because highly *nonlinear* relations drive the state's evolution, thanks to the mix of XOR, addition, and rotation. If only XORs were used, we'd still have many differences propagating, but the process would be linear and therefore insecure.

Attacking Salsa20/8

Salsa20 makes 20 rounds by default, but it's sometimes used with only 12 rounds, in a version called Salsa20/12, to make it faster. Although Salsa20/12 uses eight fewer rounds than Salsa20, it's still significantly stronger than the weaker Salsa20/8, another version with eight rounds, which is more rarely used.

Breaking Salsa20 should ideally take 2^{256} operations, thanks to its use of a 256-bit key. If the key can be recovered by performing any fewer than 2^{256} operations, the cipher is in theory broken. That's exactly the case with Salsa20/8.

The attack on Salsa20/8 (published in the 2008 paper *New Features of Latin Dances: Analysis of Salsa, ChaCha, and Rumba*, of which I'm a co-author, and for which we won a cryptanalysis prize from Daniel J. Bernstein) exploits a statistical bias in Salsa's core algorithm after four rounds to recover the key of eight-round Salsa20. In reality, this is mostly a theoretical attack: we estimate its complexity at 2^{251} operations of the core function—impossible, but less so than breaking the expected 2^{256} complexity.

The attack exploits not only a bias over the first four rounds of Salsa20/8, but also a property of the last four rounds: knowing the nonce, N, and the counter, Ctr (refer back to Figure 5-10), the only value needed to invert the computation from the keystream back to the initial state is the key, K. But as shown in Figure 5-13, if you only know some part of K, you can partially invert the computation up until the fourth round and observe some bits of that intermediate state—including the biased bit! You'll only observe the bias if you have the correct guess of the partial key; hence, the bias serves as an indicator that you've got the correct key.

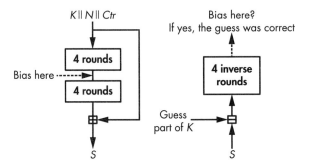

Figure 5-13: The principle of the attack on Salsa20/8

In the actual attack on Salsa20/8, in order to determine the correct guess, we need to guess 220 bits of the key, and we need 2^{31} pairs of keystream blocks, all with the same specific difference in the nonce. Once we've singled out the correct 220 bits, we simply need to brute-force 36 bits. The brute-forcing takes 2^{36} operations, a computation that dwarfs the unrealistic $2^{220} \times 2^{31} = 2^{251}$ trials needed to find the 220 bits to complete the first part of the attack.

How Things Can Go Wrong

Alas, many things can go wrong with stream ciphers, from brittle, insecure designs to strong algorithms incorrectly implemented. I'll explore each category of potential problems in the following sections.

Nonce Reuse

The most common failure seen with stream ciphers is an amateur mistake: it occurs when a nonce is reused more than once with the same key. This produces identical keystreams, allowing you to break the encryption by XORing two ciphertexts together. The keystream then vanishes, and you're left with the XOR of the two plaintexts.

For example, older versions of Microsoft Word and Excel used a unique nonce for each document, but the nonce wasn't changed once the document was modified. As a result, the clear and encrypted text of an older version of a document could be used to decrypt later encrypted versions. If even Microsoft made this kind of blunder, you can imagine how large the problem might be.

Certain stream ciphers designed in the 2010s tried to mitigate the risk of nonce reuse by building "misuse-resistant" constructions, or ciphers that remain secure even if a nonce is used twice. However, achieving this level of security comes with a performance penalty, as we'll see in Chapter 8 with the SIV mode.

Broken RC4 Implementation

Though it's already weak, RC4 can become even weaker if you blindly optimize its implementation. For example, consider the following entry in the 2007 Underhanded C Contest, an informal competition where programmers write benign-looking code that actually includes a malicious function.

Here's how it works. The naive way to implement the line swap(S[i], S[j]) in RC4's algorithm is to do the following, as expressed in this Python code:

```
buf = S[i]
S[i] = S[j]
S[j] = buf
```

This way of swapping two variables obviously works, but you need to create a new variable, buf. To avoid this, programmers often use the *XOR-swap* trick, shown here, to swap the values of the variables x and y:

```
x = x ⊕ y
y = x ⊕ y
x = x ⊕ y
```

This trick works because the second line sets y to x $\oplus$ y $\oplus$ y = x, and the third line sets x to x $\oplus$ y $\oplus$ x $\oplus$ y $\oplus$ y = y. Using this trick to implement RC4 gives the implementation shown in Listing 5-5 (adapted from Wagner and Biondi's program submitted to the Underhanded C Contest, and online at *http://www.underhanded-c.org/_page_id_16.html*).

```
# define TOBYTE(x) (x) & 255
# define SWAP(x,y) do { x^=y; y^=x; x^=y; } while (0)
```

```
static unsigned char S[256];
static int i=0, j=0;

void init(char *passphrase) {
    int passlen = strlen(passphrase);
    for (i=0; i<256; i++)
        S[i] = i;
    for (i=0; i<256; i++) {
        j = TOBYTE(j + S[TOBYTE(i)] + passphrase[j % passlen]);
        SWAP(S[TOBYTE(i)], S[j]);
    }
    i = 0; j = 0;
}

unsigned char encrypt_one_byte(unsigned char c) {
    int k;
    i = TOBYTE(i+1);
    j = TOBYTE(j + S[i]);
    SWAP(S[i], S[j]);
    k = TOBYTE(S[i] + S[j]);
    return c ^ S[k];
}
```

Listing 5-5: Incorrect C implementation of RC4, due to its use of an XOR swap

Now stop reading, and try to spot the problem with the XOR swap in Listing 5-5.

Things will go south when i = j. Instead of leaving the state unchanged, the XOR swap will set S[i] to S[i] ⊕ S[i] = 0. In effect, a byte of the state will be set to zero each time i equals j in the key schedule or during encryption, ultimately leading to an all-zero state and thus to an all-zero keystream. For example, after 68KB of data have been processed, most of the bytes in the 256-byte state are zero, and the output keystream looks like this:

00 00 00 00 00 00 00 53 53 00 00 00 00 00 00 00 00 00 00 00 00 13 13 00 5c 00 a5 00 00 . . .

The lesson here is to refrain from over-optimizing your crypto implementations. Clarity and confidence always trump performance in cryptography.

Weak Ciphers Baked Into Hardware

When a cryptosystem fails to be secure, some systems can quickly respond by silently updating the affected software remotely (as with some pay-TV systems) or by releasing a new version and prompting the users to upgrade (as with mobile applications). Some other systems are not so lucky and need to stick to the compromised cryptosystem for a while before upgrading to a secure version, as is the case with certain satellite phones.

In the early 2000s, US and European telecommunication standardization institutes (TIA and ETSI) jointly developed two standards for satellite phone (satphone) communications. Satphones are like mobile phones, except that their signal goes through satellites rather than terrestrial stations. The advantage is that you can use them pretty much everywhere in the world. Their downsides are the price, quality, latency, and, as it turns out, security.

GMR-1 and GMR-2 are the two satphone standards adopted by most commercial vendors, such as Thuraya and Inmarsat. Both include stream ciphers to encrypt voice communications. GMR-1's cipher is hardware oriented, with a combination of four LFSRs, similar to A5/2, the deliberately insecure cipher in the 2G mobile standard aimed at non-Western countries. GMR-2's cipher is software oriented, with an 8-byte state and the use of S-boxes. Both stream ciphers are insecure, and will only protect users against amateurs, not against state agencies.

This story should remind us that stream ciphers used to be easier to break than block ciphers and that they're easier to sabotage. Why? Well, if you design a weak stream cipher on purpose, when the flaw is found, you can still blame it on the weakness of stream ciphers and deny any malicious intent.

Further Reading

To learn more about stream ciphers, begin with the archives of the eSTREAM competition at *http://www.ecrypt.eu.org/stream/project.html*, where you'll find hundreds of papers on stream ciphers, including details of more than 30 candidates and many attacks. Some of the most interesting attacks are the correlation attacks, algebraic attacks, and cube attacks. See in particular the work of Courtois and Meier for the first two attack types and that of Dinur and Shamir for cube attacks.

For more information on RC4, see the work of Paterson and his team at *http://www.isg.rhul.ac.uk/tls/* on the security of RC4 as used in TLS and WPA. Also see Spritz, the RC4-like cipher created in 2014 by Rivest, who designed RC4 in the 1980s.

Salsa20's legacy deserves your attention, too. The stream cipher ChaCha is similar to Salsa20, but with a slightly different core permutation that was later used in the hash function BLAKE, as you'll see in Chapter 6. These algorithms all leverage Salsa20's software implementation techniques using parallelized instructions, as discussed at *https://cr.yp.to/snuffle.html*.

6

HASH FUNCTIONS

Hash functions—such as MD5, SHA-1, SHA-256, SHA-3, and BLAKE2—comprise the cryptographer's Swiss Army Knife: they are used in digital signatures, public-key encryption, integrity verification, message authentication, password protection, key agreement protocols, and many other cryptographic protocols. Whether you're encrypting an email, sending a message on your mobile phone, connecting to an HTTPS website, or connecting to a remote machine through IPSec or SSH, there's a hash function somewhere under the hood.

Hash functions are by far the most versatile and ubiquitous of all crypto algorithms. There are many examples of their use in the real world: cloud storage systems use them to identify identical files and to detect modified files; the Git revision control system uses them to identify files in a repository; host-based intrusion detection systems (HIDS) use them to detect modified files; network-based intrusion detection systems (NIDS) use hashes to detect known-malicious data going through a network; forensic analysts use hash values to prove that digital artifacts have not been modified; Bitcoin uses a hash function in its proof-of-work systems—and there are many more.

Unlike stream ciphers, which create a long output from a short one, hash functions take a long input and produce a short output, called a *hash value* or *digest* (see Figure 6-1).

Figure 6-1: A hash function's input and output

This chapter revolves around two main topics. First, security: what does it mean for a hash function to be secure? To that end, I introduce two essential notions—namely, collision resistance and preimage resistance. The second big topic revolves around hash functions construction. We look at the high-level techniques used by modern hash functions and then review the internals of the most common hash functions: SHA-1, SHA-2, SHA-3, and BLAKE2. Lastly, we see how secure hash functions can behave insecurely if misused.

NOTE   *Do not confuse cryptographic hash functions with* noncryptographic *ones. Noncryptographic hash functions are used in data structures such as hash tables or to detect accidental errors, and they provide no security whatsoever. For example, cyclic redundancy checks (CRCs) are noncryptographic hashes used to detect accidental modifications of a file.*

Secure Hash Functions

The notion of security for hash functions is different from what we've seen thus far. Whereas ciphers protect data confidentiality in an effort to guarantee that data sent in the clear can't be read, hash functions protect data integrity in an effort to guarantee that data—whether sent in the clear or encrypted—hasn't been modified. If a hash function is secure, two distinct pieces of data should always have different hashes. A file's hash can thus serve as its identifier.

Consider the most common application of a hash function: *digital signatures*, or just *signatures*. When digital signatures are used, applications process the hash of the message to be signed rather than the message itself, as shown in Figure 6-2. The hash acts as an identifier for the message. If even a single bit is changed in the mes-

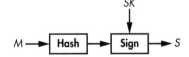

Figure 6-2: A hash function in a digital signature scheme. The hash acts as a proxy for the message.

sage, the hash of the message will be totally different. The hash function thus helps ensure that the message has not been modified. Signing a message's hash is as secure as signing the message itself, and signing a short hash of, say, 256 bits is much faster than signing a message that may be very large. In fact, most signature algorithms can only work on short inputs such as hash values.

Unpredictability Again

All of the cryptographic strength of hash functions stems from the unpredictability of their outputs. Take the 256-bit hexadecimal values shown next; these hashes are computed using the NIST standard hash function SHA-256 with the ASCII letters a, b, and c as inputs. As you can see, though the values a, b, and c differ by only one or two bits (a is the bit sequence 01100001, b is 01100010, and c is 01100011), their hash values are completely different.

```
SHA-256("a") = 87428fc522803d31065e7bce3cf03fe475096631e5e07bbd7a0fde60c4cf25c7
SHA-256("b") = a63d8014dba891345b30174df2b2a57efbb65b4f9f09b98f245d1b3192277ece
SHA-256("c") = edeaaff3f1774ad2888673770c6d64097e391bc362d7d6fb34982ddf0efd18cb
```

Given only these three hashes, it would be impossible to predict the value of the SHA-256 hash of d or any of its bits. Why? Because hash values of a secure hash function are *unpredictable.* A secure hash function should be like a black box that returns a random string each time it receives an input.

The general, theoretical definition of a secure hash function is that it behaves like a truly random function (sometimes called a *random oracle*). Specifically, a secure hash function shouldn't have any property or pattern that a random function wouldn't have. This definition is helpful for theoreticians, but in practice we need more specific notions: namely, preimage resistance and collision resistance.

Preimage Resistance

A *preimage* of a given hash value, H, is any message, M, such that **Hash**$(M) = H$. Preimage *resistance* describes the security guarantee that given a random hash value, an attacker will never find a preimage of that hash value. Indeed, hash functions are sometimes called *one-way functions* because you can go from the message to its hash, but not the other way.

First, note that a hash function can't be inverted, even given unlimited computing power. For example, suppose that I hash some message using the SHA-256 hash function and get this 256-bit hash value:

```
f67a58184cef99d6dfc3045f08645e844f2837ee4bfcc6c949c9f7674367adfd
```

Even given unlimited computing power, you would never be able to determine *the* message that I picked to produce this particular hash, since there are many messages hashing to the same value. You would therefore find *some* messages that produce this hash value (possibly including the one I picked), but would be unable to determine the message that I used.

For example, there are 2^{256} possible values of a 256-bit hash (a typical length with hash functions used in practice), but there are many more values of, say, 1024-bit messages (namely, 2^{1024} possible values). Therefore, it follows that, on average, each possible 256-bit hash value will have $2^{1024} / 2^{256} = 2^{1024 - 256} = 2^{768}$ preimages of 1024 bits each.

In practice, we must be sure that it is practically impossible to find *any* message that maps to a given hash value, not just the message that was used, which is what preimage resistance actually stands for. Specifically, we speak of first-preimage and second-preimage resistance. *First-preimage resistance* (or just *preimage resistance*) describes cases where it is practically impossible to find a message that hashes to a given value. *Second-preimage resistance*, on the other hand, describes the case that when given a message, M_1, it's practically impossible to find another message, M_2, that hashes to the same value that M_1 does.

The Cost of Preimages

Given a hash function and a hash value, you can search for first preimages by trying different messages until one hits the target hash. You would do this using an algorithm similar to find-preimage() in Listing 6-1.

```
find-preimage(H) {
    repeat {
        M = random_message()
        if Hash(M) == H then return M
    }
}
```

Listing 6-1: The optimal preimage search algorithm for a secure hash function

In Listing 6-1, random_message() generates a random message (say, a random 1024-bit value). Obviously, find-preimage() will never complete if the hash's bit length, n, is large enough, because it will take on average 2^n attempts before finding a preimage. That's a hopeless situation when working with $n = 256$, as in modern hashes like SHA-256 and BLAKE2.

Why Second-Preimage Resistance Is Weaker

I claim that if you can find first preimages, you can find second preimages as well (for the same hash function). As proof, if the algorithm solve-preimage() returns a preimage of a given hash value, you can use the algorithm in Listing 6-2 to find a second preimage of some message, M.

```
solve-second-preimage(M) {
    H = Hash(M)
    return solve-preimage(H)
}
```

Listing 6-2: How to find second preimages if you can find first preimages

That is, you'll find the second preimage by seeing it as a preimage problem and applying the preimage attack. It follows that any second-preimage resistant hash function is also preimage resistant. (Were it not, it wouldn't be second preimage resistant either, per the preceding solve-second-preimage algorithm.) In other words, the best attack we can use to find second preimages is almost identical to the best attack we can use to find first preimages (unless the hash function has some defect that allows for more efficient attacks). Also note that a preimage search attack is essentially the same as a key recovery attack on a block cipher or stream cipher—namely, a brute-force search for a single magic value.

Collision Resistance

Whatever hash function you choose to use, collisions will inevitably exist due to the *pigeonhole principle*, which states that if you have *m* holes and *n* pigeons to put into those holes, and if *n* is greater than *m*, at least one hole must contain more than one pigeon.

NOTE   *This can be generalized to other items and containers as well. For example, any 27-word sequence in the US Constitution includes at least two words that start with the same letter. In the world of hash functions, holes are the hash values, and pigeons are the messages. Because we know that there are many more possible messages than hash values, collisions* must *exist.*

However, despite the inevitable, collisions should be as hard to find as the original message in order for a hash function to be considered *collision resistant*—in other words, attackers shouldn't be able to find two distinct messages that hash to the same value.

The notion of collision resistance is related to the notion of second-preimage resistance: if you can find second preimages for a hash function, you can also find collisions, as shown in Listing 6-3.

```
solve-collision() {
    M = random_message()
    return (M, solve-second-preimage(M))
}
```

Listing 6-3: The naive collision search algorithm

That is, any collision-resistant hash is also second preimage resistant. If this were not the case, there would be an efficient solve-second-preimage algorithm that could be used to break collision resistance.

Finding Collisions

It's faster to find collisions than it is to find preimages, on the order of about $2^{n/2}$ operations instead of 2^n, thanks to the *birthday attack*, whose key idea is the following: given *N* messages and as many hash values, you can produce a total of $N \times (N-1) / 2$ potential collisions by considering each *pair* of two hash values (a number of the same order of magnitude as N^2). It's called *birthday* attack because it's usually illustrated using the so-called *birthday paradox*, or the fact that a group of only 23 persons will include two persons having the same birth date with probability 1/2.

$N \times (N - 1) / 2$ is the count of pairs of two distinct messages, where we divide by 2 because we view (M_1, M_2) and (M_2, M_1) as a same pair. In other words, we don't care about the ordering.

For the sake of comparison, in the case of a preimage search, N messages only get you N candidate preimages, whereas the same N messages give approximately N^2 potential collisions, as just discussed. With N^2 instead of N, we say that there are *quadratically* more chances to find a solution. The complexity of the search is in turn quadratically lower: in order to find a collision, you'll need to use the square root of 2^n messages; that is, $2^{n/2}$ instead of 2^n.

The Naive Birthday Attack

Here's the simplest way to carry out the birthday attack in order to find collisions:

1. Compute $2^{n/2}$ hashes of $2^{n/2}$ arbitrarily chosen messages and store all the message/hash pairs in a list.

2. Sort the list with respect to the hash value to move any identical hash values next to each other.

3. Search the sorted list to find two consecutive entries with the same hash value.

Unfortunately, this method requires a lot of memory (enough to store $2^{n/2}$ message/hash pairs), and sorting lots of elements slows down the search, requiring about $n2^n$ basic operations on average using even the quicksort algorithm.

Low-Memory Collision Search: The Rho Method

The *Rho method* is an algorithm for finding collisions that, unlike the naive birthday attack, requires only a small amount of memory. It works like this:

1. Given a hash function with n-bit hash values, pick some random hash value (H_1), and define $H_1 = H'_1$.

2. Compute $H_2 = \textbf{Hash}(H_1)$, and $H'_2 = \textbf{Hash}(\textbf{Hash}(H'_1))$; that is, in the first case we apply the hash function once, while in the second case we apply it twice.

3. Iterate the process and compute $H_{i+1} = \textbf{Hash}(H_i)$, $H'_{i+1} = \textbf{Hash}(\textbf{Hash}(H'_i))$, until you reach i such that $H_{i+1} = H'_{i+1}$.

Figure 6-3 will help you to visualize the attack, where an arrow from, say, H_1 to H_2 means $H_2 = \textbf{Hash}(H_1)$. Observe that the sequence of H_is eventually enters a loop, also called a *cycle*, which resembles the Greek letter rho (ρ) in shape. The cycle starts at H_5 and is characterized by the collision $\textbf{Hash}(H_4) = \textbf{Hash}(H_{10}) = H_5$. The key observation here is that in order to find a collision, you simply need to find such a cycle. The algorithm above allows an attacker to detect the position of the cycle, and therefore to find the collision.

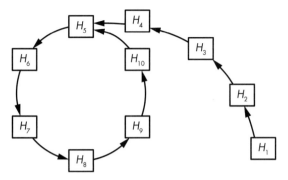

Figure 6-3: The structure of the Rho hash function. Each arrow represents an evaluation of the hash function. The cycle beginning at H_5 corresponds to a collision, **Hash**(H_4) = **Hash**(H_{10}) = H_5.

Advanced collision-finding techniques work by first detecting the start of the cycle and then finding the collision, without storing numerous values in memory and without needing to sort a long list. The Rho method takes about $2^{n/2}$ operations to succeed. Indeed, Figure 6-3 has many fewer hash values than would an actual function with digests of 256 bits or more. On average, the cycle and the tail (the part that extends from H_1 to H_5 in Figure 6-3) each include about $2^{n/2}$ hash values, where n is the bit length of the hash values. Therefore, you'll need at least $2^{n/2} + 2^{n/2}$ evaluations of the hash to find a collision.

Building Hash Functions

In the 1980s, cryptographers realized that the simplest way to hash a message is to split it into chunks and process each chunk consecutively using a similar algorithm. This strategy is called *iterative hashing*, and it comes in two main forms:

- Iterative hashing using a *compression function* that transforms an input to a *smaller output*, as shown in Figure 6-4. This technique is also known as the *Merkle–Damgård* construction (named after the cryptographers Ralph Merkle and Ivan Damgård).
- Iterative hashing using a function that transforms an input to an output of the *same size*, such that any two different inputs give two different outputs (that is, a *permutation*), as shown in Figure 6-7. Such functions are called *sponge functions*.

We'll now discuss how these constructions actually work and how compression functions look in practice.

Compression-Based Hash Functions: The Merkle–Damgård Construction

All hash functions developed from the 1980s through the 2010s are based on the Merkle–Damgård (M–D) construction: MD4, MD5, SHA-1, and the SHA-2 family, as well as the lesser-known RIPEMD and Whirlpool hash functions. The M–D construction isn't perfect, but it is simple and has proven to be secure enough for many applications.

NOTE *In MD4, MD5, and RIPEMD, the* MD *stands for* message digest, *not* Merkle–Damgård.

To hash a message, the M–D construction splits the message into blocks of identical size and mixes these blocks with an internal state using a compression function, as shown in Figure 6-4. Here, H_0 is the initial value (denoted IV) of the internal state, the values H_1, H_2, . . . are called the *chaining values*, and the final value of the internal state is the message's hash value.

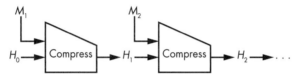

Figure 6-4: The Merkle–Damgård construction using a compression function called Compress

The message blocks are usually 512 or 1024 bits, but they can, in principle, be of any size. However, the block length is fixed for a given hash function. For example, SHA-256 works with 512-bit blocks and SHA-512 works with 1024-bit blocks.

Padding Blocks

What happens if you want to hash a message that can't be split into a sequence of complete blocks? For example, if blocks are 512 bits, then a 520-bit message will consist of one 512-bit block plus 8 bits. In such a case, the M–D construction forms the last block as follows: take the chunk of bits left (8 in our example), append 1 bit, then append 0 bits, and finally append the length of the original message, encoded on a fixed number of bits. This padding trick guarantees that any two distinct messages will give a distinct sequence of blocks, and thus a distinct hash value.

For example, if you hash the 8-bit string 10101010 using SHA-256, which is a hash function with 512-bit message blocks, the first and only block will appear, in bits, as follows:

10101010 *1000000000000000* ( ) *000000000000* 1000

Here, the message bits are the first eight bits (10101010), and the padding bits are all the subsequent bits (shown in italic). The *1000* at the end of the block (underlined) is the message's length, or 8 encoded in binary. The padding thus produces a 512-bit message composed of a single 512-bit block, ready to be processed by SHA-256's compression function.

Security Guarantees

The Merkle–Damgård construction is essentially a way to turn a secure compression function that takes small, fixed-length inputs into a secure hash function that takes inputs of arbitrary lengths. If a compression function is preimage and collision resistant, then a hash function built on it using the M–D construction will also be preimage and collision resistant. This is true because any successful preimage attack for the M–D hash could be turned into a successful preimage attack for the compression function, as Merkle and Damgård both demonstrated in their 1989 papers (see "Further Reading" on page 126). The same is true for collisions: an attacker can't break the hash's collision resistance without breaking the underlying compression function's collision resistance; hence, the security of the latter guarantees the security of the hash.

Note that the converse argument is wrong, because a collision for the compression function doesn't necessarily give a collision for the hash. A collision, $\mathbf{Compress}(X, M_1) = \mathbf{Compress}(Y, M_2)$, for chaining values X and Y, both distinct from H_0, won't get you a collision for the hash because you can't plug the collision into the iterative chain of hashes—except if one of the chaining values happens to be X and the other Y, but that's unlikely to happen.

Finding Multicollisions

A *multicollision* occurs when a set of three or more messages hash to the same value. For example, the triplet (X, Y, Z), such that $\mathbf{Hash}(X) = \mathbf{Hash}(Y) = \mathbf{Hash}(Z)$ is called a *3-collision*. Ideally, multicollisions should be much harder to find than collisions, but there is a simple trick for finding them at almost the same cost as that of a single collision. Here's how it works:

1. Find a first collision: $\mathbf{Compress}(H_0, M_{1.1}) = \mathbf{Compress}(H_0, M_{1.2}) = H_1$. Now you have a 2-collision, or two messages hashing to the same value.

2. Find a second collision with H_1 as a starting chaining value: $\mathbf{Compress}(H_1, M_{2.1}) = \mathbf{Compress}(H_1, M_{2.2}) = H_2$. Now you have a 4-collision, with four messages hashing to the same value H_2: $M_{1.1} \parallel M_{2.1}$, $M_{1.1} \parallel M_{2.2}$, $M_{1.2} \parallel M_{2.1}$, and $M_{1.2} \parallel M_{2.2}$.

3. Repeat and find N times a collision, and you'll have 2^N N-block messages hashing to the same value, or a 2^N-collision, at the cost of "only" about $N2^N$ hash computations.

In practice, this trick isn't all that practical because it requires you to find a basic 2-collision in the first place.

Building Compression Functions: The Davies–Meyer Construction

All compression functions used in real hash functions such as SHA-256 and BLAKE2 are based on block ciphers, because that is the simplest way to build a compression function. Figure 6-5 shows the most common of the block cipher–based compression functions, the *Davies–Meyer construction*.

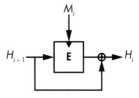

Figure 6-5: The Davies–Meyer construction. The dark triangle shows where the block cipher's key is input.

Given a message block, M_i, and the previous chaining value H_{i-1}, the Davies–Meyer compression function uses a block cipher, $\mathbf{E}$, to compute the new chaining value as

$$H_i = \mathbf{E}(M_i, H_{i-1}) \oplus H_{i-1}$$

The message block M_i acts as the block cipher key, and the chaining value H_{i-1} acts as its plaintext block. As long as the block cipher is secure, the resulting compression function is secure as well as collision and preimage resistant. Without the XOR of the preceding chaining value ($\oplus\, H_{i-1}$), Davies–Meyer would be insecure because you could invert it, going from the new chaining value to the previous one using the block cipher's decryption function.

NOTE   *The Davies–Meyer construction has a surprising property: you can find fixed points, or chaining values, that are unchanged after applying the compression function with a given message block. It suffices to take $H_{i-1} = \mathbf{D}(M_i, 0)$ as a chaining value, where $\mathbf{D}$ is the decryption function corresponding to $\mathbf{E}$. The new chaining value H_i is therefore equal to the original H_{i-1}:*

$$H_i = \mathbf{E}(M_i, H_{i-1}) \oplus H_{i-1} = \mathbf{E}(M_i, \mathbf{D}(M_i, 0)) \oplus \mathbf{D}(M_i, 0)$$
$$= 0 \oplus \mathbf{D}(M_i, 0) = \mathbf{D}(M_i, 0) = H_{i-1}$$

We get $H_i = H_{i-1}$ because plugging the decryption of zero into the encryption function yields zero—the term $\mathbf{E}(M_i, \mathbf{D}(M_i, 0))$—leaving only the $\oplus\, H_{i-1}$ part of the equation in the expression of the compression function's output. You can then find fixed points for the compression functions of the SHA-2 functions, as with the standards MD5 and SHA-1, which are also based on the Davies–Meyer construction. Fortunately, fixed points aren't a security risk.

There are many block cipher–based compression functions other than Davies–Meyer, such as those shown in Figure 6-6, but they are less popular because they're more complex or require the message block to be the same length as the chaining value.

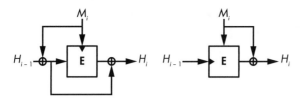

Figure 6-6: Other secure block cipher–based compression function constructions

Permutation-Based Hash Functions: Sponge Functions

After decades of research, cryptographers know everything there is to know about block cipher–based hashing techniques. Still, shouldn't there be a simpler way to hash? Why bother with a block cipher, an algorithm that takes a secret key, when hash functions don't take a secret key? Why not build hash functions with a fixed-key block cipher, a single permutation algorithm?

Those simpler hash functions are called sponge functions, and they use a single permutation instead of a compression function and a block cipher (see Figure 6-7). Instead of using a block cipher to mix message bits with the internal state, sponge functions just do an XOR operation. Sponge functions are not only simpler than Merkle–Damgård functions, they're also more versatile. You will find them used as hash functions and also as deterministic random bit generators, stream ciphers, pseudorandom functions (see Chapter 7), and authenticated ciphers (see Chapter 8). The most famous sponge function is Keccak, also known as SHA-3.

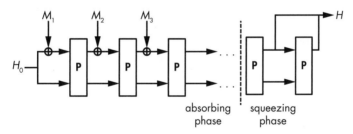

Figure 6-7: The sponge construction

A sponge function works as follows:

1. It XORs the first message block, M_1, to H_0, a predefined initial value of the internal state (for example, the all-zero string). Message blocks are all the same size and smaller than the internal state.

2. A permutation, **P**, transforms the internal state to another value of the same size.

3. It XORs block M_2 and applies **P** again, and then repeats this for the message blocks M_3, M_4, and so on. This is called the *absorbing phase*.

4. After injecting all the message blocks, it applies **P** again and extracts a block of bits from the state to form the hash. (If you need a longer hash, apply **P** again and extract a block.) This is called the *squeezing phase*.

The security of a sponge function depends on the length of its internal state and the length of the blocks. If message blocks are r-bit long and the internal state is w-bit long, then there are $c = w - r$ bits of the internal state that can't be modified by message blocks. The value of c is called a sponge's *capacity*, and the security level guaranteed by the sponge function is $c/2$. For example, to reach 256-bit security with 64-bit message blocks, the internal state should be $w = 2 \times 256 + 64 = 576$ bits. Of course, the security level also depends on the length, n, of the hash value. The complexity of a collision attack is therefore the smallest value between $2^{n/2}$ and $2^{c/2}$, while the complexity of a second preimage attack is the smallest value between 2^n and $2^{c/2}$.

To be secure, the permutation **P** should behave like a random permutation, without statistical bias and without a mathematical structure that would allow an attacker to predict outputs. As in compression function–based hashes, sponge functions also pad messages, but the padding is simpler because it doesn't need to include the message's length. The last message bit is simply followed by a 1 bit and as many zeroes as necessary.

The SHA Family of Hash Functions

The Secure Hash Algorithm (SHA) hash functions are standards defined by NIST for use by non-military federal government agencies in the US. They are considered worldwide standards, and only certain non-US governments opt for their own hash algorithms (such as China's SM3, Russia's Streebog, and Ukraine's Kupyna) for reasons of sovereignty rather than a lack of trust in SHA's security. The US SHAs have been more extensively reviewed by cryptanalysts than the non-US ones.

NOTE *Message Digest 5 (MD5) was the most popular hash function from 1992 until it was broken around 2005, and many applications then switched to one of the SHA hash functions. MD5 processes 512-bit block messages and updates a 128-bit internal state to produce a 128-bit hash, thus providing at best 128-bit preimage security and 64-bit collision security. In 1996, cryptanalysts warned of a collision for MD5's compression function, but their warning went unheeded until 2005 when a team of Chinese cryptanalysts discovered how to compute collisions for the full MD5 hash. As I write this, it takes only seconds to find a collision for MD5, yet many systems still use or support MD5, often for reasons of backward compatibility.*

SHA-1

The SHA-1 standard arose from a failure in the NSA's original SHA-0 hash function. In 1993, NIST standardized the NSA's SHA-0 hash algorithm, but in 1995 the NSA released SHA-1 to fix an unidentified security issue in SHA-0. The reason for the tweak became clear when in 1998 two researchers discovered how to find collisions for SHA-0 in about 2^{60} operations instead of the 2^{80} expected for 160-bit hash functions such as SHA-0 and SHA-1. Later attacks reduced the complexity to around 2^{33} operations, leading to actual collisions in less than an hour for SHA-0.

SHA-1 Internals

SHA-1 combines a Merkle–Damgård hash function with a Davies–Meyer compression function based on a specially crafted block cipher, sometimes called SHACAL. That is, SHA-1 works by iterating the following operation over 512-bit message blocks (M):

$$H = \mathbf{E}(M, H) + H$$

Here, the use of a plus sign (+) rather than $\oplus$ (XOR) is intentional. $\mathbf{E}(M, H)$ and H are viewed as arrays of 32-bit integers, and each two words at a same position are added together: the first 32-bit word of $\mathbf{E}(M, H)$ with the first 32-bit word of H, and so on. The initial value of H is constant for any message, then H is modified as per the above equation, and the final value of H after processing all blocks is returned as the hash of the message.

Once the block cipher is run using the message block as a key and the current 160-bit chaining value as a plaintext block, the 160-bit result is seen as an array of five 32-bit words, each of which is added to its 32-bit counterpart in the initial H value.

Listing 6-4 shows SHA-1's compression function, SHA1-compress():

```
SHA1-compress(H, M) {
    (a0, b0, c0, d0, e0) = H   // parsing H as five 32-bit big endian words
    (a, b, c, d, e) = SHA1-blockcipher(a0, b0, c0, d0, e0, M)
    return (a + a0, b + b0, c + c0, d + d0, e + e0)
}
```

Listing 6-4: SHA-1's compression function

SHA-1's block cipher SHA1-blockcipher(), shown in bold in Listing 6-5, takes a 512-bit message block, M, as a key and transforms the five 32-bit words (a, b, c, d, and e) by iterating 80 steps of a short sequence of operations to replace the word a with a combination of all five words. It then shifts the other words in the array, as in a shift register.

```
SHA1-blockcipher(a, b, c, d, e, M) {
    W = expand(M)
    for i = 0 to 79 {
        new = (a <<< 5) + f(i, b, c, d) + e + K[i] + W[i]
        (a, b, c, d, e) = (new, a, b >>> 2, c, d)
    }
    return (a, b, c, d, e)
}
```

Listing 6-5: SHA-1's block cipher

The expand() function shown in Listing 6-6 creates an array of eighty 32-bit words, *W*, from the 16-word message block by setting *W*'s first 16 words to *M* and the subsequent ones to an XOR combination of previous words, rotated one bit to the left.

```
expand(M) {
    // the 512-bit M is seen as an array of sixteen 32-bit words
    W = empty array of eighty 32-bit words
    for i = 0 to 79 {
        if i < 16 then W[i] = M[i]
        else
            W[i] = (W[i - 3] ⊕ W[i - 8] ⊕ W[i - 14] ⊕ W[i - 16]) <<< 1
    }
    return W
}
```

Listing 6-6: SHA-1's expand() function

The <<< 1 operation in Listing 6-6 is the only difference between the SHA-1 and SHA-0 functions.

Finally, the f() function (see Listing 6-7) in SHA1-blockcipher() is a sequence of basic bitwise logical operations (a Boolean function) that depends on the round number.

```
f(i, b, c, d) {
    if i < 20 then return ((b & c) ⊕ (~b & d))
    if i < 40 then return (b ⊕ c ⊕ d)
    if i < 60 then return ((b & c) ⊕ (b & d) ⊕ (c & d))
    if i < 80 then return (b ⊕ c ⊕ d)
}
```

Listing 6-7: SHA-1's f() function.

The second and fourth Boolean functions in Listing 6-7 simply XOR the three input words together, which is a linear operation. In contrast, the first and third functions use the non-linear & operator (logical AND) to protect against differential cryptanalysis, which as you recall, exploits the predictable propagation of bitwise difference. Without the & operator (in other words, if f() were always b ⊕ c ⊕ d, for example), SHA-1 would be easy to break by tracing patterns within its internal state.

Attacks on SHA-1

Though more secure than SHA-0, SHA-1 is still insecure, which is why the Chrome browser marks websites using SHA-1 in their HTTPS connection as insecure. Although its 160-bit hash should grant it 80-bit collision resistance, in 2005 researchers found weaknesses in SHA-1 and estimated that finding a collision would take approximately 2^{63} calculations. (That number would be 2^{80} if the algorithm were flawless.) A real SHA-1 collision only came twelve years later when after years of cryptanalysis, Marc Stevens and other researchers presented two colliding PDF documents through a joint work with Google researchers (see *https://shattered.io/*).

The upshot is that you should not use SHA-1. As mentioned, internet browsers now mark SHA-1 as insecure, and SHA-1 is no longer recommended by NIST. Use SHA-2 hash functions instead, or BLAKE2 or SHA-3.

SHA-2

SHA-2, the successor to SHA-1, was designed by the NSA and standardized by NIST. SHA-2 is a family of four hash functions: SHA-224, SHA-256, SHA-384, and SHA-512, of which SHA-256 and SHA-512 are the two main algorithms. The three-digit numbers represent the bit lengths of each hash.

SHA-256

The initial motivation behind the development of SHA-2 was to generate longer hashes and thus deliver higher security levels than SHA-1. For example, whereas SHA-1 has 160-bit chaining values, SHA-256 has 256-bit chaining values or eight 32-bit words. Both SHA-1 and SHA-256 have 512-bit message blocks; however, whereas SHA-1 makes 80 rounds, SHA-256 makes 64 rounds, expanding the 16-word message block to a 64-word message block using the expand256() function shown in Listing 6-8.

```
expand256(M) {
    // the 512-bit M is seen as an array of sixteen 32-bit words
    W = empty array of sixty-four 32-bit words
    for i = 0 to 63 {
        if i < 16 then W[i] = M[i]
        else {
            // the ">>" shifts instead of a ">>>" rotates and is not a typo
            s0 = (W[i - 15] >>> 7) ⊕ (W[i - 15] >>> 18) ⊕ (W[i - 15] >> 3)
            s1 = (W[i - 2] >>> 17) ⊕ (W[i - 2] >>> 19) ⊕ (W[i - 2] >> 10)
            W[i] = W[i - 16] + s0 + W[i - 7] + s1
        }
    }
    return W
}
```

Listing 6-8: SHA-256's expand256() function

Note how SHA-2's expand256() message expansion is more complex than SHA-1's expand(), shown previously in Listing 6-6, which in contrast simply performs XORs and a 1-bit rotation. The main loop of SHA-256's compression function is also more complex than that of SHA-1, performing 26 arithmetic operations per iteration compared to 11 for SHA-1. Again, these operations are XORs, logical ANDs, and word rotations.

Other SHA-2 Algorithms

The SHA-2 family includes SHA-224, which is algorithmically identical to SHA-256 except that its initial value is a different set of eight 32-bit words, and its hash value length is 224 bits, instead of 256 bits, and is taken as the first 224 bits of the final chaining value.

The SHA-2 family also includes the algorithms SHA-512 and SHA-384. SHA-512 is similar to SHA-256 except that it works with 64-bit words instead of 32-bit words. As a result, it uses 512-bit chaining values (eight 64-bit words) and ingests 1024-bit message blocks (sixteen 64-bit words), and it makes 80 rounds instead of 64. The compression function is otherwise almost the same as that of SHA-256, though with different rotation distances to cope with the wider word size. (For example, SHA-512 includes the operation a >>> 34, which wouldn't make sense with SHA-256's 32-bit words.) SHA-384 is to SHA-512 what SHA-224 is to SHA-256—namely, the same algorithm but with a different initial value and a final hash truncated to 384 bits.

Security-wise, all four SHA-2 versions have lived up to their promises so far: SHA-256 guarantees 256-bit preimage resistance, SHA-512 guarantees about 256-bit collision resistance, and so on. Still, there is no genuine proof that SHA-2 functions are secure; we're talking about probable security.

That said, after practical attacks on MD5 and on SHA-1, researchers and NIST grew concerned about SHA-2's long-term security due to its similarity to SHA-1, and many believed that attacks on SHA-2 were just a matter of time. As I write this, though, we have yet to see a successful attack on SHA-2. Regardless, NIST developed a backup plan: SHA-3.

The SHA-3 Competition

Announced in 2007, the NIST Hash Function Competition (the official name of the SHA-3 competition) began with a call for submissions and some basic requirements: hash submissions were to be at least as secure and as fast as SHA-2, and they should be able to do at least as much as SHA-2. SHA-3 candidates also shouldn't look too much like SHA-1 and SHA-2 in order to be immune to attacks that would break SHA-1 and potentially SHA-2. By 2008, NIST had received 64 submissions from around the world, including from universities and large corporations (BT, IBM, Microsoft, Qualcomm, and Sony, to name a few). Of these 64 submissions, 51 matched the requirements and entered the first round of the competition.

During the first weeks of the competition, cryptanalysts mercilessly attacked the submissions. In July 2009, NIST announced 14 second-round candidates. After spending 15 months analyzing and evaluating the performance of these candidates, NIST chose five finalists:

BLAKE An enhanced Merkle–Damgård hash whose compression function is based on a block cipher, which is in turn based on the core function of the stream cipher ChaCha, a chain of additions, XORs, and word rotations. BLAKE was designed by a team of academic researchers based in Switzerland and the UK, including myself.

Grøstl An enhanced Merkle–Damgård hash whose compression function uses two permutations (or fixed-key block ciphers) based on the core function of the AES block cipher. Grøstl was designed by a team of seven academic researchers from Denmark and Austria.

JH A tweaked sponge function construction wherein message blocks are injected before and after the permutation rather than just before.

The permutation also performs operations similar to a substitution–permutation block cipher (as discussed in Chapter 4). JH was designed by a cryptographer from a university in Singapore.

Keccak   A sponge function whose permutation performs only bitwise operations. Keccak was designed by a team of four cryptographers working for a semiconductor company based in Belgium and Italy, and included one of the two designers of AES.

Skein   A hash function based on a different mode of operation than Merkle–Damgård, and whose compression function is based on a novel block cipher that uses only integer addition, XOR, and word rotation. Skein was designed by a team of eight cryptographers from academia and industry, all but one of whom is based in the US, including the renowned Bruce Schneier.

After extensive analysis of the five finalists, NIST announced a winner: Keccak. NIST's report rewarded Keccak for its "elegant design, large security margin, good general performance, excellent efficiency in hardware, and its flexibility." Let's see how Keccak works.

Keccak (SHA-3)

One of the reasons that NIST chose Keccak is that it's completely different from SHA-1 and SHA-2. For one thing, it's a sponge function. Keccak's core algorithm is a permutation of a 1600-bit state that ingests blocks of 1152, 1088, 832, or 576 bits, producing hash values of 224, 256, 384, or 512 bits, respectively—the same four lengths produced by SHA-2 hash functions. But unlike SHA-2, SHA-3 uses a single core algorithm rather than two algorithms for all four hash lengths.

Another reason is that Keccak is more than just a hash. The SHA-3 standard document FIPS 202 defines four hashes—SHA3-224, SHA3-256, SHA3-384, and SHA3-512—and two algorithms called SHAKE128 and SHAKE256. (The name *SHAKE* stands for *Secure Hash Algorithm with Keccak*.) These two algorithms are *extendable-output functions (XOFs)*, or hash functions that can produce hashes of variable length, even very long ones. The numbers 128 and 256 represent the security level of each algorithm.

The FIPS 202 standard itself is lengthy and hard to parse, but you'll find open-source implementations that are reasonably fast and make the algorithm easier to understand than the specifications. For example, the MIT-licensed tiny_sha3 (*https://github.com/mjosaarinen/tiny_sha3/*) by Markku-Juhani O. Saarinen, explains Keccak's core algorithm in 19 lines of C, as partially reproduced in Listing 6-9.

```
static void sha3_keccakf(uint64_t st[25], int rounds)
{
    (⊕)
    for (r = 0; r < rounds; r++) {

    ❶ // Theta
        for (i = 0; i < 5; i++)
```

```
                bc[i] = st[i] ^ st[i + 5] ^ st[i + 10] ^ st[i + 15] ^ st[i + 20];

        for (i = 0; i < 5; i++) {
            t = bc[(i + 4) % 5] ^ ROTL64(bc[(i + 1) % 5], 1);
            for (j = 0; j < 25; j += 5)
                st[j + i] ^= t;
        }

❷   // Rho Pi
        t = st[1];
        for (i = 0; i < 24; i++) {
            j = keccakf_piln[i];
            bc[0] = st[j];
            st[j] = ROTL64(t, keccakf_rotc[i]);
            t = bc[0];
        }

❸   // Chi
        for (j = 0; j < 25; j += 5) {
            for (i = 0; i < 5; i++)
                bc[i] = st[j + i];
            for (i = 0; i < 5; i++)
                st[j + i] ^= (~bc[(i + 1) % 5]) & bc[(i + 2) % 5];
        }

❹   // Iota
        st[0] ^= keccakf_rndc[r];
    }
(⊕)
}
```

Listing 6-9: The tiny_sha3 implementation

The tiny_sha3 program implements the permutation, **P**, of Keccak, an invertible transformation of a 1600-bit state viewed as an array of twenty-five 64-bit words. As you review the code, notice that it iterates a series of rounds, where each round consists of four main steps (as marked by ❶, ❷, ❸, and ❹):

- The first step, Theta ❶, includes XORs between 64-bit words or a 1-bit rotated value of the words (the ROTL64(w, 1) operation left-rotates a word w of 1 bit).

- The second step, Rho Pi ❷, includes rotations of 64-bit words by constants hardcoded in the keccakf_rotc[] array.

- The third step, Chi ❸, includes more XORs, but also logical ANDs (the & operator) between 64-bit words. These ANDs are the only non-linear operations in Keccak, and they bring with them cryptographic strength.

- The fourth step, Iota ❹, includes a XOR with a 64-bit constant, hardcoded in the keccakf_rndc[].

These operations provide SHA-3 with a strong permutation algorithm free of any bias or exploitable structure. SHA-3 is the product of more than a decade of research, and hundreds of skilled cryptanalysts have failed to break it. It's unlikely to be broken anytime soon.

The BLAKE2 Hash Function

Security may matter most, but speed comes second. I've seen many cases where a developer wouldn't switch from MD5 to SHA-1 simply because MD5 is faster, or from SHA-1 to SHA-2 because SHA-2 is noticeably slower than SHA-1. Unfortunately, SHA-3 isn't faster than SHA-2, and because SHA-2 is still secure, there are few incentives to upgrade to SHA-3. So how to hash faster than SHA-1 and SHA-2 and be even more secure? The answer lies in the hash function BLAKE2, released after the SHA-3 competition.

NOTE *Full disclosure: I'm a designer of BLAKE2, together with Samuel Neves, Zooko Wilcox-O'Hearn, and Christian Winnerlein.*

BLAKE2 was designed with the following ideas in mind:

- It should be least as secure as SHA-3, if not stronger.
- It should be faster than all previous hash standards, including MD5.
- It should be suited for use in modern applications, and able to hash large amounts of data either as a few large messages or many small ones, with or without a secret key.
- It should be suited for use on modern CPUs supporting parallel computing on multicore systems as well as instruction-level parallelism within a single core.

The outcome of the engineering process is a pair of main hash functions:

- BLAKE2b (or just BLAKE2), optimized for 64-bit platforms, produces digests ranging from 1 to 64 bytes.
- BLAKE2s, optimized for 8- to 32-bit platforms, can produce digests ranging from 1 to 32 bytes.

Each function has a parallel variant that can leverage multiple CPU cores. The parallel counterpart of BLAKE2b, BLAKE2bp, runs on four cores, whereas BLAKE2sp runs on eight cores. The former is the fastest on modern server and laptop CPUs and can hash at close to 2 Gbps on a laptop CPU. In fact, BLAKE2 is the fastest secure hash available today, and its speed and features have made it the most popular non-NIST-standard hash. BLAKE2 is used in countless software applications and has been integrated into major cryptography libraries such as OpenSSL and Sodium.

You can find BLAKE2's specifications and reference code at https://blake2.net/, *and you can download optimized code and libraries from* https://github.com/ BLAKE2/. *The reference code also provides BLAKE2X, an extension of BLAKE2 that can produce hash values of arbitrary length.*

BLAKE2's compression function, shown in Figure 6-8, is a variant of the Davies–Meyer construction that takes parameters as additional input—namely, a *counter* (which ensures that each compression function behaves like a different function) and a *flag* (which indicates whether the compression function is processing the last message block, for increased security).

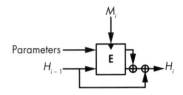

Figure 6-8: BLAKE2's compression function. The two halves of the state are XORed together after the block cipher.

The block cipher in BLAKE2's compression function is based on the stream cipher ChaCha, itself a variant of the Salsa20 stream cipher discussed in Chapter 5. Within this block cipher, BLAKE2b's core operation is composed of the following chain of operations, which transforms a state of four 64-bit words using two message words, M_i and M_j:

$$a = a + b + M_i$$
$$d = \left((d \oplus a) \ggg 32\right)$$
$$c = c + d$$
$$b = \left((b \oplus c) \ggg 24\right)$$
$$a = a + b + M_j$$
$$d = \left((d \oplus a) \ggg 16\right)$$
$$c = c + d$$
$$b = \left((b \oplus c) \ggg 63\right)$$

BLAKE2s's core operation is similar but works with 32-bit instead of 64-bit words (and thus uses different rotation values).

How Things Can Go Wrong

Despite their apparent simplicity, hash functions can cause major security troubles when used at the wrong place or in the wrong way—for example, when weak checksum algorithms like CRCs are used instead of a crypto hash to check file integrity in applications transmitting data over a network. However, this weakness pales in comparison to some others, which can cause total compromise in seemingly secure hash functions. We'll see two examples of failures: the first one applies to SHA-1 and SHA-2, but not to BLAKE2 or SHA-3, whereas the second one applies to all of these four functions.

The Length-Extension Attack

The *length-extension attack*, shown in Figure 6-9, is the main threat to the Merkle–Damgård construction.

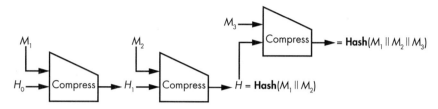

Figure 6-9: The length-extension attack

Basically, if you know **Hash**(M) for some *unknown* message, M, composed of blocks M_1 and M_2 (after padding), you can determine **Hash**($M_1 \parallel M_2 \parallel M_3$) for any block, M_3. Because the hash of $M_1 \parallel M_2$ is the chaining value that follows immediately after M_2, you can add another block, M_3, to the hashed message, even though you don't know the data that was hashed. What's more, this trick generalizes to any number of blocks in the unknown message ($M_1 \parallel M_2$ here) or in the suffix (M_3).

The length-extension attack won't affect most applications of hash functions, but it can compromise security if the hash is used a bit too creatively. Unfortunately, SHA-2 hash functions are vulnerable to the length-extension attack, even though the NSA designed the functions and NIST standardized them while both were well aware of the flaw. This flaw could have been avoided simply by making the last compression function call different from all others (for example, by taking a 1 bit as an extra parameter while the previous calls take a 0 bit). And that is in fact what BLAKE2 does.

Fooling Proof-of-Storage Protocols

Cloud computing applications have used hash functions within *proof-of-storage* protocols—that is, protocols where a server (the cloud provider) proves to a client (a user of a cloud storage service) that the server does in fact store the files that it's supposed to store on behalf of the client.

In 2007, the paper "SafeStore: A Durable and Practical Storage System" (*https://www.cs.utexas.edu/~lorenzo/papers/p129-kotla.pdf*) by Ramakrishna Kotla, Lorenzo Alvisi, and Mike Dahlin proposed a proof-of-storage protocol to verify the storage of some file, M, as follows:

1. The client picks a random value, C, as a *challenge*.
2. The server computes **Hash**($M \parallel C$) as a *response* and sends the result to the client.
3. The client also computes **Hash**($M \parallel C$) and checks that it matches the value received from the server.

The premise of the paper is that the server shouldn't be able to fool the client because if the server doesn't know M, it can't guess **Hash**($M \parallel C$).

But there's a catch: in reality, **Hash** will be an iterated hash that processes its input block by block, computing intermediate chaining values between each block. For example, if **Hash** is SHA-256 and M is 512 bits long (the size of a block in SHA-256), the server can cheat. How? The first time the server receives M, it computes $H_1 = $ **Compress**(H_0, M_1), the chaining value obtained from SHA-256's initial value, H_0, and from the 512-bit M. It then records H_1 in memory and discards M, at which point it no longer stores M.

Now when the client sends a random value, C, the server computes **Compress**(H_1, C), after adding the padding to C to fill a complete block, and returns the result as **Hash**$(M \| C)$. The client then believes that, because the server returned the correct value of **Hash**$(M \| C)$, it holds the complete message—except that it may not, as you've seen.

This trick will work for SHA-1, SHA-2, as well as SHA-3 and BLAKE2. The solution is simple: ask for **Hash**$(C \| M)$ instead of **Hash**$(M \| C)$.

Further Reading

To learn more about hash functions, read the classics from the 1980s and 90s: research articles like Ralph Merkle's "One Way Hash Functions and DES" and Ivan Damgård's "A Design Principle for Hash Functions." Also read the first thorough study of block cipher-based hashing, "Hash Functions Based on Block Ciphers: A Synthetic Approach" by Preneel, Govaerts, and Vandewalle.

For more on collision search, read the 1997 paper "Parallel Collision Search with Cryptanalytic Applications" by van Oorschot and Wiener. To learn more about the theoretical security notions that underpin preimage resistance and collision resistance, as well as length-extension attacks, search for *indifferentiability*.

For more recent research on hash functions, see the archives of the SHA-3 competition, which include all the different algorithms and how they were broken. You'll find many references on the SHA-3 Zoo at *http://ehash.iaik.tugraz.at/wiki/The_SHA-3_Zoo*, and on NIST's page, *http://csrc.nist.gov/groups/ST/hash/sha-3/*.

For more on the SHA-3 winner Keccak and sponge functions, see *http://keccak.noekeon.org/* and *http://sponge.noekeon.org/*, the official pages of the Keccak designers.

Last but not least, research these two real exploitations of weak hash functions:

- The nation-state malware Flame exploited an MD5 collision to make a counterfeit certificate and appear to be a legitimate piece of software.

- The Xbox game console used a weak block cipher (called TEA) to build a hash function, which was exploited to hack the console and run arbitrary code on it.

7

KEYED HASHING

The hash functions discussed in Chapter 6 take a message and return its hash value— typically a short string of 256 or 512 bits. Anyone can compute the hash value of a message and verify that a particular message hashes to a particular value because there's no secret value involved, but sometimes you don't want to let just anyone do that. That's where *keyed* hash functions come in, or hashing with secret keys.

Keyed hashing forms the basis of two types of important cryptographic algorithms: *message authentication codes (MACs)*, which authenticate a message and protect its integrity, and *pseudorandom functions (PRFs)*, which produce random-looking hash-sized values. We'll look at how and why MACs and PRFs are similar in the first section of this chapter; then we'll review how real MACs and PRFs work. Some MACs and PRFs are based on hash functions, some are based on block ciphers, and still others are original designs. Finally, we'll review examples of attacks on otherwise secure MACs.

Message Authentication Codes (MACs)

A MAC protects a message's integrity and authenticity by creating a value $T = \mathbf{MAC}(K, M)$, called the authentication tag of the message, M (often confusingly called the MAC of M). Just as you can decrypt a message if you know a cipher's key, you can validate that a message has not been modified if you know a MAC's key.

For example, say Alex and Bill share a key, K, and Alex sends a message, M, to Bill along with its authentication tag, $T = \mathbf{MAC}(K, M)$. Upon receiving the message and its authentication tag, Bill recomputes $\mathbf{MAC}(K, M)$ and checks that it is equal to the authentication tag received. Because only Alex could have computed this value, Bill knows that the message wasn't corrupted in transit (confirming integrity), whether accidentally or maliciously, and that Alex sent that message (confirming authenticity).

MACs in Secure Communication

Secure communication systems often combine a cipher and a MAC to protect a message's confidentiality, integrity, and authenticity. For example, the protocols in Internet Protocol Security (IPSec), Secure Shell (SSH), and Transport Layer Security (TLS) generate a MAC for each network packet transmitted.

Not all communication systems use MACs. Sometimes an authentication tag can add unacceptable overhead to each packet, typically in the range of 64 to 128 bits. For example, the 3G and 4G mobile telephony standards encrypt packets encoding voice calls but they don't authenticate them. An attacker can modify the encrypted audio signal and the recipient wouldn't notice. Thus, if an attacker damages an encrypted voice packet, it will decrypt to noise, which would sound like static.

Forgery and Chosen-Message Attacks

What does it mean for a MAC to be secure? First of all, as with a cipher, the secret key should remain secret. If a MAC is secure, an attacker shouldn't be able to create a tag of some message if they don't know the key. Such a made-up message/tag pair is called a *forgery*, and recovering a key is just a specific case of a more general class of attacks called *forgery attacks*. The security notion that posits that forgeries should be impossible to find is called *unforgeability*. Obviously, it should be impossible to recover the secret key from a list of tags; otherwise, attackers could forge tags using the key.

What can an attacker do to break a MAC? In other words, what's the attack model? The most basic model is the *known-message attack*, which passively collects messages and their associated tags (for example, by eavesdropping on a network). But real attackers often launch more powerful attacks because they can often choose the messages to be authenticated, and therefore get the MAC of the message they want. The standard model is therefore that of *chosen-message attacks*, wherein attackers get tags for messages of their choice.

Replay Attacks

MACs aren't safe from attacks involving *replays* of tags. For example, if you were to eavesdrop on Alex and Bill's communications, you could capture a message and its tag sent by Alex to Bill, and later send them again to Bill pretending to be Alex. To prevent such *replay attacks*, protocols include a message number in each message. This number is incremented for each new message and authenticated along with the message. The receiving party gets messages numbered 1, 2, 3, 4, and so on. Thus, if an attacker tries to send message number 1 again, the receiver will notice that this message is out of order and that it's a potential replay of the earlier message number 1.

Pseudorandom Functions (PRFs)

A PRF is a function that uses a secret key to return $PRF(K, M)$, such that the output looks random. Because the key is secret, the output values are unpredictable to an attacker.

Unlike MACs, PRFs are not meant to be used on their own but as part of a cryptographic algorithm or protocol. For example, PRFs can be used to create block ciphers within the Feistel construction discussed in "How to Construct Block Ciphers" on page 55. Key derivation schemes use PRFs to generate cryptographic keys from a master key or a password, and identification schemes use PRFs to generate a response from a random challenge. (Basically, a server sends a random challenge message, M, and the client returns $PRF(K, M)$ in its response to prove that it knows K.) The 4G telephony standard uses a PRF to authenticate a SIM card and its service provider, and a similar PRF also serves to generate the encryption key and MAC key to be used during a phone call. The TLS protocol uses a PRF to generate key material from a master secret as well as session-specific random values. There's even a PRF in the noncryptographic hash() function built into the Python language to compare objects.

PRF Security

In order to be secure, a pseudorandom function should have no pattern that sets its outputs apart from truly random values. An attacker who doesn't know the key, K, shouldn't be able to distinguish the outputs of $PRF(K, M)$ from random values. Viewed differently, an attacker shouldn't have any means of knowing whether they're talking to a PRF algorithm or to a random function. The erudite phrase for that security notion is *indistinguishability from a random function*. (To learn more about the theoretical foundations of PRFs, see Volume 1, Section 3.6 of Goldreich's *Foundations of Cryptography*.)

Why PRFs Are Stronger Than MACs

PRFs and MACs are both keyed hashes, but PRFs are fundamentally stronger than MACs, largely because MACs have weaker security requirements. Whereas a MAC is considered secure if tags can't be forged—that is, if the MAC's outputs can't be guessed—a PRF is only secure if its outputs are indistinguishable random strings, which is a stronger requirement. If a PRF's outputs can't be distinguished from random strings, the implication is that their values can't be guessed; in other words, any secure PRF is also a secure MAC.

The converse is not true, however: a secure MAC isn't necessarily a secure PRF. For example, say you start with a secure PRF, **PRF1**, and you want to build a second PRF, **PRF2**, from it, like this:

$$\mathbf{PRF2}(K, M) = \mathbf{PRF1}(K, M) \parallel 0$$

Because **PRF2**'s output is defined as **PRF1**'s output followed by one 0 bit, it doesn't look as random as a true random string, and you can distinguish its outputs by that last 0 bit. Hence, **PRF2** is not a secure PRF. However, because **PRF1** is secure, **PRF2** would still make a secure MAC. Why? Because if you were able to forge a tag, $T = \mathbf{PRF2}(K, M)$, for some M, then you'd also be able to forge a tag for **PRF1**, which we know to be impossible in the first place because PRF1 is a secure MAC. Thus, PRF2 is a keyed hash that's a secure MAC but not a secure PRF.

But don't worry: you won't find such MAC constructions in real applications. In fact, many of the MACs deployed or standardized are also secure PRFs and are often used as either. For example, TLS uses the algorithm HMAC-SHA-256 both as a MAC and as a PRF.

Creating Keyed Hashes from Unkeyed Hashes

Throughout the history of cryptography, MACs and PRFs have rarely been designed from scratch but rather have been built from existing algorithms, usually hash functions of block ciphers. One seemingly obvious way to produce a keyed hash function would be to feed an (unkeyed) hash function a key and a message, but that's easier said than done, as I discuss next.

The Secret-Prefix Construction

The first technique we'll examine, called the *secret-prefix construction*, turns a normal hash function into a keyed hash one by prepending the key to the message and returning **Hash**$(K \parallel M)$. Although this approach is not always wrong, it can be insecure when the hash function is vulnerable to length-extension attacks (as discussed in "The Length-Extension Attack" on page 125) and when the hash supports keys of different lengths.

Insecurity Against Length-Extension Attacks

Recall from Chapter 6 that hash functions of the SHA-2 family allow attackers to compute the hash of a partially unknown message when given a hash of a shorter version of that message. In formal terms, the *length-extension* attack allows attackers to compute $\textbf{Hash}(K \parallel M_1 \parallel M_2)$ given only $\textbf{Hash}(K \parallel M_1)$ and neither M_1 nor K. These functions allow attackers to forge valid MAC tags for free because they're not supposed to be able to guess the MAC of $M_1 \parallel M_2$ given only the MAC of M_1. This fact makes the secret-prefix construction as insecure as a MAC and PRF when, for example, it's used with SHA-256 or SHA-512. It is a weakness of Merkle–Damgård to allow length-extension attacks, and none of the SHA-3 finalists do. The ability to thwart length-extension attacks was mandatory for SHA-3 submissions.

Insecurity with Different Key Lengths

The secret-prefix construction is also insecure when it allows the use of keys of different lengths. For example, if the key K is the 24-bit hexadecimal string 123abc and M is def00, then $\textbf{Hash}()$ will process the value $K \parallel M = 123abcdef00$. If K is instead the 16-bit string 123a and M is bcdef000, then $\textbf{Hash}()$ will process $K \parallel M = 123abcdef00$, too. Therefore, the result of the secret-prefix construction $\textbf{Hash}(K \parallel M)$ will be the same for both keys.

This problem is independent of the underlying hash and can be fixed by hashing the key's length along with the key and the message, for example, by encoding the key's bit length as a 16-bit integer, L, and then hashing $\textbf{Hash}(L \parallel K \parallel M)$. But you shouldn't have to do this. Modern hash functions such as BLAKE2 and SHA-3 include a keyed mode that avoids those pitfalls and yields a secure PRF, and thus a secure MAC as well.

The Secret-Suffix Construction

Instead of hashing the key before the message as in the secret-prefix construction, we can hash it *after*. And that's exactly how the *secret-suffix construction* works: by building a PRF from a hash function as $\textbf{Hash}(M \parallel K)$.

Putting the key at the end makes quite a difference. For one thing, the length-extension attack that works against secret-prefix MACs won't work against the secret suffix. Applying length extension to a secret-suffix MAC, you'd get $\textbf{Hash}(M_1 \parallel K \parallel M_2)$ from $\textbf{Hash}(M_1 \parallel K)$, but that wouldn't be a valid attack because $\textbf{Hash}(M_1 \parallel K \parallel M_2)$ isn't a valid secret-suffix MAC; the key needs to be at the end.

However, the secret-suffix construction is weaker against another type of attack. Say you've got a collision for the hash $\textbf{Hash}(M_1) = \textbf{Hash}(M_2)$, where M_1 and M_2 are two distinct messages, possibly of different sizes. In the case of a hash function such as SHA-256, this implies that $\textbf{Hash}(M_1 \parallel K)$ and $\textbf{Hash}(M_2 \parallel K)$ will be equal too, because internally K will be processed based on the data hashed previously, namely $\textbf{Hash}(M_1)$, equal to $\textbf{Hash}(M_2)$. Hence, you'd get the same hash value whether you hash K after M_1 or after M_2, regardless of the value of K.

To exploit this property, an attacker would:

1. Find two colliding messages, M_1 and M_2
2. Request the MAC tag of M_1 **Hash**$(M_1 \parallel K)$
3. Guess that **Hash**$(M_2 \parallel K)$ is the same, thereby forging a valid tag and breaking the MAC's security

The HMAC Construction

The hash-based MAC (HMAC) construction allows us to build a MAC from a hash function, which is more secure than either secret prefix or secret suffix. HMAC yields a secure PRF as long as the underlying hash is collision resistant, but even if that's not the case, HMAC will still yield a secure PRF if the hash's compression function is a PRF. The secure communication protocols IPSec, SSH, and TLS have all used HMAC. (You'll find HMAC specifications in NIST's FIPS 198-1 standard and in RFC 2104.)

HMAC uses a hash function, **Hash**, to compute a MAC tag, as shown in Figure 7-1 and according to the following expression:

$$\textbf{Hash}((K \oplus \textit{opad}) \parallel \textbf{Hash}((K \oplus \textit{ipad}) \parallel M))$$

The term *opad* (outer padding) is a string (*5c5c5c . . . 5c*) that is as long as **Hash**'s block size. The key, K, is usually shorter than one block that is filled with 00 bytes and XORed with *opad*. For example, if K is the 1-byte string *00*, then $K \oplus \textit{opad} = \textit{opad}$. (The same is true if K is the all-zero string of any length up to a block's length.) $K \oplus \textit{opad}$ is the first block processed by the outer call to **Hash**—namely, the leftmost **Hash** in the preceding equation, or the bottom hash in Figure 7-1.

The term *ipad* (inner padding) is a string (*363636 . . . 36*) that is as long as the **Hash**'s block size and that is also completed with 00 bytes. The resulting block is the first block processed by the inner call to **Hash**—namely, the rightmost **Hash** in the equation, or the top hash in Figure 7-1.

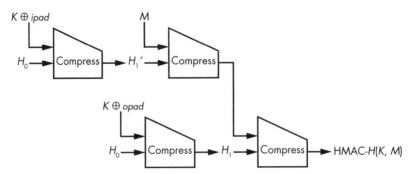

Figure 7-1: The HMAC hash-based MAC construction

NOTE *The envelope method is an even more secure construction than secret prefix and secret suffix. It's expressed as **Hash**(K ‖ M ‖ K), something called a sandwich MAC, but it's theoretically less secure than HMAC.*

If SHA-256 is the hash function used as **Hash**, then we call the HMAC instance HMAC-SHA-256. More generally, we call HMAC-*Hash* an HMAC instance using the hash function *Hash*. That means if someone asks you to use HMAC, you should always ask, "Which hash function?"

A Generic Attack Against Hash-Based MACs

There is one attack that works against all MACs based on an iterated hash function. Recall the attack in "The Secret-Suffix Construction" on page 131 where we used a hash collision to get a collision of MACs. You can use the same strategy to attack a secret-prefix MAC or HMAC, though the consequences are less devastating.

To illustrate the attack, consider the secret-prefix MAC **Hash**$(K \| M)$, as shown in Figure 7-2. If the digest is n bits, you can find two messages, M_1 and M_2, such that **Hash**$(K \| M_1) = $ **Hash**$(K \| M_2)$, by requesting approximately $2^{n/2}$ MAC tags to the system holding the key. (Recall the birthday attack from Chapter 6.) If the hash lends itself to length extension, as SHA-256 does, you can then use M_1 and M_2 to forge MACs by choosing some arbitrary data, M_3, and then querying the MAC oracle for **Hash**$(K \| M_1 \| M_3)$, which is the MAC of message $M_1 \| M_3$. As it turns out, this is also the MAC of message $M_2 \| M_3$, because the hash's internal state of M_1 and M_3 and M_2 and M_3 is the same, and you've successfully forged a MAC tag. (The effort becomes infeasible as n grows beyond, say, 128 bits.)

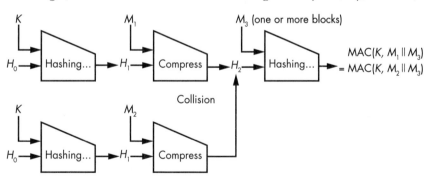

Figure 7-2: The principle of the generic forgery attack on hash-based MACs

This attack will work even if the hash function is not vulnerable to length extension, and it will work for HMAC, too. The cost of the attack depends on both the size of the chaining value and the MAC's length: if a MAC's chaining value is 512 bits and its tags are 128 bits, a 2^{64} computation would find a MAC collision but probably not a collision in the internal state, since finding such a collision would require $2^{512/2} = 2^{256}$ operations on average.

Creating Keyed Hashes from Block Ciphers: CMAC

Recall from Chapter 6 that the compression functions in many hash functions are built on block ciphers. For example, HMAC-SHA-256 PRF is a series of calls to SHA-256's compression function, which itself is a block cipher that repeats a sequence of rounds. In other words, HMAC-SHA-256 is a block cipher inside a compression function inside a hash inside the HMAC construction. So why not use a block cipher directly rather than build such a layered construction?

CMAC (which stands for *cipher-based MAC*) is such a construction: it creates a MAC given only a block cipher, such as AES. Though less popular than HMAC, CMAC is deployed in many systems, including the Internet Key Exchange (IKE) protocol, which is part of the IPSec suite. IKE, for example, generates key material using a construction called AES-CMAC-PRF-128 as a core algorithm (or CMAC based on AES with 128-bit output). CMAC is specified in RFC 4493.

Breaking CBC-MAC

CMAC was designed in 2005 as an improved version of *CBC-MAC*, a simpler block cipher–based MAC derived from the cipher block chaining (CBC) block cipher mode of operation (see "Modes of Operation" on page 65).

CBC-MAC, the ancestor of CMAC, is simple: to compute the tag of a message, M, given a block cipher, $\mathbf{E}$, you encrypt M in CBC mode with an all-zero initial value (IV) and discard all but the last ciphertext block. That is, you compute $C_1 = \mathbf{E}(K, M_1)$, $C_2 = \mathbf{E}(K, M_2 \oplus C_1)$, $C_3 = \mathbf{E}(K, M_3 \oplus C_2)$, and so on for each of M's blocks and keep only the last C_i, your CBC-MAC tag for M—simple, and simple to attack.

To understand why CBC-MAC is insecure, consider the CBC-MAC tag, $T_1 = \mathbf{E}(K, M_1)$, of a single-block message, M_1, and the tag, $T_2 = \mathbf{E}(K, M_2)$, of another single-block message, M_2. Given these two pairs, (M_1, T_1) and (M_2, T_2), you can deduce that T_2 is also the tag of the two-block message $M_1 \parallel (M_2 \oplus T_1)$. Indeed, if you apply CBC-MAC to $M_1 \parallel (M_2 \oplus T_1)$ and compute $C_1 = \mathbf{E}(K, M_1) = T_1$ followed by $C_2 = \mathbf{E}(K, (M_2 \oplus T_1) \oplus T_1) = \mathbf{E}(K, M_2) = T_2$, you can create a third message/tag pair from two message/tag pairs without knowing the key. That is, you can forge CBC-MAC tags, thereby breaking CBC-MAC's security.

Fixing CBC-MAC

CMAC fixes CBC-MAC by processing the last block using a different key from the preceding blocks. To do this, CMAC first derives two keys, K_1 and K_2, from the main key, K, such that K, K_1, and K_2 will be distinct. In CMAC, the last block is processed using either K_1 or K_2, while the preceding blocks use K.

To determine K_1 and K_2, CMAC first computes a temporary value, $L = \mathbf{E}(0, K)$, where 0 acts as the key of the block cipher and K acts as the plaintext block. Then CMAC sets the value of K_1 equal to $(L \ll 1)$ if L's most significant bit (MSB) is 0, or equal to $(L \ll 1) \oplus 87$ if L's MSB is 1. (The number 87 is carefully chosen for its mathematical properties when data blocks are 128 bits; a value other than 87 is needed when blocks aren't 128 bits.)

The value of K_2 is set equal to $(K_1 \ll 1)$ if K_1's MSB is 0, or $K_2 = (K_1 \ll 1) \oplus 87$ otherwise.

Given K_1 and K_2, CMAC works like CBC-MAC, except for the last block. If the final message chunk M_n is exactly the size of a block, CMAC returns the value $\mathbf{E}(K, M_n \oplus C_{n-1} \oplus K_1)$ as a tag, as shown in Figure 7-3. But if M_n has fewer bits than a block, CMAC pads it with a 1 bit and zeros, and returns the value $\mathbf{E}(K, M_n \oplus C_{n-1} \oplus K_2)$ as a tag, as shown in Figure 7-4. Notice that the first case uses only K_1 and the second only K_2, but both use only the main key K to process the message chunks that precede the final one.

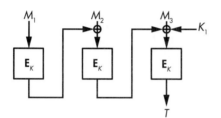

Figure 7-3: The CMAC block cipher–based MAC construction when the message is a sequence of integral blocks

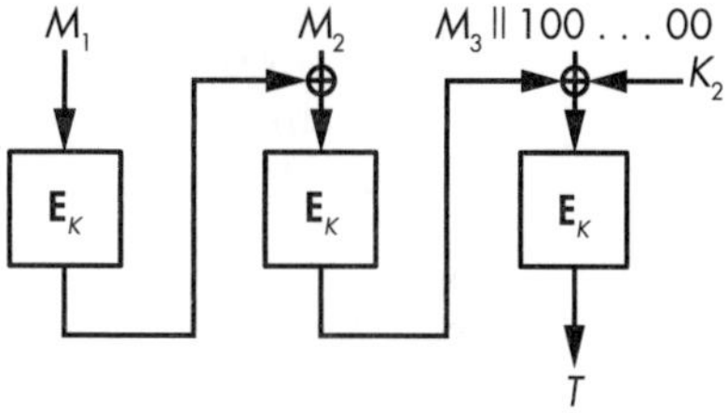

Figure 7-4: The CMAC block cipher–based MAC construction when the last block of the message has to be padded with a 1 bit and zeros to fill a block

Note that unlike the CBC encryption mode, CMAC does not take an IV as a parameter and is deterministic: CMAC will always return the same tag for a given message, M, because the computation of $\mathbf{CMAC}(M)$ is not randomized—and that's fine, because unlike encryption, MAC computation doesn't have to be randomized to be secure, which eliminates the burden of having to choose random IV.

Dedicated MAC Designs

You've seen how to recycle hash functions and block ciphers to build PRFs that are secure as long as their underlying hash or cipher is secure. Schemes such as HMAC and CMAC simply combine available hash functions or block ciphers to yield a secure PRF or MAC. Reusing available algorithms is convenient, but is it the most efficient approach?

Intuitively, PRFs and MACs should require less work than unkeyed hash functions in order to be secure—their use of a secret key prevents attackers from playing with the algorithm because they don't have the key. Also, PRFs and MACs only expose a short tag to attackers, unlike block ciphers, which expose a ciphertext that is as long as the message. Hence, PRFs and MACs should not need the whole power of hash functions or block ciphers, which is the point of *dedicated design*—that is, algorithms created solely to serve as PRFs and/or MACs.

The sections that follow focus on two such algorithms that are widely used: Poly1305 and SipHash. I'll explain their design principles and why they are likely secure.

Poly1305

The Poly1305 algorithm (pronounced *poly-thirteen-o-five*) was designed in 2005 by Daniel J. Bernstein (creator of the Salsa20 stream cipher discussed in Chapter 5 and the ChaCha cipher that inspired the BLAKE and BLAKE2 hash functions discussed in Chapter 6). Poly1305 is optimized to be super fast on modern CPUs, and as I write this, it is used by Google to secure HTTPS (HTTP over TLS) connections and by OpenSSH, among many other applications. Unlike Salsa20, the design of Poly1305 is built on techniques dating back to the 1970s—namely, universal hash functions and the Wegman–Carter construction.

Universal Hash Functions

The Poly1305 MAC uses a *universal hash function* internally that is much weaker than a cryptographic hash function, but also much faster. Universal hash functions don't have to be collision resistant, for example. That means less work is required to achieve their security goals.

Like a PRF, a universal hash is parameterized by a secret key: given a message, M, and key, K, we write $\mathbf{UH}(K, M)$, which is the computation of the output of a universal hash function, denoted $\mathbf{UH}$. A universal hash function has only one security requirement: for any two messages, M_1 and M_2, the probability that $\mathbf{UH}(K, M_1) = \mathbf{UH}(K, M_2)$ must be negligible for a random key, K. Unlike a PRF, a universal hash doesn't need to be pseudo-random; there simply should be no pair (M_1, M_2) that gives the same hash for many different keys. Because their security requirements are easier to satisfy, fewer operations are required and therefore universal hash functions are considerably faster than PRFs.

You can use a universal hash as a MAC to authenticate no more than one message, however. For example, consider the universal hash used in Poly1305, called a *polynomial-evaluation* hash. (See the seminal 1974 article "Codes Which Detect Deception" by Gilbert, MacWilliams, and Sloane for more on this notion.) This kind of polynomial-evaluation hash is parameterized by a prime number, p, and takes as input a key consisting of two numbers, R and K, in the range $[1, p]$ and a message, M, consisting of n blocks $(M_1, M_2, \ldots, M_n)$. The output of the universal hash is then computed as the following:

$$\mathbf{UH}(R, K, M) = R + M_1 K + M_2 K^2 + M_3 K^3 + \ldots + M_n K^n \bmod p$$

The plus sign (+) denotes the addition of positive integers, K^i is the number K raised to the power i, and "mod p" denotes the reduction modulo p of the result (that is, the remainder of the division of the result by p; for example, 12 mod 10 = 2, 10 mod 10 = 0, 8 mod 10 = 8, and so on).

Because we want the hash to be as fast as possible, universal hash-based MACs often work with message blocks of 128 bits and with a prime number, p, that is slightly larger than 2^{128}, such as $2^{128} + 51$. The 128-bit width allows for very fast implementations by efficiently using the 32- and 64-bit arithmetic units of common CPUs.

Potential Vulnerabilities

Universal hashes have one weakness: because a universal hash is only able to securely authenticate one message, an attacker could break the preceding polynomial-evaluation MAC by requesting the tags of only two messages. Specifically, they could request the tags for a message where $M_1 = M_2 = \ldots = 0$ (that is, whose tag is $\mathbf{UH}(R, K, 0) = R$) and then use the tags to find the secret value R. Alternatively, they could request the tags for a message where $M_1 = 1$ and where $M_2 = M_3 = \ldots = 0$ (that is, whose tag is $T = R + K$), which would allow them to find K by subtracting R from T. Now the attacker knows the whole key (R, K) and they can forge MACs for any message.

Fortunately, there's a way to go from single-message security to multi-message security.

Wegman–Carter MACs

The trick to authenticating multiple messages using a universal hash function arrived thanks to IBM researchers Wegman and Carter and their 1981 paper "New Hash Functions and Their Use in Authentication and Set Equality." The so-called Wegman–Carter construction builds a MAC from a universal hash function and a PRF, using two keys, K_1 and K_2, and it returns

$$\mathbf{MAC}\big(K_1, K_2, N, M\big) = \mathbf{UH}\big(K_1, M\big) + \mathbf{PRF}\big(K_2, N\big)$$

where N is a nonce that should be unique for each key, K_2, and where **PRF**'s output is as large as that of the universal hash function **UH**. By adding these two values, **PRF**'s strong pseudorandom output masks the cryptographic weakness of **UH**. You can see this as the encryption of the universal hash's result, where the PRF acts as a stream cipher and prevents the preceding attack by making it possible to authenticate multiple messages with the same key, K_1.

To recap, the Wegman–Carter construction $\mathbf{UH}(K_1, M) + \mathbf{PRF}(K_2, N)$ gives a secure MAC if we assume the following:

- **UH** is a secure universal hash.
- **PRF** is a secure PRF.

- Each nonce N is used only once for each key K_2.

- The output values of **UH** and **PRF** are long enough to ensure high enough security.

Now let's see how Poly1305 leverages the Wegman–Carter construction to build a secure and fast MAC.

Poly1305-AES

Poly1305 was initially proposed as Poly1305-AES, combining the Poly1305 universal hash with the AES block cipher. Poly1305-AES is much faster than HMAC-based MACs, or even than CMACs, since it only computes one block of AES and processes the message in parallel through a series of simple arithmetic operations.

Given a 128-bit K_1, K_2, and N, and message, M, Poly1305-AES returns the following:

$$\textbf{Poly}1305(K_1, M) + \textbf{AES}(K_2, N) \bmod 2^{128}$$

The mod 2^{128} reduction ensures that the result fits in 128 bits. The message M is parsed as a sequence of 128-bit blocks $(M_1, M_2, \ldots, M_n)$, and a 129th bit is appended to each block's most significant bit to make all blocks 129 bits long. (If the last block is smaller than 16 bytes, it's padded with a 1 bit followed by 0 bits before the final 129th bit.) Next, Poly1305 evaluates the polynomial to compute the following:

$$\textbf{Poly}1305(K_1, M) = M_1 K_1^n + M_2 K_1^{n-1} + \ldots + M_n K_1 \bmod 2^{130} - 5$$

The result of this expression is an integer that is at most 129-bits long. When added to the 128-bit value **AES**(K_2, N), the result is reduced modulo 2^{128} to produce a 128-bit MAC.

> **NOTE** *AES isn't a PRF; instead, it's a pseudorandom permutation (PRP). However, that doesn't matter much here because the Wegman–Carter construction works with a PRP as well as with a PRF. This is because if you're given a function that is either a PRF of a PRP, it's hard to determine whether it's a PRF of a PRP just by looking at the function's output values.*

The security analysis of Poly1305-AES (see "The Poly1305-AES Message-Authentication Code" at *http://cr.yp.to/mac/poly1305-20050329.pdf*) shows that Poly1305-AES is 128-bit secure as long as AES is a secure block cipher—and, of course, as long as everything is implemented correctly, as with any cryptographic algorithm.

The Poly1305 universal hash can be combined with algorithms other than AES. For example, Poly1305 was used with the stream cipher ChaCha (see RFC 7539, "ChaCha20 and Poly1305 for IETF Protocols"). There's no doubt that Poly1305 will keep being used wherever a fast MAC is needed.

SipHash

Although Poly1305 is fast and secure, it has several downsides. For one, its polynomial evaluation is difficult to implement efficiently, especially in the hands of many who are unfamiliar with the associated mathematical notions. (See examples at *https://github.com/floodyberry/poly1305-donna/*). Second, on its own, it's secure for only one message unless you use the Wegman–Carter construction. But in that case, it requires a nonce, and if the nonce is repeated, the algorithm becomes insecure. Finally, Poly1305 is optimized for long messages, but it's overkill if you process only small messages (say, fewer than 128 bytes). In such cases, SipHash is the solution.

I designed SipHash in 2012 with Dan Bernstein initially to address a noncryptographic problem: denial-of-service attacks on hash tables. Hash tables are data structures used to efficiently store elements in programming languages. Prior to the advent of SipHash, hash tables relied on noncryptographic keyed hash functions for which collisions were easy to find, and it was easy to exploit a remote system using a hash table by slowing it down with a denial-of-service attack. We determined that a PRF would address this problem and thus set out to design SipHash, a PRF suitable for hash tables. Because hash tables process mostly short inputs, SipHash is optimized for short messages. However, SipHash can be used for more than hash tables: it's a full-blown PRF and MAC that shines where most inputs are short.

How SipHash Works

SipHash uses a trick that makes it more secure than basic sponge functions: instead of XORing message blocks only once before the permutation, SipHash XORs them before and after the permutation, as shown in Figure 7-5. The 128-bit key of SipHash is seen as two 64-bit words, K_1 and K_2, XORed to a 256-bit fixed initial state that is seen as four 64-bit words. Next, the keys are discarded, and computing SipHash boils down to iterating through a core function called SipRound and then XORing message chunks to modify the four-word internal state. Finally, SipHash returns a 64-bit tag by XORing the four-state words together.

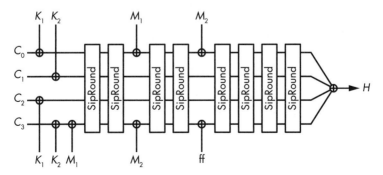

Figure 7-5: SipHash-2-4 processing a 15-byte message (a block, M_1, of 8 bytes and a block, M_2, of 7 bytes, plus 1 byte of padding)

The SipRound function uses a bunch of XORs together with additions and word rotations to make the function secure. SipRound transforms a state of four 64-bit words (a, b, c, d) by performing the following operations, top to bottom. The operations on the left and right are independent and can be carried out in parallel:

$$a \mathrel{+}= b \qquad\qquad c \mathrel{+}= d$$
$$b <<< = 13 \qquad\quad d <<< = 16$$
$$b \oplus= a \qquad\qquad d \oplus= c$$
$$a <<< = 32$$
$$c \mathrel{+}= b \qquad\qquad a \mathrel{+}= d$$
$$b <<< = 17 \qquad\quad d <<< = 21$$
$$b \oplus= c \qquad\qquad d \oplus= a$$
$$c <<< = 32$$

Here, $a \mathrel{+}= b$ is shorthand for $a = a + b$, and $b <<< = 13$ is shorthand for $b = b <<< 13$ (the 64-bit word b left-rotated 13 bits.)

These simple operations on 64-bit words are almost all you need to implement in order to compute SipHash—although you won't have to implement it yourself. You can find readily available implementations in most languages, including C, Go, Java, JavaScript, and Python.

NOTE *We write **SipHash**-x-y as the SipHash version, meaning it makes* x *SipRounds between each message block injection and then* y *rounds. More rounds require more operations, which slows down operations but also increases security. The default version is SipHash-2-4 (simply noted as SipHash), and it has so far resisted cryptanalysis. However, you may want to be conservative and opt for SipHash-4-8 instead, which makes twice as many rounds and is therefore twice as slow.*

How Things Can Go Wrong

Like ciphers and unkeyed hash functions, MACs and PRFs that are secure on paper can be vulnerable to attacks when used in a real setting, against realistic attackers. Let's see two examples.

Timing Attacks on MAC Verification

Side-channel attacks target the implementation of a cryptographic algorithm rather than the algorithm itself. In particular, *timing attacks* use an algorithm's execution time to determine secret information, such as keys, plaintext, and secret random values. As you might imagine, variable-time string comparison induces vulnerabilities not only in MAC verification, but also in many other cryptographic and security functionalities.

MACs can be vulnerable to timing attacks when a remote system verifies tags in a period of time that depends on the tag's value, thereby allowing an attacker to determine the correct message tag by trying many incorrect ones to determine the one that takes the longest amount of time to complete. The problem occurs when a server compares the correct tag with an incorrect one by comparing the two strings byte per byte, in order, until the bytes differ. For example, the Python code in Listing 7-1 compares two strings byte per byte, in variable time: if the first bytes differ, the function will return after only one comparison; if the strings x and y are identical, the function will make n comparisons against the length of the strings.

```
def compare_mac(x, y, n):
    for i in range(n):
        if x[i] != y[i]:
            return False
    return True
```

Listing 7-1: Comparison of two n-byte strings, taking variable time

To demonstrate the vulnerability of the verify_mac() function, let's write a program that measures the execution time of 100000 calls to verify_mac(), first with identical 10-byte x and y values and then with x and y values that differ in their third byte. We should expect the latter comparison to take noticeably less time than the former because verify_mac() will compare fewer bytes than the identical x and y would, as shown in Listing 7-2.

```
from time import time

MAC1 = '0123456789abcdef'
MAC2 = '01X3456789abcdef'
TRIALS = 100000

# each call to verify_mac() will look at all eight bytes
start = time()
for i in range(TRIALS):
    compare_mac(MAC1, MAC1, len(MAC1))
end = time()
print("%0.5f" % (end-start))

# each call to verify_mac() will look at three bytes
start = time()
for i in range(TRIALS):
    compare_mac(MAC1, MAC2, len(MAC1))
end = time()
print("%0.5f" % (end-start))
```

Listing 7-2: Measuring timing differences when executing compare_mac() from Listing 7-1

In my test environment, typical execution of the program in Listing 7-2 prints execution times of around 0.215 and 0.095 seconds, respectively. That difference is significant enough for you to identify what's happening within the algorithm. Now move the difference to other offsets in the string, and you'll observe different execution times for different offsets. If MAC1 is the correct MAC tag and MAC2 is the one tried by the attacker, you can easily identify the position of the first difference, which is the number of correctly guessed bytes.

Of course, if execution time doesn't depend on a secret timing, timing attacks won't work, which is why implementers strive to write *constant-time* implementations—that is, code that takes exactly the same time to complete for any secret input value. For example, the C function in Listing 7-3 compares two buffers of size bytes in constant time: the temporary variable result will be nonzero if and only if there's a difference somewhere in the two buffers.

```
int cmp_const(const void *a, const void *b, const size_t size)
{
  const unsigned char *_a = (const unsigned char *) a;
  const unsigned char *_b = (const unsigned char *) b;
  unsigned char result = 0;
  size_t i;

  for (i = 0; i < size; i++) {
    result |= _a[i] ^ _b[i];
  }

  return result; /* returns 0 if *a and *b are equal, nonzero otherwise */
}
```

Listing 7-3: Constant-time comparison of two buffers, for safer MAC verification

When Sponges Leak

Permutation-based algorithms like SHA-3 and SipHash are simple, easy to implement, and come with compact implementations, but they're fragile in the face of side-channel attacks that recover a snapshot of the system's state. For example, if a process can read the RAM and registers' values at any time, or read a core dump of the memory, an attacker can determine the internal state of SHA-3 in MAC mode, or the internal state of SipHash, and then compute the reverse of the permutation to recover the initial secret state. They can then forge tags for any message, breaking the MAC's security.

Fortunately, this attack will not work against compression function–based MACs such as HMAC-SHA-256 and keyed BLAKE2 because the attacker would need a snapshot of memory at the exact time when the key is used. The upshot is that if you're in an environment where parts of a process's memory may leak, you can use a MAC based on a noninvertible transform compression function rather than a permutation.

Further Reading

The venerable HMAC deserves more attention than I have space for here, and even more for the train of thought that led to its wide adoption, and eventually to its demise when combined with a weak hash function. I recommend the 1996 paper "Keying Hash Functions for Message Authentication" by Bellare, Canetti, and Krawczyk, which introduced HMAC and its cousin NMAC, and the 2006 follow-up paper by Bellare called "New Proofs for NMAC and HMAC: Security Without Collision-Resistance," which proves that HMAC doesn't need a collision-resistant hash, but only a hash with a compression function that is a PRF. On the offensive side, the 2007 paper "Full Key-Recovery Attacks on HMAC/NMAC-MD4 and NMAC-MD5" by Fouque, Leurent, and Nguyen shows how to attack HMAC and NMAC when they're built on top of a brittle hash function such as MD4 or MD5. (By the way, HMAC-MD5 and HMAC-SHA-1 aren't totally broken, but the risk is high enough.)

The Wegman–Carter MACs are also worth more attention, both for their practical interest and underlying theory. The seminal papers by Wegman and Carter are available at *http://cr.yp.to/bib/entries.html*. Other state-of-the-art designs include UMAC and VMAC, which are among the fastest MACs on long messages.

One type of MAC not discussed in this chapter is *Pelican*, which uses the AES block cipher reduced to four rounds (down from 10 in the full block cipher) to authenticate chunks of messages within a simplistic construction, as described in *https://eprint.iacr.org/2005/088/*. Pelican is more of a curiosity, though, and it's rarely used in practice.

Last but not least, if you're interested in finding vulnerabilities in cryptographic software, look for uses of CBC-MAC, or for weaknesses caused by HMAC handling keys of arbitrary sizes—taking **Hash**(K) as the key rather than K if K is too long, thus making K and **Hash**(K) *equivalent keys*. Or just look for systems than don't use MAC when they should—a frequent occurrence.

In Chapter 8, we'll look at how to combine MACs with ciphers to protect a message's authenticity, integrity, *and* confidentiality. We'll also look at how to do it without MACs, thanks to authenticated ciphers, which are ciphers that combine the functionality of a basic cipher with that of a MAC by returning a tag along with each ciphertext.

8

AUTHENTICATED ENCRYPTION

This chapter is about a type of algorithm that protects not only a message's confidentiality but also its authenticity. Recall from Chapter 7 that message authentication codes (MACs) are algorithms that protect a message's authenticity by creating a tag, which is a kind of signature. Like MACs, the authenticated encryption (AE) algorithms we'll discuss in this chapter produce an authentication tag, but they also encrypt the message. In other words, a single AE algorithm offers the features of both a normal cipher and a MAC.

Combining a cipher and a MAC can achieve varying levels of authenticated encryption, as you'll learn throughout this chapter. I'll review several possible ways to combine MACs with ciphers, explain which methods are the most secure, and introduce you to ciphers that produce both a ciphertext and an authentication tag. We'll then look at four important authenticated ciphers: three block cipher–based constructions, with a focus on the popular Advanced Encryption Standard in Galois Counter Mode (AES-GCM), and a cipher that uses only a permutation algorithm.

Authenticated Encryption Using MACs

As shown in Figure 8-1, MACs and ciphers can be combined in one of three ways to both encrypt and authenticate a plaintext: encrypt-and-MAC, MAC-then-encrypt, and encrypt-then-MAC.

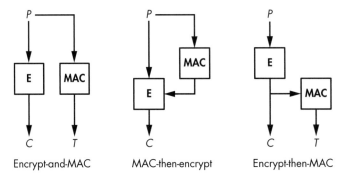

Figure 8-1: Cipher and MAC combinations

The three combinations differ in the order in which encryption is applied and the authentication tag is generated. However, the choice of a specific MAC or cipher algorithm is unimportant as long as each is secure in its own right, and the MAC and cipher use distinct keys.

As you can see in Figure 8-1, in the encrypt-and-MAC composition, the plaintext is encrypted and an authentication tag is generated from the plaintext directly, such that the two operations (encryption and authentication) are independent of each other and can therefore be computed in parallel. In the MAC-then-encrypt scheme, the tag is generated from the plaintext first, and then the plaintext and MAC are encrypted together. In contrast, in the case of the encrypt-then-MAC method, the plaintext is encrypted first, and then the tag is generated from the ciphertext.

All three approaches are about equally resource intensive. Let's see which method is likely to be the most secure.

Encrypt-and-MAC

The *encrypt-and-MAC* approach computes a ciphertext and a MAC tag separately. Given a plaintext (P), the sender computes a ciphertext $C = \mathbf{E}(K_1, P)$, where $\mathbf{E}$ is an encryption algorithm and C is the resulting ciphertext. The authentication tag (T) is calculated from the plaintext as $T = \mathbf{MAC}(K_2, P)$. You can compute C and T first or in parallel.

Once the ciphertext and authentication tag have been generated, the sender transmits both to the intended recipient. When the recipient receives C and T, they decrypt C to obtain the plaintext P by computing $P = \mathbf{D}(K_1, C)$. Next, they compute $\mathbf{MAC}(K_2, P)$ using the decrypted plaintext and compare the result to the T received. This verification will fail if either C or T was corrupted, and the message will be deemed invalid.

At least in theory, encrypt-and-MAC is the least secure MAC and cipher composition because even a secure MAC could leak information on P, which would make P easier to recover. Because the goal of using MACs is simply to make tags unforgeable, and because tags aren't necessarily random looking, the authentication tag (T) of a plaintext (P) could still leak information even though the MAC is considered secure! (Of course, if the MAC is a pseudorandom function, the tag won't leak anything on P.)

Still, despite its relative weakness, encrypt-and-MAC continues to be supported by many systems, including the secure transport layer protocol SSH, wherein each encrypted packet C is followed by the tag $T = \mathbf{MAC}(K, N \| P)$ sent in the unencrypted plaintext packet P. N in this equation is a 32-bit sequence number that is incremented for each sent packet, in order to help ensure that the received packets are processed in the right order. In practice, encrypt-and-MAC has proven good enough for use with SSH, thanks to the use of strong MAC algorithms like HMAC-SHA-256 that don't leak information on P.

MAC-then-Encrypt

The *MAC-then-encrypt* composition protects a message, P, by first computing the authentication tag $T = \mathbf{MAC}(K_2, P)$. Next, it creates the ciphertext by encrypting the plaintext and tag together, according to $C = \mathbf{E}(K_1, P \| T)$.

Once these steps have been completed, the sender transmits only C, which contains both the encrypted plaintext and tag. Upon receipt, the recipient decrypts C by computing $P \| T = \mathbf{D}(K_1, C)$ to obtain the plaintext and tag T. Next, the recipient verifies the received tag T by computing a tag directly from the plaintext according to $\mathbf{MAC}(K_2, P)$ in order to confirm that the computed tag is equal to the tag T.

As with encrypt-and-MAC, when MAC-then-encrypt is used, the recipient must decrypt C before they can determine whether they are receiving corrupted packets—a process that exposes potentially corrupted plaintexts to the receiver. Nevertheless, MAC-then-encrypt is more secure than encrypt-and-MAC because it hides the plaintext's authentication tag, thus preventing the tag from leaking information on the plaintext.

MAC-then-encrypt has been used in the TLS protocol for years, but TLS 1.3 replaced MAC-then-encrypt with authenticated ciphers (see Chapter 13 for more on TLS 1.3).

Encrypt-then-MAC

The encrypt-then-MAC composition sends two values to the recipient: the ciphertext produced by $C = \mathbf{E}(K_1, P)$ and a tag based on the ciphertext, $T = \mathbf{MAC}(K_2, C)$. The receiver computes the tag using $\mathbf{MAC}(K_2, C)$ and verifies that it equals the T received. If the values are equal, the plaintext is computed as $P = \mathbf{D}(K_1, C)$; if they are not equal, the plaintext is discarded.

One advantage with this method is that the receiver only needs to compute a MAC in order to detect corrupt messages, meaning that there is no need to decrypt a corrupt ciphertext. Another advantage is that attackers can't send pairs of C and T to the receiver to decrypt unless they have broken the MAC, which makes it harder for attackers to transmit malicious data to the recipient.

This combination of features makes encrypt-then-MAC stronger than the encrypt-and-MAC and MAC-then-encrypt approaches. This is one reason why the widely used IPSec secure communications protocol suite uses it to protect packets (for example, within VPN tunnels).

But then why don't SSH and TLS use encrypt-then-MAC? The simple answer is that when SSH and TLS were created, other approaches appeared adequate—not because theoretical weaknesses didn't exist but because theoretical weaknesses don't necessarily become actual vulnerabilities.

Authenticated Ciphers

Authenticated ciphers are an alternative to the cipher and MAC combinations. They are like normal ciphers except that they return an authentication tag together with the ciphertext.

The authenticated cipher encryption is represented as $\mathbf{AE}(K, P) = (C, T)$. The term $\mathbf{AE}$ stands for *authenticated encryption*, which as you can see from this equation is based on a key (K) and a plaintext (P) and returns a ciphertext (C) and a generated authentication tag pair (T). In other words, a single authenticated cipher algorithm does the same job as a cipher and MAC combination, making it simpler, faster, and often more secure.

Authenticated cipher decryption is represented by $\mathbf{AD}(K, C, T) = P$. Here, $\mathbf{AD}$ stands for *authenticated decryption*, which returns a plaintext (P) given a ciphertext (C), tag (T), and key (K). If either or both C and T are invalid, $\mathbf{AD}$ will return an error to prevent the recipient from processing a plaintext that may have been forged. By the same token, if $\mathbf{AD}$ returns a plaintext, you can be sure that it has been encrypted by someone or something that knows the secret key.

The basic security requirements of an authenticated cipher are simple: its authentication should be as strong as a MAC's, meaning that it should be impossible to forge a ciphertext and tag pair (C, T) that the decryption function $\mathbf{AD}$ will accept and decrypt.

As far as confidentiality is concerned, an authenticated cipher is fundamentally stronger than a basic cipher because systems holding the secret key will only decrypt a ciphertext if the authentication tag is valid. If the tag is invalid, the plaintext will be discarded. This characteristic prevents attackers from performing chosen-ciphertext queries, an attack where they create ciphertexts and ask for the corresponding plaintext.

Authenticated Encryption with Associated Data

Cryptographers define *associated data* as any data processed by an authenticated cipher such that the data is authenticated (thanks to the authentication tag) but not encrypted. Indeed, by default, all plaintext data fed to an authenticated cipher is encrypted *and* authenticated.

But what if you simply want to authenticate all of a message, including its unencrypted parts, but not encrypt the entire message? That is, you want to authenticate and transmit data in addition to an encrypted message. For example, if a cipher processes a network packet composed of a header followed by a payload, you might choose to encrypt the payload to hide the actual data transmitted, but not encrypt the header since it contains information required to deliver the packet to its final recipient. At the same time, you might still like to authenticate the header's data to make sure that it is received from the expected sender.

In order to accomplish these goals, cryptographers have created the notion of authenticated encryption with associated data (AEAD). An AEAD algorithm allows you to attach cleartext data to a ciphertext in such a way that if the cleartext data is corrupted, the authentication tag will not validate and the ciphertext will not be decrypted.

We can write an AEAD operation as $\textbf{AEAD}(K, P, A) = (C, A, T)$. Given a key ($K$), plaintext ($P$), and associated data ($A$), AEAD returns the ciphertext, the unencrypted associated data A, and an authentication tag. AEAD leaves the unencrypted associated data unchanged, and the ciphertext is the encryption of plaintext. The authentication tag depends on both P and A, and will only be verified as valid if neither C nor A has been modified.

Because the authenticated tag depends on A, decryption with associated data is computed by $\textbf{ADAD}(K, C, A, T) = (P, A)$. Decryption requires the key, ciphertext, associated data, and tag in order to compute the plaintext and associated data, and it will fail if either C or A has been corrupted.

One thing to note when using AEAD is that you can leave A or P empty. If the associated data A is empty, AEAD becomes a normal authenticated cipher; if P is empty, it's just a MAC.

NOTE *As of this writing, AEAD is the current norm for authenticated encryption. Because nearly all authenticated ciphers in use today support associated data, when referring to authenticated ciphers throughout this book, I am referring to AEAD unless stated otherwise. When discussing AEAD operations of encryption and decryption, I'll refer to them as **AE** and **AD**, respectively.*

Avoiding Predictability with Nonces

Recall from Chapter 1 that in order to be secure, encryption schemes must be unpredictable and return different ciphertexts when called repeatedly to encrypt the same plaintext—otherwise, an attacker can determine whether the same plaintext was encrypted twice. In order to be unpredictable, block ciphers and stream ciphers feed the cipher an extra parameter: the initial value (IV) or nonce—a number that can be used only once. Authenticated ciphers use the same trick. Thus, authenticated encryption can be expressed as $\mathbf{AE}(K, P, A, N)$, where N is a nonce. It's up to the encryption operation to pick a nonce that has never been used before with the same key.

As with block and stream ciphers, decryption with an authenticated cipher requires the nonce used for encryption in order to perform correctly. We can thus express decryption as $\mathbf{AD}(K, C, A, T, N) = (P, A)$, where N is the nonce used to create C and T.

What Makes a Good Authenticated Cipher?

Researchers have been struggling since the early 2000s to define what makes a good authenticated cipher, and as I write this, the answer is still elusive. Because of AEAD's many inputs that play different roles, it's harder to define a notion of security than it is for basic ciphers that only encrypt a message. Nevertheless, in this section, I'll summarize the most important criteria to consider when evaluating the security, performance, and functionality of an authenticated cipher.

Security Criteria

The most important criteria used to measure the strength of an authenticated cipher are its ability to protect the confidentiality of data (that is, the secrecy of the plaintext) and the authenticity and integrity of the communication (as with the MAC's ability to detect corrupted messages). An authenticated cipher must compete in both leagues: its confidentiality must be as strong as that of the strongest cipher, and its authenticity as strong as that of the best MAC. In other words, if you remove the authentication part in an AEAD, you should get a secure cipher, and if you remove the encryption part, you should get a strong MAC.

Another measure of the strength of an authenticated cipher's security is based on something a bit more subtle—namely, its fragility when faced with repeated nonces. For example, if a nonce is reused, can an attacker decrypt ciphertexts or learn the difference between plaintexts?

Researchers call this notion of robustness *misuse resistance*, and have designed misuse-resistant authenticated ciphers to weigh the impact of a repeated nonce and attempt to determine whether confidentiality, authenticity, or both would be compromised in the face of such an attack, as well as what information about the encrypted data would likely be leaked.

Performance Criteria

As with every cryptographic algorithm, the throughput of an authenticated cipher can be measured in bits processed per second. This speed depends on the number of operations performed by the cipher's algorithm and on the extra cost of the authentication functionality. As you might imagine, the extra security features of authenticated ciphers come with a performance hit. However, the measure of a cipher's performance isn't just about pure speed. It's also about parallelizability, structure, and whether the cipher is streamable. Let's examine these notions more closely.

A cipher's *parallelizability* is a measure of its ability to process multiple data blocks simultaneously without waiting for the previous block's processing to complete. Block cipher–based designs can be easily parallelizable when each block can be processed independently of the other blocks. For example, the CTR block cipher mode discussed in Chapter 4 is parallelizable, whereas the CBC encryption mode is not, because blocks are chained.

The internal structure of an authenticated cipher is another important performance criteria. There are two main types of structure: one-layer and two-layer. In a two-layer structure (for example, in the widely used AES-GCM), one algorithm processes the plaintext and then a second algorithm processes the result. Typically, the first layer is the encryption layer and the second is the authentication layer. But you might expect, a two-layer structure complicates implementation and tends to slow down computations.

An authenticated cipher is *streamable* (also called an *online* cipher) when it can process a message block-by-block and discard any already-processed blocks. In contrast, nonstreamable ciphers must store the entire message, typically because they need to make two consecutive passes over the data: one from the start to the end, and the other from the end to the start of the data obtained from the first pass.

Due to potentially high memory requirements, some applications won't work with nonstreamable ciphers. For example, a router could receive an encrypted block of data, decrypt it, and then return the plaintext block before moving on to decrypt the subsequent block of the message, though the recipient of the decrypted message would still have to verify the authentication tag sent at the end of the decrypted data stream.

Functional Criteria

Functional criteria are the features of a cipher or its implementation that don't directly relate to either security or performance. For example, some authenticated ciphers only allow associated data to precede the data to be encrypted (because they need access to it in order to start encryption). Others require associated data to follow the data to be encrypted or support the inclusion of associated data anywhere—even between chunks of plaintext. This last case is the best, because it enables users to protect their data in any possible situation, but it's also the hardest to design securely: as always, more features often bring more complexity—and more potential vulnerabilities.

Another piece of functional criteria to consider relates to whether you can use the same core algorithm for both encryption and decryption. For example, many authenticated ciphers are based on the AES block cipher, which specifies the use of two similar algorithms for encrypting and decrypting a block. As discussed in Chapter 4, the CBC block cipher mode requires both algorithms, but the CTR mode requires only the encryption algorithm. Likewise, authenticated ciphers may not need both algorithms. Although the extra cost of implementing both encryption and decryption algorithms won't impact most software, it's often noticeable on low-cost dedicated hardware, where implementation cost is measured in terms of logic gates, or the silicon area occupied by the cryptography.

AES-GCM: The Authenticated Cipher Standard

AES-GCM is the most widely used authenticated cipher. AES-GCM is, of course, based on the AES algorithm, and the Galois counter mode (GCM) of operation is essentially a tweak of the CTR mode that incorporates a small and efficient component to compute an authentication tag. As I write this, AES-GCM is the only authenticated cipher that is a NIST standard (SP 800-38D). AES-GCM is also part of NSA's Suite B and of the Internet Engineering Task Force (IETF) for the secure network protocols IPSec, SSH, and TLS 1.2.

NOTE *Although GCM works with any block cipher, you'll probably only see it used with AES. Some people don't want to use AES because it's American, but they won't use GCM either, for the same reason. Therefore, GCM is rarely paired with other ciphers.*

GCM Internals: CTR and GHASH

Figure 8-2 shows how AES-GCM works: AES instances parameterized by a secret key (K) transform a block composed of the nonce (N) concatenated with a counter (starting here at 1, then incremented to 2, 3, and so on) and then XOR the result with a plaintext block to obtain a ciphertext block. So far, that's nothing new compared to the CTR mode.

Next, the ciphertext blocks are mixed using a combination of XORs and multiplications (as you'll see next). You can see AES-GCM as doing 1) an encryption in CTR mode and 2) a MAC over the ciphertext blocks. Therefore, AES-GCM is essentially an encrypt-then-MAC construction, where AES-CTR encrypts using a 128-bit key (K) and a 96-bit nonce (N), with the minor difference that the counter starts from 1, not 0, as in normal CTR mode (which doesn't matter, as far as security is concerned).

To authenticate the ciphertext, GCM uses a Wegman–Carter MAC (see Chapter 7) to authenticate the ciphertext,

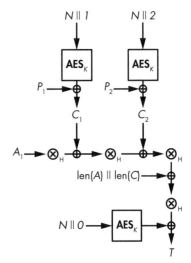

Figure 8-2: The AES-GCM mode, applied to one associated data block, A_1, and two plaintext blocks, P_1 and P_2. The circled multiplication sign represents polynomial multiplication by H, the authentication key derived from K.

which XORs the value **AES**$(K, N \| 0)$ with the output of a universal hash function called *GHASH*. In Figure 8-2, GHASH corresponds to the series of operations "$\otimes_H$" followed by the XOR with $\text{len}(A) \| \text{len}(C)$, or the bit length of A (the associated data) followed by the bit length of C (the ciphertext).

We can thus express the authentication tag's value as $T = $ **GHASH**$(H, C) \oplus$ **AES**$(K, N \| 0)$, where C is the ciphertext and H is the *hash key*, or *authentication key*. This key is determined as $H = $ **AES**$(K, 0)$, which is the encryption of the block equal to a sequence of null bytes (this step does not appear in Figure 8-2, for clarity).

NOTE *In GCM, GHASH doesn't use* K *directly in order to ensure that if GHASH's key is compromised, the master key* K *remains secret. Given* K*, you can get* H *by computing* **AES***(*K*, 0), but you can't recover* K *from that value since* K *acts here as AES's key.*

As Figure 8-2 shows, GHASH uses *polynomial notation* to multiply each ciphertext block with the authentication key H. This use of polynomial multiplication makes GHASH fast in hardware as well as in software, thanks to a special polynomial multiplication instruction available in many common microprocessors (CLMUL, for carry-less multiplication).

Alas, GHASH is far from ideal. For one thing, its speed is suboptimal. Even when the CLMUL instruction is used, the AES-CTR layer that encrypts the plaintext remains faster than the GHASH MAC. Second, GHASH is painful to implement correctly. In fact, even the experienced developers of the OpenSSL project, by far the most-used cryptographic piece of software in the world, got AES-GCM's GHASH wrong. One commit had a bug in a function called gcm_ghash_clmul that allowed attackers to forge valid MACs for the AES-GCM. (Fortunately, the error was spotted by Intel engineers before the bug entered the next OpenSSL release.)

POLYNOMIAL MULTIPLICATION

While clearly more complicated for us than classic integer arithmetic, polynomial multiplication is simpler for computers because there are no carries. For example, say we want to compute the product of the polynomials $(1 + X + X^2)$ and $(X + X^3)$. We first multiply the two polynomials $(1 + X + X^2)$ and $(X + X^3)$ as though we were doing normal polynomial multiplication, thus giving us the following (the two terms X^3 cancel each other out):

$$\left(1 + X + X^2\right) \otimes \left(X + X^3\right) = X + X^3 + X^2 + X^4 + X^3 + X^5 = X + X^2 + X^4 + X^5$$

We now apply modulo reduction, reducing $X + X^2 + X^4 + X^5$ modulo $1 + X^3 + X^4$ to give us X^2, because $X + X^2 + X^4 + X^5$ can be written as $X + X^2 + X^4 + X^5 = X \otimes (1 + X^3 + X^4) + X^2$. In more general terms, $A + BC$ modulo B is equal to A, by definition of modular reduction.

GCM Security

AES-GCM's biggest weakness is its fragility in the face of nonce repetition. If the same nonce N is used twice in an AES-GCM implementation, an attacker can get the authentication key H and use it to forge tags for any ciphertext, associated data, or combination thereof.

A look at the basic algebra behind AES-GCM's computations (as shown in Figure 8-2) will help make this fragility clear. Specifically, a tag (T) is computed as $T = \textbf{GHASH}(H, A, C) \oplus \textbf{AES}(K, N \| 0)$, where GHASH is a universal hash function with linearly related inputs and outputs.

Now what happens if you get two tags, T_1 and T_2, computed with the same nonce N? Right, the AES part will vanish. If we have two tags, $T_1 = \textbf{GHASH}(H, A_1, C_1) \oplus \textbf{AES}(K, N \| 0)$ and $T_2 = \textbf{GHASH}(H, A_1, C_1) \oplus \textbf{AES}(K, N \| 0)$, then XORing them together gives the following:

$$\textbf{GHASH}(H, A_1, C_1) \oplus \textbf{AES}(K, N \| 0) \oplus \textbf{GHASH}(H, A_2, C_2) \oplus \textbf{AES}(K, N \| 0)$$
$$= \textbf{GHASH}(H, A_1, C_1) \oplus \textbf{GHASH}(H, A_2, C_2) \oplus (\textbf{AES}(K, N \| 0) \oplus \textbf{AES}(K, N \| 0))$$
$$= \textbf{GHASH}(H, A_1, C_1) \oplus \textbf{GHASH}(H, A_2, C_2)$$

If the same nonce is used twice, an attacker can thus recover the value $\textbf{GHASH}(H, A_1, C_1) \oplus \textbf{GHASH}(H, A_2, C_2)$ for some known A_1, C_1, A_2, and C_2. The linearity of GHASH then allows an attacker to easily determine H. (It would have been worse if GHASH had used the same key K as the encryption part, but because $H = \textbf{AES}(K, 0)$, there's no way to find K from H.)

As recently as 2016, researchers scanned the internet for instances of AES-GCM exposed through HTTPS servers, in search of systems with repeating nonces (see *https://eprint.iacr.org/2016/475/*). They found 184 servers with repeating nonces, including 23 that always used the all-zero string as a nonce.

GCM Efficiency

One advantage of GCM mode is that both GCM encryption and decryption are parallelizable, allowing you to encrypt or decrypt different plaintext blocks independently. However, the AES-GCM MAC computation isn't parallelizable, because it must be computed from the beginning to the end of the ciphertext once GHASH has processed any associated data. This lack of parallelizability means that any system that receives the plaintext first and then the associated data will have to wait until all associated data is read and hashed before hashing the first ciphertext block.

Nevertheless, GCM is streamable: since the computations in its two layers can be pipelined, there's no need to store all ciphertext blocks before computing GHASH because GHASH will process each block as it's encrypted. In other words, P_1 is encrypted to C_1, then GHASH processes C_1 while P_2 is encrypted to C_2, then P_1 and C_1 are no longer needed, and so on.

OCB: An Authenticated Cipher Faster than GCM

The acronym *OCB* stands for *offset codebook* (though its designer, Phil Rogaway, prefers to simply call it OCB). First developed in 2001, OCB predates GCM, and like GCM it produces an authenticated cipher from a block cipher, though it does so faster and more simply. Then why hasn't OCB seen wider adoption? Unfortunately, until 2013, all uses of OCB required a license from the inventor. Fortunately, as I write this, Rogaway grants free licenses for non-military software implementations (see *http://web.cs.ucdavis.edu/~rogaway/ocb/license.htm*). Therefore, although OCB is not yet a formal standard, perhaps we will begin to see wider adoption.

Unlike GCM, OCB blends encryption and authentication into one processing layer that uses only one key. There's no separate authentication component, so OCB gets you authentication mostly for free and performs almost as many block cipher calls as a non-authenticated cipher. Actually, OCB is almost as simple as the ECB mode (see Chapter 4), except that it's secure.

OCB Internals

Figure 8-3 shows how OCB works: OCB encrypts each plaintext block P to a ciphertext block $C = \mathbf{E}(K, P \oplus O) \oplus O$, where $\mathbf{E}$ is a block cipher encryption function. Here, O (called the *offset*) is a value that depends on the key and the nonce incremented for each new block processed.

To produce the authentication tag, OCB first XORs the plaintext blocks together to compute $S = P_1 \oplus P_2 \oplus P_3 \oplus \ldots$ (that is, the XOR of all plaintext blocks). The authentication tag is then $T = \mathbf{E}(K, S \oplus O^*)$, where O^* is an offset value computed from the offset of the last plaintext block processed.

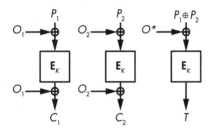

Figure 8-3: The OCB encryption process when run on two plaintext blocks, with no associated data

Like AES-GCM, OCB also supports associated data as a series of blocks, A_1, A_2, and so on. When an OCB encrypted message contains associated data, the authentication tag is calculated according to the formula

$$T = \mathbf{E}(K, S \oplus O^*) \oplus \mathbf{E}(K, A_1 \oplus O_1) \oplus \mathbf{E}(K, A_2 \oplus O_2) \oplus \ldots$$

where OCB specifies offset values that are different from those used to encrypt P.

Unlike GCM and encrypt-then-MAC, which create an authentication tag by combining ciphertext, OCB calculates the authentication tag by combining plaintext data. There's nothing wrong with this approach, and OCB is backed by solid security proofs.

NOTE *For more on how to implement OCB correctly, see either RFC 7253 or the 2011 paper "The Software Performance of Authenticated-Encryption Modes" by Krovetz and Rogaway, which covers the latest and best version of OCB, OCB3. For further details on OCB, see the OCB FAQ at* http://web.cs.ucdavis.edu/~rogaway/ocb/ocb-faq.htm.

OCB Security

OCB is a bit less fragile than GCM against repeated nonces. For example, if a nonce is used twice, an attacker that sees the two ciphertexts will notice that, say, the third plaintext block of the first message is identical to the third plaintext block of the second message. With GCM, attackers can find not only duplicates but also XOR differences between blocks at the same position. The impact of repeated nonces is therefore worse with GCM than it is with OCB.

As with GCM, repeated nonces can break the authenticity of OCB, though less effectively. For example, an attacker could combine blocks from two messages authenticated with OCB to create another encrypted message with the same checksum and tag as one of the original two messages, but the attacker would not be able to recover a secret key as with GCM.

OCB Efficiency

OCB and GCM are about equally fast. Like GCM, OCB is parallelizable and streamable. In terms of raw efficiency, GCM and OCB will make about as many calls to the underlying block cipher (usually AES), but OCB is slightly more efficient than GCM because it simply XORs the plaintext rather than performing something like the relatively expensive GHASH computation. (In earlier generations of Intel microprocessors, AES-GCM used to be more than three times slower than AES-OCB because AES and GHASH instructions had to compete for CPU resources and couldn't be run in parallel.)

One important difference between OCB and GCM implementations is that OCB needs both the block cipher's encryption and decryption functions in order to encrypt and decrypt, which increases the cost of hardware implementations when only limited silicon is available for crypto components. In contrast, GCM uses only the encryption function for both encryption and decryption.

SIV: The Safest Authenticated Cipher?

Synthetic IV, also known as *SIV*, is an authenticated cipher mode typically used with AES. Unlike GCM and OCB, SIV is secure even if you use the same nonce twice: if an attacker gets two ciphertexts encrypted using the same nonce, they'll only be able to learn whether the same plaintext was encrypted twice. Unlike with messages encrypted with GCM or OCB, the attacker would be unable to tell whether the first block of the two messages is the same because the nonce used to encrypt is first computed as a combination of the given nonce and the plaintext.

The SIV construction specification is more general than that of GCM. Instead of specifying detailed internals as with GCM's GHASH, SIV simply tells you how to combine a cipher (E) and a pseudorandom function (PRF) to get an authenticated cipher. Specifically, you compute the tag $T = PRF(K_1, N \| P)$ and then compute the ciphertext $C = E(K_2, T, P)$, where T acts as the nonce of E. Thus, SIV needs two keys (K_1 and K_2) and a nonce (N).

The major problem with SIV is that it's not streamable: after computing T, it must keep the entire plaintext P in memory. In other words, in order to encrypt a 100GB plaintext with SIV, you must first store the 100GB of plaintext so that SIV encryption can read it.

The document RFC 5297, based on the 2006 paper "Deterministic Authenticated-Encryption" by Rogaway and Shrimpton, specifies SIV as using CMAC-AES (a MAC construction using AES) as a PRF and AES-CTR as a cipher. In 2015, a more efficient version of SIV was proposed, called GCM-SIV, that combines GCM's fast GHASH function and SIV's mode and is nearly as fast as GCM. Like the original SIV, however, GCM-SIV isn't streamable. (For more information, see *https://eprint.iacr.org/2015/102/*.)

Permutation-Based AEAD

Now for a totally different approach to building an authenticated cipher: instead of building a mode of operation around a block cipher like AES, we'll look at a cipher that builds a mode around a permutation. A permutation simply transforms an input to an output of the same size, reversibly, without using a key, that's the simplest component imaginable. Better still, the resulting AEAD is fast, provably secure, and more resistant to nonce reuse than GCM and OCB.

Figure 8-4 shows how a permutation-based AEAD works: from some fixed initial state H_0, you XOR the key K followed by the nonce N to the internal state, to obtain a new value of the internal state that is the same size as the original. You then transform the new state with P and get another new value of the state. Now you XOR the first plaintext block P_1 to the current state and take the resulting value as the first ciphertext block C_1, where P_1 and C_1 are equal in size but smaller than the state.

To encrypt a second block, you transform the state with P, XOR the next plaintext block P_2 to the current state, and take the resulting value as C_2. You then iterate over all plaintext blocks and, following the last call to P, take bits from the internal state as the authentication tag T, as shown at the right of Figure 8-4.

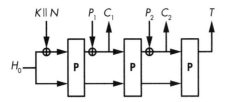

Figure 8-4: Permutation-based authenticated cipher

The mode shown in Figure 8-4 can be adapted to support associated data, but the process is a bit more complicated, so we'll skip its description.

Designing permutation-based authenticated ciphers has certain requirements in order to ensure security. For one thing, note that you only XOR input values to a part of the state: the larger this part, the more control a successful attacker has on the internal state, and thus the lower the cipher's security. Indeed, all security relies on the secrecy of the internal state.

Also, blocks must be padded properly with extra bits, in a way that ensures that any two different messages will yield different results. As a counterexample, if the last plaintext block is shorter than a complete block, it should not just be padded with zeroes; otherwise, a plaintext block of, say, two bytes (0000) would result in a complete plaintext block (0000 . . . 0000), as would a block of three bytes (000000). As a result, you'd get the same tag for both messages, although they differ in size.

What if a nonce is reused in such a permutation-based cipher? The good news is that the impact isn't as bad as with GCM or OCB—the strength of the authentication tag won't be compromised. If a nonce is repeated, a successful attacker would only be able to learn whether the two encrypted messages begin with the same value, as well as the length of this common value, or prefix. For example, although encrypting the two six-block messages *ABCXYZ* and *ABCDYZ* (each letter symbolizing a block here) with the same nonce might yield the two ciphertexts *JKLTUV* and *JKLMNO*, which have identical prefixes, attackers would not be able to learn that the two plaintexts shared the same final two blocks (*YZ*).

In terms of performance, permutation-based ciphers offer the benefits of a single layer of operations, streamable processing, and the use of a single core algorithm for encryption and decryption. However, they are not parallelizable like GCM or OCB because new calls to **P** need to wait for the previous call to complete.

If you're tempted to pick your favorite permutation and make up your own authenticated cipher, don't. You're likely to get the details wrong and end up with an insecure cipher. Read the specifications written by experienced cryptographers for algorithms such as Keyak (an algorithm derived from Keccak) and NORX (designed by Philipp Jovanovic, Samuel Neves, and myself), and you'll see that permutation-based ciphers are way more complex than they may first appear.

How Things Can Go Wrong

Authenticated ciphers have a larger attack surface than hash functions or block ciphers because they aim to achieve both confidentiality *and* authenticity. They take several different input values, and must remain secure regardless of the input—whether that contains only associated data and no encrypted data, extremely large plaintexts, or different key sizes. They must also be secure for all nonce values against attackers who collect numerous message/tag pairs and, to some extent, against accidental repetition of nonces.

That's a lot to ask, and as you'll see next, even AES-GCM has several imperfections.

AES-GCM and Weak Hash Keys

One of AES-GCM's weaknesses is found in its authentication algorithm GHASH: certain values of the hash key H greatly simplify attacks against GCM's authentication mechanism. Specifically, if the value H belongs to some specific, mathematically defined subgroups of all 128-bit strings, attackers might be able to guess a valid authentication tag for some message simply by shuffling the blocks of a previous message.

In order to understand this weakness, let's look at how GHASH works.

GHASH Internals

As you saw in Figure 8-2, GHASH starts with a 128-bit value, H, initially set to $\mathbf{AES}(K, 0)$, and then repeatedly computes

$$X_i = (X_{i-1} \oplus C_i) \otimes H$$

starting from $X_0 = 0$ and processing ciphertext blocks C_1, C_2, and so on. The final X_i is returned by GHASH to compute the final tag.

Now say for the sake of simplicity that all C_i values are equal to 1, so that for any i we have this:

$$C_i \otimes H = 1 \otimes H = H$$

Next, from the GHASH equation

$$X_i = \left(X_{i-1} \oplus C_i\right) \otimes H$$

we derive

$$X_1 = (X_0 \oplus C_1) \otimes H = (0 \oplus 1) \otimes H = H$$

substituting X_0 with 0 and C_1 with 1, to yield the following:

$$(0 \oplus 1) = 1$$

Thanks to the distributive property of $\otimes$ over $\oplus$, we substitute X with H and C_2 with 1 and then compute the next value X_2 as

$$X_2 = (X_1 \oplus C_2) \otimes H = (H \oplus 1) \otimes H = H^2 \oplus H$$

where H^2 is H squared, or $H \otimes H$.

Now we derive X_3 by substituting X_2 for its derivation, and obtain the following:

$$X_3 = \left(X_2 \oplus C_3\right) \otimes H = \left(H^2 \oplus H \oplus 1\right) \otimes H = H^3 \oplus H^2 \oplus H$$

Next, we derive X_4 to be $X_4 = H^4 \oplus H^3 \oplus H^2 \oplus H$, and so on, and eventually the last X_i is this:

$$X_n = H^n \oplus H^{n-1} \oplus H^{n-2} \oplus \ldots \oplus H^2 \oplus H$$

Remember that we set all blocks C_i equal to 1. If instead those values were arbitrary values, we would end up with the following:

$$X_n = C_1 \oplus H^n \oplus C_2 \oplus H^{n-1} \oplus C_3 H^{n-2} \oplus \ldots \oplus C_{n-1} H^2 \oplus C_n \oplus H$$

GHASH then would XOR the message's length to this last X_n, multiply the result by H, and then XOR this value with $\mathbf{AES}(K, N \| 0)$ to create the final authentication tag, T.

Where Things Break

What can go wrong from here? Let's look first at the two simplest cases:

- If $H = 0$, then $X_n = 0$ regardless of the C_i values, and thus regardless of the message. That is, all messages will have the same authentication tag if H is 0.

- If $H = 1$, then the tag is just an XOR of the ciphertext blocks, and reordering the ciphertext blocks will give the same authentication tag.

Of course, 0 and 1 are only two values of 2^{128} possible values of H, so there is only a $2/2^{128} = 1/2^{127}$ chance of these occurring. But there are other weak values as well—namely, all values of H that belong to a *short cycle* when raised to ith powers. For example, the value $H = 10d04d25f93556e69f58$ ce2f8d035a4 belongs to a cycle of length five, as it satisfies $H^5 = H$, and therefore $H^e = H$ for any e that is a multiple of five (the very definition of cycle with respect to fifth powers). Consequently, in the preceding expression of the final GHASH value X_n, swapping the blocks C_n (multiplied to H) and the block C_{n-4} (multiplied to H^5) will leave the authentication tag unchanged, which amounts to a forgery. An attacker may exploit this property to construct a new message and its valid tag without knowing the key, which should be impossible for a secure authenticated cipher.

The preceding example is based on a cycle of length five, but there are many cycles of greater length and therefore many values of H that are weaker than they should be. The upshot is that, in the unlikely case that H belongs to a short cycle of values and attackers can forge as many authentication tags as they want, unless they know H or K, they cannot determine H's cycle length. So although this vulnerability can't be exploited, it could have been avoided by more carefully choosing the polynomial used for modulo reductions.

NOTE   *For further details on this attack, read "Cycling Attacks on GCM, GHASH and Other Polynomial MACs and Hashes" by Markku-Juhani O. Saarinen, available at https://eprint.iacr.org/2011/202/.*

AES-GCM and Small Tags

In practice, AES-GCM usually returns 128-bit tags, but it can produce tags of any length. Unfortunately, when shorter tags are used, the probability of forgery increases significantly.

When a 128-bit tag is used, an attacker who attempts a forgery should succeed with a probability of $1/2^{128}$ because there are 2^{128} possible 128-bit tags. (Generally, with an n-bit tag, the probability of success should be $1/2^n$, where 2^n is the number of possible values of an n-bit tag.) But when shorter tags are used, the probability of forgery is much higher than $1/2^n$ due to weaknesses in the structure of GCM that are beyond the scope of this discussion. For example, a 32-bit tag will allow an attacker who knows the authentication tag of some 2MB message to succeed with a chance of $1/2^{16}$ instead of $1/2^{32}$.

Generally, with n-bit tags, the probability of forgery isn't $1/2^n$ but rather $2^m/2^n$, where 2^m is the number of blocks of the longest message for which a successful attacker observed the tag. For example, if you use 48-bit tags and process messages of 4GB (or 2^{28} blocks of 16 bytes each), the probability of a forgery will be $2^{28}/2^{48} = 1/2^{20}$, or about one chance in a million. That's a relatively high chance as far as cryptography is concerned. (For more information on this attack, see the 2005 paper "Authentication Weaknesses in GCM" by Niels Ferguson.)

Further Reading

To learn more about authenticated ciphers, visit the home page of CAESAR, the Competition for Authenticated Encryption: Security, Applicability, and Robustness (*http://competitions.cr.yp.to/caesar.html*). Begun in 2012, CAESAR is a crypto competition in the style of the AES and SHA-3 competitions, though it isn't organized by NIST.

The CAESAR competition has attracted an impressive number of innovative designs: from OCB-like modes to permutation-based modes, as well as new core algorithms. Examples include the previously mentioned NORX and Keyak permutation-based authenticated ciphers; AEZ (as in AEasy), which is built on a nonstreamable two-layer mode that makes it misuse resistant; AEGIS, a beautifully simple authenticated cipher that leverages AES's round function.

In this chapter, I've focused on GCM, but a handful of other modes are used in real applications as well. Specifically, the counter with CBC-MAC (CCM) and EAX modes competed with GCM for standardization in the early 2000s, and although GCM was selected, the two competitors are used in a few applications. For example, CCM is used in the WPA2 Wi-Fi encryption protocol. You may want to read these ciphers' specifications and review their relative security and performance merits.

This concludes our discussion of symmetric-key cryptography! You've seen block ciphers, stream ciphers, (keyed) hash functions, and now authenticated ciphers—or all the main cryptography components that work with a symmetric key, or no key at all. Before we move to *asymmetric* cryptography, Chapter 9 will focus more on computer science and math, to provide background for asymmetric schemes such as RSA (Chapter 10) and Diffie–Hellman (Chapter 11).

9

HARD PROBLEMS

Hard computational problems are the cornerstone of modern cryptography. They're problems that are simple to describe yet practically impossible to solve. These are problems for which even the best algorithm wouldn't find a solution before the sun burns out.

In the 1970s, the rigorous study of hard problems gave rise to a new field of science called computational complexity theory, which would dramatically impact cryptography and many other fields, including economics, physics, and biology. In this chapter, I'll give you the conceptual tools from complexity theory necessary to understand the foundations of cryptographic security, and I'll introduce the hard problems behind public-key schemes such as RSA encryption and Diffie–Hellman key agreement. We'll touch on some deep concepts, but I'll minimize the technical details and only scratch the surface. Still, I hope you'll see the beauty in the way cryptography leverages computational complexity theory to maximize security.

Computational Hardness

A computational problem is a question that can be answered by doing enough computation, for example, "Is 2017 a prime number?" or "How many *i* letters are there in *incomprehensibilities*?" *Computational hardness* is the property of computational problems for which there is no algorithm that will run in a reasonable amount of time. Such problems are also called *intractable problems* and are often practically impossible to solve.

Surprisingly, computational hardness is independent of the type of computing device used, be it a general-purpose CPU, an integrated circuit, or a mechanical Turing machine. Indeed, one of the first findings of computational complexity theory is that all computing models are equivalent. If a problem can be solved efficiently with one computing device, it can be solved efficiently on any other device by porting the algorithm to the other device's language—an exception is quantum computers, but these do not exist (yet). The upshot is that we won't need to specify the underlying computing device or hardware when discussing computational hardness; instead, we'll just discuss algorithms.

To evaluate hardness, we'll first find a way to measure the complexity of an algorithm, or its running time. We'll then categorize running times as hard or easy.

Measuring Running Time

Most developers are familiar with *computational complexity*, or the approximate number of operations done by an algorithm as a function of its input size. The size is counted in bits or in the number of elements taken as input. For example, take the algorithm shown in Listing 9-1, written in pseudocode. It searches for a value, *x*, within an array of *n* elements and then returns its index position.

```
search(x, array, n):
    for i from 1 to n {
        if (array[i] == x) {
            return i;
        }
    }
    return 0;
}
```

Listing 9-1: A simple search algorithm, written in pseudocode, of complexity linear with respect to the array length n. The algorithm returns the index where the value x is found in [1, n], or 0 if x isn't found in the array.

In this algorithm, we use a for loop to find a specific value, *x*, by iterating through an array. On each iteration, we assign the variable *i* a number starting with 1. Then we check whether the value of position *i* in array is equal to the value of *x*. If it is, we return the position *i*. Otherwise, we increment *i* and try the next position until we reach *n*, the length of the array, at which point we return 0.

For this kind of algorithm, we count complexity as the number of iterations of the for loop: 1 in the best case (if x is equal to array[1]), n in the worst case (if x is equal to array[n] or if x is not in found in array), and $n/2$ on average if x is randomly distributed in one of the n cells of the array. With an array 10 times as large, the algorithm will be 10 times as slow. Complexity is therefore proportional to n, or "linear" in n. A complexity linear in n is considered fast, as opposed to complexities exponential in n. Although processing larger input values will be slower, it will make a difference of at most just seconds for most practical uses.

But many useful algorithms are slower than that and have a complexity higher than linear. The textbook example is sorting algorithms: given a list of n values in a random order, you'll need on average $n \times \log n$ basic operations to sort the list, which is sometimes called *linearithmic complexity*. Since $n \times \log n$ grows faster than n, sorting speed will slow down faster than proportionally to n. Yet such sorting algorithms will remain in the realm of *practical* computation, or computation that can be carried out in a reasonable amount of time.

At some point, we'll hit the ceiling of what's feasible even for relatively small input lengths. Take the simplest example from cryptanalysis: the brute-force search for a secret key. Recall from Chapter 1 that given a plaintext P and a ciphertext $C = \mathbf{E}(K, P)$, it takes at most 2^n attempts to recover an n-bit symmetric key because there are 2^n possible keys—an example of a complexity that grows exponentially. For complexity theorists, *exponential complexity* means a problem that is practically impossible to solve, because as n grows, the effort very rapidly becomes infeasible.

You may object that we're comparing oranges and apples here: in the search() function in Listing 9-1, we counted the number of if (array[i] == x) operations, whereas key recovery counts the number of encryptions, each thousands of times slower than a single == comparison. This inconsistency can make a difference if you compare two algorithms with very similar complexities, but most of the time it won't matter because the number of operations will have a greater impact than the cost of an individual operation. Also, complexity estimates ignore *constant factors*: when we say that an algorithm takes time in the order of n^3 operations (which is *quadratic complexity*), it may actually take $41 \times n^3$ operations, or $12345 \times n^3$ operations—but again, as n grows, the constant factors lose significance to the point that we can ignore them. Complexity analysis is about theoretical hardness as a function of the input size; it doesn't care about the exact number of CPU cycles it will take on your computer.

You'll often find the $O()$ notation ("big O") used to express complexities. For example, $O(n^3)$ means that complexity grows no faster than n^3, ignoring potential constant factors. $O()$ denotes the *upper bound* of an algorithm's complexity. The notation $O(1)$ means that an algorithm runs in *constant time*—that is, the running time doesn't depend on the input length! For example, the algorithm that determines an integer's parity by looking at its least significant bit (LSB) and returning "even" if it's zero and "odd" otherwise will do the same thing at the same cost whatever the integer's length.

To see the difference between linear, quadratic, and exponential time complexities, look at how complexity grows for $O(n)$ (linear) versus $O(n^2)$ (quadratic) versus $O(2^n)$ (exponential) in Figure 9-1.

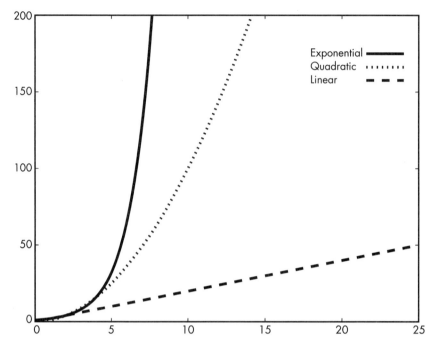

Figure 9-1: Growth of exponential, quadratic, and linear complexities, from the fastest to the slowest growing

Exponential complexity means the problem is practically impossible to solve, and linear complexity means the solution is feasible, whereas quadratic complexity is somewhere between the two.

Polynomial vs. Superpolynomial Time

The $O(n^2)$ complexity discussed in the last section (the middle curve in Figure 9-1) is a special case of the broader class of polynomial complexities, or $O(n^k)$, where k is some fixed number such as 3, 2.373, 7/10, or the square root of 17. Polynomial-time algorithms are eminently important in complexity theory and in crypto because they're the very definition of practically feasible. When an algorithm runs in *polynomial time*, or *polytime* for short, it will complete in a decent amount of time even if the input is large. That's why polynomial time is synonymous with "efficient" for complexity theorists and cryptographers.

In contrast, algorithms running in *superpolynomial time*—that is, in $O(f(n))$, where $f(n)$ is any function that grows faster than any polynomial—are viewed as impractical. I'm saying superpolynomial, and not just exponential, because there are complexities in between polynomial and the well-known exponential complexity $O(2^n)$, such as $O(n^{\log(n)})$, as Figure 9-2 shows.

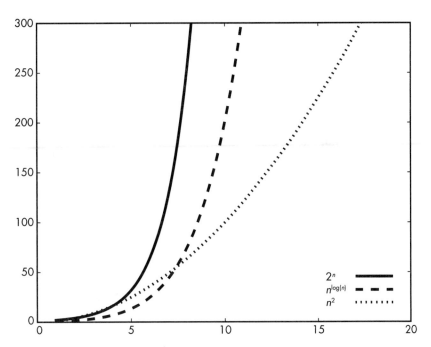

Figure 9-2: Growth of the 2^n, $n^{\log(n)}$, and n^2 functions, from the fastest to the slowest growing

NOTE   *Exponential complexity* $O(2^n)$ *is not the worst you can get. Some complexities grow even faster and thus characterize algorithms even slower to compute—for example, the complexity* $O(n^n)$ *or the exponential factorial* $O(n^{f(n-1)})$*, where for any* x*, the function* f *is here recursively defined as* $f(x) = x^{f(x-1)}$*. In practice, you'll never encounter algorithms with such preposterous complexities.*

$O(n^2)$ or $O(n^3)$ may be efficient, but $O(n^{99999999999})$ obviously isn't. In other words, polytime is fast as long as the exponent isn't too large. Fortunately, all polynomial-time algorithms found to solve actual problems do have small exponents. For example, $O(n^{1.465})$ is the time for multiplying two *n*-bit integers, or $O(n^{2.373})$ for multiplying two $n \times n$ matrices. The 2002 breakthrough polytime algorithm for identifying prime numbers initially had a complexity $O(n^{12})$, but it was later improved to $O(n^6)$. Polynomial time thus may not be the perfect definition of a practical time for an algorithm, but it's the best we have.

By extension, a problem that can't be solved by a polynomial-time algorithm is considered impractical, or *hard*. For example, for a straightforward key search, there's no way to beat the $O(2^n)$ complexity unless the cipher is somehow broken.

We know for sure that there's no way to beat the $O(2^n)$ complexity of a brute-force key search (as long as the cipher is secure), but we don't always know what the fastest way to solve a problem is. A large portion of the research in complexity theory is about proving complexity *bounds* on the running time of algorithms solving a given problem. To make their job easier, complexity theorists have categorized computational problems in different groups, or *classes*, according to the effort needed to solve them.

Complexity Classes

In mathematics, a *class* is a group of objects with some similar attribute. For example, all computational problems solvable in time $O(n^2)$, which complexity theorists simply denote $\textbf{TIME}(n^2)$, are one class. Likewise, $\textbf{TIME}(n^3)$ is the class of problems solvable in time $O(n^3)$, $\textbf{TIME}(2^n)$ is the class of problems solvable in time $O(2^n)$, and so on. For the same reason that a supercomputer can compute whatever a laptop can compute, any problem solvable in $O(n^2)$ is also solvable in $O(n^3)$. Hence, any problem in the class $\textbf{TIME}(n^2)$ also belongs to the class $\textbf{TIME}(n^3)$, which both also belong to the class $\textbf{TIME}(n^4)$, and so on. The union of all these classes of problems, $\textbf{TIME}(n^k)$, where k is a constant, is called $\textbf{P}$, which stands for polynomial time.

If you've ever programmed a computer, you'll know that seemingly fast algorithms may still crash your system by eating all its memory resources. When selecting an algorithm, you should not only consider its time complexity but also how much memory it uses, or its *space complexity*. This is especially important because a single memory access is usually orders of magnitudes slower than a basic arithmetic operation in a CPU.

Formally, you can define an algorithm's memory consumption as a function of its input length, n, in the same way we defined time complexity. The class of problems solvable using $f(n)$ bits of memory is $\textbf{SPACE}(f(n))$. For example, $\textbf{SPACE}(n^3)$ is the class of problems solvable using of the order of n^3 bits of memory. Just as we had $\textbf{P}$ as the union of all $\textbf{TIME}(n^k)$, the union of all $\textbf{SPACE}(n^k)$ problems is called $\textbf{PSPACE}$.

Obviously, the lower the memory the better, but a polynomial amount of memory doesn't necessarily imply that an algorithm is practical. Why? Well, take for example a brute-force key search: again, it takes only negligible memory but is slow as hell. More generally, an algorithm can take forever, even if it uses just a few bytes of memory.

Any problem solvable in time $f(n)$ needs at most $f(n)$ memory, so $\textbf{TIME}(f(n))$ is included in $\textbf{SPACE}(f(n))$. In time $f(n)$, you can only write up to $f(n)$ bits, and no more, because writing (or reading) 1 bit is assumed to take one unit of time; therefore, any problem in $\textbf{TIME}(f(n))$ can't use more than $f(n)$ space. As a consequence, $\textbf{P}$ is a subset of $\textbf{PSPACE}$.

Nondeterministic Polynomial Time

$\textbf{NP}$ is the second most important complexity class, after the class $\textbf{P}$ of all polynomial-time algorithms. No, $\textbf{NP}$ doesn't stand for non-polynomial time, but for *nondeterministic* polynomial time. What does that mean?

$\textbf{NP}$ is the class of problems for which a solution can be verified in polynomial time—that is, efficiently—even though the solution may be hard to find. By *verified*, I mean that given a potential solution, you can run some polynomial-time algorithm that will verify whether you've found an actual solution. For example, the problem of recovering a secret key with a known plaintext is in **NP**, because given P, $C = \mathbf{E}(K, P)$, and some candidate key K_0, you can check that K_0 is the correct key by verifying that $\mathbf{E}(K_0, P)$ equals C. The process of finding a potential key (the solution) can't be done in polynomial time, but checking whether the key is correct is done using a polynomial-time algorithm.

Now for a counterexample: what about known-ciphertext attacks? This time, you only get some $\mathbf{E}(K, P)$ values for random unknown plaintext Ps. If you don't know what the Ps are, then there's no way to verify whether a potential key, K_0, is the right one. In other words, the key-recovery problem under known-ciphertext attacks is not in **NP** (let alone in **P**).

Another example of a problem not in **NP** is that of verifying the *absence* of a solution to a problem. Verifying that a solution is correct boils down to computing some algorithm with the candidate solution as an input and then checking the return value. However, to verify that *no* solution exists, you may need to go through all possible inputs. And if there's an exponential number of inputs, you won't be able to efficiently prove that no solution exists. The absence of a solution is hard to show for the hardest problems in the class **NP**—the so-called **NP**-complete problems, which we'll discuss next.

NP-Complete Problems

The hardest problems in the class **NP** are called **NP**-complete; we don't know how to solve these problems in polynomial time. And as complexity theorists discovered in the 1970s when they developed the theory of **NP**-completeness, **NP**'s hardest problems are all equally hard. This was proven by showing that any efficient solution to any of the **NP**-complete problems can be turned into an efficient solution for any of the other **NP**-complete problems. In other words, if you can solve any **NP**-complete problem efficiently, you can solve all of them, as well as all problems in **NP**. How can this be?

NP-complete problems come in different disguises, but they're fundamentally similar from a mathematical perspective. In fact, you can reduce any **NP**-complete problem to any other **NP**-complete problem such that solving the first one depends on solving the second.

Here are some examples of **NP**-complete problems:

The traveling salesman problem　Given a set of points on a map (cities, addresses, or other geographic locations) and the distances between each point from each other point, find a path that visits every point such that the total distance is smaller than a given distance of x.

The clique problem　Given a number, x, and a graph (a set of nodes connected by edges, as in Figure 9-3), determine if there's a set of x points or less such that all points are connected to each other.

The knapsack problem　Given two numbers, x and y, and a set of items, each of a known value and weight, can we pick a group of items such that the total value is at least x and the total weight at most y?

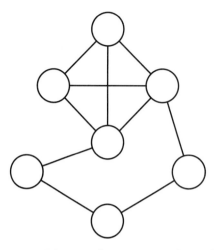

Figure 9-3: A graph containing a clique of
four points. The general problem of finding
a clique (set of nodes all connected to each
other) of given size in a graph is **NP**-complete.

Such **NP**-complete problems are found everywhere, from scheduling
problems (given jobs of some priority and duration, and one or more processors, assign jobs to the processors by respecting the priority while minimizing
total execution time) to constraint-satisfaction problems (determine values
that satisfy a set of mathematical constraints, such as logical equations). Even
the task of winning in certain video games can sometimes be proven to be
NP-complete (for famous games including *Tetris, Super Mario Bros., Pokémon,*
and *Candy Crush Saga*). For example, the article "Classic Nintendo Games
Are (Computationally) Hard" (*https://arxiv.org/abs/1203.1895*) considers "the
decision problem of reachability" to determine the possibility of reaching the
goal point from a particular starting point.

Some of these video game problems are actually even harder than
NP-complete and are called **NP**-*hard*. We say that a problem is **NP**-hard
when it's at least as hard as **NP**-complete problems. More formally, a
problem is **NP**-hard if what it takes to solve it can be proven to also solve
NP-complete problems.

I have to mention an important caveat. Not all *instances* of **NP**-complete
problems are actually hard to solve. Some specific instances, because they're
small or because they have a specific structure, may be solved efficiently.
Take, for example, the graph in Figure 9-3. By just looking at it for a few
seconds you'll spot the clique, which is the top four connected nodes—even
though the aforementioned clique problem is **NP**-hard, there's nothing hard
here. So being **NP**-complete doesn't mean that all instances of a given problem are hard, but that as the problem size grows, many of them are.

The P vs. NP Problem

If you could solve the hardest **NP** problems in polynomial time, then you
could solve *all* **NP** problems in polynomial time, and therefore **NP** would

equal **P**. That sounds preposterous; isn't it obvious that there are problems for which a solution is easy to verify but hard to find? For example, isn't it obvious that exponential-time brute force is the fastest way to recover the key of a symmetric cipher, and therefore that the problem can't be in **P**? It turns out that, as crazy as it sounds, no one has proved that **P** is different from **NP**, despite a bounty of literally one million dollars.

The Clay Mathematics Institute will award this bounty to anyone who proves that either **P** ≠ **NP** or **P** = **NP**. This problem, known as **P** vs. **NP**, was called "one of the deepest questions that human beings have ever asked" by renowned complexity theorist Scott Aaronson. Think about it: if **P** were equal to **NP**, then any easily checked solution would also be easy to find. All cryptography used in practice would be insecure, because you could recover symmetric keys and invert hash functions efficiently.

But don't panic: most complexity theorists believe **P** isn't equal to **NP**, and therefore that **P** is instead a strict subset of **NP**, as Figure 9-4 shows, where **NP**-complete problems are another subset of **NP** not overlapping with **P**. In other words, problems that look hard actually are hard. It's just difficult to prove this mathematically. While proving that **P** = **NP** would only need a polynomial-time algorithm for an **NP**-complete problem, proving the nonexistence of such an algorithm is fundamentally harder. But this didn't stop

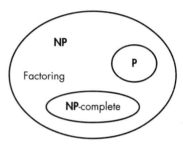

Figure 9-4: The classes **NP**, **P**, and the set of **NP**-complete problems

wacky mathematicians from coming up with simple proofs that, while usually obviously wrong, often make for funny reads; for an example, see "The P-versus-NP page" (*https://www.win.tue.nl/~gwoegi/P-versus-NP.htm*).

Now if we're almost sure that hard problems do exist, what about leveraging them to build strong, provably secure crypto? Imagine a proof that breaking some cipher is **NP**-complete, and therefore that the cipher is unbreakable as long as **P** isn't equal to **NP**. But reality is disappointing: **NP**-complete problems have proved difficult to use for crypto purposes because the very structure that makes them hard in general can make them easy in specific cases—cases that sometimes occur in crypto. Instead, cryptography often relies on problems that are *probably not* **NP**-hard.

The Factoring Problem

The factoring problem consists of finding the prime numbers p and q given a large number, $N = p \times q$. The widely used RSA algorithms are based on the fact that factoring a number is difficult. In fact, the hardness of the factoring problem is what makes RSA encryption and signature schemes secure. But before we see how RSA leverages the factoring problem in Chapter 10, I'd like to convince you that this problem is indeed hard, yet probably not **NP**-complete.

First, some kindergarten math. A *prime number* is a number that isn't divisible by any other number but itself and 1. For example, the numbers 3, 7, and 11 are prime; the numbers $4 = 2 \times 2$, $6 = 2 \times 3$, and $12 = 2 \times 2 \times 3$ are not prime. A fundamental theorem of number theory says that any integer number can be uniquely written as a product of primes, a representation called the *factorization* of that number. For example, the factorization of 123456 is $2^6 \times 3 \times 643$; the factorization of 1234567 is $= 127 \times 9721$; and so on. Any integer has a unique factorization, or a unique way to write it as a product of prime numbers. But how do we know that a given factorization contains only prime numbers or that a given number is prime? The answer is found through polynomial-time primality testing algorithms, which allow us to efficiently test whether a given number is prime. Getting from a number to its prime factors, however, is another matter.

Factoring Large Numbers in Practice

So how do we go from a number to its factorization—namely, its decomposition as a product of prime numbers? The most basic way to factor a number, N, is to try dividing it by all the numbers lower than it until you find a number, x, that divides N. Then attempt to divide N with the next number, $x + 1$, and so on. You'll end up with a list of factors of N. What's the time complexity of this? First, remember that we express complexities as a function of the input's *length*. The bit length of the number N is $n = \log_2 N$. By the basic definition of logarithm, this means that $N = 2^n$. Because all the numbers less than $N/2$ are reasonable guesses for possible factors of N, there are about $N/2 = 2^n/2$ values to try. The complexity of our naive factoring algorithm is therefore $O(2^n)$, ignoring the 1/2 coefficient in the $O()$ notation.

Of course, many numbers are easy to factor by first finding any small factors (2, 3, 5, and so on) and then iteratively factoring any other nonprime factors. But here we're interested in numbers of the form $N = p \times q$, where p and q are large, as found in cryptography.

Let's be a bit smarter. We don't need to test all numbers lower than $N/2$, but rather only the prime numbers, and we can start by trying only those smaller than the square root of N. Indeed, if N is not a prime number, then it has to have at least one factor lower than its square root $\sqrt{N}$. This is because if both of N's factors p and q are greater than $\sqrt{N}$, then their product would be greater than $\sqrt{N} \times \sqrt{N} = N$, which is impossible. For example, if we say $N = 100$, then its factors p and q can't both be greater than 10 because that would result in a product greater than 100. Either p or q has to be smaller than $\sqrt{N}$.

So what's the complexity of testing only the primes less than $\sqrt{N}$? The *prime number theorem* states that there are approximately $N/\log N$ primes less than N. Hence, there are approximately $\sqrt{N}/\log \sqrt{N}$ primes less than $\sqrt{N}$. Expressing this value, we get approximately $2^{n/2}/n$ possible prime factors and therefore a complexity of $O(2^{n/2}/n)$, since $\sqrt{N} = 2^{n/2}$ and $1/\log\sqrt{N} = 1/(n/2) = 2n$. This is faster than testing all prime numbers, but it's still painfully slow—on the order of 2^{120} operations for a 256-bit number. That's quite an impractical computational effort.

The fastest factoring algorithm is the *general number field sieve (GNFS)*, which I won't describe here because it requires the introduction of several advanced mathematical concepts. A rough estimate of GNFS's complexity is $\exp(1.91 \times n^{1/3} (\log n)^{2/3})$, where $\exp(. . .)$ is just a different notation for the exponential function e^x, with e the exponential constant approximately equal to 2.718. However, it's difficult to get an accurate estimate of GNFS's actual complexity for a given number size. Therefore, we have to rely on heuristical complexity estimates, which show how security increases with a longer n. For example:

- Factoring a **1024-bit** number, which would have two prime factors of approximately 500 bits each, will take on the order of 2^{70} basic operations.

- Factoring a **2048-bit** number, which would have two prime factors of approximately 1000 bits each, will take on the order of 2^{90} basic operations, which is about a million times slower than for a 1024-bit number.

And we estimate that at least 4096 bits are needed to reach 128-bit security. Note that these values should be taken with a grain of salt, and researchers don't always agree on these estimates. Take a look at these experimental results to see the actual cost of factoring:

- In 2005, after about 18 months of computation—and thanks to the power of a cluster of 80 processors, with a total effort equivalent to 75 years of computation on a single processor—a group of researchers factored a **663-bit** (200-decimal digit) number.

- In 2009, after about two years and using several hundred processors, with a total effort equivalent to about 2,000 years of computation on a single processor, another group of researchers factored a **768-bit** (232-decimal digit) number.

As you can see, the numbers actually factored by academic researchers are shorter than those in real applications, which are at least 1024-bit and often more than 2048-bit. As I write this, no one has reported the factoring of a 1024-bit number, but many speculate that well-funded organizations such as the NSA can do it.

In sum, 1024-bit RSA should be viewed as insecure, and RSA should be used with at least a 2048-bit value—and preferably a 4096-bit one to ensure higher security.

Is Factoring NP-Complete?

We don't know how to factor large numbers efficiently, which suggests that the factoring problem doesn't belong to **P**. However, factoring is clearly in **NP**, because given a factorization, we can verify the solution by checking that all factors are prime numbers, thanks to the aforementioned primality testing algorithm, and that when multiplied together, the factors do give the expected number. For example, to check that 3×5 is the factorization of 15, you'll check that both 3 and 5 are prime and that 3 times 5 equals 15.

So we have a problem that is in **NP** and that looks hard, but is it as hard as the hardest **NP** problems? In other words, is factoring **NP**-complete? Spoiler alert: probably not.

There's no mathematical proof that factoring isn't **NP**-complete, but we have a few pieces of soft evidence. First, all known **NP**-complete problems can have one solution, but can also have more than one solution, or no solution at all. In contrast, factoring always has exactly one solution. Also, the factoring problem has a mathematical structure that allows for the GNFS algorithm to significantly outperform a naive algorithm, a structure that **NP**-complete problems don't have. Factoring would be easy if we had a *quantum computer*, a computing model that exploits quantum mechanical phenomena to run different kinds of algorithms and that would have the capability to factor large numbers efficiently (not because it'd run the algorithm faster, but because it could run a quantum algorithm dedicated to factoring large numbers). A quantum computer doesn't exist yet, though—and might never exist. Regardless, a quantum computer would be useless in tackling **NP**-complete problems because it'd be no faster than a classical one (see Chapter 14).

Factoring may then be slightly easier than **NP**-complete in theory, but as far as cryptography is concerned, it's hard enough, and even more reliable than **NP**-complete problems. Indeed, it's easier to build cryptosystems on top of the factoring problem than **NP**-complete problems, because it's hard to know exactly how hard it is to break a cryptosystem based on some **NP**-complete problems—in other words, how many bits of security you'd get.

The factoring problem is just one of several problems used in cryptography as a *hardness assumption*, which is an assumption that some problem is computationally hard. This assumption is used when proving that breaking a cryptosystem's security is at least as hard as solving said problem. Another problem used as a hardness assumption, the *discrete logarithm problem (DLP)*, is actually a family of problems, which we'll discuss next.

The Discrete Logarithm Problem

The DLP predates the factoring problem in the official history of cryptography. Whereas RSA appeared in 1977, a second cryptographic breakthrough, the Diffie–Hellman key agreement (covered in Chapter 11), came about a year earlier, grounding its security on the hardness of the DLP. Like the factoring problem, the DLP deals with large numbers, but it's a bit less straightforward—it will take you a few minutes rather than a few seconds to get it and requires a bit more math than factoring. So let me introduce the mathematical notion of a *group* in the context of discrete logarithms.

What Is a Group?

In mathematical context, a *group* is a set of elements (typically, numbers) that are related to each other according to certain well-defined rules. An example of a group is the set of nonzero integers (between 1 and $p - 1$) modulo some prime number p, which we write $\mathbf{Z}_p^*$. For $p = 5$, we get the group $\mathbf{Z}_5^* = \{1,2,3,4\}$.

In the group $\mathbf{Z}_5^*$, operations are carried out modulo 5; hence, we don't have $3 \times 4 = 12$ but instead have $3 \times 4 = 2$, because 12 mod 5 = 2. We nonetheless use the same sign ($\times$) that we use for normal integer multiplication. Likewise, we also use the exponent notation to denote a group element's multiplication with itself mod p, a common operation in cryptography. For example, in the context of $\mathbf{Z}_5^*$, $2^3 = 2 \times 2 \times 2 = 3$ rather than 8, because 8 mod 5 is equal to 3.

To be a group, a mathematical set should have the following characteristics, called *group axioms*:

Closure   For any two x and y in the group, $x \times y$ is in the group too. In $\mathbf{Z}_5^*$, $2 \times 3 = 1$ (because 6 = 1 mod 5), $2 \times 4 = 3$, and so on.

Associativity   For any x, y, z in the group, $(x \times y) \times z = x \times (y \times z)$. In $\mathbf{Z}_5^*$, $(2 \times 3) \times 4 = 1 \times 4 = 2 \times (3 \times 4) = 2 \times 2 = 4$.

Identity existence   There's an element e such that $e \times x = x \times e = x$. In any $\mathbf{Z}_p^*$, the identity element is 1.

Inverse existence   For any x in the group, there's a y such that $x \times y = y \times x = e$. In $\mathbf{Z}_5^*$, the inverse of 2 is 3, and the inverse of 3 is 2, while 4 is its own inverse because $4 \times 4 = 16 = 1$ mod 5.

In addition, a group is called *commutative* if $x \times y = y \times x$ for any group elements x and y. That's also true for any multiplicative group of integers $\mathbf{Z}_p^*$. In particular, $\mathbf{Z}_5^*$ is commutative: $3 \times 4 = 4 \times 3$, $2 \times 3 = 3 \times 2$, and so on.

A group is called *cyclic* if there's at least one element g such that its powers (g^1, g^2, g^3, and so on) mod p span all distinct group elements. The element g is then called a *generator* of the group. $\mathbf{Z}_5^*$ is cyclic and has two generators, 2 and 3, because $2^1 = 2$, $2^2 = 4$, $2^3 = 3$, $2^4 = 1$, and $3^1 = 3$, $3^2 = 4$, $3^3 = 2$, $3^4 = 1$.

Note that I'm using multiplication as a group operator, but you can also get groups from other operators. For example, the most straightforward group is the set of all integers, positive and negative, with addition as a group operation. Let's check that the group axioms hold with addition, in the preceding order: clearly, the number $x + y$ is an integer if x and y are integers (closure); $(x + y) + z = x + (y + z)$ for any x, y, and z (associativity); zero is the identity element; and the inverse of any number x in the group is $-x$ because $x + (-x) = 0$ for any integer x. A big difference, though, is that this group of integers is of infinite size, whereas in crypto we'll only deal with *finite groups*, or groups with a finite number of elements. Typically, we'll use groups $\mathbf{Z}_p^*$, where p is *thousands* of bits long (that is, groups that contain on the order of 2^p numbers).

The Hard Thing

The DLP consists of finding the y for which $g^y = x$, given a base number g within some group $\mathbf{Z}_p^*$, where p is a prime number, and given a group element x. The DLP is called *discrete* because we're dealing with integers as opposed to real numbers (continuous), and it's called a *logarithm* because we're looking for the logarithm of x in base g. (For example, the logarithm of 256 in base 2 is 8 because $2^8 = 256$.)

People often ask me whether factoring or a discrete logarithm is more secure—or in other words, which problem is the hardest? My answer is that they're about equally hard. In fact, algorithms to solve DLP bear similarities with those factoring integers, and you get about the same security level with n-bit hard-to-factor numbers as with discrete logarithms in an n-bit group. And for the same reason as factoring, DLP isn't **NP**-complete. (Note that there are certain groups where the DLP is easier to solve, but here I'm only referring to the case of DLP groups consisting of a number modulo a prime.)

How Things Can Go Wrong

More than 40 years later, we still don't know how to efficiently factor large numbers or solve discrete logarithms. Amateurs may argue that someone may eventually break factoring—and we have no proof that it'll never be broken—but we also don't have proof that $\mathbf{P} \neq \mathbf{NP}$. Likewise, you can speculate that **P** may be equal to **NP**; however, according to experts, that surprise is unlikely. So there's no need to worry. And indeed all the public-key crypto deployed today relies on either factoring (RSA) or DLP (Diffie–Hellman, ElGamal, elliptic curve cryptography). However, although math may not fail us, real-world concerns and human error can sneak in.

When Factoring Is Easy

Factoring large numbers isn't always hard. For example, take the 1024-bit number N, which is equal to the following:

17976931348623159077293051907890247336179769789423065727343008115773934381993384298698255717419825727891725863819370926581918602662618065973066506271099555657863944771560841518689565284169198292110720231716536912489048151238855803905342712509992903154492623247093152632560831325404614070528728327909153880145 92

For 1024-bit numbers used in RSA encryption or signature schemes where $N = pq$, we expect the best factoring algorithms to need around 2^{70} operations, as we discussed earlier. But you can factor this sample number in seconds using SageMath, a piece of Python-based mathematical software. Using SageMath's factor() function on my 2015 MacBook, it took less than five seconds to find the following factorization:

$$2^{800} \times 641 \times 6700417 \times 16777388527684921553369$$
$$\times 3741405716132237595740814883432 3969$$

Right, I cheated. This number isn't of the form $N = pq$ because it doesn't have just two large prime factors but rather five, including very small ones, which makes it easy to factor. First, you'll identify the $2^{800} \times 641 \times 6700417$ part by trying small primes from a precomputed list of prime numbers, which leaves you with a 192-bit number that's much easier to factor than a 1024-bit number with two large factors.

But factoring can be easy not only when n has no small prime factors, but also when N or its factors p and q have particular forms—for example, when $N = pq$ with p and q both close to some 2^b, when $N = pq$ and some bits of p or q are known, or when N is of the form $N = p^r q^s$ and r is greater than $\log p$. However, detailing the reasons for these weaknesses is way too technical for this book.

The upshot here is that the RSA encryption and signature algorithms (covered in Chapter 10) will need to work with a value of $N = pq$, where p and q are carefully chosen, to avoid easy factorization of N, which can result in security disaster.

Small Hard Problems Aren't Hard

Computationally hard problems become easy when they're small enough, and even exponential-time algorithms become practical as the problem size shrinks. A symmetric cipher may be secure in the sense that there's no faster attack than the 2^n-time brute force, but if the key length is $n = 32$, you'll break the cipher in minutes. This sounds obvious, and you'd think that no one would be naive enough to use small keys, but in reality there are plenty of reasons why this could happen. The following are two true stories.

Say you're a developer who knows nothing about crypto but has some API to encrypt with RSA and has been told to encrypt with 128-bit security. What RSA key size would you pick? I've seen real cases of 128-bit RSA, or RSA based on a 128-bit number $N = pq$. However, although factoring is impractically hard for an N thousands of bits long, factoring a 128-bit number is easy. Using the SageMath software, the commands shown in Listing 9-2 complete instantaneously.

```
sage: p = random_prime(2**64)
sage: q = random_prime(2**64)
sage: factor(p*q)
6822485253121677229 * 17596998848870549923
```

Listing 9-2: Generating an RSA modulus by picking two random prime numbers and factoring it instantaneously

Listing 9-2 shows that a 128-bit number taken randomly as the product of two 64-bit prime numbers can be easily factored on a typical laptop. However, if I chose 1024-bit prime numbers instead by using p = random_prime(2**1024), the command factor(p*q) would never complete, at least not in my lifetime.

To be fair, the tools available don't help prevent the naive use of insecurely short parameters. For example, the OpenSSL toolkit lets you generate RSA keys as short as 31 bits without any warning; obviously, such short keys are totally insecure, as shown in Listing 9-3.

```
$ openssl genrsa 31
Generating RSA private key, 31 bit long modulus
.+++++++++++++++++++++++++++++
.+++++++++++++++++++++++++++++
e is 65537 (0x10001)
```

```
-----BEGIN RSA PRIVATE KEY-----
MCsCAQACBHHqFuUCAwEAAQIEP6zEJQIDANATAgMAjCcCAwCSBwICTGsCAhpp
-----END RSA PRIVATE KEY-----
```

Listing 9-3: Generating an insecure RSA private key using the OpenSSL toolkit

When reviewing cryptography, you should not only check the type of algorithms used, but also their parameters and the length of their secret values. However, as you'll see in the following story, what's secure enough today may be insecure tomorrow.

In 2015, researchers discovered that many HTTPS servers and email servers still supported an older, insecure version of the Diffie–Hellman key agreement protocol. Namely, the underlying TLS implementation supported Diffie–Hellman within a group, $\mathbf{Z}_p^*$, defined by a prime number, p, of only 512 bits, where the discrete logarithm problem was no longer practically impossible to compute.

Not only did servers support a weak algorithm, but attackers could force a benign client to use that algorithm by injecting malicious traffic within the client's session. Even better for attackers, the largest part of the attack could be carried out once and recycled to attack multiple clients. After about a week of computations to attack a specific group, $\mathbf{Z}_p^*$, it took only 70 seconds to break individual sessions of different users.

A secure protocol is worthless if it's undermined by a weakened algorithm, and a reliable algorithm is useless if sabotaged by weak parameters. In cryptography, you should always read the fine print.

For more details about this story, check the research article "Imperfect Forward Secrecy: How Diffie–Hellman Fails in Practice" (*https://weakdh.org/imperfect-forward-secrecy-ccs15.pdf*).

Further Reading

I encourage you to look deeper into the foundational aspects of computation in the context of computability (what functions can be computed?) and complexity (at what cost?), and how they relate to cryptography. I've mostly talked about the classes **P** and **NP**, but there are many more classes and points of interest for cryptographers. I highly recommend the book *Quantum Computing Since Democritus* by Scott Aaronson (Cambridge University Press, 2013). It's in large part about quantum computing, but its first chapters brilliantly introduce complexity theory and cryptography.

In the cryptography research literature you'll also find other hard computational problems. I'll mention them in later chapters, but here are some examples that illustrate the diversity of problems leveraged by cryptographers:

- The Diffie–Hellman problem (given g^x and g^y, find g^{xy}) is a variant of the discrete logarithm problem, and is widely used in key agreement protocols.

- Lattice problems, such as the shortest vector problem (SVP) and the learning with errors (LWE) problem, are the only examples of **NP**-hard problems successfully used in cryptography.

- Coding problems rely on the hardness of decoding error-correcting codes with insufficient information, and have been studied since the late 1970s.

- Multivariate problems are about solving nonlinear systems of equations and are potentially **NP**-hard, but they've failed to provide reliable cryptosystems because hard versions are too big and slow, and practical versions were found to be insecure.

In Chapter 10, we'll keep talking about hard problems, especially factoring and its main variant, the RSA problem.

10

RSA

The Rivest–Shamir–Adleman (RSA) cryptosystem revolutionized cryptography when it emerged in 1977 as the first public-key encryption scheme; whereas classical, symmetric-key encryption schemes use the same secret key to encrypt and decrypt messages, public-key encryption (also called *asymmetric* encryption) uses two keys: one is your public key, which can be used by anyone who wants to encrypt messages for you, and the other is your private key, which is required in order to decrypt messages encrypted using the public key. This magic is the reason why RSA came as a real breakthrough, and 40 years later, it's still the paragon of public-key encryption and a workhorse of internet security. (One year prior to RSA, Diffie and Hellman had introduced the concept of public-key cryptography, but their scheme was unable to perform public-key encryption.)

RSA is above all an arithmetic trick. It works by creating a mathematical object called a *trapdoor permutation*, a function that transforms a number x

to a number y in the same range, such that computing y from x is easy using the public key, but computing x from y is practically impossible unless you know the private key—the *trapdoor*. (Think of x as a plaintext and y as a ciphertext.)

In addition to encryption, RSA is also used to build digital signatures, wherein the owner of the private key is the only one able to sign a message, and the public key enables anyone to verify the signature's validity.

In this chapter, I explain how the RSA trapdoor permutation works, discuss RSA's security relative to the factoring problem (discussed in Chapter 9), and then explain why the RSA trapdoor permutation alone isn't enough to build *secure* encryption and signatures. I also discuss ways to implement RSA and demonstrate how to attack it.

We begin with an explanation of the basic mathematical notions behind RSA.

The Math Behind RSA

When encrypting a message, RSA sees the message as a big number, and encryption consists essentially of multiplications of big numbers. Therefore, in order to understand how RSA works, we need to know what kind of big numbers it manipulates and how multiplication works on those numbers.

RSA sees the plaintext that it's encrypting as a positive integer between 1 and $n - 1$, where n is a large number called the *modulus*. More precisely, RSA works on the numbers less than n that are co-prime with n and therefore that have no common prime factor with n. Such numbers, when multiplied together, yield another number that satisfies these criteria. We say that these numbers form a group, denoted $\mathbf{Z}_n^*$, and call the multiplicative group of integers modulo n. (See the mathematical definition of a group in "What Is a Group?" on page 174.)

For example, consider the group $\mathbf{Z}_4^*$ of integers modulo 4. Recall from Chapter 9 that a group must include an identity element (that is, 1) and that each number x in the group must have an inverse, a number y such that $x \times y = 1$. How do we determine that set that makes up $\mathbf{Z}_4^*$? Based on our definitions, we know that 0 is not in the group $\mathbf{Z}_4^*$ because multiplying any number by 0 can never give 1, so 0 has no inverse. By the same token, the number 1 belongs to $\mathbf{Z}_4^*$ because $1 \times 1 = 1$, so 1 is its own inverse. However, the number 2 does not belong in this group because we can't obtain 1 by multiplying 2 with another element of $\mathbf{Z}_4^*$ (the reason is that 2 isn't co-prime with 4, because 4 and 2 share the factor of 2.) The number 3 belongs in the group $\mathbf{Z}_4^*$ because it is its own inverse within $\mathbf{Z}_4^*$. Thus, we have $\mathbf{Z}_4^* = \{1, 3\}$.

Now consider $\mathbf{Z}_5^*$, the multiplicative group of integers modulo 5. What numbers does this set contain? The number 5 is prime, and 1, 2, 3, and 4 are all co-prime with 5, so the set of $\mathbf{Z}_5^*$ is $\{1, 2, 3, 4\}$. Let's verify this: $2 \times 3 \bmod 5 = 1$, therefore, 2 is 3's inverse, and 3 is 2's inverse; note that 4 is its own inverse because $4 \times 4 \bmod 5 = 1$; finally, 1 is again its own inverse in the group.

In order to find the number of elements in a group $\mathbf{Z}_n^*$ when n isn't prime, we use *Euler's totient function*, which is written as $\varphi(n)$, with φ representing the Greek letter phi. This function gives the number of elements co-prime with n, which is the number of elements in $\mathbf{Z}_n^*$. As a rule, if n is a product of prime numbers $n = p_1 \times p_2 \times \ldots \times p_m$, the number of elements in the group $\mathbf{Z}_n^*$ is the following:

$$\varphi(n) \;=\; (p_1 - 1) \;\times\; (p_2 - 1) \;\times\; \ldots \;\times\; (p_m - 1)$$

RSA only deals with numbers n that are the product of two large primes, usually noted as $n = pq$. The associated group $\mathbf{Z}_n^*$ will then contain $\varphi(n) = (p-1)(q-1)$ elements. By expanding this expression, we get the equivalent definition $\varphi(n) = n - p - q + 1$, or $\varphi(n) = (n+1) - (p+q)$, which expresses more intuitively the value of $\varphi(n)$ relative to n. In other words, all but $(p+q)$ numbers between 1 and $n-1$ belong to $\mathbf{Z}_n^*$ and are "valid numbers" in RSA operations.

The RSA Trapdoor Permutation

The RSA trapdoor permutation is the core algorithm behind RSA-based encryption and signatures. Given a modulus n and number e, called the *public exponent*, the RSA trapdoor permutation transforms a number x from the set $\mathbf{Z}_n^*$ into a number $y = x^e \bmod n$. In other words, it calculates the value that's equal to x multiplied by itself e times modulo n and then returns the result. When we use the RSA trapdoor permutation to encrypt, the modulus n and the exponent e make up the RSA public key.

In order to get x back from y, we use another number, denoted d, to compute the following:

$$y^d \bmod n = \left(x^e\right)^d \bmod n = x^{ed} \bmod n \;=\; x$$

Because d is the trapdoor that allows us to decrypt, it is part of the private key in an RSA key pair, and, unlike the public key, it should always be kept secret. The number d is also called the *secret exponent*.

Obviously, d isn't just any number; it's the number such that e multiplied by d is equivalent to 1, and therefore such that $x^{ed} \bmod n = x$ for any x. More precisely, we must have $ed = 1 \bmod \varphi(n)$ in order to get $x^{ed} = x^1 = x$ and to decrypt the message correctly. Note that we compute modulo $\varphi(n)$ and not modulo n here because exponents behave like the indexes of elements of $\mathbf{Z}_n^*$ rather than as the elements themselves. Because $\mathbf{Z}_n^*$ has $\varphi(n)$ elements, the index must be less than $\varphi(n)$.

The number $\varphi(n)$ is crucial to RSA's security. In fact, finding $\varphi(n)$ for an RSA modulus n is equivalent to breaking RSA, because the secret exponent d can easily be derived from $\varphi(n)$ and e, by computing e's inverse. Hence p and q should also be secret, since knowing p or q gives $\varphi(n)$ by computing $(p-1)(q-1) = \varphi(n)$.

RSA Key Generation and Security

Key generation is the process by which an RSA key pair is created, namely a public key (modulus *n* and public exponent *e*) and its private key (secret exponent *d*). The numbers *p* and *q* (such that *n* = *pq*) and the order $\varphi(n)$ should also be secret, so they're often seen as part of the private key.

In order to generate an RSA key pair, we first pick two random prime numbers, *p* and *q*, and then compute $\varphi(n)$ from these, and we compute *d* as the inverse of *e*. To show how this works, Listing 10-1 uses SageMath (*http:// www.sagemath.org/*), an open-source Python-like environment that includes many mathematical packages.

```
❶ sage: p = random_prime(2^32); p
  1103222539
❷ sage: q = random_prime(2^32); q
  17870599
❸ sage: n = p*q; n
  c
❹ sage: phi = (p-1)*(q-1); phi
  36567230045260644
❺ sage: e = random_prime(phi); e
  13771927877214701
❻ sage: d = xgcd(e, phi)[1]; d
  15417970063428857
❼ sage: mod(d*e, phi)
  1
```

Listing 10-1: Generating RSA parameters using SageMath

We use the random_prime() function to pick random primes p ❶ and q ❷, which are lower than a given argument. Next, we multiply p and q to get the modulus n ❸ and $\varphi(n)$, which is the variable phi ❹. We then generate a random public exponent, e ❺, by picking a random prime less than phi in order to ensure that e will have an inverse modulo phi. We then generate the associated private exponent *d* by using the xgcd() function from Sage ❻. This function computes the numbers *s* and *t* given two numbers, *a* and *b*, with the extended Euclidean algorithm such that *as* + *bt* = **GCD**(*a*, *b*). Finally, we check that *ed* mod $\varphi(n)$ = 1 ❼, to ensure that *d* will work correctly to invert the RSA permutation.

Now we can apply the trapdoor permutation, as shown in Listing 10-2.

```
❶ sage: x = 1234567
❷ sage: y = power_mod(x, e, n); y
   19048323055755904
❸ sage: power_mod(y, d, n)
   1234567
```

Listing 10-2: Computing the RSA trapdoor permutation back and forth

We assign the integer 1234567 to x ❶ and then use the function power_mod(x, e, n), the exponentiation modulo n, or x^e mod n in equation form, to calculate y ❷. Having computed $y = x^e$ mod n, we compute y^d mod n ❸ with the trapdoor d to return the original x.

But how hard is it to find x without the trapdoor d? An attacker who can factor big numbers can break RSA by recovering p and q and then $\varphi(n)$ in order to compute d from e. But that's not the only risk. Another risk to RSA lies in an attacker's ability to compute x from x^e mod n, or eth roots modulo n, without necessarily factoring n. Both risks seem closely connected, though we don't know for sure whether they are equivalent.

Assuming that factoring is indeed hard and that finding eth roots is about as hard, RSA's security level depends on three factors: the size of n, the choice of p and q, and how the trapdoor permutation is used. If n is too small, it could be factored in a realistic amount of time, revealing the private key. To be safe, n should at least be 2048 bits long (a security level of about 90 bits, requiring a computational effort of about 2^{90} operations), but preferably 4096 bits long (a security level of approximately 128 bits). The values p and q should be unrelated random prime numbers of similar size. If they are too small, or too close together, it becomes easier to determine their value from n. Finally, the RSA trapdoor permutation should not be used directly for encryption or signing, as I'll discuss shortly.

Encrypting with RSA

Typically, RSA is used in combination with a symmetric encryption scheme, where RSA is used to encrypt a symmetric key that is then used to encrypt a message with a cipher such as the Advanced Encryption Standard (AES). But encrypting a message or symmetric key with RSA is more complicated than simply converting the target to a number x and computing x^e mod n.

In the following subsections, I explain why a naive application of the RSA trapdoor permutation is insecure, and how strong RSA-based encryption works.

Breaking Textbook RSA Encryption's Malleability

Textbook RSA encryption is the phrase used to describe the simplistic RSA encryption scheme wherein the plaintext contains only the message you want to encrypt. For example, to encrypt the string *RSA*, we would first convert it to a number by concatenating the ASCII encodings of each of the three letters as a byte: *R* (byte 52), *S* (byte 53), and *A* (byte 41). The resulting byte string 525341 is equal to 5395265 when converted to decimal, which we might then encrypt by computing $5395265^e \bmod n$. Without knowing the secret key, there would be no way to decrypt the message.

However, textbook RSA encryption is deterministic: if you encrypt the same plaintext twice, you'll get the same ciphertext twice. That's one problem, but there's a bigger problem—given two textbook RSA ciphertexts $y_1 = x_1^e \bmod n$ and $y_2 = x_2^e \bmod n$, you can derive the ciphertext of $x_1 \times x_2$ by multiplying these two ciphertexts together, like this:

$$y_1 \times y_2 \bmod n = x_1^e \times x_2^e \bmod n = \left(x_1 \times x_2\right)^e \bmod n$$

The result is $\left(x_1 \times x_2\right)^e \bmod n$, the ciphertext of the message $x_1 \times x_2 \bmod n$. Thus an attacker could create a new valid ciphertext from two RSA ciphertexts, allowing them to compromise the security of your encryption by letting them deduce information about the original message. We say that this weakness makes textbook RSA encryption *malleable*. (Of course, if you know x_1 and x_2, you can compute $\left(x_1 \times x_2\right)^e \bmod n$, too, but if you only know y_1 and y_2, you should not be able to multiply ciphertexts and get a ciphertext of the multiplied plaintexts.)

Strong RSA Encryption: OAEP

In order to make RSA ciphertexts nonmalleable, the ciphertext should consist of the message data and some additional data called *padding*, as shown in Figure 10-1. The standard way to encrypt with RSA in this fashion is to use Optimal Asymmetric Encryption Padding (OAEP), commonly referred to as RSA-OAEP. This scheme involves creating a bit string as large as the modulus by padding the message with extra data and randomness before applying the RSA function.

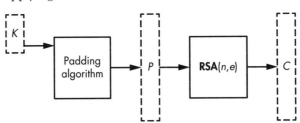

Figure 10-1: Encrypting a symmetric key, K, with RSA using (n, e) as a public key

NOTE   *OAEP is referred to as RSAES-OAEP in official documents such as the PKCS#1 standard by the RSA company and NIST's Special Publication 800-56B. OAEP improves on the earlier method now called PKCS#1 v1.5, which is one of the first in a series of Public-Key Cryptography Standards (PKCS) created by RSA. It is markedly less secure than OAEP, yet is still used in many systems.*

OAEP's Security

OAEP uses a pseudorandom number generator (PRNG) to ensure the indistinguishability and nonmalleability of ciphertexts by making the encryption
probabilistic. It has been proven secure as long as the RSA function and the
PRNG are secure and, to a lesser extent, as long as the hash functions aren't
too weak. You should use OAEP whenever you need to encrypt with RSA.

How OAEP Encryption Works

In order to encrypt with RSA in OAEP mode, you need a message (typically a symmetric key, K), a PRNG, and two hash functions. To create the
ciphertext, you use a given modulus n long of m bytes (that is, $8m$ bits, and
therefore an n lower than 2^{8m}). To encrypt K, the *encoded message* is formed
as $M = H \,\|\, 00 \ldots 00 \,\|\, 01 \,\|\, K$, where H is an h-byte constant defined by the
OAEP scheme, followed by as many 00 bytes as needed and a 01 byte. This
encoded message, M, is then processed as described next and as depicted in
Figure 10-2.

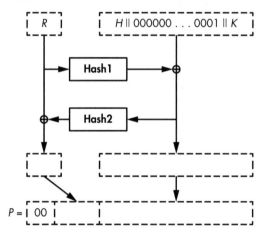

*Figure 10-2: Encrypting a symmetric key, K, with
RSA-OAEP, where H is a fixed parameter and R is
random bits*

Next, you generate an h-byte random string R and set $M = M \oplus \mathbf{Hash1}(R)$,
where $\mathbf{Hash1}(R)$ is as long as M. You then set $R = R \oplus \mathbf{Hash2}(M)$, where
$\mathbf{Hash2}(M)$ is as long as R. Now you use these new values of M and R to
form an m-byte string $P = 00 \,\|\, M \,\|\, R$, which is as long as the modulus n and
which can be converted to an integer number less than n. The result of this
conversion is the number x, which is then used to compute the RSA function $x^e \bmod n$ to get the ciphertext.

To decrypt a ciphertext y, you would first compute $x = y^d \bmod n$ and,
from this, recover the final values of M and R. Next, you would retrieve M's
initial value by computing $M \oplus \mathbf{Hash1}(R \oplus \mathbf{Hash2}(M))$. Finally, you would
verify that M is of the form $H \,\|\, 00 \ldots 00 \,\|\, 01 \,\|\, K$, with an h-byte H and 00
bytes followed by a 01 byte.

In practice, the parameters m and h (the length of the modulus and the length of **Hash2**'s output, respectively) are typically $m = 256$ bytes (for 2048-bit RSA) and $h = 32$ (using SHA-256 as **Hash2**). This leaves $m - h - 1 = 223$ bytes for M, of which up to $m - 2h - 2 = 190$ bytes are available for K (the "$- 2$" is due to the separator 01 byte in M). The **Hash1** hash value is then composed of $m - h - 1 = 223$ bytes, which is longer than the hash value of any common hash function.

NOTE   *In order to build a hash with such an unusual output length, the RSA standard documents specify the use of the* mask generating function *technique to create hash functions that return arbitrarily large hash values from any hash function.*

Signing with RSA

Digital signatures can prove that the holder of the private key tied to a particular digital signature signed some message and that the signature is authentic. Because no one other than the private key holder knows the private exponent d, no one can compute a signature $y = x^d \bmod n$ from some value x, but everyone can verify $y^e \bmod n = x$ given the public exponent e. That verified signature can be used in a court of law to demonstrate that the private-key holder did sign some particular message—a property of undeniability called *nonrepudiation*.

It's tempting to see RSA signatures as the converse of encryption, but they are not. Signing with RSA is not the same as encrypting with the private key. Encryption provides confidentiality whereas a digital signature is used to prevent forgeries. The most salient example of this difference is that it's okay for a signature scheme to leak information on the message signed, because the message is not secret. For example, a scheme that reveals parts of the messages could be a secure signature scheme but not a secure encryption scheme.

Due to the processing overhead required, public-key encryption can only process short messages, which are usually secret keys rather than actual messages. A signature scheme, however, can process messages of arbitrary sizes by using their hash values **Hash**(M) as a proxy, and it can be deterministic yet secure. Like RSA-OAEP, RSA-based signature schemes can use a padding scheme, but they can also use the maximal message space allowed by the RSA modulus.

Breaking Textbook RSA Signatures

What we call a *textbook RSA signature* is the method that signs a message, x, by directly computing $y = x^d \bmod n$, where x can be any number between 0 and $n - 1$. Like textbook encryption, textbook RSA signing is simple to specify and implement but also insecure in the face of several attacks. One such attack involves a trivial forgery: upon noticing that $0^d \bmod n = 0$, $1^d \bmod n = 1$, and $(n - 1)^d \bmod n = n - 1$, regardless of the value of the private key d, an attacker can forge signatures of 0, 1, or $n - 1$ without knowing d.

More worrying is the *blinding attack*. For example, say you want to get a third party's signature on some incriminating message, M, that you know they would never knowingly sign. To launch this attack, you could first find some value, R, such that $R^e M \bmod n$ is a message that your victim would knowingly sign. Next, you would convince them to sign that message and to show you their signature, which is equal to $S = (R^e M)^d \bmod n$, or the message raised to the power d. Now, given that signature, you can derive the signature of M, namely M^d, with the aid of some straightforward computations.

Here's how this works: because S can be written as $(R^e M)^d = R^{ed} M^d$, and because $R^{ed} = R$ is equal to $R^{ed} = R$ (by definition), we have S $= (R^e M)^d = RM^d$. To obtain M^d, we simply divide S by R, as follows, to obtain the signature:

$$S/R \;=\; RM^d/R \;=\; M^d$$

As you can see, this is a practical and powerful attack.

The PSS Signature Standard

The RSA *Probabilistic Signature Scheme (PSS)* is to RSA signatures what OAEP is to RSA encryption. It was designed to make message signing more secure, thanks to the addition of padding data.

As shown in Figure 10-3, PSS combines a message narrower than the modulus with some random and fixed bits before RSAing the results of this padding process.

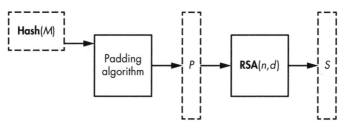

Figure 10-3: Signing a message, M, with RSA and with the PSS standard, where (n, d) is the private key

Like all public-key signature schemes, PSS works on a message's hash rather than on the message itself. Signing **Hash**(M) is secure as long as the hash function is collision resistant. One particular benefit of PSS is that you can use it to sign messages of any length, because after hashing a message, you'll obtain a hash value of the same length regardless of the message's original length. The hash's length is typically 256 bits, with the hash function SHA-256.

Why not sign by just running OAEP on **Hash**(M)? Unfortunately, you can't. Although similar to PSS, OAEP has only been proven secure for encryption, not for signature.

Like OAEP, PSS also requires a PRNG and two hash functions. One, **Hash1**, is a typical hash with h-byte hash values such as SHA-256. The other, **Hash2**, is a wide-output hash like OAEP's **Hash2**.

The PSS signing procedure for message M works as follows (where h is **Hash1**'s output length):

1. Pick an r-byte random string R using the PRNG.

2. Form an encoded message $M' = 0000000000000000 \parallel \textbf{Hash1}(M) \parallel R$, long of $h + r + 8$ bytes (with eight zero bytes at the beginning).

3. Compute the h-byte string $H = \textbf{Hash1}(M')$.

4. Set $L = 00 \dots 00 \parallel 01 \parallel R$, or a sequence of 00 bytes followed by a 01 byte and then R, with a number of 00 bytes such that L is long of $m - h - 1$ bytes (the byte width m of the modulus minus the hash length h minus 1).

5. Set $L = L \oplus \textbf{Hash2}(H)$, thus replacing the previous value of L with a new value.

6. Convert the m-byte string $P = L \parallel H \parallel BC$ to a number, x, lower than n. Here, the byte BC is a fixed value appended after H.

7. Given the value of x just obtained, compute the RSA function $x^d \bmod n$ to obtain the signature.

To verify a signature given a message, M, you compute **Hash1**(M) and use the public exponent e to retrieve L and H and then M' from the signature, checking the padding's correctness at each step.

In practice, the random string R (called a *salt* in the RSA-PSS standard) is usually as long as the hash value. For example, if you use $n = 2048$ bits and SHA-256 as the hash, the value L is long of $m - h - 1 = 256 - 32 - 1 = 223$ bytes, and the random string R would typically be 32 bytes.

Like OAEP, PSS is provably secure, standardized, and widely deployed. Also like OAEP, it looks needlessly complex and is prone to implementation errors and mishandled corner cases. But unlike RSA encryption, there's a way to get around this extra complexity with a signature scheme that doesn't even need a PRNG, thus reducing the risk of insecure RSA signatures caused by an insecure PRNG, as discussed next.

Full Domain Hash Signatures

Full Domain Hash (FDH) is the simplest signature scheme you can imagine. To implement it, you simply convert the byte string **Hash**(M) to a number, x, and create the signature $y = x^d \bmod n$, as shown in Figure 10-4.

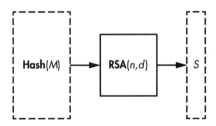

Figure 10-4: Signing a message with RSA using the Full Domain Hash technique

Signature verification is straightforward, too. Given a signature that is a number y, you compute $x = y^e \bmod n$ and compare the result with **Hash**(M). It's boringly simple, deterministic, yet secure. So why bother with the complexity of PSS?

The main reason is that PSS was released *after* FDH, in 1996, and it has a security proof that inspires more confidence than FDH. Specifically, its proof offers slightly higher security guarantees than the proof of FDH, and its use of randomness helped strengthen that proof.

These stronger theoretical guarantees are the main reason cryptographers prefer PSS over FDH, but most applications using PSS today could switch to FDH with no meaningful security loss. In some contexts, however, a viable reason to use PSS instead of FDH is that PSS's randomness protects it from some attacks on its implementation, such as the fault attacks we'll discuss in "How Things Can Go Wrong" on page 196.

RSA Implementations

I sincerely hope you'll never have to implement RSA from scratch. If you're asked to, run as fast as you can and question the sanity of the person who asked you to do so. It took decades for cryptographers and engineers to develop RSA implementations that are fast, sufficiently secure, and hopefully free of debilitating bugs, so you really don't want to reinvent RSA. Even with all the documentation available, it would take months to complete this daunting task.

Typically, when implementing RSA, you'll use a library or API that provides the necessary functions to carry out RSA operations. For example, the Go language has the following function in its crypto package (from *https://www.golang.org/src/crypto/rsa/rsa.go*):

```
func EncryptOAEP(hash hash.Hash, random io.Reader, pub *PublicKey, msg []byte,
label []byte) (out []byte, err error)
```

The function EncryptOAEP() takes a hash value, a PRNG, a public key, a message, and a label (an optional parameter of OAEP), and returns a signature and an error code. When you call EncryptOAEP(), it calls encrypt() to compute the RSA function given the padded data, as shown in Listing 10-3.

```
func encrypt(c *big.Int, pub *PublicKey, m *big.Int) *big.Int {
    e := big.NewInt(int64(pub.E))
    c.Exp(m, e, pub.N)
    return c
}
```

Listing 10-3: Implementing the core RSA encryption function from the Go language cryptography library

The main operation shown in Listing 10-3 is c.Exp(m, e, pub.N), which raises a message, m, to the power e modulo pub.N, and assigns the result to the variable c.

If you choose to implement RSA instead of using a readily available library function, be sure to rely on an existing *big-number* library, which is a set of functions and types that allow you to define and compute arithmetic operations on large numbers thousands of bits long. For example, you might use the GNU Multiple Precision (GMP) arithmetic library in C, or Go's big package. (Believe me, you don't want to implement big-number arithmetic yourself.)

Even if you just use a library function when implementing RSA, be sure that you understand how the internals work in order to measure the risks.

Fast Exponentiation Algorithm: Square-and-Multiply

The operation of raising x to the power e, when computing $x^e \bmod n$, is called *exponentiation*. When we're working with big numbers, as with RSA, this operation can be extremely slow if naively implemented. But how do we do this efficiently?

The naive way to compute $x^e \bmod n$ takes $e - 1$ multiplications, as shown in the pseudocode algorithm in Listing 10-4.

```
expModNaive(x, e, n) {
    y = x
    for i = 1 to e - 1 {
        y = y * x  mod n
    }
    return y
}
```

Listing 10-4: A naive exponentiation algorithm in pseudocode

This algorithm is simple but highly inefficient. One way to get the same result exponentially faster is to square rather than multiply exponents until the correct value is reached. This family of methods is called *square-and-multiply*, or *exponentiation by squaring* or *binary exponentiation*.

For example, say that we want to compute $3^{65537} \bmod 36567232109354321$. (The number 65537 is the public exponent used in most RSA implementations.) We could multiply the number 3 by itself 65536 times, or we could approach this problem with the understanding that 65537 can be written as $2^{16} + 1$ and use a series of squaring operations. Essentially, we do the following:

Initialize a variable, $y = 3$, and then compute the following squaring (y^2) operations:

1. Set $y = y^2 \bmod n$ (now $y = 3^2 \bmod n$).
2. Set $y = y^2 \bmod n$ (now $y = (3^2)^2 \bmod n = 3^4 \bmod n$).
3. Set $y = y^2 \bmod n$ (now $y = (3^4)^2 = 3^8 \bmod n$).
4. Set $y = y^2 \bmod n$ (now $y = (3^8)^2 = 3^{16} \bmod n$).
5. Set $y = y^2 \bmod n$ (now $y = (3^{16})^2 = 3^{32} \bmod n$).

And so on until $y = 3^{65536}$, by performing 16 squarings.

To get the final result, we return $3 \times y \bmod n = 3^{65537} \bmod n = $ 26652909283612267. In other words, we compute the result with only 17 multiplications rather than 65536 with the naive method.

More generally, a square-and-multiply method works by scanning the exponent's bits one by one, from left to right, computing the square for each exponent's bit to double the exponent's value, and multiplying by the original number for each bit with a value of 1 encountered. In the preceding example, the exponent 65537 is 1000000000000001 in binary, and we squared y for each new bit and multiplied by the original number 3 only for the very first and last bits.

Listing 10-5 shows how this would work as a general algorithm in pseudocode to compute $x^e \bmod n$ when the exponent e consists of bits $e_{m-1}e_{m-2} \cdots e_1e_0$, where e_0 is the least significant bit.

```
expMod(x, e, n) {
    y = x
    for i = m - 1 to 0 {
        y = y * y  mod n
        if e_i == 1 then
            y = y * x  mod n
    }
    return y
}
```

Listing 10-5: A fast exponentiation algorithm in pseudocode

The expMod() algorithm shown in Listing 10-5 runs in time $O(m)$, whereas the naive algorithm runs in time $O(2^m)$, where m is the bit length of the exponent. Here, $O()$ is the asymptotic complexity notation introduced in Chapter 9.

Real systems often implement variants of this simplest square-and-multiply method. One such variant is the *sliding window* method, which considers blocks of bits rather than individual bits to perform a given multiplication operation. For example, see the function expNN() of the Go language, whose source code is available at *https://golang.org/src/math/big/nat.go*.

How secure are these square-and-multiply exponentiation algorithms? Unfortunately, the tricks to speed the process up often result in increased vulnerability against some attacks. Let's see what can go wrong.

The weakness in these algorithms is due to the fact that the exponentiation operations are heavily dependent on the exponent's value. The if operation shown in Listing 10-5 takes a different branch based on whether an exponent's bit is 0 or 1. If a bit is 1, an iteration of the for loop will be slower than it will be for 0, and attackers who monitor the execution time of the RSA operation can exploit this time difference to recover a private exponent. This is called a timing attack. Attacks on hardware can distinguish 1 bit from 0 bits by monitoring the device's power consumption and observing which iterations perform an extra multiplication to reveal which bits of the private exponent are 1.

Only a minority of cryptographic libraries implement effective defenses against timing attacks, let alone against such power-analysis attacks.

Small Exponents for Faster Public-Key Operations

Because an RSA computation is essentially the computation of an exponentiation, its performance depends on the value of the exponents used. Smaller exponents require fewer multiplications and therefore can make the exponentiation computation much faster.

The public exponent e can in principle be any value between 3 and $\varphi(n) - 1$, as long as e and $\varphi(n)$ are co-prime. But in practice you'll only find small values of e, and most of the time $e = 65537$ due to concerns with encryption and signature verification speed. For example, the Microsoft Windows CryptoAPI only supports public exponents that fit in a 32-bit integer. The larger the e, the slower it is to compute x^e mod n.

Unlike the size of the public exponent, the private exponent d will be about as large as n, making decryption much slower than encryption, and signing much slower than verification. Indeed, because d is secret, it must be unpredictable and therefore can't be restricted to a small value. For example, if e is fixed to 65537, the corresponding d will usually be of the same order of magnitude as the modulus n, which would be close to 2^{2048} if n is 2048 bits long.

As discussed in "Fast Exponentiation Algorithm: Square-and-Multiply" on page 192, raising a number to the power 65537 will only take 17 multiplications, whereas raising a number to the power of some 2048-bit number will take on the order of 3000 multiplications.

One way to determine the actual speed of RSA is to use the OpenSSL toolkit. For example, Listing 10-6 shows the results of 512-, 1024-, 2048-, and 4096-bit RSA operations on my MacBook, which is equipped with an Intel Core i5-5257U clocked at 2.7 GHz.

```
$ openssl speed rsa512 rsa1024 rsa2048 rsa4096
Doing 512 bit private rsa's for 10s: 161476 512 bit private RSA's in 9.59s
Doing 512 bit public rsa's for 10s: 1875805 512 bit public RSA's in 9.68s
Doing 1024 bit private rsa's for 10s: 51500 1024 bit private RSA's in 8.97s
Doing 1024 bit public rsa's for 10s: 715835 1024 bit public RSA's in 8.45s
Doing 2048 bit private rsa's for 10s: 13111 2048 bit private RSA's in 9.65s
Doing 2048 bit public rsa's for 10s: 288772 2048 bit public RSA's in 9.68s
Doing 4096 bit private rsa's for 10s: 1273 4096 bit private RSA's in 9.71s
Doing 4096 bit public rsa's for 10s: 63987 4096 bit public RSA's in 8.50s
OpenSSL 1.0.2g  1 Mar 2016
--snip--
                sign    verify    sign/s verify/s
rsa  512 bits 0.000059s 0.000005s 16838.0 193781.5
rsa 1024 bits 0.000174s 0.000012s  5741.4  84714.2
rsa 2048 bits 0.000736s 0.000034s  1358.7  29831.8
rsa 4096 bits 0.007628s 0.000133s   131.1   7527.9
```

Listing 10-6: Benchmarks of RSA operations using the OpenSSL toolkit

How much slower is verification compared to signature generation? To get an idea, we can compute the ratio of the verification time over signature time. The benchmarks in Listing 10-6 show that I've got verification-over-signature speed ratios of approximately 11.51, 14.75, 21.96, and 57.42 for 512-, 1024-, 2048-, and 4096-bit moduli sizes, respectively. The gap grows with the modulus size because the number of multiplications for e operations will remain constant with respect to the modulus size (for example, 17 when $e = 65537$), while private-key operations will always need more multiplications for a greater modulus because d will grow accordingly.

But if small exponents are so nice, why use 65537 and not something like 3? It would actually be fine (and faster) to use 3 as an exponent when implementing RSA with a secure scheme such as OAEP, PSS, or FDH. Cryptographers avoid doing so, however, because when $e = 3$, less secure schemes make certain types of mathematical attacks possible. The number 65537 is large enough to avoid such *low-exponent attacks*, and it has just one instance in which a bit is 1, thanks to its low Hamming weight, which decreases the computational time. 65537 is also special for mathematicians: it's the fourth Fermat number, or a number of the form

$$2^{(2^n)} + 1$$

because it's equal to $2^{16} + 1$, where $16 = 2^4$, but that's just a curiosity mostly irrelevant for cryptographic engineers.

The Chinese Remainder Theorem

The most common trick to speed up decryption and signature verification (that is, the computation of $y^d \bmod n$) is the *Chinese remainder theorem (CRT)*. It makes RSA about four times faster.

The Chinese remainder theorem allows for faster decryption by computing two exponentiations, modulo p and modulo q, rather than simply modulo n. Because p and q are much smaller than n, it's faster to perform two "small" exponentiations than a single "big" one.

The Chinese remainder theorem isn't specific to RSA. It's a general arithmetic result that, in its simplest form, states that if $n = n_1 n_2 n_3 \ldots$, where the n_is are pairwise co-prime (that is, **GCD**$(n_i, n_j) = 1$ for any distinct i and j), then the value $x \bmod n$ can be computed from the values $x \bmod n_1$, $x \bmod n_2$, $x \bmod n_3$, ... For example, say we have $n = 1155$, which we write as the product of prime factors $3 \times 5 \times 7 \times 11$. We want to determine the number x that satisfies $x \bmod 3 = 2$, $x \bmod 5 = 1$, $x \bmod 7 = 6$, and $x \bmod 11 = 8$. (I've chosen 2, 1, 6, and 8 arbitrarily.)

To find x using the Chinese remainder theorem, we can compute the sum $P(n_1) + P(n_2) + \ldots$, where $P(n_i)$ is defined as follows:

$$P(n_i) = (x \bmod n_i) \times n / n_i \times \left(1 / (n / n_i) \bmod n_i\right) \bmod n$$

Note that the second term, n/n_i, is equal to the product of all other factors than this n_i.

To apply this formula to our example and recover our $x \bmod 1155$, we take the arbitrary values 2, 1, 6, and 8; we compute $P(3)$, $P(5)$, $P(7)$, and $P(8)$; and then we add them together to get the following expression:

$$\left[\begin{array}{l} 2 \times 385 \times \left(1 / 385 \bmod 3 \right) + 1 \times 231 \times \left(1 / 231 \bmod 5 \right) + 6 \\ \times 165 \times \left(1 / 165 \bmod 7 \right) + 8 \times 105 \times \left(1 / 105 \bmod 11 \right) \end{array} \right] \bmod n$$

Here, I've just applied the preceding definition of $P(n_i)$. (The math behind the way each number was found is straightforward, but I won't detail it here.) This expression can then be reduced to $[770 + 231 + 1980 + 1680]$ $\bmod n = 41$, and indeed 41 is the number I had picked for this example, so we've got the correct result.

Applying the CRT to RSA is simpler than the previous example, because there are only two factors for each n (namely p and q). Given a ciphertext y to decrypt, instead of computing $y^d \bmod n$, you use the CRT to compute $x_p = y^s \bmod p$, where $s = d \bmod (p-1)$ and $x_q = y^t \bmod q$, where $t = d \bmod (q-1)$. You now combine these two expressions and compute x to be the following:

$$x = x_p \times q \times \left(1/q \bmod p \right) + x_q \times p \times \left(1/p \bmod q \right) \bmod n$$

And that's it. This is faster than square-and-multiply because the multiplication-heavy operations are carried out on modulo p and q, numbers that are twice as small as n.

NOTE   *In the final operation, the two numbers* q × (1/q *mod* p) *and* p × (1/p *mod* q) *can be computed in advance, which means only two multiplications and an addition of modulo* n *need to be computed to find* x.

Unfortunately, there's a security caveat attached to these techniques, as I'll discuss next.

How Things Can Go Wrong

Even more beautiful than the RSA scheme itself is the range of attacks that work either because the implementation leaks (or can be made to leak) information on its internals or because RSA is used insecurely. I discuss two classic examples of these types of attacks in the sections that follow.

The Bellcore Attack on RSA-CRT

The Bellcore attack on RSA is one of the most important attacks in the history of RSA. When first discovered in 1996, it stood out because it exploited RSA's vulnerability to *fault injections*—attacks that force a part of the algorithm to misbehave and thus yield incorrect results. For example, hardware circuits or embedded systems can be temporarily perturbed by suddenly altering their voltage supply or by beaming a laser pulse to a carefully chosen part of a chip. Attackers can then exploit the resulting faults in an algorithm's internal operation by observing the impact on the final result. For example, comparing the correct result with a faulty one can provide information on the algorithm's internal values, including secret values.

The Bellcore attack is such a fault attack. It works on RSA signature schemes that use the Chinese remainder theorem and that are deterministic—meaning that it works on FDH, but not on PSS, which is probabilistic.

To understand how the Bellcore attack works, recall from the previous section that with CRT, the result that is equal to x^d mod n is obtained by computing the following, where $x_p = y^s$ mod p and $x_q = y^t$ mod q:

$$x = x_p \times q \times \left(1/q \bmod p\right) + x_q \times p \times \left(1/p \bmod q\right) \bmod n$$

Now assume that an attacker induces a fault in the computation of x_q so that you end up with some incorrect value, which differs from the actual x_q. Let's call this incorrect value x_q' and call the final result obtained x'. The attacker can then subtract the incorrect signature x' from the correct signature x to factor n, which results in the following:

$$x - x' = \left(x_q - x_q'\right) \times p \times \left(1/p \bmod q\right) \bmod n$$

The value $x - x'$ is therefore a multiple of p, so p is a divisor of $x - x'$. Because p is also a divisor of n, the greatest common divisor of n and $x - x'$ yields p, $\mathbf{GCD}(x - x', n) = p$. We can then compute $q = n/p$ and d, resulting in a total break of RSA signatures.

A variant of this attack works when you don't know the correct signature but only know the message is signed. There's also a similar fault attack on the modulus value, rather than on the CRT values computation, but I won't go into detail on that here.

Sharing Private Exponents or Moduli

Now I'll show you why your public key shouldn't have the same modulus n as that of someone else.

Different private keys belonging to different systems or persons should obviously have different private exponents, d, even if the keys use different moduli, or you could try your own value of d to decrypt messages encrypted for other entities, until you hit one that shares the same d. By the same token, different key pairs should have different n values, even if they have different ds, because p and q are usually part of the private key. Hence, if we share the same n and thus the same p and q, I can compute your private key from your public key e using p and q.

What if my private key is simply the pair (n, d_1), and your private key is (n, d_2) and your public key is (n, e_2)? Say that I know n but not p and q, so I can't directly compute your private exponent d_2 from your public exponent e_2. How would you compute p and q from a private exponent d only? The solution is a bit technical, but elegant.

Remember that d and e satisfy $ed = k\varphi(n) + 1$, where $\varphi(n)$ is secret and could give us p and q directly. We don't know k or $\varphi(n)$, but we can compute $k\varphi(n) = ed - 1$.

What can we do with this value $k\varphi(n)$? A first observation is that, according to *Euler's theorem*, we know that for any number a co-prime with n, $a^{\varphi(n)} = 1 \bmod n$. Therefore, modulo n we have the following:

$$a^{k\varphi(n)} = \left(a^{\varphi(n)}\right)^{k} = 1^{k} = 1$$

A second observation is that, because $k\varphi(n)$ is an even number, we can write it as $2^{s}t$ for some numbers s and t. That is, we'll be able to write $a^{k\varphi(n)} = 1 \bmod n$ under the form $x^{2} = 1 \bmod n$ for some x easily computed from $k\varphi(n)$. Such an x is called a *root of unity*.

The key observation is that $x^{2} = 1 \bmod n$ is equivalent to saying that the value $x^{2} - 1 = (x - 1)(x + 1)$ divides n. In other words, $x - 1$ or $x + 1$ must have a common factor with n, which can give us the factorization of n.

Listing 10-7 shows a Python implementation of this method where, in order to find the factors p and q from n and d, we use small, 64-bit numbers for the sake of simplicity.

```
from math import gcd

n = 36567232109354321
e = 13771927877214701
d = 15417970063428857

❶ kphi = d*e - 1
   t = kphi

❷ while t % 2 == 0:
       t = divmod(t, 2)[0]

❸ a = 2
   while a < 100:
     ❹ k = t
       while k < kphi:
           x = pow(a, k, n)
         ❺ if x ! = 1 and x ! = (n - 1) and pow(x, 2, n) == 1:
             ❻ p = gcd(x - 1, n)
                break
           k = k*2
       a = a + 2

   q = n//p
❼ assert (p*q) == n
   print('p = ', p)
   print('q = ', q)
```

Listing 10-7: A python program that computes the prime factors p and q from the private exponent d

This program determines $k\varphi(n)$ from e and d ❶ by finding the number t such that $k\varphi(n) = 2^s t$, for some s ❷. Then it looks for a and k such that $(a^k)^2 = 1 \bmod n$ ❸, using t as a starting point for k ❹. When this condition is satisfied ❺, we've found a solution. It then determines the factor p ❻ and verifies ❼ that the value of pq equals the value of n. It then prints the resulting values of p and q:

```
p = 2046223079
q = 17870599
```

The program correctly returns the two factors.

Further Reading

RSA deserves a book by itself. I had to omit many important and interesting topics, such as Bleichenbacher's padding oracle attack on OAEP's predecessor (the standard PKCS#1 v1.5), an attack similar in spirit to the padding oracle attack on block ciphers seen in Chapter 4. There's also Wiener's attack on RSA with low private exponents, and attacks using Coppersmith's method on RSA with small exponents that potentially also have insecure padding.

To see research results related to side-channel attacks and defenses, view the CHES workshop proceedings that have run since 1999 at *http://www.chesworkshop.org/*. One of the most useful references while writing this chapter was Boneh's "Twenty Years of Attacks on the RSA Cryptosystem," a survey that reviews and explains the most important attacks on RSA. For reference specifically on timing attacks, the paper "Remote Timing Attacks Are Practical" by Brumley and Boneh, is a must-read, both for its analytical and experimental contributions. To learn more about fault attacks, read the full version of the Bellcore attack paper "On the Importance of Eliminating Errors in Cryptographic Computations" by Boneh, DeMillo, and Lipton.

The best way to learn how RSA implementations work, though sometimes painful and frustrating, is to review the source code of widely used implementations. For example, see RSA and its underlying big-number arithmetic implementations in OpenSSL, in NSS (the library used by the Mozilla Firefox browser), in Crypto++, or in other popular software, and examine their implementations of arithmetic operations as well as their defenses against timing and fault attacks.

11

DIFFIE–HELLMAN

In November 1976, Stanford researchers Whitfield Diffie and Martin Hellman published a research paper titled "New Directions in Cryptography" that revolutionized cryptography forever. In their paper, they introduced the notion of public-key encryption and signatures, though they didn't actually have any of those schemes; they simply had what they termed a *public-key distribution scheme*, a protocol that allows two parties to establish a shared secret by exchanging information visible to an eavesdropper. This protocol is now known as the *Diffie–Hellman (DH) protocol*.

Prior to Diffie–Hellman, establishing a shared secret required performing tedious procedures such as manually exchanging sealed envelopes. Once communicating parties have established a shared secret value with the DH protocol, that secret can be used to establish a *secure channel* by turning the secret into one or more symmetric keys that are then used to encrypt and authenticate subsequent communication. The DH protocol—and its variants—are therefore called key agreement protocols.

In the first part of this chapter, I review the mathematical foundations of the Diffie–Hellman protocol, including the computational problems that DH relies on to perform its magic. I then describe different versions of the Diffie–Hellman protocol used to create secure channels in the second part of this chapter. Finally, because Diffie–Hellman schemes are only secure when their parameters are well chosen, I conclude the chapter by examining scenarios where Diffie–Hellman can fail.

NOTE *Diffie and Hellman received the prestigious Turing Award in 2015 for their invention of public-key cryptography and digital signatures, but others deserve credit as well. In 1974, two years before the seminal Diffie–Hellman paper, computer scientist Ralph Merkle introduced the idea of public-key cryptography with what are now called Merkle's puzzles. Around that same year, researchers at GCHQ (Government Communications Headquarters), the British equivalent of the NSA, had also discovered the principles behind RSA and Diffie–Hellman key agreement, though that fact would only be declassified decades later.*

The Diffie–Hellman Function

In order to understand DH key agreement protocols, you must first understand their core operation, the *DH function*. The DH function will usually work with groups denoted $\mathbf{Z}_p^*$. Recall from Chapter 9 that these groups are formed of nonzero integer numbers modulo a prime number, denoted p. Another public parameter is the *base number*, g. All arithmetic operations are performed modulo p.

The DH function involves two private values chosen randomly by the two communicating parties from the group $\mathbf{Z}_p^*$, denoted a and b. A private value a has a public value associated with $A = g^a \bmod p$, or g raised to the power a modulo p. This value is sent to the other party through a message that is visible to eavesdroppers. The public value associated with b is $B = g^b \bmod p$, or g raised to the power b modulo p, which is sent to the owner of a through a publicly readable message.

DH works its magic by combining either public value with the other private value, such that the result is the same in both cases: $A^b = (g^a)^b = g^{ab}$ and $B^a = (g^b)^a = g^{ba} = g^{ab}$. The resulting value, g^{ab}, is the *shared secret*; it is then passed to a *key derivation function (KDF)* in order to generate one or more shared symmetric keys. A KDF is a kind of hash function that will return a random-looking string the size of the desired key length.

And that's it. Like many great scientific discoveries (gravity, relativity, quantum computing, or RSA), the Diffie–Hellman trick is terribly simple in hindsight.

Diffie–Hellman's simplicity can be deceiving, however. For one thing, it won't work with just any prime p or base number g. For example, some values of g will restrict the shared secrets g^{ab} to a small subset of possible values, whereas you'd expect to have about as many possible values as elements in $\mathbf{Z}_p^*$, and therefore as many possible values for the shared secret. To ensure the highest security, safe DH parameters should work with a prime p such that $(p-1) / 2$ is also prime. Such a *safe prime* guarantees that the group doesn't have small subgroups that would make DH easier to break. With a safe prime, DH can notably work with $g = 2$, which makes computations slightly faster. But generating a safe prime p takes more time than generating a totally random prime.

For example, the `dhparam` command of the OpenSSL toolkit will only generate safe DH parameters, but the extra checks built into the algorithm result increase the execution time considerably, as shown in Listing 11-1.

```
$ time openssl dhparam 2048
Generating DH parameters, 2048 bit long safe prime, generator 2
This is going to take a long time
--snip--
-----BEGIN DH PARAMETERS-----
MIIBCAKCAQEAoSIbyA9e844q7V89rcoEV8vd/l2svwhIIjG9EPwWWr7FkfYhYkU9
fRNttmilGCTfxc9EDf+4dzw+AbRBc6oOL9gxUoPnOd1/G/YDYgyplF5M3xeswqea
SD+B7628pWTaCZGKZham7vmiN8azGeaYAucckTkjVWceHVIVXe5fvU74k7+C2wKk
iiyMFm8th2zm9W/shiKNV2+SsHtD6r3ZC2/hfu7XdOI4iT6ise83YicU/cRaDmK6
zgBKn3SlCjwL4M3+m1J+VhOUFz/nWTJ1IWAVC+aoLK8upqRgApOgHkVqzP/CgwBw
XAOE8ncQqroJOmUSB5eLqfpAvyBWpkrwQwIBAg==
-----END DH PARAMETERS-----
openssl dhparam 2048  154.53s user 0.86s system 99% cpu 2:36.85 total
```

Listing 11-1: Measuring the execution time of generating 2048-bit Diffie–Hellman parameters with the OpenSSL toolkit

As you can see in Listing 11-1, it took 154.53 seconds to generate the DH parameters using the OpenSSL toolkit. Now, for the sake of comparison, Listing 11-2 shows how long it takes on the same system to generate RSA parameters of the same size (that is, two prime numbers, p and q, each half the size of the p used for DH).

```
$ time openssl genrsa 2048
Generating RSA private key, 2048 bit long modulus
.................................................+++
.........................................................+++
e is 65537 (0x10001)
-----BEGIN RSA PRIVATE KEY-----
--snip--
-----END RSA PRIVATE KEY-----
openssl genrsa 2048  0.16s user 0.01s system 95% cpu 0.171 total
```

Listing 11-2: Generating 2048-bit RSA parameters while measuring the execution time

Generating DH parameters took about 1000 times longer than generating RSA parameters of the same security level, mainly due to the extra constraint imposed on the prime generated to create DH parameters.

The Diffie–Hellman Problems

The security of DH protocols relies on the hardness of computational problems, especially on that of the discrete logarithm problem (DLP) introduced in Chapter 9. Clearly, DH can be broken by recovering the private value a from its public value g^a, which boils down to solving a DLP instance. But we don't care only about the discrete logarithm problem when using DH to compute shared secrets. We also care about two DH-specific problems, as explained next.

The Computational Diffie–Hellman Problem

The *computational Diffie–Hellman (CDH)* problem is that of computing the shared secret g^{ab} given only the public values g^a and g^b, and not any of the secret values a or b. The motivation is obviously to ensure that even if an eavesdropper captures g^a and g^b, they should not be able to determine the shared secret g^{ab}.

If you can solve DLP, then you can also solve CDH; to put it simply, if you can solve DLP, then given g^a and g^b, you'll be able to derive a and b to compute g^{ab}. In other words, DLP is *at least* as hard as CDH. But we don't know for sure whether CDH is at least as hard as DLP, which would make the problems equally hard. In other words, DLP is to CDH what the factoring problem is to the RSA problem. (Recall that factoring allows you to solve the RSA problem, but not necessarily the converse.)

Diffie–Hellman shares another similarity with RSA in that DH will deliver the same security level as RSA for a given modulus size. For example, the DH protocol with a 2048-bit prime p will get you about the same security that RSA with a 2048-bit modulus n offers, which is about 90 bits. Indeed, the fastest way we know to break CDH is to solve DLP using an algorithm called the *number field sieve*, a method similar but not identical to the fastest one that breaks RSA by factoring its modulus: the general number field sieve (GNFS).

The Decisional Diffie–Hellman Problem

Sometimes we need something stronger than CDH's hardness assumption. For example, imagine that an attacker can compute the first 32 bits of g^{ab} given the 2048-bit values of g^a and g^b, but that they can't compute all 2048 bits. Although CDH would still be unbroken because 32 bits aren't enough to completely recover g^{ab}, the attacker would still have learned something about the shared secret, which might still allow them to compromise an application's security.

To ensure that an attacker can't learn anything about the shared secret g^{ab}, this value needs only to be indistinguishable from a random group element, just as an encryption scheme is secure when ciphertexts are indistinguishable from random strings. The computational problem formalizing this intuition is called the *decisional Diffie–Hellman (DDH)* problem. Given g^a, g^b, and a value that is either g^{ab} or g^c for some random c (each of the two with a chance of $1/2$), the DDH problem consists of determining whether g^{ab} (the shared secret corresponding to g^a and g^b) was chosen. The assumption that no attacker can solve DDH efficiently is called the *decisional Diffie–Hellman assumption.*

If DDH is hard, then CDH is also hard, and you can't learn anything about g^{ab}. But if you can solve CDH, you can also solve DDH: given a triplet (g^a, g^b, g^c), you would be able to derive g^{ab} from g^a and g^b and check whether the result is equal to the given g^c. The bottom line is that DDH is fundamentally less hard than CDH, yet DDH hardness is a prime assumption in cryptography, and one of the most studied. We can be confident that both CDH and DDH are hard when Diffie–Hellman parameters are well chosen.

More Diffie–Hellman Problems

Sometimes cryptographers devise new schemes and prove that they are at least as hard to break as it is to solve some problem related to CDH or DDH but not identical to either of these. Ideally, we'd like to demonstrate that breaking a cryptosystem is as hard as solving CDH or DDH, but this isn't always possible with advanced cryptographic mechanisms, typically because such schemes involve more complex operations than basic Diffie–Hellman protocols.

For example, in one DH-like problem, given g^a, an attacker would attempt to compute $g^{1/a}$, where $1/a$ is the inverse of a in the group (typically $\mathbf{Z}_p^*$ for some prime p). In another, an attacker might distinguish the pairs (g^a, g^b) from the pairs $(g^a, g^{1/a})$ for random a and b. Finally, in what is called the *twin Diffie–Hellman problem*, given g^a, g^b, and g^c, an attacker would attempt to compute the two values g^{ab} and g^{ac}. Sometimes such DH variants turn out to be as hard as CDH or DDH, and sometimes they're fundamentally easier—and therefore provide lower security guarantees. As an exercise, try to find connections between the hardness of these problems and that of CDH and DDH. (Twin Diffie–Hellman is actually *as hard* as CDH, but that isn't easy to prove!)

Key Agreement Protocols

The Diffie–Hellman problem is designed to build secure key agreement protocols—protocols designed to secure communication between two or more parties communicating over a network with the aid of a shared secret. This secret is turned into one or more *session keys*—symmetric keys used to encrypt and authenticate the information exchanged for the duration of the session. But before studying actual DH protocols, you should know what makes a key agreement protocol secure or insecure, and how simpler protocols work. We'll begin our discussion with a widely used key agreement protocol that doesn't rely on DH.

An Example of Non-DH Key Agreement

To give you a sense of how a key agreement protocol works and what it means for it to be secure, let's look at the protocol used in the 3G and 4G telecommunications standards to establish communication between a SIM card and a telecom operator. The protocol is often referred to as *AKA*, for *authenticated key agreement*. It doesn't use the Diffie–Hellman function, but instead uses only symmetric-key operations. The details are a bit boring, but essentially the protocol works as shown in Figure 11-1.

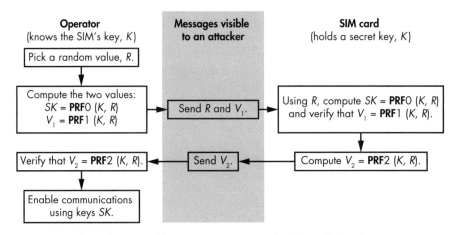

Figure 11-1: The authenticated key agreement protocol in 3G and 4G telecommunication

In this implementation of the protocol, the SIM card has a secret key, K, that the operator knows. The operator begins the session by selecting a random value, R, and then computes two values, SK and V_1, based on two pseudorandom functions, **PRF0** and **PRF1**. Next, the operator sends a message to the SIM card containing the values R and V_1, which are visible to attackers. Once the SIM card has R, it has what it needs in order to compute SK with **PRF0**, and it does so. The two parties in this session end up with a shared key, SK, that attackers are unable to determine by simply looking at the messages exchanged between the parties, or even by modifying them or injecting new ones. The SIM card verifies that it's talking to the operator by recomputing V_1 with **PRF1**, K, and R, and then checking to make sure that the calculated V_1 matches the V_1 sent by the operator. The SIM card then computes a verification value, V_2, with a new function, **PRF2**, with K and R as input, and sends V_2 to the operator. The operator verifies that the SIM card knows K by computing V_2 and checking that the computed value matches the V_2 it received.

But this protocol is not immune to all kinds of attacks: in principle there's a way to fool the SIM card with a replay attack. Essentially, if an attacker captures a pair (R, V_1), they may send it to the SIM card and trick the SIM into believing that the pair came from a legitimate operator that knows K. To prevent this attack, the protocol includes additional checks to ensure that the same R isn't reused.

Problems can also arise if K is compromised. For example, an attacker who compromises K can perform a man-in-the-middle attack and listen to all cleartext communication. Such an attacker could send messages between the two parties while pretending to be both the legitimate SIM card operator and the SIM card. The greater risk is that an attacker can record communications and any messages exchanged during the key agreement, and later decrypt those communications by using the captured R values. An attacker could then determine the past session keys and use them to decrypt the recorded traffic.

Attack Models for Key Agreement Protocols

There is no single definition of security for key agreement protocols, and you can never say that a key protocol is completely secure without context and without considering the attack model and the security goals. You can, for example, argue that the previous 3G/4G protocol is secure because a passive attacker won't find the session keys, but you could also argue that it's insecure because once the key K leaks, then all previous and future communications are compromised.

There are different notions of security in key agreement protocols as well as three main attack models that depend on the information the protocol leaks. From weakest to strongest, these are the *eavesdropper*, the *data leak*, and the *breach*:

The eavesdropper   This attacker observes the messages exchanged between the two legitimate parties running a key agreement protocol and can record, modify, drop, or inject messages. To protect against an eavesdropper, a key agreement protocol must not leak any information on the shared secret established.

The data leak   In this model, the attacker acquires the session key and all *temporary* secrets (such as SK in the telecom protocol example discussed previously) from one or more executions of the protocol, but not the long-term secrets (like K in that same protocol).

The breach (or corruption)   In this model, the attacker learns the long-term key of one or more of the parties. Once a breach occurs, security is no longer attainable because the attacker can impersonate one or both parties in subsequent sessions of the protocol. Nonetheless, the attacker shouldn't be able to recover secrets from sessions executed before gathering the key.

Now that we've looked at the attack models and seen what an attacker can do, let's explore the security goals—that is, the security guarantees that the protocol should offer. A key agreement protocol can be designed to satisfy several security goals. The four most relevant ones are described here, in order from simplest to most sophisticated.

Authentication   Each party should be able to authenticate the other party. That is, the protocol should allow for *mutual authentication*. Authenticated key agreement (AKA) occurs when a protocol authenticates both parties.

Key control   Neither party should be able to choose the final shared secret or coerce it to be in a specific subset. The 3G/4G key agreement protocol discussed earlier lacks this property because the operator chooses the value for R that entirely determines the final shared key.

Forward secrecy   This is the assurance that even if all long-term secrets are exposed, shared secrets from previous executions of the protocol won't be able to be computed, even if an attacker records all previous executions or is able to inject or modify messages from previous executions. A *forward-secret* protocol guarantees that even if you have to deliver your devices and their secrets to some authority or other, they won't be able to decrypt your prior encrypted communications. (The 3G/4G key agreement protocol doesn't provide forward secrecy.)

Resistance to key-compromise impersonation (KCI)   KCI occurs when an attacker compromises a party's long-term key and is able to use it to impersonate another party. For example, the 3G/4G key agreement protocol allows trivial key-compromise impersonation because both parties share the same key K. A key agreement protocol should ideally prevent this kind of attack.

Performance

To be useful, a key agreement protocol should be not only secure but also efficient. Several factors should be taken into account when considering a key agreement protocol's efficiency, including the number of messages exchanged, the length and number of messages, the computational effort to implement the protocol, and whether precomputations can be made to save time. A protocol is generally more efficient if fewer, shorter messages are exchanged, and it's best if interactivity is kept minimal so that neither party has to wait to receive a message before sending the next one. A common measure of a protocol's efficiency is its duration in terms of *round trips*, or the time it takes to send a message and receive a response.

Round-trip time is usually the main cause of latency in protocols, but the amount of computation to be carried out also counts; the fewer the computations required the better, and the more precomputations that can be done in advance, the better.

For example, the 3G/4G key agreement protocol discussed earlier exchanges two messages of a few hundred bits each, which must be sent in a certain order. Pre-computation can be used with this protocol to save time since the operator can pick many values of R in advance; precompute the matching values of SK, V_1, and V_2; and store them all in a database. In this case, precomputation has the advantage of reducing the exposure of the long-term key.

Diffie–Hellman Protocols

The Diffie–Hellman function is the core of most of the deployed public-key agreement protocols. However, there is no single Diffie–Hellman protocol, but rather a variety of ways to use the DH function in order to establish a shared secret. We'll review three of those protocols in the sections that follow. In each discussion, I'll stick to the usual crypto placeholder names and call the two parties Alice and Bob, and the attacker Eve. I'll write g as the basis of the group used for arithmetic operations, a value fixed and known in advance to Alice and Bob.

Anonymous Diffie–Hellman

Anonymous Diffie–Hellman is the simplest of the Diffie–Hellman protocols. It's called anonymous because it's not authenticated; the participants have no identity that can be verified by either party, and neither party holds a long-term key. Alice can't prove to Bob that she's Alice, and vice versa.

In anonymous Diffie–Hellman, each party picks a random value (a for Alice and b for Bob) to use as a private key, and sends the corresponding public key to the other peer. Figure 11-2 shows the process in a bit more detail.

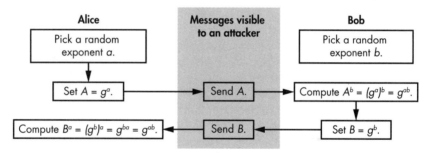

Figure 11-2: The anonymous Diffie–Hellman protocol

As you can see, Alice uses her exponent a and the group basis g to compute $A = g^a$, which she sends to Bob. Bob receives A and computes A^b, which is equal to $(g^a)^b$. Bob now obtains the value g^{ab} and computes B from his random exponent b and the value g. He then sends B to Alice and she uses it to compute g^{ab}. Alice and Bob end up with the same value, g^{ab}, after performing similar operations, which involve raising both g and the value received to their private exponent's power. Pure, simple, but only secure against the laziest of attackers.

Anonymous DH can be taken down with a man-in-the-middle attack. An eavesdropper simply needs to intercept messages and pretend to be Bob (to Alice) and pretend to be Alice (to Bob), as shown in Figure 11-3.

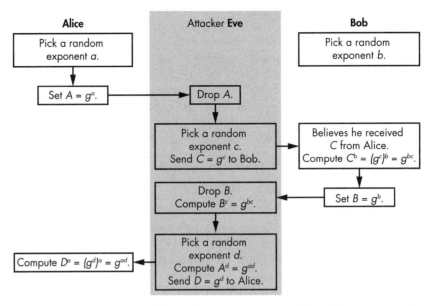

Figure 11-3: A man-in-the-middle attack on the anonymous Diffie–Hellman protocol

As in the previous exchange, Alice and Bob pick random exponents, a and b. Alice now computes and sends A, but Eve intercepts and drops the message. Eve then picks a random exponent, c, and computes $C = g^c$ to send to Bob. Because this protocol has no authentication, Bob believes he is receiving C from Alice and goes on to compute g^{bc}. Bob then computes B and sends that value to Alice, but Eve intercepts and drops the message again. Eve now computes g^{bc}, picks a new exponent, d, computes g^{ad}, computes D from g^d, and sends D to Alice. Alice then computes g^{ad} as well.

As a result of this attack, the attacker Eve ends up sharing a secret with Alice (g^{ad}) and another secret with Bob (g^{bc}), though Alice and Bob believe that they're sharing a single secret with each other. After completing the protocol execution, Alice will derive symmetric keys from g^{ad} in order to encrypt data sent to Bob, but Eve will intercept the encrypted messages, decrypt them, and re-encrypt them to Bob using another set of keys derived from g^{bc}—after potentially modifying the cleartext. All of this happens with Alice and Bob unaware. That is, they're doomed.

To foil this attack, you need a way to authenticate the parties so that Alice can prove that she's the real Alice and Bob can prove that he's the real Bob. Fortunately, there is a way to do so.

Authenticated Diffie–Hellman

Authenticated Diffie–Hellman was developed to address the sort of man-in-the-middle attacks that can affect anonymous DH. Authenticated DH equips the two parties with both a private and a public key, thereby allowing Alice and Bob to sign their messages in order to stop Eve from sending messages on their behalf. Here, the signatures aren't computed with a DH function, but a public-key signature scheme such as RSA-PSS. As a result, in order to successfully send messages on behalf of Alice, an attacker would need to forge a valid signature, which is impossible with a secure signature scheme.

Figure 11-4 shows how authenticated DH works.

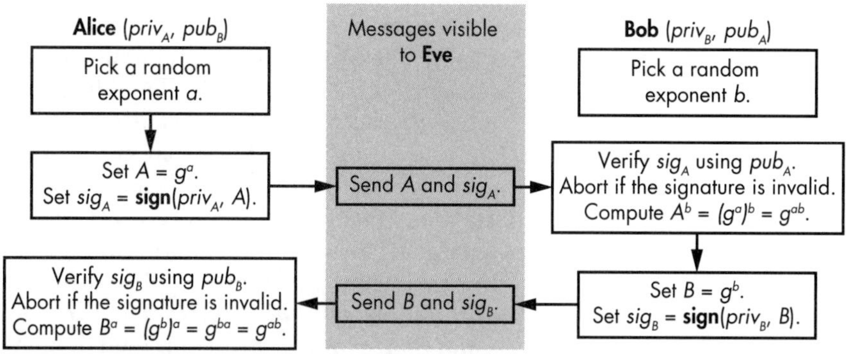

Figure 11-4: The authenticated Diffie–Hellman protocol

The **Alice** ($priv_A$, pub_B) label on the first line means that Alice holds her own private key, $priv_A$, as well as Bob's public key, pub_B. This sort of $priv/pub$ key pair is called a *long-term key* because it's fixed in advance and remains constant through consecutive runs of the protocol. Of course, these long-term private keys should be kept secret, while the public keys are considered to be known to an attacker.

Alice and Bob begin by picking random exponents, a and b, as in anonymous DH. Alice then calculates A and a signature sig_A based on a combination of her signing function **sign**, her private key $priv_A$, and A. Now Alice sends A and sig_A to Bob, who verifies sig_A with her public key pub_A. If the signature is invalid, Bob knows that the message didn't come from Alice, and he discards A.

If the signature is correct, Bob will compute g^{ab} from A and his random exponent b. He would then compute B and his own signature from a combination of the **sign** function, his private key $priv_B$, and B. Now he sends B and sig_B to Alice, who attempts to verify sig_B with Bob's public key pub_B. Alice will only compute g^{ab} if Bob's signature is successfully verified.

Security Against Eavesdroppers

Authenticated DH is secure against eavesdroppers because attackers can't learn any bit of information on the shared secret g^{ab} since they ignore the DH exponents. Authenticated DH also provides forward secrecy: even if an attacker corrupts any of the parties at some point, as in the *breach* attack model discussed earlier, they would learn the private signing keys but not any of the ephemeral DH exponents; hence, they'd be unable to learn the value of any previously shared secrets.

Authenticated DH also prevents any party from controlling the value of the shared secret. Alice can't craft a special value of a in order to predict the value of g^{ab} because she doesn't control b, which influences g^{ab} as much as a does. (One exception would be if Alice were to choose $a = 0$, in which case we'd have $g^{ab} = 1$ for any b. But 0 isn't an authorized value and should be rejected by the protocol.)

That said, authenticated DH isn't secure against all types of attack. For one thing, Eve can record previous values of A and sig_A and replay them later to Bob, in order to pretend to be Alice. Bob will then believe that he's sharing a secret with Alice when he isn't, even though Eve would not be able to learn that secret. This risk is eliminated in practice by adding a procedure called *key confirmation*, wherein Alice and Bob prove to each other that they own the shared secret. For example, Alice and Bob may perform key confirmation by sending respectively $\textbf{Hash}(pub_A \mathbin\Vert pub_B, g^{ab})$ and $\textbf{Hash}(pub_B \mathbin\Vert pub_A, g^{ab})$ for some hash function **Hash**; when Bob receives $\textbf{Hash}(pub_A \mathbin\Vert pub_B, g^{ab})$ and Alice receives $\textbf{Hash}(pub_B \mathbin\Vert pub_A, g^{ab})$, both can verify the correctness of these hash values using pub_A, pub_B, and g^{ab}. The different order of public keys ($pub_A \mathbin\Vert pub_B$ and $pub_B \mathbin\Vert pub_A$) ensures that Alice and Bob will send different values, and that an attacker can't pretend to be Alice by copying Bob's hash value.

Security Against Data Leaks

Authenticated DH's vulnerability to data leak attackers is of greater concern. In this type of attack, the attacker learns the value of ephemeral, short-term secrets (namely, the exponents a and b) and uses that information to impersonate one of the communicating parties. If Eve is able to learn the value of an exponent a along with the matching values of A and sig_A sent to Bob, she could initiate a new execution of the protocol and impersonate Alice, as shown in Figure 11-5.

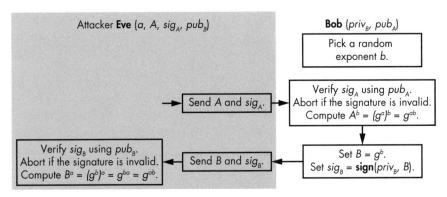

Figure 11-5: An impersonation attack on the authenticated Diffie–Hellman protocol

In this attack scenario, Eve learns the value of an a and replays the corresponding A and its signature sig_A, pretending to be Alice. Bob verifies the signature and computes g^{ab} from A and sends B and sig_B, which Eve then uses to compute g^{ab}, using the stolen a. This results in the two having a shared secret. Bob now believes he is talking to Alice.

One way to make authenticated DH secure against the leak of ephemeral secrets is to integrate the long-term keys into the shared secret computation so that the shared secret can't be determined without knowing the long-term secret.

Menezes–Qu–Vanstone (MQV)

The *Menezes–Qu–Vanstone (MQV)* protocol is a milestone in the history of DH-based protocols. Designed in 1998, MQV had been approved to protect most critical assets when the NSA included it in its Suite B, a portfolio of algorithms designed to protect classified information. (NSA eventually dropped MQV, allegedly because it wasn't used. I'll discuss the reasons why in a bit.)

MQV is Diffie–Hellman on steroids. It's more secure than authenticated DH, and it improves on authenticated DH's performance properties. In particular, MQV allows users to send only two messages, independently of each other, in arbitrary order. Other benefits are that users can send shorter messages than they would be able to with authenticated DH, and they don't need to send explicit signature or verification messages. In other words, you don't need to use a signature scheme in addition to the Diffie–Hellman function.

As with authenticated DH, in MQV Alice and Bob each hold a long-term private key as well as the long-term public key of the other party. The difference is that the MQV keys aren't signing keys: the keys used in MQV are composed of a private exponent, x, and a public value, g^x. Figure 11-6 shows the operation of the MQV protocol.

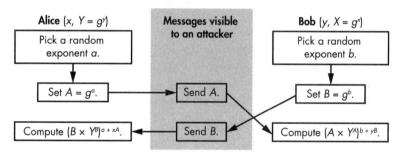

Figure 11-6: The MQV protocol

The x and y in Figure 11-6 are Alice and Bob's respective long-term private keys, and X and Y are their public keys. Bob and Alice start out with their own private keys and each other's public keys, which are g to the power of a private key. Each chooses a random exponent, and then Alice calculates A and sends it to Bob. Bob then calculates B and sends it to Alice. Once Alice gets Bob's ephemeral public key B, she combines it with her long-term private key x, her ephemeral private key a, and Bob's long-term public key Y by calculating the result of $(B \times Y^B)^{a + xA}$, as defined in Figure 11-6. Developing this expression, we obtain the following:

$$\left(B \times Y^B\right)^{a + xA} = \left(g^b \times \left(g^y\right)^B\right)^{a + xA} = \left(g^{b + yB}\right)^{a + xA} = g^{(b + yB)(a + xA)}$$

Meanwhile, Bob calculates the result of $(A \times X^A)^{b+yB}$, and we can verify that it's equal to the value calculated by Alice:

$$\left(A \times X^A\right)^{b+yB} = \left(g^a \times \left(g^x\right)^A\right)^{b+yB} = \left(g^{a+xA}\right)^{b+yB} = g^{(a+xA)(b+yB)} = g^{(b+yB)(a+xA)}$$

As you can see, we get the same value for both Alice and Bob, namely $g^{(b+yB)(a+xA)}$. This tells us that Alice and Bob share the same secret.

Unlike authenticated DH, MQV can't be broken by a mere leak of the ephemeral secrets. Knowledge of a or b won't let an attacker determine the final shared secret because they would need the long-term private keys to compute it.

What happens in the strongest attack model, the breach model, where a long-term key is compromised? If Eve compromises Alice's long-term private key x, the previously established shared secrets are safe because their computation also involved Alice's ephemeral private keys.

However, MQV doesn't provide *perfect* forward secrecy because of the following attack. Say, for example, that Eve intercepts Alice's A message and replaces it with her $A = g^a$ for some a that Eve has chosen. In the meantime, Bob sends B to Alice (and Eve records B's value) and computes the shared key. If Eve later compromises Alice's long-term private key x, she can determine the key that Bob had computed during this session. This breaks forward secrecy, since Eve has now recovered the shared secret of a previous execution of the protocol. In practice, however, the risk can be eliminated by a key-confirmation step that would have Alice and Bob realize that they don't share the same key, and they would therefore abort the protocol before deriving any session keys.

Despite its elegance and security, MQV is rarely used in practice. One reason is because it used to be encumbered by patents, which hampered its widespread adoption. Another reason is that it's harder than it looks to get MQV right in practice. In fact, when weighed against its increased complexity, MQV's security benefits are often perceived as low in comparison to the simpler authenticated DH.

How Things Can Go Wrong

Diffie–Hellman protocols can fail spectacularly in a variety of ways. I highlight some of the most common ones in the next sections.

Not Hashing the Shared Secret

I've alluded to the fact that the shared secret that concludes a DH session exchange (g^{ab} in our examples) is taken as input to derive session keys but is not a key itself. And it shouldn't be. A symmetric key should look random, and each bit should either be 0 or 1 with the same probability. But g^{ab} is not a random string; it's a random element within some mathematical group whose bits may be biased toward 0 or 1. And a random group element is different from a random string of bits.

Imagine, for example, that we're working within the multiplicative group $\mathbf{Z}_{13}^{*} = \{1, 2, 3, \ldots, 12\}$ using $g = 2$ as a generator of the group, meaning that g^i spans all values of $\mathbf{Z}_{13}^{*}$ for i in 1, 2, . . . 12: $g^1 = 2$, $g^2 = 4$, $g^3 = 8$, $g^4 = 13$, and so on. If g's exponent is random, you'll get a random element of $\mathbf{Z}_{13}^{*}$, but the encoding of a $\mathbf{Z}_{13}^{*}$ element as a 4-bit string won't be uniformly random: not all bits will have the same probability of being a 0 or a 1. In $\mathbf{Z}_{13}^{*}$, seven values have 0 as their most significant bit (the numbers from 1 to 7 in the group), but only five have 1 as their most significant bit (from 8 to 12). That is, this bit is 0 with probability $7 / 12 \approx 0.58$, whereas, ideally, a random bit should be 0 with probability 0.5. Moreover, the 4-bit sequences 1101, 1110, and 1111 will never appear.

To avoid such biases in the session keys derived from a DH shared secret, you should use a cryptographic hash function such as BLAKE2 or SHA-3—or, better yet, a key derivation function (KDF). An example of KDF construction is HKDF, or HMAC-based KDF (as specified in RFC 5869), but today BLAKE2 and SHA-3 feature dedicated modes to behave as KDFs.

Legacy Diffie–Hellman in TLS

The TLS protocol is the security behind HTTPS secure websites as well as the secure mail transfer protocol (SMTP). TLS takes several parameters, including the type of Diffie–Hellman protocol it will use, though most TLS implementations still support anonymous DH for legacy reasons, despite its insecurity.

Unsafe Group Parameters

In January 2016, the maintainers of the OpenSSL toolkit fixed a high-severity vulnerability (CVE-2016-0701) that allowed an attacker to exploit unsafe Diffie–Hellman parameters. The root cause of the vulnerability was that OpenSSL allowed users to work with unsafe DH group parameters (namely, an unsafe prime p) instead of throwing an error and aborting the protocol altogether before performing any arithmetic operation.

Essentially, OpenSSL accepted a prime number p whose multiplicative group $\mathbf{Z}_p^{*}$ (where all DH operations happen) contained small subgroups. As you learned at the beginning of this chapter, the existence of small subgroups within a larger group in a cryptographic protocol is bad because it confines shared secrets to a much smaller set of possible values than if it were to use the whole group $\mathbf{Z}_p^{*}$. Worse still, an attacker can craft a DH exponent x that, when combined with the victim's public key g^y, will reveal information on the private key y and eventually its entirety.

Although the actual vulnerability is from 2016, the principle the attack used dates back to the 1997 paper "A Key Recovery Attack on Discrete Log-based Schemes Using a Prime Order Subgroup" by Lim and Lee. The fix for the vulnerability is simple: when accepting a prime p as group modulus, the protocol must check that p is a safe prime by verifying that $(p-1) / 2$ is prime as well in order to ensure that the group $\mathbf{Z}_p^{*}$ won't have small subgroups, and that an attack on this vulnerability will fail.

Further Reading

Here's a rundown of some things that I didn't cover in this chapter but are useful to learn about.

You can dig deeper into the DH key agreement protocols by reading a number of standards and official publications, including ANSI X9.42, RFC 2631 and RFC 5114, IEEE 1363, and NIST SP 800-56A. These serve as references to ensure interoperability, and to provide recommendations for group parameters.

To learn more about advanced DH protocols (such as MQV and its cousins HMQV and OAKE, among others) and their security notions (such as unknown-key share attacks and group representation attacks), read the 2005 article "HMQV: A High-Performance Secure Diffie–Hellman Protocol" by Hugo Krawczyk (*https://eprint.iacr.org/2005/176/*) and the 2011 article "A New Family of Implicitly Authenticated Diffie–Hellman Protocols" by by Andrew C. Yao and Yunlei Zhao (*https://eprint.iacr.org/2011/035/*). You'll notice in these articles that Diffie–Hellman operations are expressed differently than in this chapter. For example, instead of g^x, you'll find the shared secret represented as xP. Generally, you'll find multiplication replaced with addition and exponentiation replaced with multiplication. The reason is that those protocols are usually not defined over groups of integers, but over *elliptic curves*, as discussed in Chapter 12.

12

ELLIPTIC CURVES

The introduction of *elliptic curve cryptography (ECC)* in 1985 revolutionized the way we do public-key cryptography. ECC is more powerful and efficient than alternatives like RSA and classical Diffie–Hellman (ECC with a 256-bit key is stronger than RSA with a 4096-bit key), but it's also more complex.

Like RSA, ECC multiplies large numbers, but unlike RSA it does so in order to combine points on a mathematical curve, called an *elliptic curve* (which has nothing to do with an ellipse, by the way). To complicate matters, there are many different types of elliptic curves—simple and sophisticated ones, efficient and inefficient ones, and secure and insecure ones.

Although first introduced in 1985, ECC wasn't adopted by standardization bodies until the early 2000s, and it wasn't seen in major toolkits until much later: OpenSSL added ECC in 2005, and the OpenSSH secure connectivity tool waited until 2011. But modern systems have few reasons not to use ECC, and you'll find it used in Bitcoin and many security components in Apple devices. Indeed, elliptic curves allow you to perform common public-key cryptography operations such as encryption, signature, and key agreement faster than their classical counterparts. Most cryptographic applications that rely on the discrete logarithm problem (DLP) will also work when based on its elliptic curve counterpart, ECDLP, with one notable exception: the Secure Remote Password (SRP) protocol.

This chapter focuses on applications of ECC and discusses why you would use ECC rather than RSA or classical Diffie–Hellman, as well as how to choose the right elliptic curve for your application.

What Is an Elliptic Curve?

An elliptic curve is a *curve* on a plane—a group of points with x and y coordinates. A curve's equation defines all the points that belong to that curve. For example, the curve $y = 3$ is a horizontal line with the vertical coordinate 3, curves of the form $y = ax + b$ with fixed numbers a and b are straight lines, $x^2 + y^2 = 1$ is a circle of radius 1 centered on the origin, and so on. Whatever the type of curve, the points on a curve are all (x, y) pairs that satisfy the curve's equation.

An elliptic curve as used in cryptography is typically a curve whose equation is of the form $y^2 = x^3 + ax + b$ (known as the *Weierstrass form*), where the constants a and b define the shape of the curve. For example, Figure 12-1 shows the elliptic curve that satisfies the equation $y^2 = x^3 - 4x$.

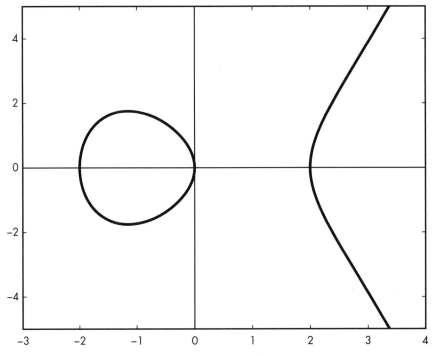

Figure 12-1: An elliptic curve with the equation $y^2 = x^3 - 4x$, shown over the real numbers

In this chapter, I focus on the simplest, most common type of elliptic curves—namely, those with an equation that looks like $y^2 = x^3 + ax + b$—but there are types of elliptic curves with equations in other forms. For example, Edwards curves *are elliptic curves whose equation is of the form $x^2 + y^2 = 1 + dx^2y^2$. Edwards curves are sometimes used in cryptography (for example, in the Ed25519 scheme).*

Figure 12-1 shows all the points that make up the curve for *x* between −3 and 4, be they points on the left side of the curve, which looks like a circle, or on the right side, which looks like a parabola. All these points have (x, y) coordinates that satisfy the curve's equation $y^2 = x^3 − 4x$. For example, when $x = 0$, then $y^2 = x^3 − 4x = 0^3 − 4 \times 0 = 0$; hence, $y = 0$ is a solution, and the point $(0, 0)$ belongs to the curve. Likewise, if $x = 2$, the solution to the equation is $y = 0$, meaning that the point $(2, 0)$ belongs to the curve.

It is crucial to distinguish points that belong to the curve from other points, because when using elliptic curves for cryptography, we'll be working with points from the curve, and points off the curve often present a security risk. However, note that the curve's equation doesn't always admit solutions, at least not in the natural number plane. For example, to find points with the horizontal coordinate $x = 1$, we solve $y^2 = x^3 − 4x$ for y^2 with $x^3 − 4x = 1^3 − 4 \times 1$, giving a result of −3. But $y^2 = −3$ doesn't have a solution because there is no number for which $y^2 = −3$. (There is a solution in the complex numbers, but elliptic curve cryptography will only deal with natural numbers—more precisely, integers modulo a prime.) Because there is no solution to the curve's equation for $x = 1$, the curve has no point at that position on the x-axis, as you can see in Figure 12-1.

What if we try to solve for $x = −1$? In this case, we get the equation $y^2 = −1 + 4 = 3$, which has two solutions ($y = \sqrt{3}$ and $y = −\sqrt{3}$), the square root of three and its negative value. Squaring a number always gives a positive number, so $y^2 = (−y)^2$ for any real number y, and as you can see, the curve in Figure 12-1 is symmetric with respect to the x-axis for all points that solve its equation (as are all elliptic curves of the form $y^2 = x^3 + ax + b$).

Elliptic Curves over Integers

Now here's a bit of a twist: the curves used in elliptic curve cryptography actually don't look like the curve shown in Figure 12-1. They look instead like Figure 12-2, which is a cloud of points rather than a curve. What's going on here?

Figures 12-1 and 12-2 are actually based on the same curve equation, $y^2 = x^3 − 4x$, but they show the curve's points with respect to different sets of numbers: Figure 12-1 shows the curve's points over the set of *real numbers*, which includes negative numbers, decimals, and so on. For example, as a continuous curve, it shows the points at $x = 2.0$, $x = 2.1$, $x = 2.00002$, and so on. Figure 12-2, on the other hand, shows only *integers* that satisfy this equation, which excludes decimal numbers. Specifically, Figure 12-2 shows the curve $y^2 = x^3 − 4x$ with respect to the integers *modulo 191*: 0, 1, 2, 3, up to 190. This set of numbers is denoted $\mathbf{Z}_{191}$. (There's nothing special with 191 here, except that it's a prime number. I picked a small number to avoid having too many points on the graph.) The points shown on Figure 12-2 therefore all have x and y coordinates that are integers modulo 191 and that satisfy the equation $y^2 = x^3 - 4x$. For example, for $x = 2$, we have $y^2 = 0$, for which $y = 0$ is a valid solution. This tells us that the point $(2, 0)$ belongs to the curve.

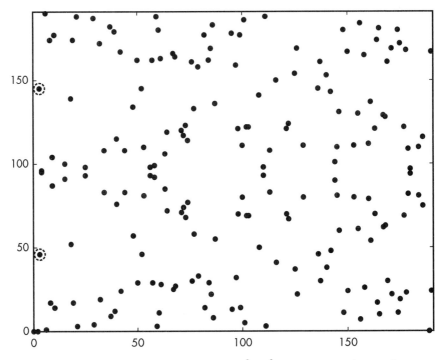

Figure 12-2: The elliptic curve with the equation $y^2 = x^3 - 4x$ over $\mathbf{Z}_{191}$, the set of integers modulo 191

What if $x = 3$? We get the equation $y^2 = 27 - 12 = 15$, which admits two solutions to $y^2 = 15$ (namely, 46 and 145), because 46^2 mod $191 = 15$ and 145^2 mod $191 = 15$ both equal 15 in $\mathbf{Z}_{191}$. Thus, the points $(3, 46)$ and $(3, 145)$ belong to the curve and appear as shown in Figure 12-2 (the two points highlighted at the left).

NOTE
Figure 12-2 considers points from the set denoted $\mathbf{Z}_{191} = \{0, 1, 2, \ldots, 190\}$, which includes zero. This differs from the groups denoted $\mathbf{Z}_p{}^*$ (with a star superscript) that we discussed in the context of RSA and Diffie–Hellman. The reason for this difference is that we'll both multiply and add numbers, and we therefore need to ensure that the set of numbers includes addition's identity element (namely 0, such that $x + 0 = x$ for every x in $\mathbf{Z}_{191}$). Also, every number x has an inverse with respect to addition, denoted $-x$, such that $x + (-x) = 0$. For example, the inverse of 100 in $\mathbf{Z}_{191}$ is 91, because $100 + 91$ mod $191 = 0$. Such a set of numbers, where addition and multiplication are possible and where each element x admits an inverse with respect to addition (denoted $-x$) as well as an inverse with respect to multiplication (denoted $1 / x$), is called a field. *When a field has a finite number of elements, as in $\mathbf{Z}_{191}$ and as with all fields used for elliptic curve cryptography, it is called a* finite field.

Adding and Multiplying Points

We've seen that the points on an elliptic curve are all coordinates (x, y) that satisfy the curve's equation, $y^2 = x^3 + ax + b$. In this section, we look at how to add elliptic curve points, a rule called the *addition law*.

Adding Two Points

Say that we want to add two points on the elliptic curve, P and Q, to give a new point, R, that is the sum of these two points. The simplest way to understand point addition is to determine the position of $R = P + Q$ on the curve relative to P and Q based on a geometric rule: draw the line that connects P and Q, find the other point of the curve that intersects with this line, and Q is the reflection of this point with respect to the x-axis. For example, in Figure 12-3, the line connecting P and Q intersects the curve at a third point between P and Q, and the point $P + Q$ is the point at the same x coordinate but the inverse y coordinate.

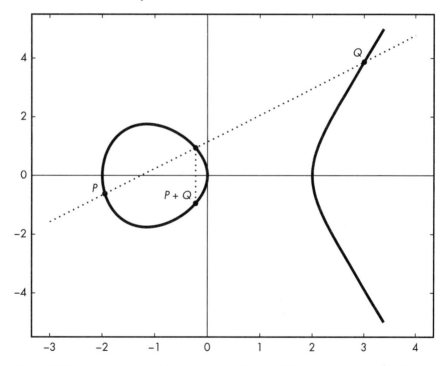

Figure 12-3: A general case of the geometric rule for adding points over an elliptic curve

This geometric rule is simple, but it won't directly give you the coordinates of the point R. We compute the coordinates (x_R, y_R) of R using the coordinates (x_P, y_P) of P and the coordinates (x_Q, y_Q) of Q using the formulas $x_R = m^2 - x_P - x_Q$ and $y_R = m(x_P - x_R) - y_P$, where the value $m = (y_Q - y_P) / (x_Q - x_P)$ is the slope of the line connecting P and Q.

Unfortunately, these formulas and the line-drawing trick shown in Figure 12-3 don't always work. If, for example, $P = Q$, you can't draw a line between two points (there's only one), and if $P = -P$, the line doesn't cross the curve again, so there is no point on the curve to mirror. We'll explore these in the next section.

Adding a Point and Its Negative

The negative of a point $P = (x_P, y_P)$ is the point $-P = (x_P, -y_P)$, which is the point mirrored around the x-axis. For any P, we say that $P + (-P) = O$, where O is called the *point at infinity*. And as you can see in Figure 12-4, the line between P and $-P$ runs to infinity and never intersects the curve. (The point at infinity is a virtual point that belongs to any elliptic curve; it is to elliptic curves what zero is to integers.)

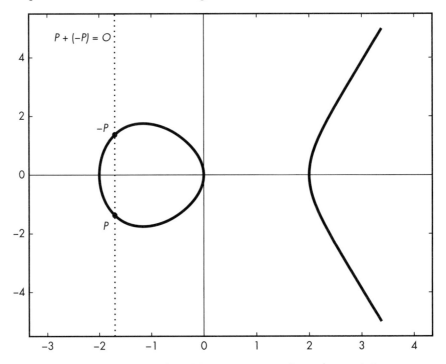

Figure 12-4: The geometric rule for adding points on an elliptic curve with the operation P + (–P) = O when the line between the points never intersects the curve

Doubling a Point

When $P = Q$ (that is, P and Q are at the same position), adding P and Q is equivalent to computing $P + P$, also denoted $2P$. This addition operation is therefore called a *doubling*.

However, to find the coordinates of the result $R = 2P$, we can't use the geometric rule from the previous section, because we can't draw a line between P and itself. Instead, we draw the line *tangent* to the curve at P, and $2P$ is the negation of the point where this line intersects the curve, as shown on Figure 12-5.

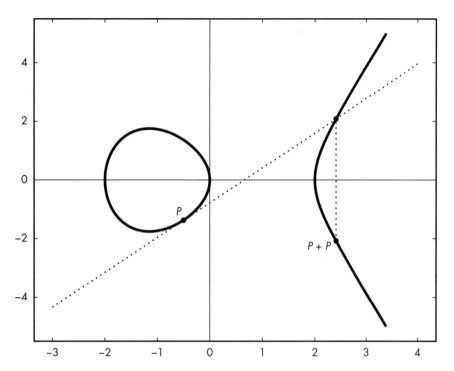

Figure 12-5: The geometric rule for adding points over an elliptic curve using the doubling operation P + P

The formula for determining the coordinates (x_R, y_R) of $R = P + P$ is slightly different from the formula we would use for a distinct P and Q. Again, the basic formula is $x_R = m^2 - x_P - x_Q$ and $y_R = m(x_P - x_R) - y_P$, but the value of m is different; it becomes $(3x_P^2 + a) / 2y_P$, where a is the curve's parameter, as in $y^2 = x^3 + ax + b$.

Multiplication

In order to multiply points on elliptic curves by a given number k, where k is an integer, we determine the point kP by adding P to itself $k - 1$ times. In other words, $2P = P + P$, $3P = P + P + P$, and so on. To obtain the x and y coordinates of kP, repeatedly add P to itself and apply the preceding addition law.

To compute kP efficiently, however, the naive technique of adding P by applying the addition law $k - 1$ times is far from optimal. For example, if k is large (of the order of, say, 2^{256}) as it occurs in elliptic curve–based crypto schemes, then computing $k - 1$ additions is downright infeasible.

But there's a trick: you can gain an exponential speed-up by adapting the technique discussed in "Fast Exponentiation Algorithm: Square-and-Multiply" on page 192 to compute $x^e \bmod n$. For example, to compute $8P$ in three additions instead of seven using the naive method, you would first compute $P_2 = P + P$, then $P_4 = P_2 + P_2$, and finally $P_4 + P_4 = 8P$.

Elliptic Curve Groups

Because points can be added together, the set of points on an elliptic curve forms a group. According to the definition of a group (see "What Is a Group?" on page 174), if the points P and Q belong to a given curve, then $P + Q$ also belongs to the curve.

Furthermore, because addition is *associative*, we have $(P + Q) + R = P + (Q + R)$ for any points P, Q, and R. In a group of elliptic curve points, the identity element is called the point at infinity, and denoted O, such that $P + O = P$ for any P. Every point $P = (x_P, y_P)$ has an inverse, $-P = (x_P, -y_P)$, such that $P + (-P) = O$.

In practice, most elliptic curve–based cryptosystems work with x and y coordinates that are numbers modulo a prime number, p (in other words, numbers in the finite field $\mathbf{Z}_p$). Just as the security of RSA depends on the size of the numbers used, the security of an elliptic curve–based cryptosystem depends on the number of points on the curve. But how do we know the number of points on an elliptic curve, or its *cardinality*? Well, it depends on the curve and the value of p.

One rule of thumb is that there are approximately p points on the curve, but you can compute the exact number of points with Schoof's algorithm, which counts points on elliptic curves over finite fields. You'll find this algorithm built in to SageMath. For example, Listing 12-1 shows how to use this algorithm to count the number of points on the curve $y^2 = x^3 - 4x$ over $\mathbf{Z}_{191}$ shown in Figure 12-1.

```
sage: Z = Zmod(191)
sage: E = EllipticCurve(Z, (-4,0))
sage: E.cardinality()
192
```

Listing 12-1: Computing the cardinality, or number of points on a curve

In Listing 12-1, we've first defined the variable Z as the set over integers modulo 191; then we defined the variable E as the elliptic curve over Z with the coefficients −4 and 0. Finally, we computed the number of points on the curve, also known as its *cardinality, group order,* or just *order.* Note that this count includes the point at infinity O.

The ECDLP Problem

Chapter 9 introduced the DLP: that of finding the number y given some base number g, where $x = g^y \bmod p$ for some large prime number p. Cryptography with elliptic curves has a similar problem: the problem of finding the number k given a base point P where the point $Q = kP$. This is called the *elliptic curve discrete logarithm problem,* or *ECDLP.* (Instead of numbers, the elliptic curve's problems operate on points, and multiplication is used instead of exponentiation.)

All elliptic curve cryptography is built on the ECDLP problem, which, like DLP, is believed to be hard and has withstood cryptanalysis since its introduction into cryptography in 1985. One important difference between ECDLP and the classical DLP is that ECDLP allows you to work with smaller numbers and still enjoy a similar level of security.

Generally, when p is n bits, you'll get a security level of about $n/2$ bits. For example, an elliptic curve taken over numbers modulo p, with a 256-bit p, will give a security level of about 128 bits. For the sake of comparison, to achieve a similar security level with DLP or RSA, you would need to use numbers of several thousands of bits. The smaller numbers used for ECC arithmetic are one reason why it's often faster than RSA or classical Diffie–Hellman.

One way of solving ECDLP is to find a collision between two outputs, $c_1P + d_1Q$ and $c_2P + d_2Q$. The points P and Q in these equations are such that $Q = kP$ for some unknown k, and c_1, d_1, c_2, and d_2 are the numbers you will need in order to find k.

As with the hash function discussed in Chapter 6, a collision occurs when two different inputs produce the same output. Therefore, in order to solve ECDLP, we need to find points where the following is true:

$$c_1P + d_1Q = c_2P + d_2Q$$

In order to find these points, we replace Q with the value kP, and we have the following:

$$c_1P + d_1kP = (c_1 + d_1k)P = c_2P + d_2kP = (c_2 + d_2k)P$$

This tells us that $(c_1 + d_1k)$ equals $(c_2 + d_2k)$ when taken modulo the number of points on the curve, which is not a secret.

From this, we can deduce the following:

$$d_2k - d_1k = c_1 - c_2$$
$$k(d_1 - d_2) = c_1 - c_2$$
$$k = (c_1 - c_2) / (d_1 - d_2)$$

And we've found k, the solution to ECDLP.

Of course, that's only the big picture—the details are more complex and interesting. In practice, elliptic curves extend over numbers of at least 256 bits, which makes attacking elliptic curve cryptography by finding a collision impractical because doing so takes up to 2^{128} operations (the cost of finding a collision over 256-bit numbers, as you learned in Chapter 6).

Diffie–Hellman Key Agreement over Elliptic Curves

Recall from Chapter 11 that in the classical Diffie–Hellman (DH) key agreement protocol, two parties establish a shared secret by exchanging non-secret values. Given some fixed number g, Alice picks a secret random number a, computes $A = g^a$, sends A to Bob, and Bob picks a secret random b and sends $B = g^b$ to Alice. Both then combine their secret key with the other's public key to produce the same $A^b = B^a = g^{ab}$.

The elliptic curve version of DH is identical to that of classical DH but with different notations. In the case of ECC, for some fixed point G, Alice picks a secret random number d_A, computes $P_A = d_A G$ (the point G multiplied by d_A), and sends P_A to Bob. Bob picks a secret random d_B, computes the point $P_B = d_B G$, and sends it to Alice. Then both compute the same shared secret, $d_A P_B = d_B P_A = d_A d_B G$. This method is called *elliptic curve Diffie–Hellman*, or *ECDH*.

ECDH is to the ECDLP problem what DH is to DLP: it's secure as long as ECDLP is hard. DH protocols that rely on DLP can therefore be adapted to work with elliptic curves and rely on ECDLP as a hardness assumption. For example, authenticated DH and Menezes–Qu–Vanstone (MQV) will also be secure when used with elliptic curves. (In fact, MQV was first defined as working over elliptic curves.)

Signing with Elliptic Curves

The standard algorithm used for signing with ECC is *ECDSA*, which stands for *elliptic curve digital signature algorithm*. This algorithm has replaced RSA signatures and classical DSA signatures in many applications. It is, for example, the only signature algorithm used in Bitcoin and is supported by many TLS and SSH implementations.

As with all signature schemes, ECDSA consists of a *signature generation* algorithm that the signer uses to create a signature using their private key and a *verification* algorithm that a verifier uses to check a signature's correctness given the signer's public key. The signer holds a number, d, as a private key, and verifiers hold the public key, $P = dG$. Both know in advance what elliptic curve to use, its order (n, the number of points in the curve), as well as the coordinates of a base point, G.

ECDSA Signature Generation

In order to sign a message, the signer first hashes the message with a cryptographic hash function such as SHA-256 or BLAKE2 to generate a hash value, h, that is interpreted as a number between 0 and $n - 1$. Next, the signer picks a random number, k, between 1 and $n - 1$ and computes kG, a point with the coordinates (x, y). The signer now sets $r = x \bmod n$ and computes $s = (h + rd) / k \bmod n$, and then uses these values as the signature (r, s).

The length of the signature will depend on the coordinate lengths being used. For example, when you're working with a curve where coordinates are 256-bit numbers, r and s would both be 256 bits long, yielding a 512-bit-long signature.

ECDSA Signature Verification

The ECDSA verification algorithm uses a signer's public key to verify the validity of a signature.

In order to verify an ECDSA signature (r, s) and a message's hash, h, the verifier first computes $w = 1 / s$, the inverse of s in the signature, which is equal to $k / (h + rd) \bmod n$, since s is defined as $s = (h + rd) / k$. Next, the verifier multiplies w with h to find u according to the following formula:

$$wh = hk / (h + rd) = u$$

The verifier then multiplies w with r to find v:

$$wr = rk(h + rd) = v$$

Given u and v, the verifier computes the point Q according to the following formula:

$$Q = uG + vP$$

Here, P is the signer's public key, which is equal to dG, and the verifier only accepts the signature if the x coordinate of Q is equal to the value r from the signature.

This process works because, as a last step, we compute the point Q by substituting the public key P with its actual value dG:

$$uG + vdG = (u + vd)G$$

When we replace u and v with their actual values, we obtain the following:

$$u + vd = hk(h + rd) + drk / (h + rd) = (hk + drk) / (h + rd) = k(h + dr) / (h + rd) = k$$

This tells us that $(u + vd)$ is equal to the value k, chosen during signature generation, and that $uG + vdG$ is equal to the point kG. In other words, the verification algorithm succeeds in computing point kG, the same point computed during signature generation. Validation is complete once a verifier confirms that kG's x coordinate is equal to the r received; otherwise, the signature is rejected as invalid.

ECDSA vs. RSA Signatures

Elliptic curve cryptography is often viewed as an alternative to RSA for public-key cryptography, but ECC and RSA don't have much in common. RSA is only used for encryption and signatures, whereas ECC is a family of algorithms that can be used to perform encryption, generate signatures, perform key agreement, and offer advanced cryptographic functionalities such as identity-based encryption (a kind of encryption that uses encryption keys derived from a personal identifier, such as an email address).

When comparing RSA and ECC's signature algorithms, recall that in RSA signatures, the signer uses their private key d to compute a signature as $y = x^d \bmod n$, where x is the data to be signed and y is the signature. Verification uses the public key e to confirm that $y^e \bmod n$ equals x—a process that's clearly simpler than that of ECDSA.

RSA's verification process is often faster than ECC's signature generation because it uses a small public key e. But ECC has two major advantages over RSA: shorter signatures and signing speed. Because ECC works with shorter numbers, it produces shorter signatures than RSA (hundreds of bits long, not thousands of bits), which is an obvious benefit if you have to store or transmit numerous signatures. Signing with ECDSA is also much faster than signing with RSA (though signature verification is about as fast) because ECDSA works with much smaller numbers than RSA does for a similar security level. For example, Listing 12-2 shows that ECDSA is about 150 times faster at signing and a little faster at verifying. Note that ECDSA signatures are also shorter than RSA signatures because they're 512 bits (two elements of 256 bits each) rather than 4096 bits.

```
$ openssl speed ecdsap256 rsa4096
                          sign      verify      sign/s    verify/s
rsa 4096 bits         0.007267s  0.000116s      137.6      8648.0
                          sign      verify      sign/s    verify/s
256 bit ecdsa (nistp256)  0.0000s    0.0001s    21074.6      9675.7
```

Listing 12-2: Comparing the speed of 4096-bit RSA signatures with 256-bit ECDSA signatures

It's fair to compare the performance of these differently sized signatures because they provide a similar security level. However, in practice, many systems use RSA signatures with 2048 bits, which is orders of magnitude less secure than 256-bit ECDSA. Thanks to its smaller modulus size, 2048-bit RSA is faster than 256-bit ECDSA at verifying, yet still slower at signing, as shown in Listing 12-3.

```
$ openssl speed rsa2048
                      sign      verify      sign/s    verify/s
rsa 2048 bits     0.000696s  0.000032s     1436.1     30967.1
```

Listing 12-3: The speed of 2048-bit RSA signatures

The upshot is that you should prefer ECDSA to RSA except when signature verification is critical *and* you don't care about signing speed, as in a sign-once, verify-many situation (for example, when a Windows executable application is signed once and then verified by all the systems executing it).

Encrypting with Elliptic Curves

Although elliptic curves are more commonly used for signing, you can still encrypt with them. But you'll rarely see people do so in practice due to restrictions in the size of the plaintext that can be encrypted: you can fit only about 100 bits of plaintext, as compared to almost 4000 in RSA with the same security level.

One simple way to encrypt with elliptic curves is to use the *integrated encryption scheme (IES)*, a hybrid asymmetric–symmetric key encryption algorithm based on the Diffie–Hellman key exchange. Essentially, IES encrypts a message by generating a Diffie–Hellman key pair, combining the private key with the recipient's own public key, deriving a symmetric key from the shared secret obtained, and then using an authenticated cipher to encrypt the message.

When used with elliptic curves, IES relies on ECDLP's hardness and is called *elliptic-curve integrated encryption scheme (ECIES)*. Given a recipient's public key, P, ECIES encrypts a message, M, as follows:

1. Pick a random number, d, and compute the point $Q = dG$, where the base point G is a fixed parameter. Here, (d, Q) acts as an ephemeral key pair, used only for encrypting M.

2. Compute an ECDH shared secret by computing $S = dP$.

3. Use a key derivation scheme (KDF) to derive a symmetric key, K, from S.

4. Encrypt M using K and a symmetric authenticated cipher, obtaining a ciphertext, C, and an authentication tag, T.

The ECIES ciphertext then consists of the ephemeral public key Q followed by C and T. Decryption is straightforward: the recipient computes S by multiplying R with their private exponent to obtain S, and then derives the key K and decrypts C and verifies T.

Choosing a Curve

Criteria used to assess the safety of an elliptic curve include the order of the group used (that is, its number of points), its addition formulas, and its origins.

There are several types of elliptic curves, but not all are equally good for cryptographic purposes. When making your selection, be sure to choose coefficients a and b in the curve's equation $y^2 = x^3 + ax + b$ carefully; otherwise, you may end up with an insecure curve. In practice, you'll use some de facto standard curve for encryption, but knowing what makes a safe curve will help you choose among the several available ones and better understand any associated risks. Here are some points to keep in mind:

- The order of the group should not be a product of small numbers; otherwise solving ECDLP becomes much easier.

- In "Adding and Multiplying Points" on page 221, you learned that adding points $P + Q$ required a specific addition formula when $Q = P$. Unfortunately, treating this case differently from the general one may leak critical information if an attacker is able to distinguish doublings from additions between distinct points. Some curves are secure *because* they use a single formula for all point addition. (When a curve does not require a specific formula for doublings, we say that it admits a *unified* addition law.)

- If the creators of a curve don't explain the origin of a and b, they may be suspected of foul play because you can't know whether they may have chosen weaker values that enable some yet-unknown attack on the cryptosystem.

Let's review some of the most commonly used curves, especially ones used for signatures or Diffie–Hellman key agreement.

NOTE *You'll find more criteria and more details about curves on the dedicated website* https://safecurves.cr.yp.to/.

NIST Curves

In 2000, the NIST curves were standardized by the US NIST in the FIPS 186 document under "Recommended Elliptic Curves for Federal Government Use." Five NIST curves work modulo a prime number (as discussed in "Elliptic Curves over Integers" on page 219), called *prime curves*. Ten other NIST curves work with binary polynomials, which are mathematical objects that make implementation in hardware more efficient. (We won't cover binary polynomials in further detail because they're seldom used with elliptic curves.)

The most common NIST curves are the prime curves. Of these, one of the most common is P-256, a curve that works over numbers modulo the 256-bit number $p = 2^{256} - 2^{224} + 2^{192} + 2^{96} - 1$. The equation for P-256 is $y^2 = x^3 - 3x + b$, where b is a 256-bit number. NIST also provides prime curves of 192 bits, 224 bits, 384 bits, and 521 bits.

NIST curves are sometimes criticized because only the NSA, creator of the curves, knows the origin of the b coefficient in their equations. The only explanation we've been given is that b results from hashing a random-looking constant with SHA-1. For example, P-256's b parameter comes from the following constant: c49d3608 86e70493 6a6678e1 139d26b7 819f7e90.

No one knows why the NSA picked this particular constant, but most experts don't believe the curve's origin hides any weakness.

Curve25519

Daniel J. Bernstein brought Curve25519 (pronounced *curve-twenty-five-five-nineteen*) to the world in 2006. Motivated by performance, he designed Curve25519 to be faster and use shorter keys than the standard curves. But Curve25519 also brings security benefits, because unlike the NIST curves it has no suspicious constants and can use the same unified formula for adding distinct points or for doubling a point.

The form of Curve25519's equation, $y^2 = x^3 + 486662x^2 + x$, is slightly different from that of the other equations you've seen in this chapter, but it still belongs to the elliptic curve family. The unusual form of this equation allows for specific implementation techniques that make Curve25519 fast in software.

Curve25519 works with numbers modulo the prime number $2^{255} - 19$, a 256-bit prime number that is as close as possible to 2^{255}. The b coefficient 486662 is the smallest integer that satisfies the security criteria set by Bernstein. Taken together, these features make Curve25519 more trustworthy than NIST curves and their fishy coefficients.

Curve25519 is used everywhere: in Google Chrome, Apple systems, OpenSSH, and many other systems. However, because Curve25519 isn't a NIST standard, some applications stick to NIST curves.

NOTE *To learn all the details and rationale behind Curve25519, view the 2016 presentation "The first 10 years of Curve25519" by Daniel J. Bernstein, available at* http://cr.yp.to/talks.html#2016.03.09/.

Other Curves

As I write this, most cryptographic applications use NIST curves or Curve25519, but there are other legacy standards in use, and newer curves are being promoted and pushed within standardization committees. Some of the old national standards include France's ANSSI curves and Germany's Brainpool curves: two families that don't support complete addition formulas and that use constants of unknown origins.

Some newer curves are more efficient than the older ones and are clear of any suspicion; they offer different security levels and various efficiency optimizations. Examples include Curve41417, a variant of Curve25519, which works with larger numbers and offers a higher level of security (approximately 200 bits); Ed448-Goldilocks, a 448-bit curve first proposed in 2014 and considered to be an internet standard; as well as six curves proposed by Aranha et al. in "A note on high-security general-purpose elliptic curves" (see *http://eprint.iacr.org/2013/647/*), though these curves are rarely used. The details specific to all these curves are beyond the scope of this book.

How Things Can Go Wrong

Elliptic curves have their downsides due to their complexity and large attack surface. Their use of more parameters than classical Diffie–Hellman brings with it a greater attack surface with more opportunities for mistakes and abuse—and possible software bugs that might affect their implementation. Elliptic curve software may also be vulnerable to side-channel attacks due to the large numbers used in their arithmetic. If the speed of calculations depends on inputs, attackers may be able to obtain information about the formulas being used to encrypt.

In the following sections, I discuss two examples of vulnerabilities that can occur with elliptic curves, even when the implementation is safe. These are protocol vulnerabilities rather than implementation vulnerabilities.

ECDSA with Bad Randomness

ECDSA signing is randomized, as it involves a secret random number k when setting $s = (h + rd) / k \bmod n$. However, if the same k is reused to sign a second message, an attacker could combine the resulting two values, $s_1 = (h_1 + rd) / k$ and $s_2 = (h_2 + rd) / k$, to get $s_1 - s_2 = (h_1 - h_2) / k$ and then $k = (h_1 - h_2) / (s_1 - s_2)$. When k is known, the private key d is easily recovered by computing the following:

$$\left(k s_1 - h_1\right) / r = \left(\left(h_1 + rd\right) - h_1\right) / r = rd / r = d$$

Unlike RSA signatures, which won't allow the key to be recovered if a weak pseudorandom number generator (PRNG) is used, the use of non-random numbers can lead to ECDSA's k being recoverable, as happened with the attack on the PlayStation 3 game console in 2010, presented by the fail0verflow team at the 27th Chaos Communication Congress in Berlin, Germany.

Breaking ECDH Using Another Curve

ECDH can be elegantly broken if you fail to validate input points. The primary reason is that the formulas that give the coordinates for the sum of points $P + Q$ never involve the b coefficient of the curve; instead, they rely only on the coordinates of P and Q and the a coefficient (when doubling a point). The unfortunate consequence of this is that when adding two points, you can never be sure that you're working on the right curve because you may actually be adding points on a different curve with a different b coefficient. That means you can break ECDH as described in the following scenario, called the *invalid curve attack*.

Say that Alice and Bob are running ECDH and have agreed on a curve and a base point, G. Bob sends his public key $d_B G$ to Alice. Alice, instead of sending a public key $d_A G$ on the agreed upon curve, sends a point on a different curve, either intentionally or accidentally. Unfortunately, this new curve is weak and allows Alice to choose a point P for which solving ECDLP is easy. She chooses a point of low order, for which there is a relatively small k such that $kP = O$.

Now Bob, believing that he has a legitimate public key, computes what he thinks is the shared secret $d_B P$, hashes it, and uses the resulting key to encrypt data sent to Alice. The problem is that when Bob computes $d_B P$, he is unknowingly computing on the weaker curve. As a result, because P was chosen to belong to a small subgroup within the larger group of points, the result $d_B P$ will also belong to that small subgroup, allowing an attacker to determine the shared secret $d_B P$ efficiently if they know the order of P.

One way to prevent this is to make sure that points P and Q belong to the right curve by ensuring that their coordinates satisfy the curve's equation. Doing so would prevent this attack by making sure that you're only able to work on the secure curve.

Such an invalid curve attack was found in 2015 on certain implementations of the TLS protocol, which uses ECDH to negotiate session keys. (For details, see the paper "Practical Invalid Curve Attacks on TLS-ECDH" by Jager, Schwenk, and Somorovsky.)

Further Reading

Elliptic curve cryptography is a fascinating and complex topic that involves lots of mathematics. I've not discussed important notions such as a point's order, a curve's cofactor, projective coordinates, torsion points, and methods for solving the ECDLP problem. If you are mathematically inclined, you'll find information on these and other related topics in the *Handbook of Elliptic and Hyperelliptic Curve Cryptography* by Cohen and Frey (Chapman and Hall/CRC, 2005). The 2013 survey "Elliptic Curve Cryptography in Practice" by Bos, Halderman, Heninger, Moore, Naehrig, and Wustrow also gives a good illustrated introduction with practical examples (*https://eprint.iacr.org/2013/734/*).

13

TLS

The *Transport Layer Security (TLS) protocol*, also known as *Secure Socket Layer (SSL)*, which is the name of its predecessor, is the workhorse of internet security. TLS protects connections between servers and clients, whether that connection is between a website and its visitors, email servers, a mobile application and its servers, or video game servers and players. Without TLS, there would be no secure online commerce, secure online banking, or for that matter secure online anything.

TLS is application agnostic; it doesn't care about the type of content encrypted. This means that you can use it for web-based applications that rely on the HTTP protocol, as well as for any system where a client computer or device needs to initiate a connection with a remote server. For example, TLS is widely used for machine-to-machine communications in so-called internet of things (IoT) applications.

This chapter provides you with an abbreviated view of TLS. As you'll see, TLS has become increasingly complex over the years. Unfortunately, complexity and bloat brought multiple vulnerabilities, and bugs found in its cluttered implementations have made headlines—think Heartbleed, BEAST, CRIME, and POODLE, all vulnerabilities that impacted millions of web servers.

In 2013, engineers tired of fixing new cryptographic vulnerabilities in TLS overhauled it and started working on TLS 1.3. As you'll learn in this chapter, TLS 1.3 ditched unnecessary features and insecure ones, and replaced old algorithms with state-of-the-art ciphers. The result is a simpler, faster, and more secure protocol.

But before we explore how TLS 1.3 works, let's review the problem that TLS aims to solve in the first place, and the reason for its very existence.

Target Applications and Requirements

TLS is best known for being the *S* in HTTPS websites, and the padlock in a browser's address bar indicating that a page is secure. The primary driver for creating TLS was to enable secure browsing in applications such as e-commerce or e-banking by encrypting website connections to protect credit card numbers, user credentials, and other sensitive information.

TLS also helps to protect internet-based communication in general by establishing a *secure channel* between a client and a server that ensures the data transferred is confidential, authenticated, and unmodified.

One of TLS's security goals is to prevent man-in-the-middle attacks, wherein an attacker intercepts encrypted traffic from the transmitting party, decrypts the traffic to capture the clear content, and re-encrypts it to send to the receiving party. TLS defeats man-in-the-middle attacks by authenticating servers (and optionally clients) using certificates and trusted certificate authorities, as we'll discuss in more detail in the section "Certificates and Certificate Authorities" on page 238.

To ensure wide adoption, TLS needed to satisfy four more requirements: it needed to be efficient, interoperable, extensible, and versatile.

For TLS, efficiency means minimizing the performance penalty compared with unencrypted connections. This is good for both the server (to reduce the cost of hardware for the service providers) and for clients (to avoid perceptible delays or the reduction of mobile devices' battery life). The protocol needed to be interoperable so that it would work on any hardware and any operating system. It was to be extensible so that it could support additional features or algorithms. And it had to be versatile—that is, not bound to a specific application (this parallels something like Transport Control Protocol, which doesn't care about the application protocol used on top of it).

The TLS Protocol Suite

To protect client–server communications, TLS is made up of multiple versions of several protocols that together form the TLS protocol *suite*. And although *TLS* stands for *Transport Layer Security*, it's actually not a transport protocol. TLS usually sits between the transport protocol TCP and an application layer protocol such as HTTP or SMTP, in order to secure data transmitted over a TCP connection.

TLS can also work over the *User Datagram Protocol (UDP)* transport protocol, which is used for "connectionless" transmissions such as voice or video traffic. However, unlike TCP, UDP doesn't guarantee delivery or correct packet ordering. The UDP version of TLS is therefore slightly different and is called *DTLS (Datagram Transport Layer Security)*. For more on TCP and UDP, see Charles Kozierok's *The TCP/IP Guide* (No Starch Press, 2005.)

The TLS and SSL Family of Protocols: A Brief History

TLS began life in 1995 when Netscape, developer of the Netscape browser, developed TLS's ancestor, the Secure Socket Layer (SSL) protocol. SSL was far from perfect, and both SSL 2.0 and SSL 3.0 had security flaws. The upshot is that you should never use SSL, you should always use TLS—what adds to the confusion is that TLS is often referred to as "SSL," even by security experts.

Moreover, not all versions of TLS are secure. TLS 1.0 (1999) is the least secure TLS version, though it's still more secure than SSL 3.0. TLS 1.1 (2006) is better but includes a number of algorithms known today to be weak. TLS 1.2 (2008) is better yet, but it's complex and only gets you high security if configured correctly (which is no simple matter). Also, its complexity increases the risk of bugs in implementations and the risk of incorrect configurations. For example, TLS 1.2 supports AES in CBC mode, which is often vulnerable to padding oracle attacks.

TLS 1.2 inherited dozens of features and design choices from earlier versions of TLS that make it suboptimal, both in terms of security and performance. To clean up this mess, cryptography engineers reinvented TLS—keeping only the good parts and adding security features. The result is TLS 1.3, an overhaul that has simplified a bloated design and made it more secure, more efficient, and simpler. Essentially, TLS 1.3 is mature TLS.

TLS in a Nutshell

TLS has two main protocols: one determines how to transmit data, and the other what data to transmit. The *record protocol* defines a packet format to encapsulate data from higher-level protocols and sends this data to another party. It's a simple protocol that people often forget is part of TLS.

The *handshake protocol*—or just *handshake*—is TLS's key agreement protocol. It's often mistaken for "the" TLS protocol but the record protocol and the handshake can't be separated.

The handshake is started by a client to initiate a secure connection with a server. The client sends an initial message called ClientHello with parameters that include the cipher it wants to use. The server checks this message and its parameters and then responds with a message called ServerHello. Once both the client and the server have processed each other's messages, they're ready to exchange encrypted data using session keys established through the handshake protocol, as you'll see in the section "The TLS Handshake Protocol" on page 241.

Certificates and Certificate Authorities

The most critical step in the TLS handshake, and the crux of TLS's security, is the *certificate validation step*, wherein a server uses a *certificate* to authenticate itself to a client.

A certificate is essentially a public key accompanied by a signature of that key and associated information (including the domain name). For example, when connecting to *https://www.google.com/*, your browser will receive a certificate from some network host and will then verify the certificate's signature, which reads something like "I am *google.com* and my public key is [*key*]." If the signature is verified, the certificate (and its public key) are said to be *trusted*, and the browser can proceed with establishing the connection. (See Chapters 10 and 12 for details about signatures.)

How does the browser know the public key needed to verify the signature? That's where the concept of *certificate authority* (*CA*) comes in. A CA is essentially a public key hard coded in your browser or operating system. The public key's private key (that is, its signing capability) belongs to a trusted organization that ensures the public keys in certificates that it issues belong to the website or entity that claims them. That is, a CA acts as a *trusted third party*. Without CAs, there would be no way to verify that the public key served by *google.com* belongs to Google and not to an eavesdropper performing a man-in-the-middle attack.

For example, the command shown in Listing 13-1 shows what happens when we use the OpenSSL command-line tool to initiate a TLS connection to *www.google.com* on port 443, the network port used for TLS-based HTTP connections (that is, HTTPS.):

```
$ openssl s_client -connect www.google.com:443
CONNECTED(00000003)
--snip--
---
Certificate chain
❶ 0 s:/C=US/ST=California/L=Mountain View/O=Google Inc/CN=www.google.com
   i:/C=US/O=Google Inc/CN=Google Internet Authority G2
❷ 1 s:/C=US/O=Google Inc/CN=Google Internet Authority G2
   i:/C=US/O=GeoTrust Inc./CN=GeoTrust Global CA
❸ 2 s:/C=US/O=GeoTrust Inc./CN=GeoTrust Global CA
   i:/C=US/O=Equifax/OU=Equifax Secure Certificate Authority
---
Server certificate
-----BEGIN CERTIFICATE-----
MIIEgDCCA2igAwIBAgIISCr6QCbz5rowDQYJKoZIhvcNAQELBQAwSTELMAkGA1UE
BhMCVVMxEzARBgNVBAoTCkdvb2dsZSBJbmMxJTAjBgNVBAMTHEdvb2dsZSBJbnRl
--snip--
cb9reU8in8yCaH8dtzrFyUracpMureWnBeajOYXRPTdCFccejAh/xyH5SKDOOZ4v
3TP9GBtClAH1mSXoPhX73dp7jipZqgbY4kiEDNx+hformTUFBDHDOeO/s2nqwuWL
pBH6XQ==
```

```
-----END CERTIFICATE-----
subject=/C=US/ST=California/L=Mountain View/O=Google Inc/CN=www.google.com
issuer=/C=US/O=Google Inc/CN=Google Internet Authority G2
--snip--
```

Listing 13-1: Establishing a TLS connection with www.google.com *and receiving certificates to authenticate the connection*

I've trimmed the output to show only the interesting part, which is the certificate. Notice that before the first certificate (which starts with the BEGIN CERTIFICATE tag) is a description of the *certificate chain*, where the line starting with s: describes the subject name and the line starting with i: describes the issuer of the signature. Here, certificate 0 is the one received by *google.com* ❶, certificate 1 ❷ belongs to the entity that signed certificate 0, and certificate 2 ❸ belongs to the entity that signed certificate 1. The organization that issued certificate 2 (GeoTrust) granted permission to Google Internet Authority to issue a certificate (certificate 1) for the domain name *www.google.com*, thereby transferring trust to Google Internet Authority.

Obviously, these CA organizations must be trustworthy and only issue certificates to trustworthy entities, and they must protect their private keys in order to prevent an attacker from issuing certificates on their behalf (for example, in order to impersonate a legitimate *google.com* server).

To see what's in a certificate, we enter the command shown in Listing 13-2 into a Linux terminal and then paste the first certificate shown in Listing 13-1.

```
$ openssl x509 -text -noout
-----BEGIN CERTIFICATE-----
--snip--
-----END CERTIFICATE-----
Certificate:
    Data:
        Version: 3 (0x2)
        Serial Number: 5200243873191028410 (0x482afa4026f3e6ba)
    Signature Algorithm: sha256WithRSAEncryption
        Issuer: C=US, O=Google Inc, CN=Google Internet Authority G2
        Validity
            Not Before: Dec 15 14:07:56 2016 GMT
            Not After : Mar  9 13:35:00 2017 GMT
        Subject: C=US, ST=California, L=Mountain View, O=Google Inc,
CN=www.google.com
        Subject Public Key Info:
            Public Key Algorithm: rsaEncryption
                Public-Key: (2048 bit)
                Modulus:
                    00:bc:bc:b2:f3:1a:16:3b:c6:f6:9d:28:e1:ef:8e:
                    92:9b:13:b2:ae:7b:50:8f:f0:b4:e0:36:8d:09:00:
--snip--

                    8f:e6:96:fe:41:41:85:9d:a9:10:9a:09:6e:fc:bd:
                    43:fa:4d:c6:a3:55:9a:9e:07:8b:f9:b1:1e:ce:d1:
                    22:49
                Exponent: 65537 (0x10001)
--snip--
    Signature Algorithm: sha256WithRSAEncryption
```

```
94:cd:66:55:83:f1:16:7d:46:d8:66:21:06:ec:c6:9d:7c:1c:
2b:c1:f6:4f:b7:3e:cd:01:ad:69:bd:a1:81:6a:7c:96:f5:9c:
--snip--
85:fa:2b:99:35:05:04:31:c3:d1:e3:bf:b3:69:ea:c2:e5:8b:
a4:11:fa:5d
```

Listing 13-2: Decoding a certificate received from www.google.com

What you see in Listing 13-2 is the command `openssl x509` decoding a certificate, originally provided as a block of base64-encoded data. Because OpenSSL knows how this block of data is structured, it can tell us what's inside the certificate, including a serial number and version information, identifying information, validity dates (the Not Before and Not After lines), a public key (here as an RSA modulus and its public exponent), and a signature of the preceding information.

Although security experts and cryptographers often claim the whole certificate system is broken by design, it's one of the best solutions we have, along with the trust-on-first-use (TOFU) policy adopted by SSH, for example.

The Record Protocol

All data exchanged through TLS 1.3 communications is transmitted as sequences of *TLS records*, the data packets used by TLS. The TLS record protocol (the *record layer*) is essentially a transport protocol, agnostic of the transported data's meaning; this is what makes TLS suitable for any application.

The TLS record protocol is first used to carry the data exchanged during the handshake. Once the handshake is complete and both parties share a secret key, application data is fragmented into chunks that are transmitted as part of the TLS records.

Structure of a TLS Record

A TLS record is a chunk of data of at most 16 kilobytes, structured as follows:

- The first byte represents the type of data transmitted and is set to the value 22 for handshake data, 23 for encrypted data, and 21 for alerts. In the TLS 1.3 specifications, this value is called ContentType.

- The second and third byte are set to 3 and 1, respectively. These bytes are fixed for historical reasons and are not unique to TLS version 1.3. In the specifications, this 2-byte value is called ProtocolVersion.

- The fourth and fifth bytes encode the length of the data to transmit as a 16-bit integer, which can be no larger than 2^{14} bytes (16KB).

- The rest of the bytes are the data to transmit (also called the *payload*), of a length equal to the value encoded by the record's fourth and fifth bytes.

NOTE *A TLS record has a relatively simple structure. As we've seen, a TLS record's header includes only three fields. For comparison, an IPv4 packet includes 14 fields before its payload and a TCP segment includes 13 fields.*

When the first byte of a TLS 1.3 record (ContentType) is set to 23, its payload is encrypted and authenticated using an authenticated cipher. The payload consists of a ciphertext followed by an authentication tag, which the receiving end will decrypt. But then how does the recipient know which cipher and key to decrypt with? That's the magic of TLS: if you receive an encrypted TLS record, you already know the cipher and key, because they are established when the TLS handshake protocol is executed.

Nonces

Unlike many other protocols such as IPsec's Encapsulating Security Payload (ESP), TLS records don't specify the nonce to be used by the authenticated cipher.

The nonces used to encrypt and decrypt TLS records are derived from 64-bit sequence numbers, maintained locally by each party, and incremented for each new record. When the client encrypts data, it derives a nonce by XORing the sequence number with a value called client_write_iv, itself derived from the shared secret. The server uses a similar method but with a different value, called server_write_iv.

For example, if you transmit three TLS records, you'll derive a nonce from 0 for the first record, from 1 for the second, and from 2 for the third; if you then receive three records, you'll also use nonces 0, 1, and 2, in this order. Reuse of the same sequence numbers values for encrypting transmitted data and decrypting receiving data isn't a weakness because they are XORed with different constants (client_write_iv and server_write_iv) and because you use different secret keys for each direction.

Zero Padding

TLS 1.3 records support a nice feature known as *zero padding* that mitigates traffic analysis attacks. *Traffic analysis* is a method that attackers use to extract information from traffic patterns using timing, volume of data transferred, and so on. For example, because ciphertexts are approximately the same size as plaintexts, even when strong encryption is used, attackers can determine the approximate size of your messages simply by looking at the length of their ciphertext.

Zero padding adds zeros to the plaintext in order to inflate the ciphertext's size, and thus to fool observers into thinking that an encrypted message is longer than it really is.

The TLS Handshake Protocol

The *handshake* is the key TLS agreement protocol—the process by which a client and server establish shared secret keys in order to initiate secure communications. During the course of a TLS handshake, the client and server play different roles. The client proposes some configurations (the TLS version and a suite of ciphers, in order of preference) and the server chooses the configuration to be used. The server should follow the client's preferences, but it may do otherwise. In order to ensure interoperability between implementations and to guarantee that any server implementing TLS 1.3 will be able to read TLS 1.3 data sent by any client implementing TLS 1.3 (even if it's using a different library or programming language), the TLS 1.3 specifications also describe the format in which data should be sent.

Figure 13-1 shows how data is exchanged in the handshake process, as described in the TLS 1.3 specifications. As you can see, in the TLS 1.3 handshake, the client sends a message to the server saying, "I want to establish a TLS connection with you. Here are the ciphers that I support to encrypt TLS records, and here is a Diffie–Hellman public key." The public key must be generated specifically for this TLS session, and the client keeps the associated private key. The message sent by the client also includes a 32-byte random value and optional information (additional parameters and such). This first message is called *ClientHello*, and it must follow a specific format when transmitted as a series of bytes, as defined in the TLS 1.3 specification.

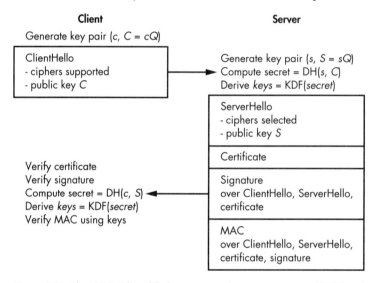

Figure 13-1: The TLS 1.3 handshake process when connecting to HTTPS websites

But note that the specifications also describe in what format data should be sent, in order to ensure interoperability between implementations by guaranteeing that any server implementing TLS 1.3 will be able to read TLS 1.3 data sent by any client implementing TLS 1.3, possibly using a different library or programming language.

The server receives the ClientHello message, verifies that it's correctly formatted, and responds with a message called *ServerHello*. The ServerHello message is loaded with information: it contains the cipher to be used to encrypt TLS records, a Diffie–Hellman public key, a 32-byte random value (discussed in "Downgrade Protection" on page 244), a certificate, a signature of all the previous information in ClientHello and ServerHello messages (computed using the private key associated with the certificate's public key), a MAC of that same information plus the signature. The MAC is computed using a symmetric key derived from the Diffie–Hellman shared secret, which the server computes from its Diffie–Hellman private key and the client's public key.

When the client receives the ServerHello message, it verifies the certificate's validity, verifies the signature, computes the shared Diffie–Hellman secret and derives symmetric keys from it, and verifies the MAC sent by the server. Once everything has been verified, the client is ready to send encrypted messages to the server.

Note, however, that TLS 1.3 supports many options and extensions, so it may behave differently than what has been described here (and shown in Figure 13-1). You can, for example, configure the TLS 1.3 handshake to require a client certificate so that the server verifies the identity of the client. TLS 1.3 also supports a handshake with pre-shared keys.

NOTE   *TLS 1.3 supports many options and extensions, so it may behave differently than what has been described here (and shown in Figure 13-1). You can, for example, configure the TLS 1.3 handshake to require a client certificate so that the server verifies the identity of the client. TLS 1.3 also supports a handshake with pre-shared keys.*

Let's look at this in practice. Say you've deployed TLS 1.3 to provide secure access to the website *https://www.nostarch.com/*. When you point your browser (the client) to this site, your browser sends a ClientHello message to the site's server that includes the ciphers that it supports. The website responds with a ServerHello message and a certificate that includes a public key associated with the domain *www.nostarch.com*. The client verifies the certificate's validity using one of the certificate authorities embedded in the browser (the received certificate should be signed by a trusted certificate authority, whose certificate should be included in the browser's certificate store in order to be validated). Once all checks are passed, the browser requests the site's initial page from the *www.nostarch.com* server.

Upon a successful TLS 1.3 handshake, all communications between the client and the server are encrypted and authenticated. An eavesdropper can learn that a client at a given IP address is talking to a server at another given IP address, and can observe the encrypted content exchanged, but won't be able to learn the underlying plaintext or modify the encrypted messages (if they do, the receiving party will notice that the communication has been tampered with, because messages are not only encrypted but also authenticated). That's enough security for many applications.

TLS 1.3 Cryptographic Algorithms

We know that TLS 1.3 uses authenticated encryption algorithms, a key derivation function (a hash function that derives secret keys from a shared secret), as well as a Diffie–Hellman operation. But how exactly do these work, what algorithms are used, and how secure are they?

With regard to the choice of authenticated ciphers, TLS 1.3 supports only three algorithms: AES-GCM, AES-CCM (a slightly less efficient mode than GCM), and the ChaCha20 stream cipher combined with the Poly1305

MAC (as defined in RFC 7539). Because TLS 1.3 prevents you from using an unsafe key length such as 64 or 80 bits (which are both too short), the secret key can be either 128 bits (AES-GCM or AES-CCM) or 256 bits (AES-GCM or ChaCha20-Poly1305).

The key derivation operation (KDF) in Figure 13-1 is based on HKDF, a construction based on HMAC (discussed in Chapter 7) and defined in RFC 5869 that uses either the SHA-256 or the SHA-384 hash function.

Your options for performing the Diffie–Hellman operation (the core of the TLS 1.3 handshake) are limited to elliptic curve cryptography and a multiplicative group of integers modulo a prime number (as in traditional Diffie–Hellman). But you can't use just any elliptic curve or group: the supported curves include three NIST curves as well as Curve25519 (discussed in Chapter 12) and Curve448, both defined in RFC 7748. TLS 1.3 also supports DH over groups of integers, as opposed to elliptic curves. The groups supported are the five groups defined in RFC 7919: groups of 2048, 3072, 4096, 6144, and 8192 bits.

The 2048-bit group may be TLS 1.3's weakest link. Whereas the other options provide at least 128-bit security, 2048-bit Diffie–Hellman is believed to provide less than 100-bit security. Supporting a 2048-bit group can therefore be seen as inconsistent with other TLS 1.3 design choices.

TLS 1.3 Improvements over TLS 1.2

TLS 1.3 is very different from its predecessor. For one thing, it gets rid of weak algorithms like MD5, SHA-1, RC4, and AES in CBC mode. Also, whereas TLS 1.2 often protected records using a combination of a cipher and a MAC (such as HMAC-SHA-1) within a MAC-then-encrypt construction, TLS 1.3 only supports the more efficient and more secure authenticated ciphers. TLS 1.3 also ditches elliptic curve point encoding negotiation, and defines a single point format for each curve.

One of the main development goals of TLS 1.3 was to remove features in 1.2 that weakened the protocol and to reduce the protocol's overall complexity and thereby its attack surface. For example, TLS 1.3 ditches optional data compression, a feature that enabled the CRIME attack on TLS 1.2. This attack exploited the fact that the length of the compressed version of a message leaks information on the content of the message.

But TLS 1.3 also brings new features that make connections either more secure or more efficient. I'll discuss three of these features briefly: downgrade protection, the single round-trip handshake, and session resumption.

Downgrade Protection

TLS 1.3's *downgrade protection* feature is designed as a defense against *downgrade attacks*, wherein an attacker forces the client and server to use a weaker version of TLS than 1.3. To carry out a downgrade attack, an attacker forces the server to use a weaker version of TLS by intercepting and modifying the ClientHello message to tell the server that the client doesn't support TLS 1.3. Now the attacker can exploit vulnerabilities in earlier versions of TLS.

In an effort to defeat downgrade attacks, the TLS 1.3 server uses three types of patterns in the 32-byte random value sent within the ServerHello message to identify the type of connection requested. The pattern should match the client's request for a specific type of TLS connection. If the client receives the wrong pattern, it knows that something is up.

Specifically, if the client asks for a TLS 1.2 connection, the first eight of the 32 bytes are set to 44 4F 57 4E 47 52 44 01, and if it asks for a TLS 1.1 connection, they're set to 44 4F 57 4E 47 52 44 00. However, if the client requests a TLS 1.3 connection, these first eight bits should be random. For example, if a client sends a ClientHello asking for a TLS 1.3 connection, but an attacker on the network modifies it to ask for a TLS 1.1 connection, when the client receives the ServerHello with the wrong pattern, it will know that its ClientHello message was modified. (The attacker can't arbitrarily modify the server's 32-byte random value because this value is cryptographically signed.)

Single Round-Trip Handshake

In a typical TLS 1.2 handshake, the client sends some data to the server, waits for a response, and then sends more data and waits for the server's response before sending encrypted messages. The delay is that of two round-trip times (RTT). In contrast, TLS 1.3's handshake takes a single round-trip time, as shown in Figure 13-1. The time saved can be in the hundreds of milliseconds. That may sound small, but its actually significant when you consider that servers of popular services handle thousands of connections per second.

Session Resumption

TLS 1.3 is faster than 1.2, but it can be made even faster (on the order of hundreds of milliseconds) by completely eliminating the round trips that precede an encrypted session. The trick is to use *session resumption,* a method that leverages the pre-shared key exchanged between the client and server in a previous session to bootstrap a new session. Session resumption brings two major benefits: the client can start encrypting immediately, and there is no need to use certificates in these subsequent sessions.

Figure 13-2 shows how session resumption works. First, the client sends a ClientHello message that includes the identifier of the key already shared (denoted *PSK* for *pre-shared key*) with the server, along with a fresh DH public key. The client can also include encrypted data in this first message (such data is known as *0-RTT data*). When the server responds to a ClientHello message, it provides a MAC over the data exchange. The client verifies the MAC and knows that it's talking to the same server as it did previously, thus rendering certificate validation somewhat superfluous. The client and the server perform a Diffie–Hellman key agreement as in the normal handshake, and subsequent messages are encrypted using keys that depend on both the PSK and the newly computed Diffie–Hellman shared secret.

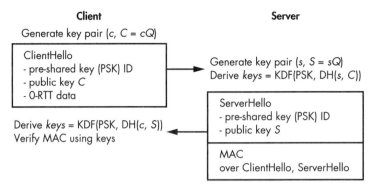

Client

Generate key pair $(c, C = cQ)$

ClientHello
- pre-shared key (PSK) ID
- public key C
- 0-RTT data

Derive *keys* = KDF(PSK, DH(c, S))
Verify MAC using keys

Server

Generate key pair $(s, S = sQ)$
Derive *keys* = KDF(PSK, DH(s, C))

ServerHello
- pre-shared key (PSK) ID
- public key S

MAC
over ClientHello, ServerHello

Figure 13-2: The TLS 1.3 session resumption handshake. The 0-RTT data is the session resumption data sent along with the ClientHello.

The Strengths of TLS Security

We'll evaluate the strengths of TLS 1.3 with respect to two main security notions discussed in Chapter 11: authentication and forward secrecy.

Authentication

During the TLS 1.3 handshake, the server authenticates to the client using the certificate mechanism. However, the client is not authenticated, and clients may authenticate with a server-based application (such as Gmail) by providing a username and password in a TLS record after performing the handshake. If the client has already established a session with the remote service, it may authenticate by sending a *secure cookie*, one that can only be sent through a TLS connection.

In certain cases, clients can authenticate to a server using a certificate-based mechanism similar to what the server uses in order to authenticate to the client: the client sends a *client certificate* to the server, which in turn verifies this certificate before authorizing the client. However, client certificates are rarely used because they complicate things for both clients and the server (that is, the certificate issuer): clients need to perform complex operations in order to integrate the certificate into their system and to protect its private key, while the issuer needs to make sure that only authorized clients received a certificate, among other requirements.

Forward Secrecy

Recall from "Key Agreement Protocols" on page 205 that a key agreement is said to provide forward secrecy if previous sessions aren't compromised when the present session is compromised. In the data leak model, only temporary secrets are compromised, whereas in the breach model, long-term secrets are exposed.

Thankfully, TLS 1.3 forward secrecy holds up in the face of both a data leak and a breach. In the case of the data leak model, the attacker recovers temporary secrets such as the session keys or Diffie–Hellman private keys of a specific session (the values *c*, *s*, *secret*, and *keys* in Figure 13-1 on page 242). However, they can only use these values to decrypt communications from the present session, but not from previous sessions, because different values of *c* and *s* were used (thus yielding different keys).

In the breach model, the attacker also recovers long-term secrets (namely, the private key that corresponds to the public key in the certificate). However, this is no more useful when decrypting previous sessions than temporary secrets, because this private key only serves to authenticate the server, and forward secrecy holds up again.

But what happens in practice? Say an attacker compromises a client's machine and gains access to all of its memory. Now the attacker may recover the client's TLS session keys and secrets for the current session from memory. But more importantly, if previous keys are still in memory, the attacker may be able to find them too and use them to decrypt previous sessions, thereby bypassing the theoretical forward secrecy. Therefore, in order for a TLS implementation to ensure forward secrecy, it must properly erase keys from memory once they are no longer used, typically by zeroing out the memory.

How Things Can Go Wrong

TLS 1.3 fits the bill as a general-purpose secure communications protocol, but it's not bulletproof. Like any security system, it can fail under certain circumstances (for example, when the assumptions made by its designers about real attacks turn out to be wrong). Unfortunately, even the latest version of TLS 1.3, configured with the most secure ciphers, can still be compromised. For example, TLS 1.3 security relies on the assumption that all three parties (the client, the server, and the certificate authority) will behave honestly, but what if one party is compromised or the TLS implementation itself is poorly implemented?

Compromised Certificate Authority

Root certificate authorities (root CAs) are organizations that are trusted by browsers to validate certificates served by remote hosts. For example, if your browser accepts the certificate provided by *www.google.com*, the assumption is that a trusted CA has verified the legitimacy of the certificate owner. The browser verifies the certificate by checking its CA-issued signature. Since only the CA knows the private key required to create this signature, we assume that others can't create valid certificates on behalf of the CA. Very often a website's certificate won't be signed by a root CA but by an intermediate CA, which is connected to the root CA through a certificate chain.

But let's say that a CA's private key is compromised. Now the attacker will be able to use the CA's private key to create a certificate for any URLs in, say, the *google.com* domain without Google's approval. What happens then? The attacker can use those certificates to pretend to host a legitimate server or subdomain like *mail.google.com* and intercept a user's credentials and communications. That's exactly what happened in 2011 when an attacker hacked into the network of the Dutch certificate authority DigiNotar and was able to create certificates that appeared to have been legitimate DigiNotar certificates. The attacker then used these fake certificates for several Google services.

Compromised Server

If a server is compromised and fully controlled by an attacker, all is lost: the attacker will be able to see all transmitted data before it's encrypted, and all received data once it has been decrypted. They will also be able to get their hands on the server's private key, which could allow them to impersonate the legitimate server using their own malicious server. Obviously, TLS won't save you in this case.

Fortunately, such security disasters are rarely seen in high-profile applications such as Gmail and iCloud, which are well protected and sometimes have their private keys stored in a separate security module. Attacks on web applications via vulnerabilities such as database query injections and cross-site scripting are more common, because they are mostly independent of TLS's security and are carried out by attackers over a legitimate TLS connection. Such attacks may compromise usernames, passwords, and so on.

Compromised Client

TLS security is also compromised when a client, such as a browser, is compromised by a remote attacker. Having compromised the client, the attacker will be able to capture session keys, read any decrypted data, and so on. They could even install a rogue CA certificate in the client's browser to have it silently accept otherwise invalid certificates, thereby letting attackers intercept TLS connections.

The big difference between the compromised CA or server scenarios and the compromised client scenario is that in the case of the compromised client, only the targeted client will be affected, instead of potentially *all* the clients.

Bugs in Implementations

As with any cryptographic system, TLS can fail when there are bugs in its implementation. The poster child for TLS bugs is Heartbleed (see Figure 13-3), a buffer overflow in the OpenSSL implementation of a minor TLS feature known as heartbeat. Heartbleed was discovered in 2014, independently by a Google researcher and by the Codenomicon company, and affected millions of TLS servers and clients.

As you can see in Figure 13-3, a client first sends a buffer along with a buffer length to the server to check whether the server is online. In this example, the buffer is the string *BANANAS*, and the client explicitly says that this word is seven letters long. The server reads the seven-letter word and returns it to the client.

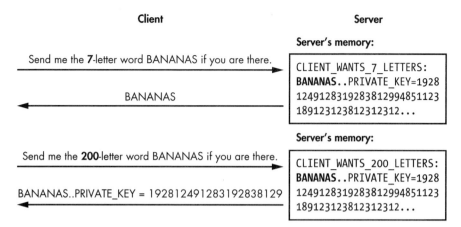

Figure 13-3: The Heartbleed bug in OpenSSL implementations of TLS

The problem is that the server doesn't confirm that the length is correct, and will attempt to read as many characters as the client tells it to. Consequently, if the client provides a length that is longer than the string's actual length, the server reads too much data from memory and will return it to the client, together with any extra data that may contain sensitive information, such as private keys or session cookies.

It won't surprise you to hear that the Heartbleed bug came as a shock. To avoid similar future bugs, OpenSSL and other major TLS implementations now perform rigorous code reviews and use automated tools such as fuzzers in order to identify potential issues.

Further Reading

As I stated at the outset, this chapter is not a comprehensive guide to TLS, and you may want to dig deeper into TLS 1.3. For starters, the complete TLS 1.3 specifications include everything about the protocol (though not necessarily about its underlying rationale). You can find that on the home page of the TLS Working Group (TLSWG) here: *https://tlswg.github.io/*.

In addition, let me cite two important TLS initiatives:

- SSL Labs TLS test (*https://www.ssllabs.com/ssltest/*) is a free service by Qualys that lets you test a browser's or a server's TLS configuration, providing a security rating as well as improvement suggestions. If you set up your own TLS server, use this test to make sure that everything is safe and that you get an "A" rating.
- Let's Encrypt (*https://letsencrypt.org/*) is a nonprofit that offers a service to "automagically" deploy TLS on your HTTP servers. It includes features to automatically generate a certificate and configure the TLS server, and it supports all the common web servers and operating systems.

14

QUANTUM AND POST-QUANTUM

Previous chapters focused on cryptography today, but in this chapter I'll examine the future of cryptography over a time horizon of, say, a century or more—one in which *quantum computers* exist. Quantum computers are computers that leverage phenomena from quantum physics in order to run different kinds of algorithms than the ones we're used to. Quantum computers don't exist yet and look very hard to build, but if they do exist one day, then they'll have the potential to break RSA, Diffie–Hellman, and elliptic curve cryptography—that is, all the public-key crypto deployed or standardized as of this writing.

To insure against the risk posed by quantum computers, cryptography researchers have developed alternative public-key crypto algorithms called *post-quantum* algorithms that would resist quantum computers. In 2015, the NSA called for a transition to quantum-resistant algorithms designed to be safe even in the face of quantum computers, and in 2017 the US standard-ization agency NIST began a process that will eventually standardize post-quantum algorithms.

This chapter will thus give you a nontechnical overview of the principles behind quantum computers as well as a glimpse of post-quantum algorithms. There's some math involved, but nothing more than basic arithmetic and linear algebra, so don't be scared by the unusual notations.

How Quantum Computers Work

Quantum computing is a model of computing that uses quantum physics to compute differently and do things that classical computers can't, such as breaking RSA and elliptic curve cryptography efficiently. But a quantum computer is not a super-fast normal computer. In fact, quantum computers can't solve any problem that is too hard for a classical computer, such as brute force search or **NP**-complete problems.

Quantum computers are based on quantum mechanics, the branch of physics that studies the behavior of subatomic particles, which behave truly randomly. Unlike classical computers, which operate on bits that are either 0 or 1, quantum computers are based on *quantum bits* (or *qubits*), which can be both 0 and 1 simultaneously—a state of ambiguity called *superposition*. Physicists discovered that in this microscopic world, particles such as elec-trons and photons behave in a highly counterintuitive way: before you observe an electron, the electron is not at a definite location in space, but in several locations at the same time (that is, in a state of superposition). But once you observe it—an operation called *measurement* in quantum physics—then it stops at a fixed, random location and is no longer in superposition. This quantum magic is what enables the creation of qubits in a quantum computer.

But quantum computers only work because of a crazier phenomenon called *entanglement*: two particles can be connected (entangled) in a way that observing the value of one gives the value of the other, even if the two particles are widely separated (kilometers or even light-years away from each other). This behavior is illustrated by the *Einstein–Podolsky–Rosen (EPR) paradox* and is the reason why Albert Einstein initially dismissed quantum mechanics. (See *https://plato.stanford.edu/entries/qt-epr/* for an in-depth explanation of why.)

To best explain how a quantum computer works, we should distinguish the actual quantum computer (the hardware, composed of quantum bits) from quantum algorithms (the software that runs on it, composed of *quantum gates*). The next two sections discuss these two notions.

Quantum Bits

Quantum bits (qubits), or groups thereof, are characterized with numbers called *amplitudes*, which are akin to probabilities but aren't *exactly* probabili-ties. Whereas a probability is a number between 0 and 1, an amplitude is a complex number of the form $a + b \times i$, or simply $a + bi$, where a and b are real numbers, and *i* is an *imaginary unit*. The number *i* is used to form *imaginary numbers*, which are of the form *bi*, with *b* a real number. When *i* is multiplied by a real number, we get another imaginary number, and when it is multiplied by itself it gives –1; that is $i^2 = -1$.

Unlike real numbers, which can be seen as belonging to a line (see Figure 14-1), *complex numbers* can be seen as belonging to a plane (a space with two dimensions), as shown in Figure 14-2. Here, the x-axis in the figure corresponds to the *a* in *a + bi*, the y-axis corresponds to the *b*, and the dotted lines correspond to the real and imaginary part of each number. For example, the vertical dotted line going from the point 3 + 2*i* down to 3 is two units long (the 2 in the imaginary part 2*i*).

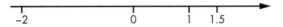

Figure 14-1: View of real numbers as points on an infinite straight line

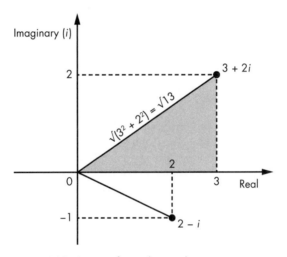

Figure 14-2: A view of complex numbers as points in a two-dimensional space

As you can see in Figure 14-2, you can use the Pythagorean theorem to compute the length of the line going from the origin (0) to the point *a + bi* by viewing this line as the diagonal of a triangle. The length of this diagonal is equal to the square root of the sum of the squared coordinates of the point, or $\sqrt{(a^2 + b^2)}$, which we call the *modulus* of the complex number *a + bi*. We denote the modulus as |*a + bi*| and can use it as the length of a complex number.

In a quantum computer, registers consist of 1 or more qubits in a state of superposition characterized by a set of such complex numbers. But as we'll see, these complex numbers—the amplitudes—can't be any numbers.

Amplitudes of a Single Qubit

A single qubit is characterized by two amplitudes that I'll call α (alpha) and β (beta). We can then express a qubit's state as α |0⟩ + β |1⟩, where the "| ⟩" notation is used to denote vectors in a quantum state. This notation then means that when you observe this qubit it will appear as 0 with a probability $|\alpha|^2$ and 1 with a probability $|\beta|^2$. Of course, in order for these to be actual probabilities, $|\alpha|^2$ and $|\beta|^2$ must be numbers between 0 and 1, and $|\alpha|^2 + |\beta|^2$ must be equal to 1.

For example, say we have the qubit Ψ (psi) with amplitudes of α = 1/√2 and β = 1/√2. We can express this as follows:

$$\Psi = \left(1 \,/\, \sqrt{2}\right)|0\rangle + \left(1 \,/\, \sqrt{2}\right)|1\rangle = \left(|0\rangle + |1\rangle\right) \,/\, \sqrt{2}$$

This notation means that in the qubit Ψ, the value 0 has an amplitude of 1/√2, and the value 1 has the same amplitude, 1/√2. To get the actual probability from the amplitudes, we compute the modulus of 1/√2 (which is equal to 1/√2, because it has no imaginary part), then square it: $(1/\sqrt{2})^2 = 1/2$. That is, if you observe the qubit Ψ, you'll have a 1/2 chance of seeing a 0, and the same chance of seeing a 1.

Now consider the qubit Φ (phi), where

$$\Phi = \left(i \,/\, \sqrt{2}\right)|0\rangle - \left(1 \,/\, \sqrt{2}\right)|1\rangle = \left(i|0\rangle - |1\rangle\right) \,/\, \sqrt{2}, \text{ or } |\Phi\rangle = \left(i \,/\, \sqrt{2}, 1 \,/\, \sqrt{2}\right)$$

The qubit Φ is fundamentally distinct from Ψ because unlike Ψ, where amplitudes have equal values, the qubit Φ has distinct amplitudes of α = i/√2 (a positive imaginary number) and β = –1/√2 (a negative real number). If, however, you observe Φ, the chance of your seeing a 0 or 1 is 1/2, the same as it is with Ψ. Indeed, we can compute the probability of seeing a 0 as follows, based on the preceding rules:

$$|\alpha|^2 = \left(\sqrt{\left(1 \,/\, \sqrt{2}\right)^2}\right)^2 = 1 \,/\, \sqrt{2}^2 = 1 \,/\, 2$$

NOTE   *Because* α = i/√2, α *can be written as* a + bi *with* a = 0 *and* b = 1/√2, *and computing* |α| = √(a² + b²) *yields 1/√2.*

The upshot is that different qubits can behave similarly to an observer (with the same probability of seeing a 0 for both qubits) but have different amplitudes. This tells us that the actual probabilities of seeing a 0 or a 1 only partially characterize a qubit; just as when you observe the shadow of an object on a wall, the shape of the shadow will give you an idea of the object's width and height, but not of its depth. In the case of qubits, this hidden dimension is the value of its amplitude: Is it positive or negative? Is it a real number or an imaginary number?

To simplify notations, a qubit is often simply written as its pair of amplitudes (α, β). Our previous example can then be written $|\Psi\rangle = (1/\sqrt{2}, 1/\sqrt{2})$.

Amplitudes of Groups of Qubits

We've explored single qubits, but how do we understand multiple qubits? For example, a *quantum byte* can be formed with 8 qubits, when put into a state where the quantum states of these 8 qubits are somehow connected to each other (we say that the qubits are entangled, which is a complex physical phenomenon). Such a quantum byte can be described as follows, where the αs are the amplitudes associated with each of the 256 possible values of the group of 8 qubits:

$$\alpha_0 |00000000\rangle + \alpha_1 |00000001\rangle + \alpha_2 |00000010\rangle + \alpha_3 |00000011\rangle + \ldots + \alpha_{255} |11111111\rangle$$

Note that we must have $|\alpha_0|^2 + |\alpha_1|^2 + \ldots + |\alpha_{255}|^2 = 1$, so that all probabilities sum to 1.

Our group of 8 qubits can be viewed as a set of $2^8 = 256$ amplitudes, because it has 256 possible configurations, each with its own amplitude. In physical reality, however, you'd only have eight physical objects, not 256. The 256 amplitudes are an implicit characteristic of the group of 8 qubits; each of these 256 numbers can take any of infinitely many different values. Generalizing, a group of n qubits is characterized by a set of 2^n complex numbers, a number that grows exponentially with the numbers of qubits.

This encoding of exponentially many high-precision complex numbers is a core reason why a classical computer can't simulate a quantum computer: in order to do so, it would need an unfathomably high amount of memory (of size around 2^n) to store the same amount of information contained in only n qubits.

Quantum Gates

The concepts of amplitude and quantum gates are unique to quantum computing. Whereas a classical computer uses registers, memory, and a microprocessor to perform a sequence of instructions on data, a quantum computer transforms a group of qubits reversibly by applying a series of quantum gates, and then measures the value of one or more qubits. Quantum computers promise more computing power because with only n qubits, they can process 2^n numbers (the qubits' amplitudes). This property has profound implications.

From a mathematical standpoint, quantum algorithms are essentially a circuit of *quantum gates* that transforms a set of complex numbers (the amplitudes) before a final measurement where the value of 1 or more qubits is observed (see Figure 14-3). You'll also see quantum algorithms referred to as *quantum gate arrays* or *quantum circuits*.

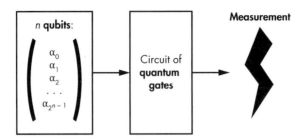

Figure 14-3: Principle of a quantum algorithm

Quantum Gates as Matrix Multiplications

Unlike the Boolean gates of a classical computer (AND, XOR, and so on), a quantum gate acts on a group of amplitudes just as a matrix acts when multiplied with a vector. For example, in order to apply the simplest quantum gate, the *identity* gate, to the qubit Φ, we see I as a 2×2 matrix and multiply it with the column vector consisting of the two amplitudes of Φ, as shown here:

$$I|\Phi\rangle = \begin{pmatrix} 1 & 0 \\ 0 & 1 \end{pmatrix} \begin{pmatrix} i / \sqrt{2} \\ -1 / \sqrt{2} \end{pmatrix} = \begin{pmatrix} 1 \times \dfrac{i}{\sqrt{2}} + 0 \times \left(-\dfrac{1}{\sqrt{2}} \right) \\ 0 \times \dfrac{i}{\sqrt{2}} + 1 \times \left(-\dfrac{1}{\sqrt{2}} \right) \end{pmatrix} = \begin{pmatrix} i / \sqrt{2} \\ -1 / \sqrt{2} \end{pmatrix} = \Phi\rangle$$

The result of this matrix–vector multiplication is another column vector with two elements, where the top value is equal to the dot product of the *I* matrix's first line with the input vector (the result of adding the product of the first elements 1 and $i/\sqrt{2}$ to the product of the second elements 0 and $-1/\sqrt{2}$), and likewise for the bottom value.

NOTE *In practice, a quantum computer wouldn't explicitly compute matrix–vector multiplications because the matrices would be way too large. (That's why quantum computing can't be simulated by a classical computer.) Instead, a quantum computer would transform qubits as physical particles through physical transformations that are equivalent to a matrix multiplication. Confused? Here's what Richard Feynman had to say: "If you are not completely confused by quantum mechanics, you do not understand it."*

The Hadamard Quantum Gate

The only quantum gate we've seen so far, the identity gate *I*, is pretty useless because it doesn't do anything and leaves a qubit unchanged. Now we're going to see one of the most useful quantum gates, called the *Hadamard gate*, usually denoted *H*. The Hadamard gate is defined as follows (note the negative value in the bottom-right position):

$$H = \begin{pmatrix} 1 / \sqrt{2} & 1 / \sqrt{2} \\ 1 / \sqrt{2} & -1 / \sqrt{2} \end{pmatrix}$$

Let's see what happens if we apply this gate to the qubit $|\Psi\rangle = (1/\sqrt{2}, 1/\sqrt{2})$:

$$H|\Psi\rangle = \begin{pmatrix} 1/\sqrt{2} & 1/\sqrt{2} \\ 1/\sqrt{2} & -1/\sqrt{2} \end{pmatrix}\begin{pmatrix} 1/\sqrt{2} \\ 1/\sqrt{2} \end{pmatrix} = \begin{pmatrix} 1/2+1/2 \\ 1/2-1/2 \end{pmatrix} = \begin{pmatrix} 1 \\ 0 \end{pmatrix} = 0$$

By applying the Hadamard gate H to $|\Psi\rangle$, we obtain the qubit $|0\rangle$ for which the value $|0\rangle$ has amplitude 1, and $|1\rangle$ has amplitude 0. This tells us that the qubit will behave deterministically: that is, if you observe this qubit, you would always see a 0 and never a 1. In other words, we've lost the randomness of the initial qubit $|\Psi\rangle$.

What happens if we apply the Hadamard gate again to the qubit $|0\rangle$?

$$H|0\rangle = \begin{pmatrix} 1/\sqrt{2} & 1/\sqrt{2} \\ 1/\sqrt{2} & -1/\sqrt{2} \end{pmatrix}\begin{pmatrix} 1 \\ 0 \end{pmatrix} = \begin{pmatrix} 1/\sqrt{2} \\ 1/\sqrt{2} \end{pmatrix} = |\Psi\rangle$$

This brings us back to the qubit $|\Psi\rangle$ and a randomized state. Indeed, the Hadamard gate is often used in quantum algorithms to go from a deterministic state to a uniformly random one.

Not All Matrices are Quantum Gates

Although quantum gates can be seen as matrix multiplications, not all matrices correspond to quantum gates. Recall that a qubit consists of the complex numbers α and β and the amplitudes of the qubit, such that they satisfy the condition $|\alpha|^2 + |\beta|^2 = 1$. If after multiplying a qubit by a matrix we get two amplitudes that don't match this condition, the result can't be a qubit. Quantum gates can only correspond to matrices that preserve the property $|\alpha|^2 + |\beta|^2 = 1$, and matrices that satisfy this condition are called *unitary matrices*.

Unitary matrices (and quantum gates by definition) are *invertible*, meaning that given the result of an operation, you can compute back the original qubit by applying the *inverse* matrix. This is the reason why quantum computing is said to be a kind of *reversible computing*.

Quantum Speed-Up

A *quantum speed-up* occurs when a problem can be solved faster by a quantum computer than by a classical one. For example, in order to search for an item among n items of an unordered list on a classical computer, you need on average $n/2$ operations, because you need to look at each item in the list before finding the one you're looking for. (On average, you'll find that item after searching half of the list.) No classical algorithm can do better than $n/2$. However, a quantum algorithm exists to search for an item in only about $\sqrt{n}$ operations, which is orders of magnitude smaller than $n/2$. For example, if n is equal to 1000000, then $n/2$ is 500000, whereas $\sqrt{n}$ is 1000.

We attempt to quantify the difference between quantum and classical algorithms in terms of *time complexity*, which is represented by $O()$ notation.

In the previous example, the quantum algorithm runs in time $O(\sqrt{n})$ but the classical algorithm can't be faster than $O(n)$. Because the difference in time complexity here is due to the square exponent, we call this *quadratic speed-up*. But while such a speed-up will likely make a difference, there are much more powerful ones.

Exponential Speed-Up and Simon's Problem

Exponential speed-ups are the Holy Grail of quantum computing. They occur when a task that takes an exponential amount of time on a classical computer, such as $O(2^n)$, can be performed on a quantum computer with polynomial complexity—namely $O(n^k)$ for some fixed number k. This exponential speed-up can turn a practically impossible task into a possible one. (Recall from Chapter 9 that cryptographers and complexity theorists associate exponential time with the impossible, and they associate polynomial time with the practical.)

The poster child of exponential speed-ups is *Simon's problem*. In this computational problem, a function, $\mathbf{f}()$, transforms n-bit strings to n-bit strings, such that the output of $\mathbf{f}()$ looks random except that there is a value, m, such that any two values x, y that satisfies $\mathbf{f}(x) = \mathbf{f}(y)$, then $y = x \oplus m$. The way to solve this problem is to find m.

The route to take when solving Simon's problem with a classical algorithm boils down to finding a collision, which takes approximately $2^{n/2}$ queries to $\mathbf{f}()$. However, a quantum algorithm (shown in Figure 14-4) can solve Simon's problem in approximately n queries, with the extremely efficient time complexity of $O(n)$.

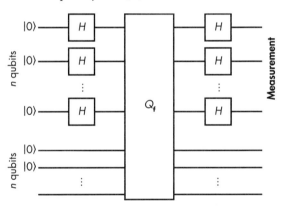

Figure 14-4: The circuit of the quantum algorithm that solves Simon's problem efficiently

As you can see in Figure 14-4, you initialize $2n$ qubits to $|0\rangle$, apply Hadamard gates (H) to the first n qubits, then apply the gate $Q_{\mathbf{f}}$ to the two groups of all n qubits. Given two n-qubit groups x and y, the gate $Q_{\mathbf{f}}$ transforms the quantum state $|x\rangle|y\rangle$ to the state $|x\rangle|\mathbf{f}(x) \oplus y\rangle$. That is, it computes the function $\mathbf{f}()$ on the quantum state reversibly, because you can go from the new state to the old one by computing $\mathbf{f}(x)$ and XORing it to $\mathbf{f}(x) \oplus y$. (Unfortunately, explaining why all of this works is beyond the scope of this book.)

The exponential speed-up for Simon's problem can be used against symmetric ciphers only in very specific cases, but in the next section you'll see some real crypto-killer applications of quantum computing.

The Threat of Shor's Algorithm

In 1995, AT&T researcher Peter Shor published an eye-opening article titled "Polynomial-Time Algorithms for Prime Factorization and Discrete Logarithms on a Quantum Computer." *Shor's algorithm* is a quantum algorithm that causes an exponential speed-up when solving the factoring, discrete logarithm (DLP), and elliptic curve discrete logarithm (ECDLP) problems. You can't solve these problems with a classical computer, but you could with a quantum computer. That means that you could use a quantum computer to solve any cryptographic algorithm that relies on those problems, including RSA, Diffie–Hellman, elliptic curve cryptography, and all currently deployed public-key cryptography mechanisms. In other words, you could reduce the security of RSA or elliptic curve cryptography to that of Caesar's cipher. (Shor might as well have titled his article "Breaking All Public-Key Crypto on a Quantum Computer.") Shor's algorithm has been called "one of the major scientific achievements of the late 20th century" by renowned complexity theorist Scott Aaronson.

Shor's algorithm actually solves a more general class of problems than factoring and discrete logarithms. Specifically, if a function $\mathbf{f}()$ is *periodic*—that is, if there's a ω (the period) such that $\mathbf{f}(x + \omega) = \mathbf{f}(x)$ for any x, Shor's algorithm will efficiently find ω. (This looks very similar to Simon's problem discussed previously, and indeed Simon's algorithm was a major inspiration for Shor's algorithm.) The ability of Shor's algorithm to efficiently compute the period of a function is important to cryptographers because that ability can be used to attack public-key cryptography, as I'll discuss next.

A discussion of the details of how Shor's algorithm achieves its speed-up is far too technical for this book, but in this section I'll show how you could use Shor's algorithm to attack public-key cryptography. Let's see how Shor's algorithm could be used to solve the factoring and discrete logarithm problems (as discussed in Chapter 9), which are respectively the hard problems behind RSA and Diffie–Hellman.

Shor's Algorithm Solves the Factoring Problem

Say you want to factor a large number, $N = pq$. It's easy to factor N if you can compute the period of $a^x \bmod N$, a task that is hard to do with a classical computer but easy to do on a quantum one. You first pick a random number a less than N, and ask Shor's algorithm to find the period ω of the function $\mathbf{f}(x) = a^x \bmod N$. Once you've found the period, you'll have

$a^x \bmod N = a^{x+\omega} \bmod N$ (that is, $a^x \bmod N = a^x a^\omega \bmod N$), which means that $a^\omega \bmod N = 1$, or $a^\omega - 1 \bmod N = 0$. In other words, $a^\omega - 1$ is a multiple of N, or $a^\omega - 1 = kN$ for some unknown number k.

The key observation here is that you can easily factor the number $a^\omega - 1$ as the product of two terms, where $a^\omega - 1 = (a^{\omega/2} - 1)(a^{\omega/2} + 1)$. You can then compute the greatest common divisor (GCD) between $(a^{\omega/2} - 1)$ and N, and check to see if you've obtained a nontrivial factor of N (that is, a value other than 1 or N). If not, you can just rerun the same algorithm with another value of a. After a few trials, you'll get a factor of N. You've now recovered the private RSA key from its public key, which allows you to decrypt messages or forge signatures.

But just how easy is this computation? Note that the best classical algorithm to use to factor a number N runs in time exponential in n, the bit length of N (that is, $n = \log_2 N$). However, Shor's algorithm runs in time *polynomial* in n—namely, $O(n^2 (\log n)(\log \log n))$. This means that if we had a quantum computer, we could run Shor's algorithm and see the result within a reasonable amount of time (days? weeks? months, maybe?) instead of thousands of years.

Shor's Algorithm and the Discrete Logarithm Problem

The challenge in the discrete logarithm problem is to find y, given $y = g^x \bmod p$, for some known numbers g and p. Solving this problem takes an exponential amount of time on a classical computer, but Shor's algorithm lets you find y easily thanks to its efficient period-finding technique.

For example, consider the function $\mathbf{f}(a, b) = g^a y^b$. Say we want to find the period of this function, the numbers ω and ω', such that $\mathbf{f}(a + \omega, b + \omega') = \mathbf{f}(a, b)$ for any a and b. The solution we seek is then $x = -\omega / \omega'$ modulo q, the order of g, which is a known parameter. The equality $\mathbf{f}(a + \omega, b + \omega') = \mathbf{f}(a, b)$ implies $g^\omega y^{\omega'} \bmod p = 1$. By substituting y with g^x, we have $g^{\omega + x\omega'} \bmod p = 1$, which is equivalent to $\omega + x\omega' \bmod q = 0$, from which we derive $x = -\omega / \omega'$.

Again, the overall complexity is $O(n^2 (\log n)(\log \log n))$, with n the bit length of p. This algorithm generalizes to find discrete logarithms in any commutative group, not just the group of numbers modulo a prime number.

Grover's Algorithm

After Shor's algorithm exponential speed-up for factoring, another important form of quantum speed-up is the ability to search among n items in time proportional to the square root of n, whereas any classical algorithm would take time proportional to n. This quadratic speed-up is possible thanks to *Grover's algorithm*, a quantum algorithm discovered in 1996 (after Shor's algorithm). I won't cover the internals of Grover's algorithm because they're essentially a bunch of Hadamard gates, but I'll explain what kind of problem Grover solves and its potential impact on cryptographic security. I'll also show why you can salvage a symmetric crypto algorithm from quantum computers by doubling the key or hash value size, whereas asymmetric algorithms are destroyed for good.

Think of Grover's algorithm as a way to find the value x among n possible values, such that $\mathbf{f}(x) = 1$, and where $\mathbf{f}(x) = 0$ for most other values. If m values of x satisfy $\mathbf{f}(x) = 1$, Grover will find a solution in time $O(\sqrt{(n\ /\ m)})$; that is, in time proportional to the square root of n divided by m. In comparison, a classical algorithm can't do better than $O(n\ /\ m)$.

Now consider the fact that $\mathbf{f}()$ can be any function. It could be, for example, "$\mathbf{f}(x) = 1$ if and only if x is equal to the unknown secret key K such that $\mathbf{E}(K, P) = C$" for some known plaintext P and ciphertext C, and where $\mathbf{E}()$ is some encryption function. In practice, this means that if you're looking for a 128-bit AES key with a quantum computer, you'll find the key in time proportional to 2^{64}, rather than 2^{128} if you had only classical computers. You would need a large enough plaintext to ensure the uniqueness of the key. (If the plaintext and ciphertext are, say, 32 bits, many candidate keys would map that plaintext to that ciphertext.) The complexity 2^{64} is much smaller than 2^{128}, meaning that a secret key would be much easier to recover. But there's an easy solution: to restore 128-bit security, just use 256-bit keys! Grover's algorithm will then reduce the complexity of searching a key to "only" $2^{256\ /\ 2} = 2^{128}$ operations.

Grover's algorithm can also find preimages of hash functions (a notion discussed in Chapter 6). To find a preimage of some value h, the $\mathbf{f}()$ function is defined as "$\mathbf{f}(x) = 1$ if and only if $\mathbf{Hash}(x) = h$, otherwise $\mathbf{f}(x) = 0$." Grover thus gets you preimages of n-bit hashes at the cost of the order of $2^{n/2}$ operations. As with encryption, to ensure 2^n *post-quantum* security, just use hash values twice as large, since Grover's algorithm will find a preimage of a $2n$-bit value in at least 2^n operations.

The bottom line is that you can salvage symmetric crypto algorithms from quantum computers by doubling the key or hash value size, whereas asymmetric algorithms are destroyed for good.

NOTE *There is a quantum algorithm that finds hash function collisions in time $O(2^{n/3})$, instead of $O(2^{n/2})$, as with the classic birthday attack. This would suggest that quantum computers can outperform classical computers for finding hash function collisions, except that the $O(2^{n/3})$-time quantum algorithm also requires $O(2^{n/3})$ space, or memory, in order to run. Give $O(2^{n/3})$ worth of computer space to a classic algorithm and it can run a parallel collision search algorithm with a collision time of only $O(2^{n/6})$, which is much faster than the $O(2^{n/3})$ quantum algorithm. (For details of this attack, see "Cost Analysis of Hash Collisions" by Daniel J. Bernstein at* http://cr.yp.to/papers.html#collisioncost.*)*

Why Is It So Hard to Build a Quantum Computer?

Although quantum computers can in principle be built, we don't know how hard it will be or when that might happen, if at all. And so far, it looks really hard. As of early 2017, the record holder is a machine that is able to keep 14 (fourteen!) qubits stable for only a few milliseconds, whereas we'd need to keep millions of qubits stable for weeks in order to break any crypto. The point is, we're not there yet.

Why is it so hard to build a quantum computer? Because you need extremely small things to play the role of qubits—about the size of electrons or photons. And because qubits must be so small, they're also extremely fragile.

Qubits must also be kept at extremely low temperatures (close to absolute zero) in order to remain stable. But even at such a freezing temperature, the state of the qubits decays, and they eventually become useless. As of this writing, we don't yet know how to make qubits that will last for more than a couple of seconds.

Another challenge is that qubits can be affected by the environment, such as heat and magnetic fields, which can create noise in the system, and hence computation errors. In theory, it's possible to deal with these errors (as long as the error rate isn't too high), but it's hard to do so. Correcting qubits' errors requires specific techniques called quantum error-correcting codes, which in turn require additional qubits and a low enough rate of error. But we don't know how to build systems with such a low error rate.

At the moment, there are two main approaches to forming qubits, and therefore to building quantum computers: superconducting circuits and ion traps. Using *superconducting circuits* is the approach championed by labs at Google and IBM. It's based on forming qubits as tiny electrical circuits that rely on quantum phenomena from superconductor materials, where charge carriers are pairs of electrons. Qubits made of superconducting circuits need to be kept at temperatures close to absolute zero, and they have a very short lifetime. The record as of this writing is nine qubits kept stable for a few microseconds.

Ion traps, or trapped ions, are made up of ions (charged atoms) and are manipulated using lasers in order to prepare the qubits in specific initial states. Using ion traps was one of the first approaches to building qubits, and they tend to be more stable than superconducting circuits. The record as of this writing is 14 qubits stable for a few milliseconds. But ion traps are slower to operate and seem harder to scale than superconducting circuits.

Building a quantum computer is really a moonshot effort. The challenge comes down to 1) building a system with a handful of qubits that is stable, fault tolerant, and capable of applying basic quantum gates, and 2) scaling such a system to thousands or millions of qubits to make it useful. From a purely physical standpoint, and to the best of our knowledge, there is nothing to prevent the creation of large fault-tolerant quantum computers. But many things are possible in theory and prove hard or too costly to realize in practice (like secure computers). Of course, the future will tell who is right—the quantum optimists (who sometimes predict a large quantum computer in ten years) or the quantum skeptics (who argue that the human race will never see a quantum computer).

Post-Quantum Cryptographic Algorithms

The field of *post-quantum cryptography* is about designing public-key algorithms that cannot be broken by a quantum computer; that is, they would be quantum safe and able to replace RSA and elliptic curve–based algorithms in a future where off-the-shelf quantum computers could break 4096-bit RSA moduli in a snap.

Such algorithms should not rely on a hard problem known to be efficiently solvable by Shor's algorithm, which kills the hardness in factoring and discrete logarithm problems. Symmetric algorithms such as block ciphers and hash functions would lose only half their theoretical security in the face of a quantum computer but would not be badly broken as RSA. They might constitute the basis for a post-quantum scheme.

In the following sections, I explain the four main types of post-quantum algorithms: code-based, lattice-based, multivariate, and hash-based. Of these, hash-based is my favorite because of its simplicity and strong security guarantees.

Code-Based Cryptography

Code-based post-quantum cryptographic algorithms are based on *error-correcting codes*, which are techniques designed to transmit bits over a noisy channel. The basic theory of error-correcting codes dates back to the 1950s. The first code-based encryption scheme (the *McEliece* cryptosystem) was developed in 1978 and is still unbroken. Code-based crypto schemes can be used for both encryption and signatures. Their main limitation is the size of their public key, which is typically on the order of a hundred kilobytes. But is that really a problem when the average size of a web page is around two megabytes?

Let me first explain what error-correcting codes are. Say you want to transmit a sequence of bits as a sequence of (say) 3-bit words, but the transmission is unreliable and you're concerned that 1 or more bits may be incorrectly transmitted: you send 010, but the receiver gets 011. One simple way to address this would be to use a very basic error-correction code: instead of transmitting 010 you would transmit 000111000 (repeating each bit three times), and the receiver would decode the received word by taking the majority value for each of the three bits. For example, 100110111 would be decoded to 011 because that pattern appears twice. But as you can see, this particular error-correcting code would allow a receiver to correct only up to one error per 3-bit chunk, because if two errors occur in the same 3-bit chunk, the majority value would be the wrong one.

Linear codes are an example of less trivial error-correcting codes. In the case of linear codes, a word to encode is seen as an n-bit vector v, and encoding consists of multiplying v with an $m \times n$ matrix G to compute the code word $w = vG$. (In this example, m is greater than n, meaning that the code word is longer than the original word.) The value G can be structured such that for a given number t, any t-bit error in w allows the recipient to recover the correct v. In other words, t is the maximum number of errors that can be corrected.

In order to encrypt data using linear codes, the McEliece cryptosystem constructs *G* as a secret combination of three matrices, and encrypts by computing $w = vG$ plus some random value, *e*, which is a fixed number of 1 bit. Here, *G* is the public key, and the private key is composed of the matrices *A*, *B*, and *C* such that $G = ABC$. Knowing *A*, *B*, and *C* allows one to decode a message reliably and retrieve *w*. (You'll find the decoding step described online.)

The security of the McEliece encryption scheme relies on the hardness of decoding a linear code with insufficient information, a problem known to be **NP**-complete and therefore out of reach of quantum computers.

Lattice-Based Cryptography

Lattices are mathematical structures that essentially consist of a set of points in an *n*-dimensional space, with some periodic structure. For example, in dimension two ($n = 2$), a lattice can be viewed as the set of points shown in Figure 14-5.

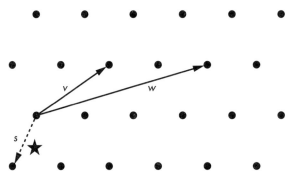

Figure 14-5: Points of a two-dimensional lattice, where v and w are basis vectors of the lattice, and s is the closest vector to the star-shaped point

Lattice theory has led to deceptively simple cryptography schemes. I'll give you the gist of it.

A first hard problem found in lattice-based crypto is known as *short integer solution* (SIS). SIS consists of finding the secret vector *s* of *n* numbers given (*A*, *b*) such that $b = As \bmod q$, where *A* is a random $m \times n$ matrix and *q* is a prime number.

The second hard problem in lattice-based cryptography is called *learning with errors* (LWE). LWE consists of finding the secret vector *s* of *n* numbers given (*A*, *b*), where $b = As + e \bmod q$, with *A* being a random $m \times n$ matrix, *e* a random vector of noise, and *q* a prime number. This problem looks a lot like noisy decoding in code-based cryptography.

SIS and LWE are somewhat equivalent, and can be restated as instances of the *closest vector problem (CVP)* on a lattice, or the problem of finding the vector in a lattice closest to a given point, by combining a set of basis vectors. The dotted vector *s* in Figure 14-5 shows how we would find the closest vector to the star-shaped point by combining the basis vectors *v* and *w*.

CVP and other lattice problems are believed to be hard both for classical and quantum computers. But this doesn't directly transfer to secure cryptosystems, because some problems are only hard in the worst case (that is, for their hardest instance) rather than the average case (which is what we need for crypto). Furthermore, while finding the exact solution to CVP is hard, finding an approximation of the solution can be considerably easier.

Multivariate Cryptography

Multivariate cryptography is about building cryptographic schemes that are as hard to break as it is to solve systems of multivariate equations, or equations involving multiple unknowns. Consider, for example, the following system of equations involving four unknowns x_1, x_2, x_3, x_4:

$$x_1 x_2 + x_3 x_4 + x_2 = 1$$
$$x_1 x_3 + x_1 x_4 + x_2 x_3 = 12$$
$$x_1^2 + x_3^2 + x_4 = 4$$
$$x_2 x_3 + x_2 x_4 + x_1 + x_4 = 0$$

These equations consist of the sum of terms that are either a single unknown, such as x_4 (or terms of degree one), or the product of two unknown values, such as $x_2 x_3$ (terms of degree two or *quadratic* terms). To solve this system, we need to find the values of x_1, x_2, x_3, x_4 that satisfy all four equations. Equations may be over all real numbers, integers only, or over finite sets of numbers. In cryptography, however, equations are typically over numbers modulo some prime numbers, or over binary values (0 and 1).

The problem here is to find a solution that is **NP**-hard given a *random* quadratic system of equations. This hard problem, known as *multivariate quadratics (MQ) equations*, is therefore a potential basis for post-quantum systems because quantum computers won't solve **NP**-hard problems efficiently.

Unfortunately, building a cryptosystem on top on MQ isn't so straightforward. For example, if we were to use MQ for signatures, the private key might consist of three systems of equations, L_1, N, and L_2, which when combined in this order would give another system of equations that we'll call P, the public key. Applying the transformations L_1, N, and L_2 consecutively (that is, transforming a group of values as per the system of equations) is then equivalent to applying P by transforming x_1, x_2, x_3, x_4 to y_1, y_2, y_3, y_4, defined as follows:

$$y_1 = x_1 x_2 + x_3 x_4 + x_2$$
$$y_2 = x_1 x_3 + x_1 x_4 + x_2 x_3$$
$$y_3 = x_1^2 + x_3^2 + x_4$$
$$y_4 = x_2 x_3 + x_2 x_4 + x_1 + x_4$$

In such a cryptosystem, L_1, N, and L_2 are chosen such that L_1 and L_2 are linear transformations (that is, having equations where terms are only added, not multiplied) that are invertible, and where N is a quadratic system of equations that is also invertible. This makes the combination of the three a quadratic system that's also invertible, but whose inverse is hard to determine without knowing the inverses of L_1, N, and L_2.

Computing a signature then consists of computing the inverses of L_1, N, and L_2 applied to some message, M, seen as a sequence of variables, x_1, x_2, ...

$$S = L_2^{-1}\left(N^{-1}\left(L_1^{-1}(M)\right)\right)$$

Verifying a signature then consists of verifying that $P(S) = M$.

Attackers could break such a cryptosystem if they manage to compute the inverse of P, or to determine L_1, N, and L_2 from P. The actual hardness of solving such problems depends on the parameters of the scheme, such as the number of equations used, the size and type of the numbers, and so on. But choosing secure parameters is hard, and more than one multivariate scheme considered safe has been broken.

Multivariate cryptography isn't used in major applications due to concerns about the scheme's security and because it's often slow or requires tons of memory. A practical benefit of multivariate signature schemes, however, is that it produces short signatures.

Hash-Based Cryptography

Unlike the previous schemes, hash-based cryptography is based on the well-established security of cryptographic hash functions rather than on the hardness of mathematical problems. Because quantum computers cannot break hash functions, they cannot break anything that relies on the difficulty of finding collisions, which is the key idea of hash function–based signature schemes.

Hash-based cryptographic schemes are pretty complex, so we'll just take a look at their simplest building block: the one-time signature, a trick discovered around 1979, and known as *Winternitz one-time signature* (WOTS), after its inventor. Here "one-time" means that a private key can be used to sign only one message; otherwise, the signature scheme becomes insecure. (WOTS can be combined with other methods to sign multiple messages, as you'll see in the subsequent section.)

But first, let's see how WOTS works. Say you want to sign a message viewed as a number between 0 and $w - 1$, where w is some parameter of the scheme. The private key is a random string, K. To sign a message, M, with $0 \le M < w$, you compute $\textbf{Hash}(\textbf{Hash}(. . .(\textbf{Hash}(K))))$, where the hash function $\textbf{Hash}$ is repeated M times. We denote this value as $\textbf{Hash}^M(K)$. The public key is $\textbf{Hash}^w(K)$, or the result of w nested iterations of $\textbf{Hash}$, starting from K.

A WOTS signature, S, is verified by checking that $\textbf{Hash}^{w-M}(S)$ is equal to the public key $\textbf{Hash}^w(K)$. Note that S is K after M applications of $\textbf{Hash}$, so if we do another $w - M$ applications of $\textbf{Hash}$, we'll get a value equal to K hashed $M + (w - M) = w$ times, which is the public key.

This scheme looks rather dumb, and it has significant limitations:

Signatures can be forged

From $\mathbf{Hash}^M(K)$, the signature of M, you can compute $\mathbf{Hash}(\mathbf{Hash}^M(K))$ = $\mathbf{Hash}^{M+1}(K)$, which is a valid signature of the message $M + 1$. This problem can be fixed by signing not only M, but also $w - M$, using a second key.

It only works for short messages

If messages are 8 bits long, there are up to $2^8 - 1 = 255$ possible messages, so you'll have to compute $\mathbf{Hash}$ up to 255 times in order to create a signature. That might work for short messages, but not for longer ones: for example, with 128-bit messages, signing the message $2^{128} - 1$ would take forever. A workaround is to split longer messages into shorter ones.

It works only once

If a private key is used to sign more than one message, an attacker can recover enough information to forge a signature. For example, if $w = 8$ and you sign the numbers 1 and 7 using the preceding trick to avoid trivial forgeries, the attacker gets $\mathbf{Hash}^1(K)$ and $\mathbf{Hash}^7(K')$ as a signature of 1, and $\mathbf{Hash}^7(K)$ and $\mathbf{Hash}^1(K')$ as a signature of 7. From these values, the attacker can compute $\mathbf{Hash}^x(K)$ and $\mathbf{Hash}^x(K')$ for any x in $[1;7]$ and thus forge a signature on behalf of the owner of K and K'. There is no simple way to fix this.

State-of-the-art hash-based schemes rely on more complex versions of WOTS, combined with tree data structures and sophisticated techniques designed to sign different messages with different keys. Unfortunately, the resulting schemes produce large signatures (on the order of dozens of kilobytes, as with SPHINCS, a state-of-the-art scheme at the time of this writing), and they sometimes have a limit on the number of messages they can sign.

How Things Can Go Wrong

Post-quantum cryptography may be fundamentally stronger than RSA or elliptic curve cryptography, but it's not infallible or omnipotent. Our understanding of the security of post-quantum schemes and their implementations is more limited than for not-post-quantum cryptography, which brings with it increased risk, as summarized in the following sections.

Unclear Security Level

Post-quantum schemes can appear deceptively strong yet prove insecure against both quantum and classical attacks. Lattice-based algorithms, such as the ring-LWE family of computational problems (versions of the LWE problem that work with polynomials), are sometimes problematic.

Ring-LWE is attractive for cryptographers because it can be leveraged to build cryptosystems that are in principle as hard to break as it is to solve the hardest instances of Ring-LWE problems, which can be **NP**-hard. But when security looks too good to be true, it often is.

One problem with security proofs is that they are often asymptotic, meaning that they're true only for a large number of parameters such as the dimension of the underlying lattice. However, in practice, a much smaller number of parameters is used.

Even when a lattice-based scheme looks to be as hard to break as some **NP**-hard problem, its security remains hard to quantify. In the case of lattice-based algorithms, we rarely have a clear picture of the best attacks against them and the cost of such an attack in terms of computation or hardware, because of our lack of understanding of these recent constructions. This uncertainty makes lattice-based schemes harder to compare against better-understood constructions such as RSA, and this scares potential users. However, researchers have been making progress on this front and hopefully in a few years, lattice problems will be as well understood as RSA. (For more technical details on the Ring-LWE problem, read Peikert's excellent survey at *https://eprint.iacr.org/2016/351/*.)

Fast Forward: What Happens if It's Too Late?

Imagine this CNN headline: April 2, 2048: "ACME, Inc. reveals its secretly built quantum computer, launches break-crypto-as-a-service platform." Okay, RSA and elliptic curve crypto are screwed. Now what?

The bottom line is that post-quantum encryption is way more critical than post-quantum signatures. Let's look at the case of signatures first. If you were still using RSA-PSS or ECDSA as a signature scheme, you could just issue new signatures using a post-quantum signature scheme in order to restore your signatures' trust. You would revoke your older, quantum-unsafe public keys and compute fresh signatures for every message you had signed. After a bit of work, you'd be fine.

You would only need to panic if you were encrypting data using quantum-unsafe schemes, such as RSA-OAEP. In this case all transmitted ciphertext could be compromised. Obviously, it would be pointless to encrypt that plaintext again with a post-quantum algorithm since your data's confidentiality is already gone.

But what about key agreement, with Diffie–Hellman (DH) and its elliptic curve counterpart (ECDH)?

Well, at first glance, the situation looks to be as bad as with encryption: attackers who've collected public keys g^a and g^b could use their shiny new quantum computer to compute the secret exponent a or b and compute the shared secret g^{ab}, and then derive from it the keys used to encrypt your traffic. But in practice, Diffie–Hellman isn't always used in such a simplistic fashion. The actual session keys used to encrypt your data may be derived from both the Diffie–Hellman shared secret and some internal state of your system.

For example, that's how state-of-the-art mobile messaging systems work, thanks to a protocol pioneered with the Signal application. When you send a new message to a peer with Signal, a new Diffie–Hellman shared secret is computed and combined with some internal secrets that depend on the previous messages sent within that session (which can span long periods of time). Such advanced use of Diffie–Hellman makes the work of an attacker much harder, even one with a quantum computer.

Implementation Issues

In practice, post-quantum schemes will be code, not algorithms; that is, software running on some physical processor. And however strong the algorithms may be on paper, they won't be immune to implementation errors, software bugs, or side-channel attacks. An algorithm may be completely post-quantum in theory but may still be broken by a simple classical computer program because a programmer forgot to enter a semicolon.

Furthermore, schemes such as code-based and lattice-based algorithms rely heavily on mathematical operations, the implementation of which uses a variety of tricks to make those operations as fast as possible. But by the same token, the complexity of the code in these algorithms makes implementation more vulnerable to side-channel attacks, such as timing attacks, which infer information about secret values based on measurement of execution times. In fact, such attacks have already been applied to code-based encryption (see *https://eprint.iacr.org/2010/479/*) and to lattice-based signature schemes (see *https://eprint.iacr.org/2016/300/*).

The upshot is that, ironically, post-quantum schemes will be less secure in practice at first than non-post-quantum ones, due to vulnerabilities in their implementations.

Further Reading

To learn the basics of quantum computation, read the classic *Quantum Computation and Quantum Information* by Nielsen and Chuang (Cambridge, 2000). Aaronson's *Quantum Computing Since Democritus* (Cambridge, 2013), a less technical and more entertaining read, covers more than quantum computing.

Several software simulators will allow you to experiment with quantum computing. The Quantum Computing Playground at *http://www.quantum playground.net/* is particularly well designed, with a simple programming language and intuitive visualizations.

For the latest research in post-quantum cryptography, see *https://pqcrypto .org/* and the associated conference PQCrypto.

The coming years promise to be particularly exciting for post-quantum crypto thanks to NIST's Post-Quantum Crypto Project, a community effort to develop the future post-quantum standard. Be sure to check the project's website *http://csrc.nist.gov/groups/ST/post-quantum-crypto/* for the related algorithms, research papers, and workshops.

INDEX

authenticated encryption (AE),
continued
permutation-based AEAD, 157–158
SIV, 156–157
using MACs, 146–148
authenticated encryption with
associated data (AEAD), 16,
149, 157–158
authenticated key agreement
(AKA), 205–207
authentication tag, 16. *See also*
authenticated encryption
(AE); MACs (message
authentication codes)
AVX (Advanced Vector Extensions), 55

Micali, Silvio, 19
Microsoft, 65
Microsoft Windows CryptoAPI, 194
misuse resistance, 150
MitM (meet-in-the-middle) attacks,
72–74
mode of operation, 4, 5, 65
Moore, Jonathan, 233
most significant bit (MSB), 28, 135,
138, 215
MQ (multivariate quadratics), 265
MQV (Menezes–Qu–Vanstone),
213–214, 226
MT (Mersenne Twister) algorithm,
28, 36
mt_rand, 28
multicollisions, 113
multivariate cryptography, 265–266
multivariate problems, 179
multivariate quadratics (MQ), 265

N

Naehrig, Michael, 233
National Institute of Standards and
Technology (NIST), 29, 53,
59, 120–121
National Security Agency (NSA), 59,
116, 213, 251
Netscape, 35, 237
network-based intrusion detection
systems (NIDS), 105
Neves, Samuel, 123, 158
NFSR (nonlinear feedback shift
register), 86
Nguyen, Phong Q., 143
Nielsen, Michael, 269
NIST (National Institute of Standards
and Technology), 29, 53, 59,
120–121
NM (non-malleability), 13
nonces, 71–72, 78–79
predictability, 149–150
reuse, 101
in TLS records, 241
WEP insecurity and, 93–94
nondeterministic polynomial time class.
See NP (nondeterministic
polynomial time) class
nonlinear equation, 29
nonlinear feedback shift register
(NFSR), 86

non-malleability (NM), 13
nonrepudiation, 188
non-uniform distribution, 23
NP (nondeterministic polynomial
time) class, 168–169
NP-complete problem, 169–170
NP-hard problem, 170
NSA (National Security Agency), 59,
116, 213, 251
NSS library, 199
number field sieve, 204

O

OAEP. See Optimal Asymmetric
Encryption Padding
(OAEP)
OCB (offset codebook)
efficiency, 156
internals, 155–156
security, 156
one-time pad, 7
encrypting with, 7–8
security, 8–9, 13, 40
one-way function, 107
opad, 132
OpenSSH, 136, 217, 231
OpenSSL toolkit
generating DH parameters, 203
generating keys, 30, 49, 177–178
GHASH bug, 153
Heartbleed, 248–249
unsafe DH group parameters,
215–216
Optimal Asymmetric Encryption
Padding (OAEP), 52, 186
encoded message, 187
mask generating function, 188

P

P (polynomial time) class, 166–168,
168–169
padding, 19, 69–70, 112–113
OAEP, 52, 186–188
zero padding, 241
padding oracle attacks, 19, 74–75
parallelism, 43
parallelizability, 151, 154, 156
parent process ID (PPID), 35
password, 49, 129
Paterson, Kenny, 103

random oracle, 107
Ray, Marsh, 65
RC4, 79, 92–93
    broken implementation, 101–102
    in TLS, 94–95
    in WEP, 93–94
RDRAND instruction, 34–35
RDSEED instruction, 34
reduction, 46
replay attacks, 129, 206
Rho method, 110–111
Rijndael, 59
ring-LWE, 267
Rivest, Ron, 92, 103
Rivest–Shamir–Adleman. *See* RSA
    (Rivest–Shamir–Adleman)
Rogaway, Phillip, 155, 156, 157
RNGs (random number generators),
    24–25
root of unity, 198
rounds, 48
round trips, 208
round-trip times (RTT), 245
RSA (Rivest–Shamir–Adleman),
    181–182
    Bellcore attack, 196–197
    CRT, 195–196
    vs. ECDSA, 227–228
    encryption, 185
    and factoring problem, 46–47, 177
    FDH, 190–191
    groups, 182–183
    implementations, 191–192
    key generation, 184–185
    modulus, 182
    OEAP, 186–188
    private exponents, 197–199
    private keys, 50, 183, 184
    problem, 204
    PSS, 189–190, 191
    public exponents, 183
    public keys, 183
    secret exponents, 183
    security, 185
    shared moduli, 197
    signatures, 188–189
    small exponents, 194–195
    speed, 194–196
    square-and-multiply, 192–193
    textbook encryption, 185–186

textbook signature, 188
trapdoor permutation, 183
RSAES-OAEP, 186
RSA Security, 92
RTT (round-trip times), 245

S

Saarinen, Markku-Juhani O., 121, 166
safe prime, 203
SageMath, 176, 184
Salsa20, 95
    attacking, 99–100
    column-round function, 97
    double-round function, 97
    internal state, 96
    and nonlinear relations, 98–99
    quarter-round function, 96
    row-round function, 97
    Salsa20/8, 99
salt, 190
sandwich MAC, 133
satellite phone (satphone), 102
S-boxes (substitution boxes), 57
scheduling problems, 170
Schneier, Bruce, 26, 38, 121
Schwenk, Jörg, 233
searchable encryption, 17
search algorithm, 164
second-preimage resistance, 108
secret-prefix MAC, 130, 133
secret-suffix MAC, 131
secure channel, 201, 236
secure cookie, 246
Secure Hash Algorithms (SHAs), 116
Secure Hash Algorithm with Keccak
    (SHAKE), 121
Secure Shell (SSH), 51–52, 128, 132,
    147, 148, 152, 226, 240
Secure Socket Layer (SSL), 35, 235, 237
security
    bit, 42–43
    computational, 40–41
    cryptographic, 39
    goals, 10, 12–13
    heuristic, 46, 48–49
    informational, 40
    levels, choosing, 44–45
    margin, 48–49
    notions, 10, 13–15

Serious Cryptography is set in New Baskerville, Futura, TheSansMono Condensed, and Dogma. This book was printed and bound at Sheridan Books, Inc. in Chelsea, Michigan. The paper is 60# Finch Smooth, which is certified by the Forest Stewardship Council (FSC).

The book uses a layflat binding, in which the pages are bound together with a cold-set, flexible glue and the first and last pages of the resulting book block are attached to the cover. The cover is not actually glued to the book's spine, and when open, the book lies flat and the spine doesn't crack.

RESOURCES

Visit *https://www.nostarch.com/seriouscrypto/* for resources, errata, and more information.

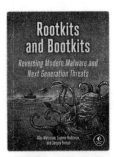
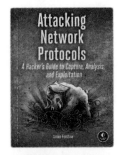

The Electronic Frontier Foundation (EFF) is the leading organization defending civil liberties in the digital world. We defend free speech on the Internet, fight illegal surveillance, promote the rights of innovators to develop new digital technologies, and work to ensure that the rights and freedoms we enjoy are enhanced — rather than eroded — as our use of technology grows.

EFF.ORG

ELECTRONIC FRONTIER FOUNDATION

Protecting Rights and Promoting Freedom on the Electronic Frontier